Awakening Christian Ministry
The Call To Serve Others As We Serve Jesus Christ

Dr. Lee Ann B. Marino, Ph.D., D.Min., D.D.

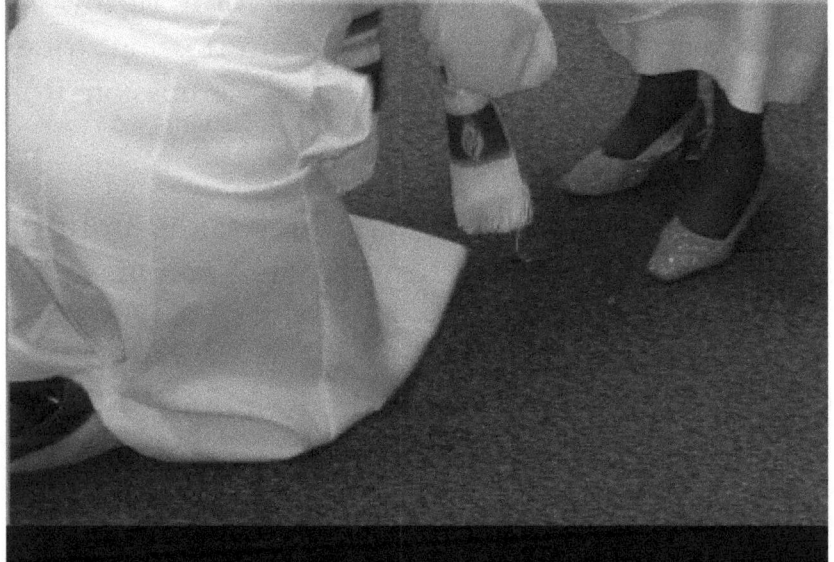

Awakening Christian Ministry
The Call To Serve Others As We Serve Jesus Christ

Dr. Lee Ann B. Marino, Ph.D., D.Min., D.D.

Published by:
RIGHTEOUS PEN PUBLICATIONS
www.righteouspenpublications.com

All rights reserved. No part of this book may be reproduced or transmitted in any form or by any means, electronic or mechanical, or information storage and retrieval system without written permission from the author.

Unless otherwise noted, Scriptures taken from the Holy Bible, Authorized King James Version,
   Public Domain.

Complete Scripture Copyright Reference List can be found on the preceding page.

Copyright © 2014, 2017 by Lee Ann B. Marino.

ISBN: 1940197155
13-Digit: 978-1-940197-15-9

Printed in the United States of America.

Lord, I give up
All my own plans and purposes,
All my own desires and hopes
And accept Thy will for my life.
I give myself, my life, my all,
Utterly to Thee
To be Thine forever.
Fill me and seal me with Thy Holy Spirit.
Use me as Thou wilt,
Send me where Thou wilt,
Work out Thy whole will in my life
At any cost,
Now and forever.

- Betty Scott Stam (Martyred in China, in the 1930s)

Dr. Lee Ann B. Marino, Ph.D., D.Min., D.D.

Scripture Copyright Reference List

Scriptures marked **AMP** are taken from the **Amplified®** Bible, Copyright © 1954, 1958, 1962, 1964, 1965, 1987 by The Lockman Foundation. Used by permission. (www.Lockman.org)

Scriptures marked **ASV** are from the American Standard Version of the Holy Bible, 1901. Public domain.

Scriptures marked **CEB** are taken from the Common English Bible®, CEB® Copyright © 2010, 2011 by Common English Bible. ™ Used by permission. All rights reserved worldwide. The "CEB" and "Common English Bible" trademarks are registered in the United States Patent and Trademark Office by Common English Bible. Use of either trademark requires the permission of Common English Bible.

Scripture quotations marked **CEV** are from the Contemporary English Version Copyright © 1991, 1992, 1995 by American Bible Society, Used by Permission.

Scriptures marked **DARBY** are from The Holy Scriptures: A New Translation from the Original Languages by J.N. Darby, 1890. Public domain.

Scriptures marked **ERV** are taken from the HOLY BIBLE: EASY-TO-READ VERSION © 2006 by World Bible Translation Center, Inc. Used by permission.

Scriptures marked **ESV** are taken from the Holy Bible, English Standard Version®, Copyright © 2001 by Crossway, a publishing ministry of Good News Publishers. All rights reserved. Used by permission.

Scripture quotations marked **GNT** are from the Good News Translation in Today's English Version-Second Edition Copyright © 1992 by American Bible Society. Used by Permission.

Scriptures marked GOD'S WORD are a copyrighted work of God's Word to the Nations. Quotations are used by permission. Copyright 1995 by God's Word to the Nations. All rights reserved.

Scripture quotations marked **HCSB** are taken from the Holman Christian Standard Bible®, Copyright © 1999, 2000, 2002, 2003, 2009 by Holman Bible Publishers. Used by permission. Holman Christian Standard Bible®, Holman CSB®, and HCSB® are federally registered trademarks of Holman Bible Publishers.

Scripture quotations marked **LEB** are from the *Lexham English Bible.* Copyright 2012 Logos Bible Software. Lexham is a registered trademark of Logos Bible Software.

Scriptures marked **NASB** are taken from The New American Standard Bible®, Copyright © 1960, 1962, 1963, 1968, 1971, 1972, 1973, 1975, 1977, 1995 by The Lockman Foundation. Used by permission.

Scriptures marked **NCV** are from the New Century Version®. Copyright © 2005 by Thomas Nelson, Inc. Used by permission. All rights reserved.

Scriptures marked **NIV** are taken from the Holy Bible, New International Version ®, NIV®, Copyright © 1973, 1978, 1984 by Biblica, Inc. ™ Used by permission of Zondervan. All rights reserved worldwide.

Scriptures marked **NLT** are taken from the Holy Bible, New Living Translation copyright © 1996, 2004, 2007 by the Tyndale House Foundation. Used by permission of Tyndale House Publishers, Inc., Carol Stream, Illinois 60188. All rights reserved.

Scriptures marked **PHILLIPS** are taken from The New Testament in Modern English, copyright © 1958, 1959, 1960 J.B. Phillips and 1947, 1952, 1955, 1957 The Macmillian Company, New York. Used by permission. All rights reserved.

Scriptures marked **WE** are from THE JESUS BOOK - The Bible in Worldwide English. Copyright SOON Educational Publications, Derby DE65 6BN, UK. Used by permission.

Scriptures marked **WYC** are from The Wycliffe Bible © 2001 by Terence P. Noble.

Scriptures marked **YLT** are from Young's Literal Translation, 1898, Public domain.

Table Of Contents

Acknowledgments... i
Foreword... 1
Introduction.. 5

Section 1: Discovering Principles Of Christian Leadership

1. What Is Ministry?....................................... 13
2. Principles For Christian Leadership..................... 31
3. The Call To Serve Others As We Serve Jesus Christ....... 47
4. Selecting A Christian Leader............................ 63

Section 2: The Five-Fold Ministry

5. Building Up The Body Of Christ.......................... 85
6. The Office Of The Apostle............................... 115
7. The Office Of The Prophet............................... 141
8. The Office Of The Evangelist............................ 163
9. The Office Of The Pastor................................ 177
10. The Office Of The Teacher.............................. 193

Section 3: The Appointments Of Bishop, Elder, And Deacon

11. Deacons: An Appointment Of Service..................... 209
12. Bishops And Elders..................................... 223

Section 4: Ministry And Church Order

13. Discussing Proper Understandings Of Christian Ministry With Others.. 245
14. The Forum-Driven Church................................ 253
15. One Universal Church: The Church Beyond The Local Community.. 269

Section 5: Thoughts For Christian Leaders

16. Things Ministers Should Consider Before Getting Married... 273
17. Ten Realities Of Ministry You Need To Embrace To Run Your Race... 281

18	Identifying Judas...	289

Section 6: Covering

19	The Things I Wish People Would Recognize About Covering..	303
20	More Things I Wish People Would Recognize About Covering..	315
21	The Things I Wish Coverings Knew About Covering.........	327
22	Covering: An Assignment Of Love............................	337
23	Becoming All Things To All People............................	343
24	A Guide To International Covering: Covering People Overseas..	349
25	Leaders To Beware And Avoid..................................	359
26	Six Types Of People Every Leaders Needs In Their Lives And Ministries..	367
27	A Million Reasons...	377

Section 7: Apostle Marino's Apostolic Testimony

28	Crossing The Jordan: My Testimony As An Apostle.........	385
	References..	445
	About The Author..	451

Acknowledgements

I first recognize that I cannot write this book without acknowledging Jesus Christ, the One Who called me to the office of the apostle. As difficult and arduous a journey as it has been, I am grateful that the Lord trusts me to lead His people.

I thank and acknowledge every leader I have ever had, though I do not name them here. Whether we are still connected in some way or our season has long passed, I haven't a single doubt that you have been instrumental and foundational in my purposes of ministry, down to the present day. I thank those of you who helped inspire me to write and publish this word, things that were long overdue to write and publish, especially here in these words.

To all those who are somehow a part of, covered by, or in connection with this ministry, Apostolic Fellowship International Ministries: I think about something Apostle Yolanda Y. Davis once said about us: *"We represent the church the way it is supposed to be. We are one."* For that, and for all of you – I am eternally grateful. It is an honor to stand as your leader, both in service and in purpose. We learn from one another, and I learn just as much from all of you as I hope you learn from me.

To the many others who have stood by me through this journey of ministry: those who have shared with me, talked with me, carried me, encouraged me, corrected me, and helped me get to this point today…

And to the many friends, supporters, and fans of this ministry in the US and abroad…I stand here, forever your servant, forever a leader to the Body, forever your apostle.

With love,

+Apostle Dr. Lee Ann B. Marino, Ph.D., D.Min, D.D.

Foreword

REFLECTIONS ON THE JOURNEY

The past seven years it took to write this book – and now the subsequent three years since – have been an interesting time in my life. I moved from Kentucky to North Carolina after only spending about two and a half years in western Kentucky. I got two dogs, who are now approaching the end of their lives. I began to fully embrace the call God placed on my life as an apostle. I was ordained as an apostle, after holding credentials as a pastor for eight years. I've watched my perspectives and opinions on things start in one place, and shake up totally different, only to come out on a different side of the issue all together. I've studied, I've learned, I've stepped out in faith more times than I can even remember, and I've seen so many changes occur in the church, it's not funny anymore. I've seen many ministers come and go, even unto the demise of their own ministries and well-being. I've seen friends turn quickly into enemies, distance grow between close friends, spiritual sons and daughters turn on their leaders (including me), victories and defeats, and the "turning," yet again, of lives and situations into different things as we continue to advance in this specific era of the church.

It was only recently that I realized while, reviewing through the pages of this book in its manuscript form, how much this book has become a product of my own ministry journey of the past seven years. It is my own awakening, my own realization of the importance of proper leadership and leadership conduct in the church. Prior to this point in time, I didn't think a lot about church structure or the need for specified conduct among leaders. I was someone who, more or less, adapted the perspective that we should all just do whatever "God" called us to do, however He called us to do it. I didn't think that much about order or the fact that God operates according to certain precepts and methods. If you would have asked me, "Without order, how will it be accomplished?" I wouldn't have had an answer for you.

I might not have had the leadership answers I needed once upon a time, but the circumstances of the past seven years have forced me to find them. As I have been a leader now for seventeen years (almost exactly to the day, in fact), I have spent a good part of the past seven years documenting and addressing issues affecting the church. The studies and writings contained herein carefully document commonly asked questions, issues, studies, and problems that have needed addressing within the church. It's a story; a chronicling; a biography of what I have seen, encountered, and experienced – and my response to it under the guidance of the Holy Ghost. My life, my ministry, my work is not that which it once was, but it is somehow the same. It is the plan God had for me all along and the product of each step taken unto the truth of that discovery for all these years.

At the same time, I recognize it is not only my story, but the story of all of us. It is the story of how a few people, all ministers, several of whom were women, started using internet podcasting, social media, and blogging to change the way the church perceived the five-fold ministry. It is the story of every minister who has discovered their call to ministry in some way, and to every individual called to assist or help in ministry, as well. These pages are an unveiling of the church; of the ways in which ministry has changed, and still needs to change, over the past several years. It is the story of the church, of the work of ministry, of the five-fold, and of the appointments. It is our biography, our pursuit of true and sustainable leadership in a time where ministries are fleeting and leadership is quickly failing to produce results.

This book is not just a word of correction, but a mark of success. It's not just about the way it should be, but in many churches and ministries in the world, it reflects the way it is. If it's not how it is, it's how it can become. For those who are in process, it represents their transition, their own awakening to the fullness of Christian leadership and all it is supposed to be.

For almost three years, I have struggled to finish this book, feeling it not complete in its existing forms. I realize now that this struggle ensued because it is never over. We are all continuing in the discovery of just what it means to be in ministry. We are figuring out progressively what it means to be an apostle, a prophet, an evangelist, a pastor, and a teacher. We are re-thinking what it means to be a bishop, elder, and deacon, re-examining those works and seeing how they apply to ministry in a Biblically relevant way. We are looking long and hard at leadership, examining the issues that exist and finding comprehensive answers to address them. There will always be a call to find a new answer for a new question or issue, but as of right now, the way to address where we are is to publish what I have.

If you are seeking, I encourage you to read, and seek. If you are studying, I encourage you to read, and learn even more. If you are already there, read and confirm. Wherever you are in the awakening, there is something for you in this book. Whether discerning the call, in leadership yourself, or looking for good signs of a great leader…this book has the answers…to help you discover the awakening of Christian ministry for yourself.

Dr. Lee Ann B. Marino, Ph.D., D.Min., D.D.

Introduction

During the summer of 2010, the Lord gave me a lesson about leadership I will never forget. I was on my way home from an Apostolic Fellowship meeting in Raleigh, North Carolina when I realized how uncomfortable I was in my dress suit. It was the middle of July and the middle of what seemed to be a never-ending heat wave. As I drove home in a car with no functional air conditioning, I got hotter and more uncomfortable. All I wanted to do was take off my suit, whether it would get me arrested for public indecency or not. I waited, and continued driving, totally distracted by how uncomfortable I was.

I selected the suit I had on for one reason: it was a cheap suit. I have far better suits I could have worn, but I chose to wear this suit because it was inexpensive. I could throw it in the washing machine when I got home and not worry it needed to go to the dry cleaners. If it got dirty, soiled, or became damaged for any reason, it wasn't a big loss. In the middle of scorching heat, I didn't want to damage a good suit...so I wore a cheap one.

It is a pretty suit, indeed: wrap-around style in baby blue with a white accent collar, white décor buttons, and a long skirt with white accent trim on the side walking vent. It presents well. It travels well, and has been to many conferences. On first glance, nobody would ever know it is one of the cheapest suits I own.

On closer inspection, however, the suit doesn't quite measure up. The cheap fabric and materials explained why I suffered so on a ninety-seven-degree day. It was heavy and coarse, rather than subtle and refined. The zipper is just an ordinary zipper, not what is often called a "hidden zipper," which is less noticeable on formal clothing. The suit is not lined. While it is pretty to the untrained eye, the suit itself was made...well...cheap.

As I got home and prepared to wash the suit (at this point I had thoughts about burning it), the Lord began to reveal to me a powerful comparison between the suit I'd worn that day and Christian leadership in our modern times. Much of Christian leadership today is like my cheap suit. On the outside, Christian leaders may seem like they have it all together: they may have large congregations, plenty of financial support, and are popular. Then there are those who seem to say all the right things, do all the right things, and carry themselves in just the right way....but something is just not adding up. If we judge what we see by the exterior, they seem to be great leaders. Just like my suit, however, they are merely presenting well. While they look pretty on the outside to the untrained eye, they are not as substantial as they could be. There are issues of disorder, lack of authority, disrespect, and lack of God's implemented structure. Some of the most popular church leaders in the world hold offices that in no way resemble God's order for Christian ministry. The more we study Christian leadership, we find many leaders represent something, but they are not standing up to present the best of God or Christian leadership.

The original purpose in this book was a thorough study on the five-fold ministry. That still remains a purpose in this book, but not its exclusive purpose. I can't rightly teach on the five-fold ministry without recognizing the five-fold as God's purpose for Christian leadership. Sometimes I think, in modern fervor to understand the five-fold, we forget apostles, prophets, evangelists, pastors, and teachers are God's appointed leaders. If we don't understand the five-fold in terms of God's established leadership, we are unable to understand God's ministry.

In November 2008, I set out to design a Bible study on the five-fold ministry for our weekly ministry study. While I had studied the five-fold ministry somewhat prior to this point, I did not know much about any office beyond the apostle and prophet. It is also noteworthy to mention that some of what I knew about both the apostle and prophet were incorrect. In our modern church, apostles and prophets are given great relevance and focus in study and ministry, although what we learn is not always right. This is an important step for the church, as the offices of apostle and prophet were denied overall for several hundred years. For this reason, the majority of questions I have received over the past few years almost exclusively relate to that of apostles and prophets. As I did not receive many questions, introspection, or interest in the other offices, I did not study them as thoroughly. Like many out there, I made the assumption that while apostles and prophets were misunderstood, the offices of evangelist, pastor, and teacher were understood and functioning correctly. My study on the five-fold ministry caused me to stand corrected. I recognized the great importance in studying the full five-fold ministry to learn, not just about what the offices are called to do individually, but what every part of the five-fold is called to do corporally.

This book is an expansion of that original Bible study on the five-fold ministry. Here we explore the purpose of its offices, individually and working together as the leadership of the body. We cannot in good conscience say we believe in church ministry and then abandon the five-fold ministry or uphold incorrect concepts of its offices. The Bible identifies five-fold ministry as foundational to church doctrine, function, and establishment. We cannot have a functioning church without the full five-fold ministry, working in cooperation together. It is also essential we understand the purpose in each office and identify the duties of the five-fold ministry offices to discern claims in our modern day. While there is no doubt that solid, sincere, and anointed ministers are alive and well in the church, there are plenty of ministers who use titles to gain followings and mislead people. I believe there is also general confusion about what it means to be an apostle, prophet, evangelist, pastor, or teacher. With crossover roles and general religious assimilation in every aspect of ministry life, copycat ministries using titles (or rather, misusing them) cause people to be uncertain as to what such terms and titles mean in an actual sense.

In keeping with our emphasis on Christian leadership and ministry, I am also including studies on the role of deacons, bishops, and elders, general principles for Christian leadership, true Christian service, and guidelines to select a Christian leader. It has come to my attention since I wrote the original study on the five-fold ministry how deeply confused the church is about service, leadership, and submission to authority. If someone is called to serve in an office of the five-fold ministry or an office of appointment, that individual needs to understand true service and authority. Serving in the five-fold ministry is not a license to have a personal servant or slave, nor is it an excuse to mistreat people. Church leaders need to recognize their purpose as just that – leaders - not religious powers or figureheads.

This book is divided into twenty-eight chapters and seven sections. The first section includes four chapters on ministry and principles of leadership, service, and leadership selection. The second section includes six chapters on the five-fold ministry. he third section includes two chapters on appointments. The studies present within chapters one through twelve contain several parts, including summaries, studies of the topics at hand according to the Bible, questions and answers about common subjects related to the topic, vocabulary, and discussion and review questions, perfect for individual or group study. The remaining chapters of this book are divided up into four sections and are composed of writings about ministry and leadership. The last section and chapter of this book is my personal testimony as an apostle, which provides purpose for teaching and experience.

To fully participate in the studies contained within this book, you will need the following:

- **A copy of The King James Version of the Holy Bible** – The Bible translation used in this study is the King James Version, unless otherwise noted. For the key texts in each study, cross-references are made to other translations which translate the text differently. In our pursuit for accuracy and understanding, it is vital we see how verses are translated into English in different versions. The Authorized Version was not selected based on a belief that it is superior to other translations, but because of its common usage among much of today's church. Its common usage makes it a meeting ground for people of many different perspectives to come together and truly study the issues presented in a serious and discerning matter.

- **A notebook for writing notes on the text for later study and review** – When reading and studying, making notations and devising questions or thoughts for further study are a very essential aspect to developing ministerial knowledge and discernment. This book is established for study and review, and is here to facilitate study and discussion as well as personal discernment over ministerial callings and claims. This is the start of study, not the end.

- **A prayerful attitude and focused mind** – Many people come into studies on the five-fold ministry with preconceived attitudes and ideas about the topic. Instead of coming to search the Scriptures and align with the Word, many come with the intent to prove themselves right and walk away with a distorted view of truth. If we are going to truly understand the inspired Word and its benefit for ministry today, we must be open to what the Word teaches on the topic. The Word does not have to conform to religious doctrine; rather, our doctrine and deeply held beliefs must conform to the Word.

It is my prayer that, through deep study and understanding, this text can be of benefit in developing ministries and ministerial understanding for today's church.

Section 1

Discovering Principles of Christian Leadership

Chapter One

WHAT IS MINISTRY?

A successful woman preacher was once asked, "What special obstacles have you met as a woman in the ministry?" "Not one," she answered, "except the lack of a minister's wife."
– Anna Garlin Spencer[1]

It's not uncommon to meet people of all sorts today who identify themselves as "ministers." They may do one thing or another, whether it's preaching, altar work, an online ordination, or maybe even believe they have a call to ministry, but not have it fully developed yet. Whatever the situation may be, it is most common that in our current day and age, you will meet someone who identifies themselves with ministry.

The word "ministry" tends to mean different things to different people. Some people think ministry is all about church work. Other people think it is about social work. Many people think ministry is about having a formal ordination with a denomination, wearing a collar or black outfit, or wearing a robe. The truth is that ministry is not necessarily identified by any of these things. Those who are ministers of God are in service to the people of God and the world at large.

Ministry is a service. If we desire to understand about ministry in a specific sense, such as the five-fold ministry or appointments, we must understand about ministry in a general sense: its purpose, power, and function to transform the world.

Text study

2 Corinthians 3:1-10

Supplementary texts

Exodus 28:35-43, Exodus 40:12-16, Deuteronomy 18:1-4, 1 Samuel 2:18, 1 Samuel 3:1-10, Matthew 8:14-15, Matthew 20:20-28, Acts 26:10-16, Romans 13:1-4.

Key verse

2 Corinthians 3:6:

- *"Who also hath made us able ministers of the new testament; not of the letter, but of the Spirit: for the letter killeth, but the Spirit giveth life."*

- *"He has made us competent as ministers of a new covenant—not of the letter but of the Spirit; for the letter kills, but the Spirit gives life."* (NIV)

- *"He has enabled us to be ministers of his new covenant. This is a covenant not of written laws, but of the Spirit. The old written covenant ends in death; but under the new covenant, the Spirit gives life."* (NLT)

- *"He has also qualified us to be ministers of a new promise, a spiritual promise, not a written one. Clearly, what was written brings death, but the Spirit brings life."* (GOD'S WORD)

- *"Who also made us adequate as servants of a new covenant, not of the letter but of the Spirit; for the letter kills, but the Spirit gives life."* (NASB)

- *"Which also made us able ministers of the new testament, not by letter, but by Spirit; for the letter slayeth, but the Spirit quickeneth."* (WYC)

Power words

- **Made us able** – From the Greek word *"hikanoo"* which means, "to make sufficient, render fit."[2]

- **Ministers** – From the Greek word *"diakonos"* which means, "one who executes the commands of another, especially of a master, a servant, attendant, minister."[3]

- **New Testament** – From two Greek words: *"kainos,"* which means, "new;"[4] and *"diatheke,"* which means, "a disposition, arrangement of any sort, which one wishes to be valid, the last disposition which one makes of his earthly possessions after his death, a testament or will; a compact, a covenant, a testament."[5]

- **Letter** – From the Greek word *"gramma"* which means, "a letter; any writing, a document or record; letters, i.e., learning."[6] (compare to the English word, "grammar.")

- **Spirit** – From the Greek word *"pneuma"* which means, "a movement of air (a gentle blast); the spirit, i.e., the vital principle by which the body is animated; a spirit, i.e., a simple essence, devoid of all or at least all grosser matter, and possessed of the power of knowing, desiring, deciding, and acting; of God; the disposition or influence which governs or fills the soul of any one."[7]

- **Killeth** – From the Greek word *"apokteino"* which means, "to kill in any way whatever; metaphorically, to extinguish, abolish."[8]

- **Gives life** – From the Greek word *"zoopoieo"* which means, "to produce alive, begat or bear living young; to cause to live, make alive, give life; metaphorically, of seeds quickened into life, i.e., germinating, springing up, growing."[9]

Historical context

The church in Corinth came as called out of pagan culture. The people within that fellowship were familiar with pagan temple priests and priestesses and the way pagan leaders conducted themselves. Pagan priests and priestesses conducted various ceremonies, especially sexual rites, and offered sacrifices to the various pagan gods. The priests were believed to be facilitators between the spiritual realm and the physical realm, and catalysts for rites and spells. While the people of Corinth understood the pagan priesthood – and the way pagan religion functioned – they were not familiar with the concept of ministry service as was present in Old Testament Jewish culture. In learning of God, they learned of the law, but they needed to see the Old Testament "type" present in the Word, pertaining to Christian ministry. The Corinthian church needed an understanding of the command to be in ministry and the vision of New Testament ministry. Here, in his words to them, the Apostle Paul provides that understanding.

Notes on text

Understanding Christian ministry is the essence of understanding service to others. Christian ministry is a calling, something one answers. God calls His workers, He equips them, and He establishes them as competent. Christian ministry is not about the re-imposition of the law or establishment of the law in our day and age, but is about proclaiming the New Covenant, the work of God's grace through Christ, and the work of the Spirit in each believer. In Christian ministry, ministers are called to bring forth practical life understanding and application.

Power points

- The word "ministry" is found throughout the Bible to refer to service. It is used in three contexts: to be of service to God, to be of service to a leader, or to be of service one to another (2 Chronicles 7:6, Hosea 12:10, Matthew 8:14-15, Romans 13:1-4). These three understandings of the word "ministry" give us a profound understanding of the purpose in Christian ministry. Ministers are those appointed by God for service to Him, as our Highest Leader, to leaders in the faith, and to one another (2 Corinthians 3:1-10). Jesus Himself proclaimed His ministry to be one of service, rather than being served, and that the greatest among us is the one who becomes the servant of all (Matthew 20:20-28).

- Christian ministry varies in its function, but has one specific purpose: to bring forth the New Covenant (2 Corinthians 3:1-10). In our understanding of the new covenant, we recognize the proclamation of the grace of God, received by faith in Jesus Christ (Ephesians 2:1-10). The new covenant minister uses the competencies and abilities he or she has received from the Lord to live, work, and proclaim the new covenant through Kingdom work and service (Acts 26:10-16).

- Ministry service is not random (1 Samuel 2:18). A minister has a set purpose, and is on a course for the Lord. A minister's service is fulfilled in doing whatever the Lord commands them to do. This is done through both a larger ministry purpose and obedience in executing smaller tasks that are a part of that greater vision. While a minister may not understand every order of the Lord, a minister of the Lord understands all of their steps are ordered by Him (1 Samuel 3:1-10).

- Being in ministry is a serious command, in which one must be set apart, and unctioned, or anointed, for such service (Exodus 28:35-43, Exodus 40:12-16). God calls those who are appointed into His service, and they are prepared for competence. Those who are in the ministry of the Lord are called by God to study and learn, preparing themselves for every powerful and purposed work. Kingdom ministry requires a call, many years of preparation, and a humble spirit which never ceases to pursue all the things of God as He orders (Psalm 119:7, Proverbs 16:21, Isaiah 26:9, Daniel 1:17, Matthew 9:13, 2 Timothy 2:15).

- The work of ministry bears its own inheritance: the inheritance of the Lord. God's ministers stand as His representatives, and the Lord therefore provides for the needs of those in His service through His Kingdom system. In His provision, part comes through the offerings received by those who benefit from the ministry work and service. (Deuteronomy 18:1-4).

Characteristics of Christian ministry

In looking at examples of Christian ministry in action and different combinations of ministry gifts, we can clearly see the characteristics essential to Christian ministry:

- **The Apostle Peter's mother-in-law, Matthew 8:14-15 (ministry service and hospitality)** – Most Bible students and even scholars don't give much relevance to the experience of Peter's mother-in-law. It is not incorrect to make it a story about the healing power of Jesus, but it is incorrect to make it about nothing more. The mere fact that the Apostle Peter brought the Savior to his mother-in-law is most relevant, showing her prominence in his life and his respect and love for his wife and her family. It is also not an accident that, once healed, she immediately attended to "ministry." It is undeniable she most likely sought to be hospitable, through food and beverage. Yet if we consider the experience of Martha and Mary (Luke 10:38-42), which we will discuss shortly, meeting a cultural expectation to serve does not qualify as Kingdom service. The Apostle Peter's mother-in-law didn't just serve according to custom, she ministered! She shared with them, in learning and teaching, and was of service to her Savior and her son-in-law. In her, we see the important elements of service, duty, hospitality, sharing, learning, encouraging, and holiness in the role of a minister of the Lord.

- **The twelve, and then the seventy-two, sent out, Matthew 10:1-42 and Luke 10:1-24 (the first work and foundations of Christian ministry)** – When Jesus Christ sent out the twelve, He sent them out with power and order. He also sent them out with specific instructions to be of service and receive back from those who embrace God's ministers: proclaim the Kingdom of heaven is near, heal the sick, raise the dead, cleanse the lepers, drive out demons; give freely, and receive from those who honor the work of ministry. We can see in this the same heart of the Levitical priesthood, which did not receive a land inheritance as the Lord was their inheritance. As they went about ministering, they were to receive for their service as the Lord provided it through those who embraced their work. If the work was not embraced, they were to kick the dust off their feet (an ancient sign of contempt), and keep going. Even though everyone does not receive Christian service, Christian ministers are to persevere and keep going in obedience to wherever the Lord would have them minister next.

- **Mary, Luke 10:38-42 (ministry purpose, heart, and focus)** – Martha and Mary are two of the most talked-about women in the Bible. Sermons abound – and debate – about the purpose of this story and why Martha stood corrected, while Mary did not. Martha did what was expected of her within her culture – and, within much of the world today, what is still expected of women – whereas Mary sat at the feet of Jesus. Ancient societies prided themselves in hospitality. One's reputation and the reputation of their household rested in the type of hospitality extended to guests. To be a bad host or hostess, be deemed inhospitable, or gain a reputation as a bad host or hostess was considered one of the worst things that could happen. Martha did things for Jesus: she ran around, preparing the house, cooking, cleaning, and beyond, because that was what her culture told her to do. Even though there is nothing wrong with hospitality or with serving others, there is something wrong with doing it if it is done with no heart or purpose because it is being done to satisfy a custom or cultural rule. Martha had never delved into herself, examining her purpose or what the Lord genuinely asked of her to do. She was angry that she was left to meet a customary expectation alone, because she felt that duty should extend beyond her. Mary, on the other hand, waited for the Lord's command. If it was the Lord's will that she sat and be taught, then that was what she, as His servant, was going to do. I have no doubt that if the Lord had asked Mary for something, she would not have hesitated to get it for Him. Culture wasn't on Mary's mind; she was not concerned what anyone would think of her, save the Savior. Mary displayed the heart of a true servant and exposed the power of purpose and focus in ministry. For God's servants to be effective, they must hold Him above all worldly expectation.

- **The five-fold ministry, Ephesians 4:11-16 (apostles, prophets, evangelists, pastors, and teachers)** – The standard for modern-day Christian leadership in ministry is found in the five-fold ministry of apostles, prophets, evangelists, pastors, and teachers. Each office of the five-fold is powerfully invested with gifts and abilities to lead the Kingdom of God until the time when Jesus Christ returns. As we will be looking in-depth at the five-fold ministry in this book and at each office, it is essential for readers to connect the five-fold and Christian ministry in order to understand God's order in the church.

- **Deacons, Acts 6:1-7 (service to leaders and to the needs of the church)** – We will be looking at deacons more in-depth later in this book. Often the role of the deacon is crafted into something other than its divinely ordained purpose, creating an intense confusion in the modern understanding of the deacon. The word "deacon" literally means "minister" or "servant." They are so-called because they are called to church service, to assist with the needs of the church, and assist the five-fold in its ministry.

Types of Christian ministry

- **The book of Leviticus; also found in Exodus, Numbers, and Deuteronomy** – *The Levitical priesthood*, a type of Christian ministry. The major type found in the Old Testament revealing the shadow of Christian ministry lies in the Levitical priesthood. It was the duty of the Levites to stand in the service of the Lord and of the people, performing sacrificial offerings and ministering to various needs pertaining to questions of cleanliness or spiritual matters. The Levites also ministered in word and song, in the maintenance of the temple, and in the care of holy and sacred things. The Levites were the spiritual leaders of Israel, just as Christian ministers are the leaders of the Body of Christ.

- **Esther 2:1-6** – *The king's ministers*, a type of Christian ministry. As was stated earlier, the term "minister" as is found in the Bible refers to any type of servant, especially in the Old Testament. Those who were in service to ancient kings followed their orders, operated in certain functions, and lived by a sense of loyalty to the king at all costs. Certain orders within the king's ministry were required to be willing to die for the king in service. We can see this type actively pointing to Christian ministry, as ministry service takes many forms, and the ultimate action of Christian service is to die for our heavenly King, whether through physical death or through the death of self and the flesh unto following the will of the Father as we walk through this life.

Questions and answers

- **Why is ministry needed?**

In reviewing history, especially Biblical history, the concept of service has been required in a number of different callings and professions. This is especially true in areas of work where one is of service to a group or nation of people. Those who served in political or governmental offices provided a service to the people they led. Those who worked in the area of stewardship, whether of food or domestic work, provided a service to whoever owned the household. This same principle applies for the house of God. God's ministers serve His people and work as His governing leaders within His Kingdom.

Ministry is needed because service is needed. Just as with any other service-minded area of life, God's Kingdom needs people who are active within His work as leaders and servers both full and part time. This enables the work of the Kingdom to remain solid, ensure it has what it needs, and ensure its growth, as the people within God's Kingdom receive the necessary structure and discipline they need. The Kingdom of God needs leadership; it needs godly leaders who do their best to implement Kingdom structure and order and who follow the Lord out of love. They must be people who seek to bring about the Kingdom of God within the lives and hearts of people, and who are not afraid to confront the challenges that arise from living in the world. Ministry is a powerful call, not something to be taken lightly.

- **I've seen people online refer to themselves as "Minister" and then their name rather than referring to themselves by an office of the five-fold ministry. What is the difference?**

Any individual who is called of God and operating in the office of apostle, prophet, evangelist, pastor, or teacher is technically a "minister." The term "minister" can also be used by extension to refer to an individual who is serving as a bishop, elder, or even a deacon, because the word "deacon" means "minister." The term "minister" is often used in a general sense to refer to someone who holds a ministry or an office of service within the church. Today, some use the term "minister" to describe themselves if they have received an ordination or affirmation, but the credentials they have are non-specific. For example, if one receives a non-specific online ordination that just issues a certificate to the holder, they aren't commissioned to any specific ministerial office. Even though they may be called to serve in a certain office of the five-fold, that distinction has not been made in their status as a minister. Sometimes people just use the classification of minister to distinguish themselves from other people, or to draw attention to education, training, or certification. Some people genuinely don't know what else to call themselves, drawing on years of misunderstanding about leadership and ministry and the call to minister with specified orders. The main difference between calling one's self a "minister" as a title and identifying one's self as an office of the five-fold is the specification of the calling. "Minister" is also used as a non-specific legal distinction, bearing with it the legal right to serve in ministerial functions, such as baptisms, communion, ordinations, funerals, and weddings. Many who are in training for other functions of service or who hold credentials without a specified office may also go by "minister."

It's very important that matters of ordination and appointment are taken seriously. Random, non-specific online ordinations may seem like a good legal option, but they do not uphold Kingdom dignity and echo the service of ministry. They also do not edify, train, or affirm an individual to their area of Kingdom service. A minister of God should know their calling in Him.

- **What about the title "Reverend?"**

The term "Reverend" is from the Latin and literally means "the respected." Its usage indicated a revered and respected status. Historically, it comes from Roman Catholic and Anglican usage. It was used for the ordained clergy of those denominations, and not used to refer to non-ordained or untrained lay ministers, despite their function or work. In more modern times, using the term "Reverend" to indicate any minister of any denomination has grown in popularity. Individuals use it to refer to any service, even when they are not formally ordained or affiliated with a denomination.

I think we should be very careful when using terminology that is not Biblical to refer to a ministry work. I understand that when dealing with the world (such as in prison or hospital ministry), our specific ministerial offices may not receive the proper acknowledgement they should and we may be designated to a non-specific role, such as that of "reverend." I also acknowledge that many use the term because that is what is listed on their ordination credentials from a denomination. In this vein, there is nothing wrong with its usage. There is no question that ministers of God should be individuals who are respectable and therefore, worthy of respect. The term is often used to indicate an individual's qualification to ministry or to just describe an ordination requirement rather than describe their ministry – and, thus, there is no minister in the Bible identified as "reverend." While I do not feel using such a title should cause fuss or offense (i.e., it is not improper to work with a minister who uses the title "reverend"), using such a non-Biblical title should never be the first usage by those who embrace the five-fold ministry.

- **How do ministers make their money?**

Let's start by answering this one with a fact: the majority of ministers are not individuals who "make money" in the context of having tons of it to throw around. Megachurch leaders represent less than five percent of all ministries worldwide, if even that much. The genuine call to ministry is not one based on financial gain. In the Old Testament, the Levite priesthood (the first ministry) did not receive a land inheritance among their brethren. Instead of receiving a land inheritance, the Lord Himself was to be the inheritance of the Levites (Joshua 13:33). They were to receive tithes as a part of their ministry service (Numbers 18:21,24). The purpose of tithes was to continue the temple ministry work and provide for the Levites and their families. This established pattern for ministerial support extends over into Christian ministry. The purpose of bringing in offerings to the Christian church is for the support of its ministries and ministers (Matthew 10:10, John 4:36). We see the command for Christians to support their leaders financially in the New Testament in several places (1 Corinthians 9:1-22, Philippians 4:14-19). We must also recognize that many first-century five-fold ministry leaders maintained jobs to help support themselves financially (Acts 18:3). Ideally, those who follow ministries should support their leaders, and their leaders should not need to work a separate job to support their ministries. This is not always the case, such as the Apostle Paul recognizes, and when ministers must work, they require extra support and assistance in their lives from those who follow their ministries.

In today's society, many have foregone the idea that congregants and church members need to support their leaders, whatever their office may be. Many believe it is the job of congregants to support only their local congregation and pastor, but this is untrue. Any ministry sowing into the life of a Christian should be supported. This includes ministries heard on the radio, internet, itinerant ministers visiting congregations, or those ministers watched regularly on television. Special consideration should go to ministries without regular congregations to support them. It is also important that, when holding conferences or events, provisions are made for invited speakers and ministers (including offering, accommodations and travel).

We've all seen the big-name television ministries on various networks. Sometimes we erroneously believe all five-fold ministers have the same lifestyle accommodations as those on television. Every minister of the Gospel has a set of circumstances which we cannot measure by the way a few live. Whatever circumstance you may perceive in some ministers does not change the basic command to support your leaders and those who provide Word teaching in your life.

- **Should ministers wear robes or clerical wear?**

The Old Testament priests wore elaborate robes to perform their ministry duties (Exodus 28:1-43). Those who study Biblical shadows and types know the purpose in these robes: they served to teach and point to Christ and His new covenant ministers. Recognizing these garments as a type indicates they are not the fulfillment of such, but only things which point toward a reality. As Christ is the reality, and we are the reality of His ministry in Him, the wearing of such robes is unnecessary for salvation or an understanding of salvation. We find no evidence that New Testament ministers ever wore such garments, as the only High Priest in the New Testament was

Christ (Hebrews 4 and 5).

It is also worth noting that first-century ministers, such as the Apostles Peter, Paul, Timothy, and others, would most likely not have worn traditional Jewish robes in their ministries. They recognized they were free from the law, and such garments were a part of the law. For example, traditional robes were also a sign of the "old life" in the Apostle Paul, who would have worn robes as part of his Pharisee office. Wanting to divorce himself from that life, the Apostle Paul would most likely not have worn his Pharisee robe as an apostle. His work as a Pharisee reflected the ministry of men, and his apostolic office was appointed by God. Wearing a robe as an apostle to just "wear one" would have been inappropriate.

That having been said, the development of clerical wear is something that has evolved through the ages in order to identify clergy members in their respective offices. There are many different schools of thought on the reasons why clerical wear and robes are important for certain occasions in the walk of the ministry. Some of these theories have merit, while others do seem unbiblical and farfetched. If one properly understands the meaning behind clerical garments, it is for the purpose of identifying one's profession as a minister and making the minister's work visible by attire. The system also helps to create distinctions between offices (by color and garment) when in ceremonial situations and distinctions.

I do believe that clerical and ceremonial attire have their place in the church, and can also be misused. I was one who was highly opposed to any sort of ceremonial or clerical attire until I reached a place where I could see the need for both in the life of a minister. Sometimes that means we need to put our own ideas about things aside and become *"all things to all people,"* as the Apostle Paul commands us to do (1 Corinthians 9:22). This means rather than argue over attire, when ceremonial or clerical attire is required, we need to dress ourselves appropriately and follow the guidelines laid out, that we may minister the Gospel in any environment. When we are in formal situations (ordinations, appointments, convocations, communion gatherings, weddings, funerals, and other formal occasions), our attire must match that of the occasion, and the way such is matched as a minister is by clerical or ceremonial attire. Many ministers also wear their clerical attire when travelling, in certain professional settings (such as lobbying or other events) or in gatherings of ministers of differing denominations, in keeping with the requirements therein. Civic attire is also important for ministry activities when working in things such as prison ministry, as a hospital chaplain, or other ministry works that occur outside the church walls.

There are also instances were such attire is highly inappropriate. While some ministers do wear their collars and robes on a weekly basis, I believe we should reserve such attire for more formal occasions. Weekly services, street witnessing, youth ministry, children's ministry, and other occasions often demand different clothing and it is important to attire ourselves appropriately, representing the ministry in the best light possible.

The short answer to this question: we need to dress ourselves appropriately for each and every situation. In my books, *Ministry School Boot Camp: Training For Helps Ministries, Appointments, And Beyond* and *About My Father's Business: Professional Ministry For Kingdom Leaders*, I detail the different meanings of ceremonial and clerical attire and what is appropriate for each office. (For further information on this topic, feel free to reference those books.) Every minister should have at least one white clergy robe and at least two minister's shirts with collar (one in the color of their designated office and one black) for occasions that call for such attire. Different organizations have different specifications on the requirements for such, so if you are required to wear something specific to be in attendance at a certain type of event, it is best to be in contact with the host organization to align with those specifications.

- **Do Christian ministers need to be married?**

The call to be in ministry is both public and personal at the same time. Those who are called to be leaders are walking out something God called them to in private. In a sense, ministers walk a fine line between the professional and the personal.

Often ministers go through private things very publicly, and that gives people the idea they know or can legislate for the making private decisions. One such area pertains to ministry, marriage, family, and how the three may intertwine or not intertwine.

In the Bible, we see a variety of personal circumstances when it comes to marriage and family. Deborah, the great judge and prophetess of the Old Testament, was married, but we have no record that she ever had children (Judges 4:4). Knowing ministry as I do, I believe we have no record of Deborah's children because she never had any. Jeremiah was commanded to be single because of his prophetic call (Jeremiah 16:2-4). Hosea, on the other hand, was called to marry a prostitute and have children as an illustration of the spiritual situation present in Israel at the time (Hosea 1:2). Peter had a mother-in-law, and obviously, a wife (Luke 4:38). Priscilla and Aquila were a husband and wife team in the ministry (Acts 18:24-26). Apostles Andronicus and Junia had a relationship, either by blood or marriage (Romans 16:7). The Apostle Paul specifically states he was unmarried at the time he was an apostle (1 Corinthians 7:8). Philip's four daughters were prophetesses and unmarried (Acts 21:8-9). There are specific guidelines for married pastors, deacons, and deaconesses in the New Testament (1 Timothy 3:1-13).

It is obvious that God has room in ministry for all personal circumstances that uphold the Word and are honorable in their conduct. As the call to leadership starts out on a personal level, the personal circumstances by which we are able to execute our call vary by our needs and abilities. It is not an easy thing to have a leadership call from God, and having such means we need to make choices about what we will do, have, and be in our personal lives. While the standards for the five-fold ministry do not change, the circumstances we may have in our personal lives do change and depend on the minister's purpose, duty, and call from God.

The church today tends to be in a hurry to pair off people into marriage, especially women and men in ministry. We all need to step back and mind our business when it comes to people's personal relationships, allowing God to speak into an individual's life about what their personal circumstances should be.

Discussion, study and review questions

- What culture did the church at Corinth derive from? What would the people of that fellowship have been familiar with? What was believed about the pagan priests and the purpose of their service? What were the people of Corinth unfamiliar with? When they learned about God, what else did they learn about? Beyond seeing the law, what did the people of Corinth need to see in Christian ministry? What did they need to understand?

- If we understand Christian ministry, what else do we understand? What is Christian ministry? What does God do for His ministers? What is Christian ministry not about? What is Christian ministry about? What are ministers called to bring forth?

- How does the Bible use the word "ministry?" What three contexts exist for the word "ministry?" What are ministers appointed to do? What did Jesus proclaim His ministry to be? What is the greatest among us appointed to do?

- Does Christian ministry vary in function? No matter the function, what is its one specific purpose? What does the minister of the New Covenant use, and why?

- Is ministry service random? In contrast to randomness, what does the minister of God have? How is a minister's service fulfilled? How is this accomplished? Does a minister understand every order of God? What does the minister of God understand?

- Is being in ministry a serious command? What must a minister be for such service? Who calls those appointed to ministry? What are those called to ministry required to do? What does Kingdom ministry require?

- What is the inheritance of ministry work? Who provides for ministers, and why? How does part of the Lord's provision come?

- What are some characteristics of Christian ministry? What are some specific Biblical examples of the characteristics of Christian ministry in action?

- What are some Old Testament types of Christian ministry? How do these types shadow what Christian ministry is to represent?

- Discuss and share some of the questions and answers found in the "Questions and Answers" section. What did you learn that you did not know about Christian ministry? What did you learn that changed your mind about an opinion you might have had prior about Christian ministry? How did learning about specific issues related to Christian ministry help you to grow in your understanding of ministry? The church? Your own relationship with God?

Chapter Two

PRINCIPLES FOR CHRISTIAN LEADERSHIP

He who has never learned to obey cannot be a good commander."
– Aristotle[1]

It's great to be called to serve in God's ministry. Discerning a ministerial call is one of the most incredible things that can happen in the life of a minister. The connection we often fail to make is the call to be a minister is a call to be a Christian leader. When somebody is called to ministry, they are called to spend their lives in the service of the Lord for the purpose of building His Kingdom and edifying His people. This is not an easy task, nor one at which we should minimize or scoff. Examining and re-examining a call to Christian leadership is a deep, introspective, and reflective process. It calls the leader to examine their motives, thoughts, self, and relationship to both God and the body of Christ.

Some aspects of a leadership call vary, depending on the office or ministry one is called to have. If one is an apostle, the way they lead is different than the way a pastor or prophet leads. It's important we acknowledge that not every type of leadership is exactly the same. At the same time, we can get so caught up in the differences of offices we forget there are many essential components to Christian leadership that remain the same, no matter what office we may be called to walk in as the Lord leads. Here we are going to look at principles of Christian leadership – the essential components that make for good Christian leaders, no matter what office they may called to serve in or what stage of development they are at in their call of Christian leadership.

Text study

Numbers 11:10-17

Supplementary texts

Exodus 28:36, 1 Chronicles 16:10-11, Hosea 4:4-9, Matthew 10:38-39, 1 Corinthians 14:40, 2 Corinthians 4:1-18, Ephesians 4:3, 1 Thessalonians 3:12, Hebrews 12:5-14, 1 Peter 2:19-21, Revelation 3:9.

Power verse

Numbers 11:17:

- *"I will come down and talk with thee there: and I will take of the Spirit which is upon thee, and will put it upon them; and they shall bear the burden of the people with thee, that thou bear it not thyself alone."*

- *"And I will come down and talk with you there; and I will take of the Spirit which is upon you and will put It upon them; and they shall bear the burden of the people with you, so that you may not have to bear it yourself alone."* (AMP)

- *"And I will come down and talk with you there; and I will take of the Spirit which is upon you and will put It upon them; and they shall bear the burden of the people with you, so that you may not have to bear it yourself alone."* (NIV)

- *"And I will come down and talk with you there; and I

will take of the Spirit which is upon you and will put It upon them; and they shall bear the burden of the people with you, so that you may not have to bear it yourself alone." (NASB)

- *"Then I will come down and speak with you there. I will take some of the Spirit who is on you and put [the Spirit] on them. They will help you bear the burden of the people, so that you do not have to bear it by yourself."* (HCSB)

- *"While I am talking with you there, I will give them some of your authority, so they can share responsibility for my people. You will no longer have to care for them by yourself."* (CEV)

Power words

- **Come down** – From the Hebrew word *"yarad"* which means, "to go down, descend, decline, march down, sink down."[2]

- **Talk** – From the Hebrew word *"dabar"* which means, "to speak, declare, converse, command, promise, warn, threaten, sing."[3]

- **Spirit** – From the Hebrew word *"ruwach"* which means, "wind, breath, mind, spirit."[4]

- **Put it upon them** – From the Hebrew word *"suwm"* which means, "to put, place, set, appoint, make."[5]

- **Bear** – From the Hebrew word *"nasa'"* which means, "to lift, bear, carry up, take."[6]

- **Burden of the people** – From two Hebrew words: *"massa,"* which means, "load, bearing, tribute, burden, lifting; utterance, oracle, burden;"[7] and *"am,"* which means, "nation, people; kinsman, kindred."[8]

Historical context

The Israelites gave Moses a run for his money out in the wilderness. Between their disobedience, griping, complaining, arguing, and lack of faith, Moses truly had his hands full as the singular leader of God's people. God recognized the burden present on Moses and saw fit to lift his burden with these people by establishing other leaders who would carry the same authority and leadership ability to assist in leading the people. In ancient cultures, such was common. Tribal heads or elders were given the power to lead and make certain decisions over groups of people and then functioned as a leadership body for making decisions.

Notes on text

Numbers 11 gives us intense and powerful insight into God's principles for leadership. Leadership is to be multiplied, that ample leadership may abound and extend to all. It has always been God's will that His people were governed and led by His precepts, and in turn, by leaders that uphold His precepts and His Spirit. Serving as Kingdom leaders is an appointment and a spiritual operation, not a worldly one. To qualify for leadership in God's Kingdom, one must have His Spirit.

Power points

- Kingdom leadership comes from God's giving. It is recognized by those who are also in Kingdom leadership, as Kingdom leaders know there is only one Spirit by which we live and lead in God's Kingdom (Numbers 11:17, Ephesians 4:3). Those who are called to operate as Christian leaders bear the Spirit of God for the purposes of leadership. One cannot be a Christian leader because someone appoints them without God's seal, but only because God appoints them (Numbers 10:16).

- A Christian leader must hear from God (Numbers 11:17, 1 Chronicles 16:10-11). While there are many ways by which this is accomplished, a true leader of God will have a solid prayer life and spend time hearing from God in His Word (Isaiah 34:16). Leaders are learners, seeking the revelation of God through the Holy Spirit, essential learning about the things of God and the things of this world, and learning about people (Proverbs 28:5, Hosea 4:4-9). Christian leaders are service-minded, not seeking to help others for personal gain, but for the glory and praise of our Father in heaven (Matthew 5:16).

- The basic principle of any Christian leader is to work, live, and abide in love (2 Corinthians 8:24, Galatians 5:13). It's great to operate a pulpit ministry, but more important that love backs up the teaching. Christian leaders must be accessible to people, not to the point of wearing out or being abused, but taking a genuine interest in the issues, concerns, and lives those who follow Christian ministry have (Numbers 11:10-17, 1 Thessalonians 3;12).

- Christian leaders must have the courage of conviction to stand in faith and make faith real to those who follow their ministries (2 Corinthians 4:1-5). They must be able to speak and teach (2 Corinthians 4:5, 13), to witness (2 Corinthians 4:1-4), and to rise up as leaders, without complaining about the cost (2 Corinthians 4:7-12). They are called to not just claim to be people of faith, but stand up in solid character (2 Corinthians 4:11-18). It is essential for leaders to know who they are in Christ, know their identity in Him, and make their calling sure as they step out in faith and walk the path of ministry (2 Corinthians 4:1-18).

- As Christian ministry stands upon decency, order, and discipline (1 Corinthians 14:40), Christian ministers must exemplify these characteristics in their own lives and their own ministries. Such gives legitimacy to the Kingdom of God, maintaining order, decency and discipline while upholding principles of freedom and grace (Revelation 3:19). Christian leadership is not an avenue for being a tyrant or controlling other people, but is one in which the same principles are taught and implemented within the faith and lives of those who believe (Hebrews 12:5-13).

- One of the most important precepts of Christian leadership is holiness (Exodus 28:36). Holiness puts the burden on the individual to live according to the calling God has placed upon them. In the calling to ministry, leaders are set apart for their service and called to exemplify the lifestyle to which God has called them. Christian leaders must be people of God both in and out of the pulpit, setting an example to others about what God asks of each of us in the Christian life (Hebrews 12:14).

- Christian leaders must be unselfish. They are commanded to deny themselves, take up the difficulties of their lives and their calling, and follow Him (Matthew 10:38-39). Christian ministry is a constant call to die to self, seek the face of God, repent and intercede. Beyond being a job, being a Christian minister is a lifestyle principle: it is a way of living for the Lord in His service (1 Peter 2:19-21).

The characteristics of Christian leadership found in Jesus

Jesus Christ offers us the perfect example of Christian leadership. Even though we often don't think of Him as such, Jesus modeled the essential characteristics leaders need to embody within His ministry work. Within Jesus, we find the entire five-fold ministry and appointments and that means the characteristics He displays are beneficial for every type of Christian leader:

- **Teaching** – Jesus was, first and foremost, a teacher throughout His three-year ministry (Matthew 5-7, Mark 6:34, Luke 21:29-38, Luke 4:14-30, John 3:1-8, 7:50-51). It was His desire that people would discover the truth about God and come into the fullness of life with God. This was accomplished as Jesus taught the people spiritual truths in ways they could understand. The purpose of teaching is to make the things of God plain to people, so they may hear and understand. A leader's message is conveyed through their ability to teach. When teaching, a leader must relate through mannerisms, items, and style in a way that they can understand. When teaching, we must understand different cultures, language usage, and presentation to make sure the message transcends cultures and reaches people's heads, hearts, and souls.

- **Understanding** – Jesus not only understood others, He also conveyed understanding (Matthew 7:1-6, Mark 12:41-44, Luke 7:1-10, Luke 7:36-50, John 4:1-26, John 8:1-11). Science is full of studies on human behavior and primes psychologists, advertisers, and marketers in how to read, manipulate, and appeal to varied perspectives of human thinking. This is, indeed, a way of understanding other people – but it does not convey understanding to those on the receiving end. Understanding is about more than just knowing how people think or trying to work someone to an end goal – it is also about being able to impact someone else's life so your understanding and theirs meet for a purpose.

- **Empathy** – It's easy to become so hardened and fast on principal issues that you forget about and miss the human element in ministry. Endless parades of political viewpoints, protests, debates, and opinions on different matters cause ministers to become more about the drama of belief than the simple, everyday perspective that the world has various hurts, requiring healing. Jesus definitely held fast to His Father's principles, but He also remembered people were people and had needs to be met (Matthew 14:13-21, Matthew 15:21-28, Mark 5:21-43, Luke 7:11-17). Herein, in Christ, lies the basis of empathy. Empathy maintains principle while also upholding the relevance of human need. When we empathize with a person, we understand their position, suffering, hurt, or thinking about a current situation or condition. Instead of taking that upon ourselves, empathy allows objectivity and spiritual movement for a true rectification to any situation.

- **Compassion** – In modern society, we are desensitized to suffering. Every time someone turns on the television, they see another story of someone's plight or misfortune. Seeing so much suffering so frequently creates a lack of urgency within us to reach out and help others. In its essence, compassion is a deepened sense of empathy, creating a desire to help someone else. The Bible describes Jesus' compassion as "doing good" – wherever He went, He did good (Acts 10:38). As ministers of the Gospel, we have a call to compassion – to do good – wherever we go.

- **Principle** – Jesus was influential because He represented powerful ideas. Representing powerful ideas is principle. When we stand for principle, we are standing for and representing something greater than ourselves. The world's reaction to principle is often mixed – some love it, some hate it, and, as in the case of Christ, some persecute it (Matthew 12:1-14, Mark 3:1-6, Mark 3:20-35, John 11:45-57). For this reason, principle must be intricately connected to both purpose and compassion – because without this combination, principle can be ineffective.

- **Discipline** – Jesus was a disciplinarian (Luke 9:46-48, Luke 22:24-30). Before you do a double-take at that statement, think about what a disciplinarian is: it is an individual who both promotes and enforces discipline. Being a disciplinarian means that discipline is a value both upheld and enforced by an individual. The ultimate goal of discipline is to create self-discipline in others. One of a minister's prime goals should always be to create disciples well-disciplined and purposed for the work of Christ in this world.

- **Character** – Jesus didn't do one thing and then claim to be about something else (Colossians 1:17, Matthew 5:37, Matthew 6:24, Luke 16:13). In a world of utter confusion, character needs to be a trait of God's ministers. Character does not mean that we never falter or fail, but it does mean that we are not hypocrites. Don't proclaim to believe in one thing, and then live a way contrary to that statement. High character means being people of integrity, purpose, and discipline, seeing to it that God's work is done, and realizing that doing the work of God needs to mean something to the man or woman of God that does it.

- **Insight** – Perhaps the hardest thing for a leader to do is figure out how to handle everyone. Not everyone requires the same handling in every situation. It is through insight that we learn how to read people's needs and special circumstances. Jesus was a master at insight. He knew when the circumstances required directness (Matthew 9:16-17), sarcasm (John 2:1-5), illustration (Matthew 13:1-52), correction (Mark 10:17-31), compassion (Mark 6:30-44), and every other conceivable situation. Christian ministers need to seek insight – or knowledge of a person or situation by the Spirit of God – in order to lead God's people more effectively and with greater empowerment.

Exemplary characteristics present in types of Christian ministry

- **Joshua 10:1-11** – *Joshua's obedience*, a type of the Christian minister's need for obedience. Anyone who has ever read the books of Exodus, Leviticus, Numbers, and Deuteronomy can discern the wandering Israelites weren't the most fun group of people to deal with on a regular basis. I have no question that the leaders of the Israelites probably found themselves quite frustrated as the children of Israel whined, complained, and found fault after fault with their circumstances, no matter what was done for them. In the mist of these negative attitudes, there was Joshua, who was faithful, committed, and sincere, right through to the end. Joshua's obedience to God is noted in his total devotion to bring the children of God right into God's promise for them, despite the naysayers, the obvious reminders that Joshua was not Moses and never would be, and any personal doubts of fears he might have had. Joshua was a true leader in the face of difficulty and adversity. Christian ministers need to hold this same commitment to obedience. If God has called us to it, there is a definite purpose behind it. Obedience is the bridge between faith unseen and revelation revealed. If Christian leaders want to see the fruit of their work, obedience is essential. Too many leaders fall by the wayside because they don't see desired results. We will never see what we want if we falter in obedience.

- **1 Samuel 17:1-58** –*David's courage*, a type of Christian minister's need for courage. King David is a common figure when we examine Biblical leadership. He is noted for many things – giant-slaying, ruling Israel during its greatest historical period, his young age, even his affair with Bathsheba – but we seldom consider David's incredible courage as a powerful leadership characteristic equally worthy of emulation. David wasn't a man who backed down from a challenge. While many modern Christian figures often discourage courage, citing it as "confrontational" or a "lack of faith," David's life bespeaks the total opposite. It takes more faith, trust, and belief in God to step out and speak about wrong, confront issues that need confronting, and deal with issues head-on than it does to sit back and leave things to their own devices. Christian ministers are called to have this courage; to step up and be counted when everyone else would rather sit back and ignore what needs to be addressed. God calls the Christian minister to be proactive: to go where others dare not go, speak what others dare not speak, and handle issues that others dare not touch. No Christian minister can live this life and stand up and be counted in this powerful way without courage!

- **1 Kings 3:16-28** – *Solomon's wisdom*, a type of the Christian minister's need for wisdom. Do you understand the power and relevance of wisdom in a minister's life? Whenever we see a minister "caught" in the act of trouble (whether it is adultery, abuse, theft, fraud, or something else), we are seeing the consequences of operating a life and ministry without the exercise of wisdom. Wisdom is the ability to see things with spiritual foresight, and the application of that foresight to whatever situation warrants or calls for it. Christian ministers need to walk in wisdom for two reasons. The first is obvious: to exercise fairness, righteousness, and purpose in and throughout their ministries. Ministry growth, expansion, planning, and maintenance all come about by revelation assessed in wisdom. God certainly gives us vision, but He also gives us wisdom by which we are able to assess that revelation and make it practical. The second is obvious, but understated: to exercise good and sound judgment both in the professional and personal arenas of life. The decisions we make today will impact the results we see tomorrow. This requires God's Christian leaders to walk in purpose, on purpose, in wisdom, at all times.

- **Esther 2:10-22** – *Mordecai's skillfulness*, a type of the Christian minister's need for skill. I believe heavily in the power of God's anointing, but I also believe that we are anointed for a purpose. The purpose of God's anointing is not to bolster our self-esteem, make us feel good about ourselves, or impress other people with our spiritual gifts. In Mordecai's humility, we see his purpose and skill. Mordecai didn't act haphazardly or randomly pick up one thing and then something else to try and get results. One thing Mordecai recognized that would do all Christian ministers good to recognize in their ministries is the power of skillfulness is persistence. What we do should be carefully examined and planned as God guides. We should never be running many steps ahead of God, or randomly trying to pursue various things in the hopes one of them will work out. Walking by skill gives the Christian minister a powerful edge over the enemy.

- **Judges 4:4-10** – *Deborah's forcefulness*, a type of the Christian minister's need for force. If there was ever a Biblical leader whose work is distorted in modern context, it's Deborah. We don't hear much about Deborah in the context of her leadership ability. What many try to do is slant Deborah one way or another, using her to push an agenda based on personal conviction rather than truth. Deborah was, yes, a woman who was also a leader – and a military leader, at that. She didn't shy away from controversy, and didn't retreat when things got hard or became more than she wanted to deal with. We know from the New Testament that *"...The* *kingdom of heaven suffereth violence, and the violent take it by force."* (Matthew 11:12). There are many ways to understand this passage, but the one we need to see right here and now is the Christian minister's command of the Kingdom of God. Taking the Kingdom by force doesn't mean being rude or nasty, or operating a ministry that is up in everyone's face at all times. What it means is being about the Father's business in any and all necessary situations. Deborah knew what she needed to do it and she was not afraid to exert influence and power to do it. The Christian minister can't shy back because they fear the front lines.

Questions and answers

- **How does a Christian minister prepare for ministry?**

There are many different levels of preparation for Christian ministry, all of which are contingent upon the level of service and purpose in an individual's ministry work.

Ministers begin their ministerial preparations through God's call and deep, introspective prayer. This aspect of preparation may take a short period of time or a long period of time, but it is the first stage of ministry preparation. In this initial stage, the minister seeks God about his or her ministry purpose. This stage is fundamental because it revives throughout the ministry walk in periods of discernment.

The second phase of ministry preparation comes through sharing about the call with others. In this phase, the minister of God begins their walk in their respective ministry. There will be both encouragement and discouragement from different sources, but the minister of God must maintain balance. They are neither called to run, nor called to grow in conceit, but called to find their own purpose, place, and positioning within the church. This phase is an intermediary one, an in-between place between where the minister of God is going and where they have been. It is a time to find out what is needed to further develop the call.

The third stage of ministry is often skipped due to doctrinal beliefs or excitement, and that stage is education. When a minister of God has a call, they must prepare for that call practically as well as spiritually. Every minister needs to learn about the Word beyond church services and books written by popular preachers. History, context, culture, original languages, and varied perspectives must all be considered when ministering or writing on the Word. Ministers must also be prepared for the legal side of ministry, through ordination and licensing. Whatever ministry call a person has, they must pursue the necessary education to operate in their ministry gift with grace and poise.

The fourth stage of ministry preparation is a combination of all reached to this point, and it is one of maintenance. Ministers are ever called to learn, expand their education, network with others, learn about changing understandings of ministry in church, and discern with the Lord about the direction of their call. Ministry preparation is constant, rather than static, in continuing process.

- **Is ministry a burden for the minister?**

Sorting out the call of ministry is a challenge for the minister. It is not simple, nor is acceptance of a ministry call instantaneous. There may be years where ministry is viewed as a burden by the minister who walks in that ministry, for any number of reasons. Some people have a hard time accepting the ministry God has for them. Some people have difficulty balancing life with ministry, and falter in the lack of support they may receive from others in their lives. Some people find ministry itself overwhelming, and others walk in callings they should not pursue, thus making ministry burdensome.

We associate the word "burden" in a negative connotation today. The word for "prophecy" and "vision" in the Old Testament also means "burden" by extension. If we carefully study the prophecies of the prophets, we understand why this was. The prophecies received by the prophets brought with them heavy understanding and intense introspection. They saw the coming fall and rise of nations, the destruction of their people, the sinfulness and offenses committed against God, and the way all these things impacted the spiritual state of the people. Being a prophet was a serious responsibility, and not to be taken lightly. For this reason, it was a "burden" to receive the message from God. It was not something that made neither the prophet, nor the people feel particularly good about themselves or their situations.

In understanding the word "burden" in this sense, it means the prophetic word itself and the office did not serve to personally bolster the prophet. In this sense, ministry is, indeed, a divine "burden." The goal of ministry is not the personal gain of the minister, but the purpose of God in that ministry. It may not always be easy to execute, and may ask a lot of that individual. They may have to sacrifice personal relationships, finances, prestige, even things they desire in this life that may not be bad for someone else. Understanding ministry as a "burden" doesn't mean it is tiresome or unwanted – it means that the call itself is difficult. It is not easy to walk in ministry. What God asks of a person is not always easy for that individual to do.

Seeing ministry in this way gives us a greater respect for leaders, especially good Christian ministers who are solid in their faith and in their work. There is a reason the Word tells us to esteem leadership. True ministers make great sacrifices to see to the spiritual well-being of those assigned under their care. They are worthy of respect and honor because the work they do is difficult, honorable and unselfish.

- **Should ministers support one another?**

Yes, they should. If we rightly understand ministry offices, there is no need for competition. Each office has its own function and when we are duly called to an office, we walk in that office by the Spirit of God. We see competition in offices today because we don't understand the true work of the five-fold ministry and the differences of each of those offices.

If the ministers of God will step back and see ministry for what it is, and uphold the principles of Christian leadership, Christian ministers will realize the need for other ministers in Christ to stand behind them and with them. God does not call us to a spirit of competition, but one of love and mutual respect. When we start esteeming the work that others do as much as we esteem the work God is doing in us, ministry life of all sorts will change for the better.

- **How can a Christian minister gain a better sense of principles for Christian ministry?**

Christian ministers need to understand the power and purpose in their call. If a Christian minister can see the relevance and importance in the way they carry themselves, the principles follow. Being a Christian minister means having a walk of integrity – and we find that unconditional, unrelenting integrity present in the principles purposed for Christian ministry.

Discussion, study and review questions:

- Why did Moses have his hands full as leader of the Israelites? How did God recognize and lift the burden from Moses? Was this common? What purpose did tribal heads and elders serve?

- Should leadership be multiplied? Why or why not? What has always been God's will for His people and, in turn, His leaders? What two things mark Kingdom service? What is the qualification for leadership in God's Kingdom?

- How are Kingdom leaders chosen? Who recognizes Kingdom leaders? Why? What do Christian leaders bear, and why? Who must appoint a Christian leader?

- Who must a Christian leader hear from? What are some ways this is accomplished? What kind of people are leaders? Where do they seek their revelation from? What do they seek to learn? What kind of mindset do Christian ministers have? How does this manifest?

- What is the basic principle of a Christian leader? Which is more important: pulpit ministry or working love? Why? Should Christian leaders be accessible? In what way? Why?

- What courage should Christian leaders have? How does it manifest? What must they be able to do? What else should they display? What should Christian leaders know about themselves and their calling?

- What does Christian ministry stand upon? How does this principle relate to Christian leaders? Why is this important? How should Christian ministers deal with areas that do not line up with holiness, decency, and order?

- What is one of the most important precepts of Christian ministry? In the call of ministry, what are leaders set apart for and called to exemplify? What kind of people should Christian leaders be?

- Should Christian leaders be unselfish? Why or why not? What are Christian leaders commanded to do? What is Christian ministry? What kind of lifestyle is demanded of a Christian minister?

- What are some characteristics present in the ministry of Jesus that can benefit the Christian leader?

- What are some illustrations of types present for Christian leadership? How do these types shadow what Christian ministry is to represent?

- Discuss and share some of the questions and answers found in the "Questions and Answers" section. What did you learn that you did not know about Christian ministry? What did you learn that changed your mind about Christian leadership? How did learning about specific issues related to Christian ministry help you to grow in your understanding of ministry? The church? Your own relationship with God?

Chapter Three

THE CALL TO SERVE OTHERS AS WE SERVE JESUS CHRIST

There have been meetings of only a moment which have left impressions for life...for eternity. No one can understand that mysterious thing we call 'influence'...yet everyone of us continually exerts influence, either to heal, to bless, to leave marks of beauty; or to wound, to hurt, to poison, to stain other lives.
– J.B. Miller[1]

What does it mean to be a servant? In most societies, being a servant has a negative connotation. It is associated with having to wait on others who may be rude, abusive, or ill-tempered. Being a servant is associated with living in poverty, and receiving little pay for a lot of hard work. A servant may be forced to do work that is beneath their station, and may cause them to feel badly about themselves. Yet, they continue in their work, because their work is not about them – it is about the one or ones they serve.

Now, imagine having a life-long call to service. Your work is never going to be about you. What your Master asks of you may be less than desirable, and it may take you to places and to do things you never imagined. You may have financial struggles. You may experience rejection and hardship. Your master lets you know that your work as a servant will not be easy. Do you still answer the call?

Ministry is any number of different concepts, concoctions, and conceptions. Some believe the life of ministry serves to be served, rather than be of service. Some think ministry should be materially rewarding. Still others think ministry is all about suffering and poverty. The truth lies somewhere in the middle of all these different concepts and ideas. Ministry is the call of servanthood. It is a life based in trusting God, and living in obedience to Him. The true minister of God lives not for themselves, but for God, and those they too are called to serve.

Christian ministers are called to serve others as they serve Jesus Christ. We often talk about serving the Lord, but serving God is about serving more than just personal interest for reward. It's about far more than just ministering to be noticed or become famous. In Christian service, we humble ourselves to obey the work of God in our everyday lives, and in every task He calls us unto, and to bless those we are sent to with the Gospel in word and action.

Text study

John 13:1-17

Supplementary texts

Daniel 3:1-20, Matthew 20L20-28, Luke 22:24-30, John 12:23-32, Romans 7:5-6, Romans 14:16-19, Galatians 5:13-14, Hebrews 9:1-15

Power verse

John 13:13-15:

- *"Ye call Me Master and Lord; and ye say well; for so I am. If I then, your Lord and Master, have washed your feet; ye also ought to wash one another's feet. For I have given you an example, that ye should do as I have done to you."*

- *"You call Me 'Teacher' and 'Lord,' and you speak correctly, because I am. If I, your Lord and teacher, have washed your feet, you too must wash each other's feet. I have given you an example: just as I have done, you also must do."* (CEB)

- *"You call Me Teacher and Lord, and it is right that you do so, because that is what I am. I, your Lord and Teacher, have just washed your feet. You, then, should wash one another's feet. I have set an example for you, so that you will do just what I have done for you."* (GNT)

- *"You call Me 'Teacher' and 'Lord,' and rightly so, for that is what I am. Now that I, your Lord and Teacher, have washed your feet, you also should wash one another's feet. I have set you an example that you should do as I have done for you."* (NIV)

- *"You call Me the Teacher (Master) and the Lord, and you are right in doing so, for that is what I am. If I then, your Lord and Teacher (Master), have washed your feet, you ought [it is your duty, you are under obligation, you owe it] to wash one another's feet. For I have given you this as an example, so that you should do [in your turn] what I have done to you."* (AMP)

- *"You call Me teacher and Lord, and you're right because that's what I am. So if I, your Lord and teacher, have washed your feet, you must wash each other's feet. I've given you an example that you should follow."* (GOD'S WORD)

Power words

- **Master** – From the Greek word *"didaskalos"* which means, "a teacher; in the New Testament, one who teaches concerning the things of God, and the duties of man."[2]

- **Lord** – From the Greek word *"kurios"* which means, "he to whom a person or thing belongs, about which he has the power of deciding; master, lord."[3]

- **Wash one another's feet** – From three Greek words: *"nipto,"* which means, "to wash, to wash oneself;"[4] *"allelon,"* which means, "one another, reciprocally, mutually;"[5] and *"pous,"* which means, "a foot, both of men or beast."[6]

- **Given** – From the Greek word *"didomi"* which means, "to give, to give something to someone; to give; to grant or permit one."[7]

- **Example** – From the Greek word *"hupodeigma"* which means, "a sign suggestive of anything, delineation of a thing, representation, figure, copy; an example; for imitation." [8]

Historical context

Ancient Middle Eastern culture emphasized hospitality. When one was invited to another's house, they were accustomed to certain actions considered hospitable. As everyone wore sandals or went without shoes in the hot, desert sands, feet were easily dirtied. With no brooms or vacuum cleaners, floors also quickly got dirty. This was a particular issue for eating areas, which were also on the floor. A ritual washing was done prior to eating for hygienic purposes. When one was a guest in another's home, it was the job of the servants to wash the feet of the guests. This was regarded as the lowest possible position for someone to be in. For Jesus to willingly take up this position and wash the feet of His disciples displayed His true humility and also showed us the heart of a servant leader.

Notes on text

Christian leaders are called to be servant leaders, modeling the faith and humility of our Leader, Jesus Christ. This gives us a powerful illustration of what Christian leaders are supposed to be about. Christian leadership is not about personal glory or gain; it's not about being the star; it is about serving others just as Christ has called us to serve: with humility, love, and grace.

Power points

- Christian leadership is ministry based in service. This means the Christian leader provides a service for the people who receive and embrace their leadership. While Christian leaders may require assistance, the purpose of Christian leadership is not to be served – it is to provide this service for God's people. In providing this service, leaders are an example of humility, transformation, and true spiritual empowerment. Just as Jesus came not to be served, but to serve (Luke 13:1-17), Christian leaders come for the same purpose. It is a work about others rather than selfish ambitions (Matthew 20:20-28).

- In Christian service, leaders do not bow down to the idols or falsehoods of this world. Even when everyone else around them succumbs to idols, they refuse. No matter what form the idol may take, they trust God. This happens even in the face of rejection or threat. This proves in Christian leadership, action speaks louder than words. Christian leaders must back up every claim they make about faith and about God in their lives and choices (Daniel 3:1-20).

- The service demanded of a Christian leader requires sacrifice. It is not an easy call, and not one to be taken lightly. There will be many circumstances by which the Christian leader is forced to die to himself or herself and sacrifice personal interest for the Kingdom of God (Matthew 20:20-28). If Christian leaders are to point to Christ, they must follow His lead, deny themselves, take up their cross, and follow Him, dying daily that Christ may live in them as others may come to know Him (Luke 22:24-30).

- Christian ministry is a "drawing" of people to Christ. People learn of that drawing as both followers and leaders are drawn together in Kingdom service. Such is achieved only as the minister dies to the flesh and glorifies God in a more powerful and upstanding way (John 12:23-32). A minister's life is not their own, as they live by the Spirit (Romans 7:5-6).

- Being a Christian leader is about Kingdom service. A Christian leader is not to be exceedingly preoccupied with worldly things. Christian ministers should never allow good to be spoken of as evil, and should be focused with a Kingdom mindset and vision. Christian service is pleasing before God and human beings when it reflects righteousness, peace and joy in the Holy Spirit, and when it pursues peace and mutual edification (Romans 14:16-19).

- Christian service works for and advocates freedom in Christ and serves in love. It is essential Christian leaders love their neighbors as themselves, both Christian and non-Christian neighbors alike. Such love must be shown, rather than just a mere lip-service of speech (Galatians 5:13-14).

- Christian leaders are advocates and representatives of the new covenant present in Christ Jesus. That new covenant makes the work of Jesus Christ real, living, and applicable to people today. Rather than being about exterior things, Christian leaders realize how important it is to focus on the true things, the things of God, and His eternal truth (Hebrews 9:1-15).

Attitudes of servanthood

How do leaders display their heart of service? This is a question that has been examined and re-examined throughout the ages. Some leaders don't do nearly enough, while some go over the top in their efforts to assist and help other people. The truth is that servant-hood is an attitude as well as a way of operating ministry. If one carefully examines the attitudes present in a leader, they can determine whether or not that leader is servant-minded.

- **Balance** – Perhaps the most difficult thing for a minister to maintain is a good sense of balance within ministry. Most often, I see varied extremes: ministers who are either burning themselves out or completely burnt out, or ministers who simply do not do enough in their work of service. A true servant needs to find balance, because in the state of extremes, they are no good to anybody. A solid, servant-minded leader knows the relevance of prayer, rest, refreshment, and active, visible service through the ministry God has given them (Deuteronomy 4:9-14, Deuteronomy 11:18-19, Matthew 6:33, Matthew 10:37, John 15:5).

- **Boundaries** – One of the first things God established with the Israelites was a good sense of boundaries (Exodus 19:16-25). Telling the Israelites that they could not go beyond a certain point or do certain things was not to be mean – it was to help the people have a greater sense of limits and boundaries in their spiritual lives. God went beyond boundaries in the spiritual realm and also set up boundaries in the natural realm as well, through dietary laws, hygiene laws, and relational guidelines (Exodus 21:1-36, Leviticus 11:1-47, Leviticus 15:1-33). Even though the boundaries leaders enforce today may be different than these literal guidelines established once upon a time, the principles behind them are the same. Boundaries are enforced by godly leaders because they help people to know their limits with God, one another, with leaders, and within themselves. As a teaching tool, boundaries serve to be one of the most effective impacts a leader can have in service to others.

- **Interest** – Ministers today tend to limit themselves to only the preaching aspect of ministry, and ignore other aspects of ministry, such as counseling, leadership training, and both social and community action. Preaching is definitely a part of ministry (Ezra 6:14, Matthew 12:41, Luke 4:44, Acts 8:25, Acts 17:13), but it is not all of ministry (Romans 12:1-8). Our first purpose in ministry should be toward the people, and meeting the needs of the church and community as God has graced us within our office or appointment. We need to be interested in people beyond pulpit preaching or ministering, on a level that will impact them in varied areas of their lives.

- **Attentiveness** – Have you ever seen a minister who was clearly uninterested in what they were doing? They don't want to talk to the people, or care if the message or work impacts lives. They go about ministry as if it is a chore to complete. The people they lead are considered a burden, and they are never available beyond pulpit preaching for issues that may arise. This is an inattentive leader – one who is genuinely not interested in ministry aside from its gains. When I say "gains," I am not just referring to money, but also the sense of power, importance, and notability a minister may get from the job. They aren't in ministry to serve, but to be noticed. A true servant is attentive to the needs of the people God has assigned them to and interested in making sure their ministry is a good fit for those individuals (Proverbs 12:15, Mark 4:21-25, Hebrews 2:1, James 1:19-25). A good leader knows, within the realms of balance, how to be attentive to what the people need without burning out.

- **Grace** – Grace is over-used and, as a result, misunderstood in modern society. Grace is not getting the first parking spot at the mall, an extra portion of dessert, or a television on sale. Grace is the unmerited favor of God working in our lives to remove the effects and cost of sin. Grace also works as we walk in the Spirit, giving us the ability to walk in God's ways and live in holiness and purpose consistently (Zechariah 12:10, Acts 13:43, Romans 1:7, Romans 12:3, 1 Corinthians 15:10, 2 Corinthians 12:9). A leader's work is a part of that ministry of grace, and the Christian minister is called to walk in God's grace throughout their work. It's tempting to be people who are judgmental, harsh, and punitive on matters of sin, especially when doing so gets a leader attention. Ministers of God are required to flow in God's grace as they hear about the hurts, sins, and offenses of God's people. There is a sacred trust that flows back and forth between the minister and the person who is in need of ministry. The confidence of someone in need of ministering should never be broken, and the minister should listen, offer realistic perspective, and always keep both love and principle in mind when offering advice or perspective.

- **Involvement** – Being in ministry should be a proactive experience, not static (Numbers 4:27, 1 Chronicles 18:14, Matthew 21:24, Matthew 24:46, 1 Corinthians 4:20, 2 Corinthians 11:12). If a minister covers other leaders, he or she should know what those leaders are doing and be involved in support and covering of that work. Leaders should be taught and instructed in the Word, rather than left to their own devices. If a minister covers a church or group of people, the leader should be involved in the church's activities, actively participating in the works and life of the church. An uninvolved, distant leader is a leader void of impact.

- **Objectivity** – It is essential that a leader maintain objectivity with those they lead. It is fine to love the people you lead, as you are their leader, but it is not appropriate to become emotionally, sexually, or physically involved with them. Ethics must be kept in proper perspective, especially when one is working with individuals who may be hurting, damaged, or otherwise unwell (Exodus 20:1-21, Deuteronomy 5:1-22, 2 Corinthians 4:1-6).

- **Correction and encouragement** – I have listed correction and encouragement together because they go together, hand-in-hand. Ministers who seek to only correct become discouraging task-masters, while ministers who only encourage bring up undisciplined individuals in the faith. Both correction and encouragement are needed as balancing points with those a leader leads. No leader enjoys the prospect of correction, but that does not make it any less necessary. A right leader will view both correction and encouragement as essential parts of service (Proverbs 10:17, Job 5:17, 2 Timothy 3:16, 2 Timothy 4:2).

Types of Christian service present in the Old Testament

- **Genesis 14:20** – *Abraham's tithe before Melchizedek*, a type of financial service between leaders. We know that tithes and offerings are the way God's church functions...but do we ever forget that tithing is everyone's responsibility? Both members and church leaders alike are required to tithe. Bringing forth tithes and offerings is a required part of ministry service!

- **Ruth 2:8-16** –*Boaz and Ruth,* a type of the Christian minister's call to work hard, trust in God, and attend to needs. Ruth is the first example of service in the book of Ruth, and she works tirelessly to ensure her mother-in-law, Naomi, and her, have enough to eat. Ruth takes a consistent leadership role throughout the book of Ruth, making the commitment to Naomi to remain with her until the end, and then following through with her commitment. Then Boaz enters the picture, also stepping up and taking a leadership role, as he sees to the care and needs of Ruth and Naomi. Throughout Ruth we see the principle of hard work, dedication, meeting needs, and consistent trust in God – even when trust was hard.

- **2 Samuel 11:1-12:25** – *David's repentance,* a type of the Christian minister's humility. David's affair with Bathsheba is, perhaps, one of the lowest points of David's work and ministry. Not only did David sin in his affair, he also sinned trying to cover it up. After David cried out to God in repentance, it took a lot for him to gather himself together and move on...but he still did it. God doesn't ask leaders to be perfect; He asks them to be humble. This is not a condoning of any sinful behavior, but an awareness that the leader has to rely on God for their very existence and ministry. We operate, move on, function, and follow through on ministry commitments via God's Spirit, not our own doings. Repentance for wrongdoing shows a leader is humble enough to follow God and admit their faults as a person, ever-more relying on God.

- **The books of Ezra and Nehemiah** – *The rebuilding of the wall,* a type of Christian ministry correction and encouragement. The call to rebuild the wall was not an easy one. In order to get to the point where the Israelites were able to build the wall, they had to be extensively corrected and then encouraged. Before the people could get to the right thing, the people needed to deal with having done the wrong thing. This is why correction comes before edification: in order for edification to be effective, it must be in what's right, rather than what's wrong. Building the Kingdom of God means we correct first, and encourage in all that is right. This way, the Kingdom of God continues.

- **The book of Haggai** – *The rebuilding of the temple*, a type of the Christian minister's need to focus on spiritual matters in service. The Prophet Haggai had a difficult task to complete: telling the Israelites that they were self-centered and ignoring their divine Kingdom commands pertaining to worship. This literal work of correction shows the essence of the Christian minister's call to serve in spiritual matters. Many leaders have taken on so many diverse social causes and political issues that they forget and forego the essential work and call to present spiritual matters. It is true that a Christian minister is an advocate of what is right in any setting, whether sacred or secular – but the true Christian leader is aware that sacred issues are of far more relevance. Christian ministers need to always keep in mind that encouraging people to seek first the Kingdom of God will help other issues of this world to align with right. Attending to spiritual needs in spiritual service must always be the first priority of the Christian minister, modeling the way for those who follow that leader to do in kind.

Questions and answers

- **Should ministries be involved in community outreach and service?**

The Scriptures clarify that Christian ministry is, in and of itself, a service for God's people. All the way back to the tabernacle, the Scriptures spoke of the priest's work as "service." Whether a minister engages in community outreach or spiritual operation, a minister is operating service.

Ministers are given different gifts and different operations within the Body of Christ. Some ministries are totally centered on community outreaches, such as ministry to the homeless or community feeding programs. Some ministries are predominately teaching ministries, functioning within the church to ensure leaders and ministers are brought up properly in the Word and are able to effectively teach and reach out to others. There are also ministries that do a combination of both – they work within the church and also do outreaches of any variety, along with their instructional work.

The minister of God needs to make sure that, if they are engaging in outreach ministry, they do not forget their spiritual duties. Operating a ministry for the homeless is a good work, but anybody from any spiritual background can do charity work. There are many secular works in this world that are extremely charitable, so we need to keep in mind that simply doing charity work or community outreach is not enough. It is also noteworthy to suggest that community outreach by itself can become an enabling force, something utilized by people to avoid getting their lives together instead of helping them to get it together. The reason the Word calls people to various outreaches is simple: people have natural needs that must be met along with spiritual needs. The church cannot talk about the spiritual realm and ignore what is right in front of its face in the natural realm.

The Word instructs those who are truly believers to reach out to the hungry, the thirsty, those who are sick, the imprisoned, the stranger or foreigner, and those who are in need. Meeting these practical needs opens the door for deeper spiritual needs to be addressed and purposed.

As a rule, I say that ministries should have at least one outreach ministry as a part of their work. This helps keep a ministry current in their communities and nations as well as keeping the door open for proper perspective between the natural and the spiritual.

- **Is there such a thing as a minister doing too much for their people?**

If a minister is going above and beyond to the point where the people are taking advantage of that leader, that leader is doing too much for their people.

God does not ask His ministers to be floor-mats – He asks them to be servants. There is a radical difference between being a servant and being used and abused by people. Some things people need to figure out and learn on their own. While a minister is there to be a help and support to people, and to be a great instructor, guide, and mentor in their lives, a minister can't make decisions or choices for their people. A minister should, likewise, avoid enabling the people they minister. When a minister becomes sexually or overly emotionally involved with someone they cover, the temptation exists to make excuses for that person. The minister of God should never be in this position. If someone is doing the wrong thing, it is the minister's job to warn them, not intervene in the process of due consequence.

There is also the situation that arises when a minister works so hard to make their own ministry work, they do too much for the people they lead. It's not the minister's job to pick everyone up from church, pay everyone's medical bills out of pocket, or see to it that someone's rent is paid on a regular basis. If a leader has to do this to keep people coming back to service or ministry events, then they aren't there because they hold to the Kingdom vision. Ministry is not a bribe. If this is going on, the minister is both enabling the people and killing their vision with people who don't share the vision. Very politely set the boundaries between a handout and ministerial help. If everyone leaves, everyone leaves – God will send new people.

- **Should leaders operate in service to one another?**

Ministers should hold general respect to one another and be willing to assist and serve each other as God duly appoints and calls. When a minister is holding a meeting, fellow ministers should show up not just to attend, but to assist as needed. No minister should ever have an attitude about assisting people at the altar, helping out a preaching minister, or refrain from doing what is needed because of their so-called position.

Ministers are also of service to one another by being a support. It is not easy to be in ministry. People demand of time, there is always difficulty in maintaining finances to bring forth vision, people constantly back out of things, and there is often little help or support for the work. With the new modern attitudes about ministry and the notion that everyone believes they should be in it, it is more competitive and discouraging than ever before. It really says something when a minister can be trusted as a colleague and friend with confidences, personal issues, and encouragement. Such behavior is far more encouraging to a minister than just offering a Bible verse or a generic word that is given to everybody, all of the time. To me, as one who has numerous years in the ministry, this is far more encouraging than many other things that could be done, and an invaluable service.

- **Should ministers literally perform foot-washing among their congregations or those they work with?**

Some denominations believe that a foot-washing ceremony should accompany communion. When done, it is not just the minister who does the foot-washing, but all of the members, as well. There is nothing wrong with this, and it is a great way to mime the Gospel. We do need to remember, however, that Jesus was illustrating a point when He washed the disciples' feet. The point He was illustrating is the need to be of service, so the rite needs to reflect the service associated with it. As long as foot-washing doesn't become more about performing a rite than the need to be of service, having a foot-washing ceremony is a great way to remember our need to serve others.

Discussion, study and review questions:

- What aspect of life did ancient Middle Eastern culture emphasize? What happened when one was invited to someone else's house? Why was ritual foot washing performed prior to eating? Whose job was it to wash feet? How was this job regarded? Why was it so significant for Jesus to take on this role with His disciples?

- What kind of leaders are Christian leaders supposed to be? Whose faith and humility do we follow? What is Christian leadership not about? What is it about?

- What kind of leadership is Christian ministry based in? What does this mean? What is the purpose of Christian ministry? In providing this service, what kind of example do Christian leaders become? Why did Jesus come? In this heritage, why do Christian leaders serve? What kind of work is Christian ministry?

- In Christian ministry, what do Christian leaders never succumb to? What does this prove in Christian leadership? What must Christian leaders do in their claims?

- What does Christian service demand of a leader? Is it an easy call? Why or why not? What circumstances will a Christian leader face? If Christian leaders point to Christ, what must they do?

- What is Christian ministry? How do people learn about what it is about? What should Christian ministries never allow? When is Christian service pleasing?

- What does Christian service work for and advocate? What is essential for Christian leaders to do?

- What are Christian leaders representatives and advocates of? What does the New Covenant do? What do Christian ministers focus on, and why?

- What are some types of Christian service present in the Old Testament?

- Discuss and share some of the questions and answers found in the "Questions and Answers" section. What did you learn that you did not know about Christian ministry and service? What did you learn that changed your mind about ministry service? How did learning about specific issues related to Christian ministry help you to grow in your understanding of ministry? The church? Your own relationship with God?

Chapter Four

SELECTING A CHRISTIAN LEADER

He who thinks he leads and has no one following him is only taking a walk.
- Anonymous [1]

So you're a Christian, you're in the Kingdom, and you're growing in the Lord...now what? Whether you have been a Christian for ten minutes or twenty years, you are in need of a Christian leader to help you develop your Christian life and walk. This is true for ministers as well as those who never serve in Christian ministry. Every one of us has the need for teaching, blessing, correcting, encouragement, and accountability as part of God's established system of ministry.

Christian leadership has been established by God for our benefit. This means leadership, in and of itself, is a good thing in God's Kingdom. However...this does not mean that bad leaders do not exist, and it certainly does not mean that every person who claims to be a leader should be trusted. It is also important to realize different leaders serve different people, callings, and yes, even ministries. How do we select the right leader? The Scriptures help us to realize what we need, what we seek, and how to find it in our leader.

Text study

Hebrews 13:7-9

Supplementary texts

Exodus 18:17-23, Micah 3:1-12, 1 Corinthians 3:1-22, 1 Corinthians 4:14-21, Galatians 2:1-9, Hebrews 13:17-24

Power verse

Hebrews 13:7:

- *"Remember them which have the rule over you, who have spoken unto you the Word of God: whose faith follow, considering the end of their conversation."*

- *"Remember your leaders, who spoke the Word of God to you; considering the outcome of their way of life, imitate their faith."* (LEB)

- *"Remember your leaders. They taught God's message to you. Remember how they lived and died, and copy their faith."* (ERV)

- *"Remember your leaders. They taught God's message to you. Remember how they lived and died, and copy their faith."* (GNT)

- *"Remember your leaders, who spoke the Word of God to you. Consider the outcome of their way of life and imitate their faith."* (NIV)

- *"Remember those who led you, who spoke the Word of God to you; and considering the result of their conduct, imitate their faith."* (NASB)

Power words

- **Remember** – From the Greek word *"mnemonueo"* which means, "to be mindful of, to remember, to call to mind, to make mention of."[1] (Compare to the English word, "mnemonic.")

- **Rule** – From the Greek word *"hegeomai"* which means, "to lead; to consider, deem, account, think."[3]

- **Spoken** – From the Greek word *"laleo"* which means, "to utter a voice or emit a sound; to speak; to talk; to utter, tell; to use words in order to declare one's mind and disclose one's thoughts."[4]

- **Word of God** – From two Greek words: *"logos,"* which means, "of speech; its use as respect to MIND alone; in John, it denotes the essential Word of God, Jesus Christ, the personal wisdom and power in union with God, His minister in creation and government of the universe, the cause of all the world's life, both physical and ethical, which for the procurement of man's salvation put on human nature in the person of Jesus the Messiah;"[5] and *"theos,"* which means, "a god or goddess, a general name for deities or divinities; the Godhead; spoken of the only and true God; whatever can in any respect be likened unto God, or resemble Him in any way."[6]

- **Faith follow** – From two Greek words: *"pistis,"* which means, "conviction of the truth of anything, belief; in the New Testament, of a conviction of belief respecting man's relationship to God and divine things, generally with the included idea of trust and holy fervor born of faith and joined with it; fidelity, faithfulness;"[7] and *"mimeomai,"* which means, "to imitate; any one."[8]

- **Conversation** – From the Greek word *"anastrophe"* which means, "manner of life, conduct, behavior, deportment."[9]

Historical context

Leaders were an honored part of ancient culture. Schools of philosophy and thought existed and thrived, whereby one was educated in the thought and art of debate unique to that specific teacher or leader. The author of Hebrews encourages the same type of honor and modeling among the church: that those who are in leadership should be leaders worthy of imitation in the faith, and that those under good leaders should honor their leaders, apply the Word of God they have taught, and imitate them in the faith.

Notes on text

The balance of leadership and selecting a leader is presented well in Hebrews, because it gives us an idea of what is required on both sides; the leaders are to be solid in their faith, good as leaders, solid teachers of the Word, and worthy of imitation in their conduct. With such good examples of leadership, those who are under their leaders should follow their leaders in example, teaching, conduct, and faith.

Power points

- Everyone in the Body of Christ requires leadership for the purpose of learning and training. When selecting a leader, we should recognize the process is a drawing. God establishes those for us in our lives that, while we may have many spiritual teachers, we only have a few fathers and mothers. Fathers and mothers in the faith are those men and women of God who establish us in our calling and help us to develop in the foundational and essential areas of our faith. Leaders should walk in humility, refrain from being puffed up, and love those they lead. While there are different types of leadership, one who follows a leader should listen to that leader, as they come both with correction and edification (1 Corinthians 4:14-21).

- Leaders should be individuals who teach the ordinances and regulations of God, showing the way others must walk. As leaders, this means the leader must walk in the way of faith, showing as much by example as by word. Leaders must also be workers in God's way, exemplifying the best possible leadership available. They must be people of truth, hating theft and dishonest secrecy, and be prepared to handle the matters brought before them. It is clear some will lead over many and some will lead over few, but all are still expected to uphold proper leadership conduct (Exodus 18:17-23).

- Leaders should never be hung up on themselves or try to point people unto themselves. Instead, good leaders point their followers to Jesus Christ and uphold the principles of God. Godly leaders do not attend to nonsense, but to the things of God (1 Corinthians 3:1-22). When a question arises, the true leader of God stands for truth and what is true, and does not compromise, no matter what the issue presented may be (Galatians 2:1-9).

- The leaders of God are worthy of our remembrance. We should bring to mind their teachings in the Word, and uphold them in all we do. We are to remember their faith, and follow in that faith. One of the best ways we can uphold the teaching of a leader is to refrain from falling into strange doctrines, away from the truth we have been taught (Hebrews 13:7-9). It's also essential we obey what we are taught, and willingly allow ourselves to be taught by our leaders, not displaying pride or rebellion against them. It is essential our prayers go up for our godly leaders, live honestly, work toward the transformation needed in Christ, and salute our leaders, honoring them with respect (Hebrews 13:17-24).

- The Scriptures cautions us strongly against following false leaders. In selecting a good leader, we should watch for the signs of a bad leader, to avoid being drawn in by such. Some signs of a bad leader include: loving evil, demoralizing those under their watch, falsely prophesying or giving words, conduct contrary to that required of a leader, causing those under them to err in faith, perverting equality, giving prophesies for money, and basing judgments on financial gain (Micah 3:1-12).

Signs of a false leader

When selecting a leader, there are many important characteristics to watch for. When it comes to avoiding a leader, there are also things to beware. Nine times out of ten, people are taken in by false leaders because something about that leader appeals to them on an emotional level. There is a reason we are advised against making faith-oriented decisions based on feelings and emotions! The Word offers us practical advice to avoid being taken in by false leaders. The practical signs given in the Word help us to remain level-headed and observant of things we need to recognize.

- **False prophecy** – There is no "fleshly prophecy." Prophecy doesn't succeed some times, and fail other times. You can't have a prophecy that's "half-right" (Deuteronomy 18:14-22, Jeremiah 5:30). Keeping all of this in mind, prophecy is not purposed to be something that appeals to people's emotional states. Yes, as much as we don't like to consider it, there are plenty of people who claim to have this gift, that gift, and some other gift, but in reality, have no such gift except for emotional sway (2 Timothy 3:6-9). If someone spoke something over you that was obviously false, or spoke a word over a region that was false, or gave a series of specified predictions that also never came to pass, this individual is guilty of false prophecy. Such a leader needs not be followed, no matter how good you may think they are at making you feel a certain way.

- **Emotionalism** – When the Word of the Prophet Malachi went forth to the leaders of his day, there was a specific statement about God's dislike when a leader *"floods the altar with tears"* (Malachi 2:13). This is a statement against emotionalism, or using certain emotional behaviors, actions, and cues to illicit a desired response from an audience. There are very well-known ministers who know how to cry, yell, speak-sing, or stir up a crowd, right on cue. The only thing behind their display is a desire to work up their audiences. Emotionalism is dangerous because it can create a false spiritual state or appearance. There's no question that being in the presence of God can fill us with certain responses and emotions. Keeping this in mind, emotionalism is the creation of those responses and emotions without the presence or Spirit of God behind them (2 Timothy 3:5-9). Beware leaders that stir a good crowd, but lack Spirit, truth and teaching in their messages.

- **False teaching** – Classifying a teacher as "false" is a serious charge. All sorts of accusations are made against leaders today, classifying this one or that one as "false" simply because someone doesn't like something about the work they do. This is unfair and misleading, because it gives people the wrong idea about what truly marks false teaching. An individual is not a false teacher because they are female, wear pants to teach, wear make-up, use translations of the Bible besides the King James Version, have a different view of politics, or don't use hymnals during services. False teaching is the teaching of beliefs and principles contrary to the Word of God while claiming to be teaching the Word. There are two possible reasons why a false teacher is a false teacher. The first is that the individual has been taught incorrectly themselves about spiritual matters. The second reason is that the individual deliberately intends to deceive. Whether or not a leader intends to teach falsely does not nullify the need for correction, but it does alert us to the heart of the leader in question. False teachers need to be corrected – and that is why God gave the church apostles and prophets (Ephesians 4:11-16). If a leader is teaching something notably false, or you just don't feel comfortable with something about their teaching, it is best to avoid that leader. In this case, certainly do not follow or submit to their ministry. If you aren't sure about something they are teaching, find someone who can help explain the situation to you better, and either confirm or correct your doubts.

- **Lack of humility** – Pride takes a lot of forms. Sometimes leaders aren't visibly proud on the surface, at least in the traditional ways we tend to regard pride. Sometimes there is pride in a leader, bubbling just under the surface, as they outlay their empires built on sand. Are you in the midst of a leader who has no time to help someone else? Do they brush off people who have genuine need under their ministries? Are they intolerant of the issues people have, even if the issues are new or not the fault of that person? Do they fail to keep their word, return phone calls, or honor their commitments? Do they have a large number of people in the congregation who seem to cater to the leader's needs, wants, and whims? Do they seem to seek people out who can benefit them, but they really don't seem to be benefiting anyone else? If you answered "yes" to these questions – even any one of these questions – you may be dealing with a leader who struggles with pride (2 Peter 2:18; Jude 1:16). Often this comes about due to the stresses of ministry early-on that turn later into issues with entitlement. A leader who is not humble is not a servant (Matthew 20:20-28), and therefore, can't effectively minister to the people of God.

- **Everyone around them seems to be an extension of them** – This is an interesting phenomenon that I never thought much about until a few years ago. Have you ever heard the expression, "Birds of a feather flock together?" If you think about this expression and then look around the modern church, you will see its incarnation. People today go through a number of leaders before finding one that reflects their own thoughts and interests, and then they keep that leader around. They've gone through so many leaders because they haven't been able to find one prior who would allow them to do what they want without consequences. Now, even though these individuals might have a leader they claim as their own and many friends, the people they surround themselves with are all reflections of them. Their leader doesn't challenge or correct them on matters, they keep themselves exclusive to their own community, and their world does not grow. Their covering, friends, and associates in ministry all sound exactly like them, including holding and sharing the same opinions. You need to beware a leader who shows no diversity within their circles, i.e., everyone seems to agree with everyone else, all the time, and about everything. I'm not talking unity here – I'm talking the leader has created a universe where what they think goes, no matter what the topic may be (2 Thessalonians 2:10).

- **They have a history of being stripped of credentials** – Many today argue the validity of credentials and whether or not Christian ministers need them. If we look in the Old Testament and New Testaments alike, leaders had to meet certain criteria to hold their offices (Numbers 8:5-25, Acts 1:8, Acts 1:12-26, Acts 8:1-31). It wasn't as simple as someone declaring one's self to be something and then going out and doing it. All throughout history, people who were called needed to have that calling tested and proven by human beings (1 Corinthians 3:1-23, 1 Corinthians 4:1-21). This doesn't mean everyone always accepts the office, nor does it mean that those who doubt it are correct – but it does mean that when it comes to ministry, standards must exist. In our modern day and age, the standards we have in place for ministry are ministerial credentials in the form of a minister's license and ordination. I do not question that ministers are sometimes stripped of credentials unjustly, nor do I question that sometimes credentials are given on conditions that later invalidate them. The reality, however, is that the majority of times credentials are revoked, there is usually a reason why. It is usually because the minister who granted those credentials does not feel comfortable with the individual in question doing work in ministry. If this is the case, that's a very serious situation indeed, and the leader in question needs to be examined, with caution, from a distance.

- **The usurping of authority** – God has established order and authority for a reason. The reason is not to invalidate gifts, but to give each individual minister a sense of purpose and vision in ministry (Acts 1:8, Ephesians 4:11-16, 1 Corinthians 12:28). If you encounter a minister who is dead-set on getting his or her point, message, or work across, with no sense of decency and order according to the Word, the odds are good you've got a false leader in your midst. The veracity of a leader is not found in just what they teach, but in how they interact with others in the Body of Christ, as well (Jeremiah 5:26-27). Does the leader have a leader to whom they are accountable? Do they understand the relevance of submitting to a vision when participating in an event hosted by someone else? Do they understand that they are required to submit to a leader that is of a higher office in ministry, even if that leader is not their own personal leader? Do they try to be in control, no matter where they are? Leaders who don't submit to authority make terrible leaders themselves.

- **Questionable integrity** – All ministers make mistakes. No leader on this earth was born sanctified, and there are always points in a minister's walk where they will experience trial, temptation – and possibly even succumb to such. How the matters are handled afterwards tell a lot about the kind of leader a person is and claims to be. Can the leader apologize? Ask for forgiveness? On the other hand, does the leader have repeated issues? Are they shady financially or in some other issue within the ministry? Do they constantly succumb to various temptations? Are they always trying to hide things? If you answered "yes" to any of these (Psalm 12:3, Luke 12:15)…it's time to find a new leader.

Types of leadership selection in the Old Testament

- **1 Kings 10:1-13** – *The Queen of Sheba before Solomon*, a type of leadership interaction and selection among leaders. I love the interaction present between the queen and Solomon because we see two leaders showing complete honor and respect to one another. The Queen of Sheba was a leader, equal to Solomon as ruler – but came forth to hear and test his wisdom. In other words, the Queen of Sheba came with respect, but didn't just accept hearsay about Solomon – she sought to see him in action, herself. She followed the customs of her day, coming forth with gifts, and offering additional gifts after she saw the leadership ability present in Solomon. The honor, respect, and yes, testing all show forth the proper way for leaders to interact with one another, both when a leader is covered by that leader or the leaders are colleagues in ministry.

- **1 Samuel 18:1-4, 19:1-6, 20:1-42** –*Jonathan and David*, a type of leadership order and interaction, both among leaders and when one is friends with their leader. Some people believe you should never cover friends. I think David and Jonathan are a perfect example that you can be the friend of someone you cover, as long as the relationship parameters are kept in proper view. We often regard David and Jonathan as close friends, but we forget that David was also Jonathan's leader. This means their relationship had a special edge to it: both David and Jonathan had to know when it was time to be friends, or time to be leader and follower. This means a covering can be someone's friend, just with limitations. The person needs to know when the leader is speaking as a leader, and understand the boundaries of leadership that exist in the relationship. It's also essential to have a heart for the leader and remain obedient as needed. We also see that long-term leadership is possible with the right leader, in keeping with balance, purpose, and humility.

- **Judges 4:1-24** – *Deborah and Barak*, a type of leadership order. There are numerous theories behind Barak's motives when he came before Deborah. Some people think he was weak, others think he was lazy, and some think he was just doing his job. The Bible doesn't give us insight into his motives, because they aren't relevant. What is relevant is Barak was faced with a situation and he clearly wasn't sure how to handle it without his leader's guidance – and his leader recognized this. In turn, Deborah called for him to make sure he got the needed information to move forward. When we are covered by our leader, we should be able to seek them out, receive direction and guidance, and move forward with the advice and foresight we are given. As we can see in Barak's case, the word we receive may not be what we always want – but that does not make it any less needed.

- **Daniel 1:1-21** – *Daniel and King Nebuchadnezzar*, a type of a proper leadership attitude in the face of persecution. Most people wouldn't find themselves persecuted by their leaders today, so the word "persecution" is exclusive to Daniel's experience. Lesser forms related to persecution, however – such as harassment, betrayal, intimidation, or threats – are a serious matter. In this particular situation, Daniel didn't have the option to up and leave his leader. Even in the face of severe trial, Daniel held fast and handled the situation as he was able. There are too many accounts of individuals who blame their personal sins on their leaders…but Daniel proves you do not need to be under a good leader to refrain from sin. When you're in a situation that you just can't get out of, you hold fast to God, while remaining respectful of the authority that is in place.

- **Numbers 18:1-32, Nehemiah 10:1-39** – *The Israelites and the priests*, a type of people and their leaders. The Levites were the priests of ancient Israel. It was their job to serve as the spiritual leaders of the people. They functioned as workers of God's service, offering sacrifices, instructing in matters of the law, and seeing to it that the spiritual needs of the people were met. In return, the people were responsible to meet the practical needs of the priests, by providing tithes and offerings. The Old Testament shows us what happens when the people are wrong, and the consequences of wrong leadership among the Levites. In a completely fair and balanced perspective, God's Word shows us the need to be both good leaders, and good followers.

Questions and answers

- **What do I do if I feel it's time to move on from a leader?**

If you feel it is time to move on to a different leader, or move on from a leader, you need to seek God, first and foremost. There may be any number of reasons why you feel it is time to move on, but it is important those reasons have spiritual and practical purposes rather than emotional ones. It's not right to leave a situation without divine reassurance, or based on mere feelings or thoughts that can change and pass with time. If you are feeling this way about your situation, it's important to communicate. Even if you don't bring forth everything you may be thinking about the situation, talk to your leader about things. Discuss with your leader about feeling restless in the Spirit, and see what they recommend for that. Ask questions about things you seek to do in ministry that you don't feel you can do right now, and seek your leader's perspective about how you can do those things. If the situation continues and God is the One Who is prompting the movement forward, handle the situation with grace and tact. Follow the regulations for release and behave in decency and order.

It's also important to make sure you are not leaving a ministry or minister's guidance out of selfishness. It is easy to grow jealous or envious of the way in which a leader interacts with someone else in a ministry or feel like you are being overlooked or treated unfairly, when this may not even be the case. Examining one's own heart and motives is always key to such a situation, as God calls us to examine ourselves first.

The bottom line of what you do in this situation boils down to respect. We need to honor the time we've had with a leader, even if that time is up. We need to remember that until God moves us on, we need to learn from our leaders in faith and practice. If we ourselves are looking to move on, then we ourselves need to be people to emulate in faith and practice. This is especially relevant in our conduct with a leader. How ready you are to move forward shows in how you carry yourself: in the pulpit, out of the pulpit, and in your interactions with other leaders. This doesn't just show God, but also shows your leaders just how ready you are to do whatever it is you feel it is time to do.

- **What do I do if I feel I am being held back by a leader?**

If you are feeling held back by a leader, there are three possible explanations for the feeling. First, a leader might truly be sensing something in God, or something in you, that isn't ready to go to the next level. Before you write this off as "not the case," listen to me for a minute. When we start to get excited about our calling, we aren't always the most objective people in the world about it. God shows us an end result, or a long-term product, of our ministry work as motivational action to help us take steps to get to that place. Just because we have a call on our lives does not mean we are ready to go out tomorrow and start pursuing every single grand thing God shows us in our ministry vision. Our walk with God is a process, and ministry is no different. So, in the case of a leader, you may go and tell your leader that God's called you to have an international ministry and you're going to go and preach before the masses…but it would be unwise for your leader to take you to the airport the next day and send you to do a crusade in India before forty thousand people. Why is this? Because even though God might have shown you something you will one day do, you haven't done anything to prepare for that purpose – you haven't done Bible training, haven't studied the Word as a minister, you've just seen a call – and you aren't prepared to walk in it yet. This is obviously not always the case – however, even if we've been in ministry for a while, a leader may be seeing something in us that needs to be worked out before we can take the next steps to go where we need to be. In this particular instance, what the leader needs to do is explain what they are seeing or sensing, and work with you as a leader to overcome those issues. It's not acceptable for a leader to just say, "Oh, you're not ready yet" and not explain, in at least some semblance of understanding, why. If they acknowledge the goal, they need to help you work toward that goal – so this is not a no, it's a not yet – and they need to help you get to the next place so you can get where you need to be and do what you need to do.

Second, a leader might not be able to take you to the next point in your journey. Leaders are human, and they have their limitations. Leaders also have their own calling from God. The calling they have may be perfectly good for the point you've been at for a while, but may not serve well for the level God is calling you to go to. Unfortunately, there aren't many leaders who understand this kind of dynamic and may take it personally, and try to hold on. Yes, it's hard to leave a covering in this situation, because hard feelings will most likely result, no matter what is done. I would like to believe there are still many leaders who would release you to where you believe you need to go, especially if they are asked with order and decency. In this instance, with great prayer and respect, the leader should be approached, once again, after thoroughly seeking God. This is especially true if you have met someone that can take you to the next level. Don't put the person you want to be covered by in the position of having to feel like they are "stealing" you from someone else, nor make the person who is covering you feel as if someone is "stealing" you.

The third reason may be that a leader may want to hold onto you for his or her own reasons. In this instance, the tie that binds isn't so holy, and it can actually be bad for both the leader and the person they are covering. God will guide you in how to handle this leader, especially given the complications of the situation.

What do I recommend? Talk to your leader! The Word tells us there is wisdom in counsel, and there is definitely something to be said for examining a situation from all possible angles. If you still have questions, feel free to talk to a leader or a trusted friend. The only thing you need to be sure to not do: do not leave out details that make your leaders look like they are right about your situation, simply because you don't want to do what you have been told. Examine yourself and your relationship with your leader. It's true that there are leaders who aren't good for us, or maybe have served their purpose in our lives – but it's also true that we may be walking in pride and sour because we can't do as we want. I know there are many who may not have this issue, but even if this is not the case, we still need to examine ourselves and what God requires of our situation. This is truly how we discern where God wants us to be. Are you not really growing anymore under your leader? Do you feel like it's time to do something different, that your leader can't help you with? Do you just want to do, without having to wait? Whatever it is…seek out God's guidance and, with the help of a good leader, other leader, friend, or all of the above…start to work it out. Whatever you do, remember, once again, to maintain proper respect and behave in a way that imitates faith and practice.

- **How do I approach a leader I would like to cover me?**

In keeping with what we have already discussed, respect is key when dealing with a leader or a potential leader. Be honest with a leader about what God has spoken to you and the role you believe they are to play in your ministry and/or spiritual development. Meet and talk with them in some way, even if it's online or over the phone. Share with them what God has revealed to you about that leader. Learn about the criteria they have established to be under their leadership, and why they have the guidelines they have. Get feedback from the leader. Establish relationship, and show eagerness for covenant. Let God do the rest!

- **My leader is teaching error. How do I handle this? Should they continue to be my leader?**

Saying that a leader is teaching error is a serious accusation. I recognize, however, that most making this accusation do not do so lightly. It is often a difficult experience to come forth and say such about a leader, especially when a leader has been important in one's life and development.

The first thing I advise is the individual in question thoroughly examines the statement or teaching they believe is false. It's important to review notes, audio, and Scriptures to make sure what was said was properly understood. If there is no question about what was said, the first step is to approach the leader directly. Ask your leader, with respect and honor, about the issue you see. This does not have to be done with an attitude. Something to the extent of, "Recently I heard you teach on (insert topic). I wondered if you could clarify what you were speaking of for me." If you feel there is a contradiction in the Word, ask about the Scripture that contradicts what was said. It's important not to argue, and not offer hostility. In doing this, the goal is to learn more about what was said and clarify there was no misunderstanding.

If it is clear there was no misunderstanding, there are two

options. The first is, most obviously, to dismiss one's self from the situation. If it doesn't appear it will be fruitful to pursue the situation further within the minister's walls or within the leader's authority, then leaving is a good option. The second option is to try and bring about correction, or more relevantly, bring the situation before someone who can bring about correction. I agree that truth is truth, but it may sound different coming from someone's leader than someone's follower. In my own ministry, I believe in knowing those people covered by the people I cover. They know if something comes up, they are free to come and talk to me about it. If there is something that comes up and you genuinely want to see it corrected, try bringing it to a leader's leader, with order and concern.

- **Do different types of leaders serve different purposes?**

Yes, and such should be considered when selecting a leader.

Apostles and prophets are called to lead other leaders. While the apostle and prophet surely do bless and impact the lives of leaders and non-leaders alike, the apostle and prophet are leaders designated to lead others in the five-fold ministry. This means their leadership style is stronger, tougher, harsher, and more impacting than that of another type of leader. Evangelists are called to the unsaved, the lukewarm, and the backslidden, and thus have a style that is more dramatic and entertaining than other ministers. Evangelists do not "cover" people, as apostles, prophets, and pastors do. Pastors are called to love and shepherd those who are not called to ministry or those who may be discerning a call. Teachers are called to teach, and also do not serve in a covering office. These different leadership styles relate directly to what one is called to do, and in many ways, what one is not called to do. If you are not called for leadership, an apostle or prophet is not the right kind of leader for you. If you are called to be a ministry leader, an evangelist, pastor, or teacher is going to be the wrong kind of leader for you. Carefully considering these options ensures your leader will be a good fit to you, and you will be a good match for your leader.

Discussion, study and review questions

- Why were leaders honored in ancient culture? Why does the author of Hebrews encourage the same type of honor and modeling among the church? How should Christian leaders be? How should those under good leaders be?

- How are the issues of good leadership and being under a good leader presented?

- Who in the Body of Christ requires leadership? What kind of a process is the selection of a leader? What is a spiritual father or mother? How should leaders conduct themselves? What should those under a leader do?

- What should leaders do? Do numbers of people change what a leader does? Why or why not?

- Who do good leaders point their followers toward? Do they attend to nonsense? When an issue arises, what do godly leaders stand for?

- What are leaders of God worthy of? What should we bring to mind, and why? What is one of the best ways to uphold the teachings of a leader? How do we walk in obedience and submission with our leaders?

- What does the Word caution us against? What are some of the signs of a bad leader?

- What are some characteristics of false leaders? Why are these characteristics important?

- What are some Old Testament types present for Christian leadership interactions? How do these types shadow Christian leadership, and all it is to represent?

- Discuss and share some of the questions and answers found

in the "Questions and Answers" section. What did you learn that you did not know about Christian ministry? What did you learn that changed your mind about Christian leadership? How did learning about specific issues related to Christian ministry help you to grow in your understanding of ministry? The church? Your own relationship with God?

Section 2

THE FIVE-FOLD MINISTRY

Chapter Five

BUILDING UP THE BODY OF CHRIST

The Christian ministry is the worst of all trades, but the best of all professions.
— John Newton [1]

What does it mean to be part of the Body of Christ? Many teachings in the Bible are devoted to discovering what it means to stand as a member of Christ's church. As individual members, we learn we are called to represent and live God's higher purpose for believers. What does belonging to the Body of Christ mean for us beyond individual obedience? The church and church membership are not just about us as individuals. If we live the Christian life isolated, without structure or function, Christianity quickly becomes something to debate. Such debates reduce Christianity to a personal level of who is right in personal opinion. With no focus, structure, or discipline, Christianity becomes a concept rather than a living reality.

It is for this reason that, from the beginning of the church, God established authority and functional ministry for the church. The church has been created and established by Christ to function as His Body in the world, not to be a connection of personal dealings based on opinions. In order to bring structure, God established leadership present in what we call the five-fold ministry. The five-fold ministry is God's established function, order, and leadership structure for the Body of Christ, the church. Church leadership is designed to bring people into the Kingdom of God and equip the saints in their calling from God. Through solid teaching, correction, encouragement, and Kingdom-building, apostles, prophets, evangelists, pastors, and teachers equip and build the body of Christ from the ground up.

The church is to be Kingdom-minded and about the business of expanding and maintaining the Kingdom of God. From this revelation, we understand Kingdom leaders to be purposeful in this work. Kingdom leaders are purposeful in the ministry office God has called them for in this time. Understanding the five-fold ministry is understanding the essence of Kingdom mentality in terms of leadership positioning. If we seek to be good leaders or follow good leaders, we have to first identify the purpose and cooperation of the five-fold ministry.

Text study

Ephesians 4:7-16

Supplementary texts

Romans 11:28-29, 2 Corinthians 5:18-21, 2 Corinthians 6:1-3, Ephesians 3:4-9, Colossians 4:16-18, 2 Peter 2:1-10.

Power verse

Ephesians 4:11:

- *"And He gave some, apostles; and some, prophets; and some, evangelists; and some, pastors and teachers."*

- *"It was He Who gave some to be apostles, some to be prophets, some to be evangelists, and some to be pastors and teachers..."* (NIV)

- *"Now these are the gifts Christ gave to the church: the apostles, the prophets, the evangelists, and the pastors and teachers."* (NLT)

- "And His gifts were [varied; He Himself appointed and gave men to us] some to be apostles (special messengers), some prophets (inspired preachers and expounders), some evangelists (preachers of the Gospel, traveling missionaries), some pastors (shepherds of His flock) and teachers." (AMP)

- "And Christ gave gifts to people—He made some to be apostles, some to be prophets, some to go and tell the Good News, and some to have the work of caring for and teaching God's people." (NCV)

- "And He gave some [as] apostles, and some [as] prophets, and some [as] proclaimers of good news, and some [as] shepherds and teachers..." (YLT)

Power words

- **Gave** – From the Greek word *"didomi"* which means, "to give; to give something to someone; to give; to grant or permit one."[2]

- **Apostles** – From the Greek word *"apostolos"* which means, "a delegate, a messenger, one sent forth with orders."[3]

- **Prophets** – From the Greek word *"prophetes"* which means, "in Greek writings, an interpreter of oracles or other hidden things; one who, moved by the Spirit of God and hence his organ, solemnly declares to men what he has received by inspiration, especially concerning future events, and in particular the cause and Kingdom of God and human salvation; a poet (because poets were believed to sing under divine inspiration)."[4]

- **Evangelists** – From the Greek word *"euaggelistes"* which means, "a bringer of good tidings, an evangelist; the name given to the New Testament heralds of salvation who were not apostles."⁵

- **Pastors** – From the Greek word *"poimen"* which means, "a herdsman, especially a shepherd; metaphorically."⁶

- **Teachers** – From the Greek word *"didaskalos"* which means, "a teacher; in the New Testament one who teaches concerning the things of God, and the duties of man."⁷

Historical context

Throughout religious history, many offices arose to govern different religious groups. We've seen tyrants, control freaks, and abuses of power. We have also seen the other extreme: people who advocated a lack of government in religion or a governing system where everyone participates. We've seen elections, councils, and similar structures of authority, active and ready for modern leadership. What we often don't see is the structure of governing put into place in the New Testament. This structure is revolutionary, both for the first century and today, because it provides a balance of authority for the full covering of the church. The five-fold ministry contrasts centralized power (one or only a few leaders) and an electoral government (electing leaders through a voting process involving all members or a selection of members). Challenging the historical emperor's power, the Kingdom of God offered and continues to offer a new approach to leadership and qualification to be in leadership.

Notes on text

If we are to understand Christian leadership, we must understand the importance of the five-fold ministry. The five-fold ministry is not just for a distant time, but must work completely and in unity throughout every church age until the time when Jesus returns. Many claim the five-fold ministry has ceased; but this would mean the body has reached full maturity, perfection, and edification, with the work of ministry being completed. We know this is not so, and will not be so until Jesus returns. Therefore, we need to understand far more about the five-fold ministry and its purpose for the church.

Power points

- The Scriptures tell us the Lord has given grace according to the measure of the gift of Christ to everyone in the church (Ephesians 4:7-10). For everything God gifts and appoints us to do, we receive grace to exercise that gift by divine purpose (Ephesians 3:4-9, Colossians 4:16-18).

- In the case of church leadership, the offices to which apostles, prophets, evangelists, pastors, and teachers are called are a gift. They are a gift to the individual that walks in the calling and a gift to the church. To reject these offices, declare they are no longer necessary, or to try and say the number of offices we have today is reduced to only a few is to reject the gift of God placed in church leadership (Ephesians 4:11, Romans 11:28-29).

- The purposes of the five-fold ministry are: to perfect the saints; do the work of the ministry; and edify the body of Christ until the entire church comes to a place of unity in faith, full knowledge of the Son of God, unto a perfect man, with the church walking in the full stature of Christ (Ephesians 4:12-13). As we have not reached this point, one cannot argue against the validity of the five-fold ministry for this age and every age until the return of Christ (2 Corinthians 5:18-21).

- The church has the command to be mature. We often see Christians never maturing to a full place of spiritual growth in Christ. Part of the reason for Christian immaturity lies with unscriptural church leadership. Many churches and ministries today follow leadership patterns that are not found in the New Testament and are not appointed by God to bring maturity to the church. Papal offices, cardinals, and the Roman curia all follow the structure of the ancient Roman Empire – not the New Testament. Churches that employ election for leaders are not following a New Testament structure. Eliminating Scriptural leadership offices or trying to replace Scriptural offices with others leaves the church open to invasion of false teachers, as proper discernment for leadership becomes muddled (Ephesians 4:14, 2 Peter 2:1-10).

- Those in the five-fold ministry are to execute their offices in love. We recognize the purpose in the five-fold ministry is to bring together the body of Christ and grow it to full maturity. The purpose of ministry is not to walk in an office to exercise power and control, dominating and intimidating followers. The ministry offices edify the church by teaching truth in love (Ephesians 4:15-16, 2 Corinthians 6:1-3).

Characteristics of the five-fold ministry

In looking at examples of the five-fold ministry in action and different combinations of five-fold ministry gifts, we can clearly see the characteristics essential to the five-fold ministry:

- **The Council Meeting at Jerusalem, Acts 15:1-35 (apostles working with elders)** – The meeting at Jerusalem displays the powerful characteristics present in the synergy of cooperation between apostles and appointment ministries. As we can see upon examining the text, the apostles were brought an issue still in debate within the church: what role does the law of Moses play in the life of a Christian believer? While circumcision might have been the subject, the purpose of the law was the real issue. To resolve this issue, apostles and elders were brought together. The apostles displayed discernment skills, the ability to analyze situations, the ability to speak and present on important matters, define terminology, clarify questions, and the ability to function with other ministers. The elders present were able to discuss, to listen with humility, to accept correction as necessary, to analyze the situation, and then return with the information present and teach it to their appointed congregations.

- **The revelation given, Ephesians 3:1-5 (apostles and prophets)** – Apostles and prophets are designed by God's purpose to work together in a special way because they receive God's divine revelation. They must have the ability to convey that revelation, through speech and writing. They must be strong in the things of God, a knowledgeable people, and focused.

- **The appointment of ministry offices, 1 Corinthians 12:28 (apostles, prophets, and teachers)** – Apostles, prophets, and teachers are primary foundations to the success of proclaiming the Gospel. The apostle must be willing to move with God's revelation, the prophet must be willing to proclaim that revelation, and teachers must be willing to teach the revelation. To do this, all three must equip themselves with that revelation: the apostles and prophets by receiving and accepting it, and the teacher by learning it from apostles and prophets.

- **The call to do the work of an evangelist, 2 Timothy 4:1-5 (apostles and evangelists)** – We see in 2 Timothy 4:1-5 the wonderful way in which revelation was given by an apostle, to another apostle, who was directed to do the work of an evangelist. As we've already seen characteristics of apostles, evangelists must be ready to, at any time, proclaim the Gospel. They must be a prepared people, ready in every circumstance. They must be well-educated, well-versed in the Scriptures, and love people. Evangelists must have a heart of compassion, be moved by human suffering with a heart of empathy, and care deeply for those who do not know God.

Types of the five-fold ministry

- **Genesis 47:2** –*Joseph's five brothers selected to go before Pharaoh*, a type of the responsible five-fold ministry. These brothers were presented to Pharaoh as family leaders to ask for the favor to relocate. They were to be responsible for caring for their families and had to step up, accepting the duty as leaders to go before Pharaoh and receive favor from their government official. Leaders in the five-fold ministry are called to be responsible, standing up for what is needed for the people they care for and to go before the Lord boldly, seeking favor and blessing wherever they go.

- **Leviticus 26:8** – *The five who will chase one hundred,* a type of the authority-leading five-fold ministry. Too often Christians feel intimidated by the ungodly, who seem to be greater in number. Christian leaders are often no different. If five who stand up for the Lord can chase one hundred, imagine the power of five offices that stand up for the Lord! We are commanded to not be afraid, not back down, and trust that God will handle our enemies as we attend to Kingdom matters.

- **Numbers 27:1-11** – *The five daughters of Zelophehad,* a type of the female five-fold ministry. These women were denied their legal rights of inheritance according to interpretations of the law. Instead of accepting this denial, they fought for what was theirs…and won. They were pioneers, leaders, and radical changers. By virtue of their actions, they overcame the power of legalism and introduced a spirit of virtue and freedom to legalistic mindsets. They stand as a relevant signpost for women called to the five-fold ministry today, who fight the legalism of religious mindsets and exclusionary law to proclaim the Gospel as free in Christ.

- **Judges 18:2** – *The five Danite spies,* a type of the territorial claim of the five-fold ministry. We can see from this story that these spies were sent out to inspect land because the tribe of Dan did not have a land inheritance. They had to have a critical eye, analyze situations, and work together for the good of the mission. United in their common cause of claiming their land within the Kingdom, the five-fold ministry must view their calling likewise: we are united, not one more important than another, to claim territory for the Kingdom.

- **1 Chronicles 2:4** – *Judah, father of the Messianic tribe, fathers five sons,* as a type of the divine authority and lineage of the five-fold ministry. We are sons and daughters of God through Christ, and all true five-fold ministers acknowledge we receive our calling through Christ. The five-fold ministry bears authority we have received from Christ, the Messiah. Just as Judah birthed five sons, so did God birth five ministry offices through Christ, designed to bring forth the praise of God and the leadership jurisdiction of His Kingdom. Even though other tribal leaders and familial heads did birth five children, it is most significant that Judah, the tribe of messianic leadership, would have a type of the five-fold ministry in his familial lineage.

- **Psalm 68:11** – *The great host of women who bear and publish the good news*, a type of the female five-fold ministry. The good news of salvation comes through the Gospel, and Psalm 68:11 specifically mentions a great host of women who bear and publish the Gospel. We know these women are ministers as they have the specific command to bear and publish the news, indicating a specific calling beyond a general believer. The command to bear and publish the news implies five-fold ministry, respect, and authority in the presentation of the Gospel. These women are apostles, prophets, evangelists, pastors, and teachers, each walking in their God-appointed office.

- **Jeremiah 31:22** – *The woman who shall woo, win, and compass a man*, a type of the female five-fold ministry. It is uncommon to hear messages on Jeremiah 31:22 due to the intense nature and strength of its words. The prophecy of a woman having power over a man is not one most churches are apt to preach. Even though no one wants to talk about it, it is a Bible prophecy speaking of the rise of women to the five-fold ministry in the last days. As Israel is an Old Testament type of the church, the backslidden virgin daughter in this passage is clearly today's church. We know the church is backslidden as it is marked by confusion, error, and untruth. The promise of its restoration lies in women who shall rise up and educate, protect, and lead men, both those who are learning and those who have led the church into error.

Questions and answers

- **Why do we need to study the five-fold ministry?**

It is not uncommon to meet people who display confusion about church leadership. As the church has often abandoned Kingdom mindsets and priorities, many have come to obey and follow leadership that is clearly unscriptural. Numerous denominations, claiming to be Christian and Biblical, adhere to a number of leadership offices that are neither Biblical nor rooted in Biblical truth. Even though denominational leadership may be, false leadership claims of being Biblical have caused people to believe that such are Biblical offices. A few oddly placed Bible verses here and there, conveniently taken out of context, add to the confusion about leadership. The mere suggestion of Biblical leadership when such is not present misleads those new in the faith or unknowing about Bible leadership. The result is a situation where what is Biblical is not discerned from what is unbiblical. This state of confusion is unacceptable. True leaders cannot turn our heads the other way and allow people to be led into deception.

The first reason we need to study the five-fold ministry is because leadership in and of itself is essential in the Body of Christ. Not just any leadership is suited for the church established by Christ. We cannot divorce Scriptural leadership from a Scriptural church structure. Christians need to ensure the leadership to which we both adhere and ascribe is Scriptural. If we claim to be a Scriptural people, we must have Scriptural leadership. Believing in the five-fold ministry as a nice idea or a nice concept is not enough; it must be the solid foundation for effective leadership ministry by which we seek in every era of church life.

The second reason why studying the five-fold ministry is important is because the five-fold ministry is the standard for Biblical leadership. Any church minister claiming an office in the church must measure up to the criteria established for their office as laid out in the five-fold ministry. For example, someone claiming to be an apostle must meet the standards for being an apostle according to the Word. A prophet cannot idly speak any word and be called a prophet; he or she must meet the criteria established for being a prophet according to the Word. A pastor can't be a pastor of they are not a pastor according to Biblical standards. The same is true with the offices of evangelist and teacher. Even though many deviate and attempt to disclaim themselves from various responsibilities or duties of ministry, a Christian leader cannot rightly do so and consider themselves Christian leaders.

The third reason why studying the five-fold ministry is important goes hand-in-hand with the second reason: False leadership must be identified and rooted out as it arises. False leaders cannot be rooted out if we do not know how to recognize true leaders. To recognize true leadership, we must all know the signs, duties, callings, and responsibilities of the five-fold ministry.

- **I have a personal relationship with Christ. Why do I need leadership?**

The very nature of this question is the essence of why we need the five-fold ministry. I laud your personal relationship with Christ and pray you continue to be edified in that relationship. The answer to your question, however, lies in the question itself. The purpose in having a personal relationship with God through Jesus Christ is to know, on a personal level, what is true through Christ. It is accepting Christ as the way, truth, and life (John 14:6) with understanding that because we have believed and experienced it personally, no one can take it away from us. It is personally accepting the knowledge of Christ's sacrifice for sins, and that we are saved by the grace of God, through faith (Ephesians 2:8). A personal relationship is our individual assurance of our righteousness of God through Christ (Romans 3:22).

However, a personal relationship with Christ is not the end of our striving toward relationship, right living, and knowledge of the truth. We aren't given a license to personally decide what is true or final. We are not given the right to establish personal doctrine, or to stand as our own personal "pope" to lead ourselves. It is possible to read the Bible incorrectly, failing to rightly divide the Word of truth (2 Timothy 2:15). It is not just a matter of "us and Jesus;" when we are truly born again, we are a part of the Body, His Body. In His Body, He has established leadership to help it function here on earth. If we rely on ourselves to lead ourselves, we will rely on our own personal understanding rather than that which will lead to life.

Another reason why a personal relationship with Christ is not sufficient for Christian living is because it is very possible, living insularly in the concept that it's just "you and Jesus," will become seriously isolating. We are believers, brought into the Kingdom, to reveal Christ to others and establish the Kingdom of heaven on earth. Isolating the relationship to self, where it is solely about personal understanding, revelation, knowledge, and opinion, reduces the Kingdom to an individual experience rather than one composed of a body of believers. A personal relationship with Jesus does not nullify us from our connection to the rest of the church. When we are saved, God puts us in the Body – His Body. He does not intend a relationship with Him to be isolating or disconnecting, and our opinions to be the final authority.

The biggest temptation we have when we isolate ourselves from the Body of Christ is to make our opinions doctrinal. Opinions are not doctrines, they are not facts – they are personal opinions. Any one of us can read something and develop a feeling about it. No matter how much we may want to take our opinions as faith, they aren't! We can hold to an opinion and believe in it firmly, only for it to be totally and completely false. That is why leadership is a gift – it keeps the Body from being lost in a sea of self-importance and self-opinion, both of which lead to destruction.

As a result, God has established individuals who are called by Him and recognized by their ministries to bring empowerment to the body of Christ. Leadership clarifies what is true, establishes the true teaching, corrects misconceptions, assists believers in their Kingdom journey, and stands to equip the church by bringing believers together as one body.

- **If everyone needs leadership, who leads five-fold ministers?**

There are many different terms to describe five-fold ministry leadership. The most common term is "covering," in which one leader is "covered" spiritually by another leader. The way covering is interpreted differs among leaders. Some people interpret covering to mean that one ministry becomes an extension of another, and the covered ministry becomes a smaller version of the covering ministry. The smaller ministry is then given access to the "circle" of churches and ministries which fellowship with the covering ministry. Within this interpretation of covering, the covered ministry submits to the covering ministry, accepting this ministry as their spiritual "parentage" and being called in all things to obey them, even unto the point of ministry sacrifice or failure. In many instances, such ministries are subject to ask for permission before moving higher, changing direction, or fellowshipping with others. One cannot do anything in ministry without the expressed consent of the leader. This type of controlled covering is an extension of the Shepherding Movement, and does reach points where it becomes unscriptural and controlling.

To say that this is an extreme, however, does not nullify the reality that "covering," as an illustration of leadership authority, is very telling and very poignant. We talk about our leaders "covering us because they do just that – they offer us a protection, both in the spiritual and natural worlds, from invading forces. Through mentorship, leadership, education, and guidance, a leader prepares those under them for their lives, spiritual walks, and ministry assignments, however it is that those individuals are called to function or operate. While expecting people to operate in self-discipline, respect for leadership, honor, and consideration, this type of covering (even though the term "covering" is used here to describe something Scriptural, the term itself is not in the Word in the exact same usage) is indeed Scriptural (1 Corinthians 4:17, 1 Corinthians 16:10, Hebrews 12:9). If leaders recognize Bible understanding, leaders are covered by other leaders who are found within the order of the five-fold. It is servant-based leadership designed to develop other leaders. It is not an exclusive club, but one which follows divine order.

Leaders, therefore, are led by other leaders who are guided by God and who are proved in their ministries. Apostles are authorized to cover and lead any member of the five-fold or the appointments of bishop, elder, and deacon. As a leadership office, one of the apostle's primary jobs is to both develop and support leaders in their ministries. It is not a matter of laying on hands and then running off, but a continual drawing by which new things are discovered and prepared as the individual develops in their respective office. Prophets exist to cover and train other prophets in the work of the prophetic. Evangelists and teachers, though vital and important to the ministry work, are not covering offices. Individuals should not be covered by those who claim such offices, because their work does not demand such a relationship with individuals. Pastors cover individuals who are not called to ministry (at least at the present time – when they discover that call, they are called to move on to a new leader) and those who are walking out their lives on a laity basis. The established structure God has enacted for the body of Christ is complete and strong in every way.

- **Are you saying leaders can only learn things from other leaders?**

No. As a minister, I have learned just as much, if not more, from people who were not in church leadership. This question is different, however, from the issue of having a leader. There is a difference between learning from someone and embracing someone as a leader. There are many different kinds of learning necessary for leaders and for human beings in general. When a leader needs to learn something, God will have a leader learn from whomever He appoints. In terms of learning the specifics about being in ministry and what it means to be in ministry, leaders must go to the source for mentoring and education. The world cannot educate Christian leaders in ways it does not understand or know.

There is also the issue of accountability to consider.

Accountability begins with leadership, but extends outward to all we lead. Ministers need to learn accountability from other leaders – and that starts from the leaders we, ourselves have. God provides leaders so others can learn about their offices and how to be accountable and responsible in ministry – and leaders teach that to one another as much as to those who are not in ministry.

- **How do I know if I am called to an office in the five-fold ministry?**

When I am contacted by someone new, more than half of the time they are inquiring with this question. Many are curious in their own self-discovery to ministry and think that by talking to me and hearing what an apostle is called to do, they will know whether or not they are called to ministry. In truth, discerning a call to the five-fold ministry is not this simple. Sometimes people are called to an office in the ministry, but pursue the wrong office for some reason. Even though in this example someone may definitely have a call from God, they don't have the call they are pursuing. Sometimes people desire to have a call or think they should have a call, so they give themselves a title and pursue something that is not God-ordained. They often have ministerial struggles with purpose, anointing, ministry organization and direction, and lack divine direction in their decisions. These issues manifest to those who are assured of the Word and know solid leadership when it arises. Then there are those who have a call, but are unsure about it, what it means, and how to pursue it.

A calling indicates one has been called by God to do something. This means one knows of their call from God Himself. While the calling one has is confirmed by leaders and members of the church, the basic knowing of ministry purpose comes from God. Even though one may not understand all the duties of their office (or what it is called) in the beginning, one has some revelation of their purpose in that ministry calling. They are called to the duties of the office and are strong in areas demanding that specific ministry leadership. Through prayer, acknowledgement, and trust of God, developing confirmation of one's calling enhances the steps one is called to take in ministry.

A person who is called to ministry needs to know they are chosen for that work. God calls many, but we know from the Word, that few are chosen. Are you willing to make the commitment and necessary sacrifices to bring forth ministry work? Do you have what it takes to be the kind of leader God needs? Are you ready, willing, and able to handle disappointments and joys? What about the necessary study and dedication? Will you be able to handle this, even after it starts to get hard? What do you understand of the office you believe you're called to serve? All of these things must be taken into serious consideration when considering a call to ministry, and even more sincerely when answering that call.

- **Can't you just do ministry work? Why do you need a title?**

The use of ministry terms (apostle, prophet, evangelist, pastor, and teacher) and appointments (bishop, deacon, and elder) as "titles" is not forbidden in the Bible. Having a negative attitude about their use, however, comes from the world.

The use of titles is a sign of respect that has always conveyed respect, and always will convey respect. It shows respect for the work one has been called to (thereby honoring God) and the work one is walking in through divine obedience (thereby honoring the ministry). In the New Testament, none of the disciples ever approached Jesus, calling Him by His first Name – it was always Lord, Rabboni, Master, or Teacher. The modern church would do well to remember this, for a few reasons. First, in our pursuit of a personal relationship with the Lord, we have gotten too casual in our approach with Him. The majority of people do not approach the sacred with a sense of awe or respect. The second reason they referred to Jesus by title was to make it clear to Who they were speaking. Jesus was a common name in the first century, and thus identifying the Savior meant He needed a distinguishing mark – a title. "Christ" is a title, not a last name. Christ distinguishes Jesus as our Messiah, anointed Lord and Savior. We can see in this example the necessity and relevance of titles. Jesus was known by His ministry, and thus called by it. Those who have been gifted for ministry by Him, nonetheless, should be known by the same. It connects ministry to generations past, and to the Lord Who gives those gifts.

If we look at church history, obtainment of a ministry title came when a specific denomination appointed someone to fill a role within the organization. This is titling that was used to distinguish a person for position within an organization. Such is unbiblical in its motive and approach, as are many of the offices individuals operate in such a setting. Even though the method by which such is done is not Biblical, the principle behind it is the same; the organization seeks to make those it has acknowledged notable by their work.

We do not see the lax "let's just do ministry work and not call it what it is" mentality present in the Bible. Not calling forth a ministry for what it is, is just as dishonest as being in a ministry under false pretenses. People who were called to be apostles were called just that. The same is true of the other offices in the New Testament. What one was called for, chosen to be, and operating in is what an individual was noted by throughout their ministry.

We must distinguish genuine ministry calling – where a ministry calling is identified for what it is – from individuals who just appoint themselves to be something and treat a ministry office calling as a title. Just because someone may misuse a ministry calling does not mean ministry callings are abolished all together. To compare, people likewise misuse or take the Name of the Lord in vain, but that does not mean we stop calling on Jesus! Referring to someone by their five-fold ministry office is acknowledging what God has called an individual to do, not a formalized title.

It is a very big step for a minister to call himself or herself what God has already called him or her to be as ministers of the Kingdom. For many ministers, it is a struggle to refer to themselves by their ministry calling, at first. There is so much heard about false teachers, and often true ministers have many issues with bad examples in ministry. True leaders are too often hesitant to use a title which perhaps may associate a ministry with confusing leadership in any way. It is a powerful identity for true leaders show forth the ministry gift which God has placed in their lives for the edification and building up of His church.

- **Didn't the five-fold ministry cease?**

The doctrine of cessationalism teaches the gifts of the Spirit have ceased, ending at the close of the first century. Such teaching cites we now have the Bible and do not need the gifts of the Spirit or the five-fold ministry any longer because we can now read what is true for ourselves. A by-product of this doctrine teaches all expressions of spiritual gifts occurring since the first century are demonic counterfeits. Is this doctrine correct?

Many believe it is a matter of personal opinion whether or not one accepts the gifts of the Spirit and the five-fold ministry. As an apostle, I believe such an attitude is dangerous. If the gifts and five-fold ministry are appointed to be active and vital in our time, there is no opinion as to the essential nature of their function in the church. This makes discovery of whether or not spiritual activity has ceased of relevance for Christians today.

The first thing we must do is examine the New Testament. Is there a verse stating the gifts would cease because of the printed Bible? Many are surprised to learn the Bible gives no such verse stating the gifts (leadership included) to cease at the end of the first century. Likewise, we have no indication spiritual gifts or leadership began to fade as New Testament books were authored.

1 Corinthians 13:8-10 is the one universal passage invoked by cessationalists: *"Charity never faileth: but whether there be prophecies, they shall fail; whether there be tongues, they shall cease; whether there be knowledge, it shall vanish away. For we know in part, and we prophesy in part. But when that which is perfect is come, then that which is in part shall be done away."*

On the surface, this passage doesn't challenge a cessationalist view. At the same time, it does not affirm such a view, either. 1 Corinthians 13:8 correctly states that one day prophesies, tongues, and knowledge will cease. However, this passage, does not state when this ceasing shall occur. 1 Corinthians 13:8 identifies the cessation, or ending, of such gifts will be at a future time. The Apostle Paul does not indicate from his words that the gifts would be ceasing in the near future, such at the time of his death or the other apostles. If indeed that were the case, the Apostle Paul would have specified the gifts were ceasing due to the end of the New Testament era. He makes no such specification.

We also need to consider the point of this passage, which is clarified by reading verses 9 and 10. The Apostle Paul's purpose was not to create debate about whether or not the gifts were continuing, but to teach about the eternity of love. In that being the purpose of this passage, we see the gifts will cease when they are no longer needed. When will they cease? The passage answers that question: when the perfect is come! The "perfect" is a reference to the time when Jesus will return, as He is the Perfect, and all things will be restored (Acts 3:21). "The perfect" was not the closing of the Bible canon. Since the perfect has not yet arrived, the time for the cessation of spiritual gifts and offices has not yet arrived, either!

There is no Biblical prophecy telling the church to beware leaders because the five-fold ministry (a part of the spiritual gifts) would cease. We find warning of false leaders and false prophets to come (2 Peter 2:1, 1 John 4:1) – not people who claim to have an office that ceased. If indeed such was to happen, surely there would have been warning that false leadership wasn't a matter of counterfeit faith, but of following offices no longer in place. Since no such warning, prophecy, or promise exists, we can safely say there is no New Testament prophecy, promise, or verse telling of a ceasing five-fold ministry.

If there is no promise, prophecy, warning, or verse – or even the context of such – then we can safely say the five-fold ministry, as part of the gifts of the Spirit, will not cease until the time when Jesus returns. Any teaching that states otherwise is unscriptural and out of order for church structure. As the church pulled farther and farther away from the truth over the first few centuries, the five-fold ministry was one of the first things to disappear. Once disordered and maligned men removed apostles, prophets, evangelists, pastors, and teachers from the church, they replaced the Bible offices with ministry offices of their own making. The church then fell into serious doctrinal, moral, and ethical error. The five-fold ministry structure is essential to keep church leadership and authority intact.

On a deeper level, we must also examine Romans 10:14: ***"Faith cometh by hearing, and hearing by the Word of God."*** The Bible itself states faith comes by hearing, not by reading. Part of the reason evangelistic fruits are now low today is due to promoting evangelization through reading rather than hearing. The "reading method" of evangelization is when individuals hand out Bibles and tracts to a large group of people. They hope that by reading the Word or information provided, they will come to accept church teachings. This is not Biblical! It depends on an individual's ability to both read and understand what they read. As literacy is a relatively new facet to society, that would mean the majority of people throughout history had no chance of ever being saved. Faith comes by hearing, meaning it comes by the process of hearing the Word in preaching, testimony, and action. This means our effort is involved, and the Spirit is involved in the reception process. If there is anything I have learned from studying religion, it is that anyone can read the Bible, and walk away with little faith and lots of thoughts from self-interpretation. Faith comes by hearing, not reading!

If we believe faith continues to be real and valid in the church today, then we cannot deny the gifts of the Spirit. Why is that, you ask? Faith is identified as a spiritual gift, one which the Holy Spirit is a part of as one accepts and comes to live in faith (1 Corinthians 12:9). We can't pick and choose what is relevant or active today because it makes the most sense to our natural minds. If faith is active, so are the rest of the spiritual gifts – (Romans 12:6-8, 1 Corinthians 12:1-11) – and so is the five-fold ministry and its spiritual gifts of apostle, prophet, evangelist, pastor, and teacher (Ephesians 4:7-16).

Another necessary proof the five-fold ministry is found in

Ephesians 4:11-16 itself: *"And He gave some, apostles; and some, prophets; and some, evangelists; and some, pastors and teachers; for the perfecting of the saints, for the work of the ministry, for the edifying of the body of Christ: till we all come in the unity of the faith, and of the knowledge of the Son of God, unto a perfect man, unto the measure of the stature of the fulness of Christ: That we henceforth be no more children, tossed to and fro, and carried about with every wind of doctrine, by the sleight of men, and cunning craftiness, whereby they lie in wait to deceive; but speaking the truth in love, may grow up into Him in all things, which is the head, even Christ: from whom the whole body fitly joined together and compacted by that which every joint supplieth, according to the effectual working in the measure of every part, maketh increase of the body unto the edifying of itself in love."* The purpose of the five-fold ministry is to build up the church until the time when it reaches full unity of faith, unto Christ, the Head, is no longer tossed by false doctrine, or given to false teachers. Last time I checked, this has not yet happened. If the purpose of the ministry is not fulfilled, the five-fold ministry is still vital and relevant for today. The fulfillment will come when Christ returns and all is restored, when the "perfect" arrives.

It is also notable to recognize Revelation 18:20, in speaking of the fall of Babylon in the last days: *"Rejoice over her, thou heaven, and ye holy apostles and prophets; for God hath avenged you on her."* If heaven was to rejoice separately from the apostles and prophets, this tells us Revelation is not speaking of first-century apostles and prophets, but of apostles and prophets living in that day. No matter how we understand that: to indicate a restoration of apostles and prophets or a continuation of them, we can surely say apostles and prophets will be present at the fall of Babylon. This means the offices have not ceased and will not until the perfect, Jesus Christ, arrives.

While there are a few other passages occasionally cited by cessationalists, they prove the cessationalist point as little as 1 Corinthians 13:8-10. Passages such as Ephesians 4:11-17 and

Ephesians 2:20 uphold the order of the five-fold ministry and its necessity, not its cessation. We can see clearly from this examination that a cessationalist point of view is ignorant of the Word.

It is also relevant to note where cessationalism has its strongholds. Cessationalism is strongest within Jehovah's Witnesses, Church of Christ adherents, the Orthodox Church, and many mainline, dispensational, and evangelical non-denominational Protestant groups. Examination of the legalism, false teaching, and rigorous structural replacement of God's order speaks loudly to the problems existing in these denominations. The display of disunity, disobedience, and man-made rules taught as those of God (Matthew 15:6, Mark 7:13) are thorough evidence of a man-made leadership structure. There are also individuals who do not claim membership with such groups who hold a cessationalist viewpoint. There are many of varying denominational positions who also reject the notion of five-fold ministry leadership and the exercise of spiritual gifts. Often they doubt the gifts because they themselves have not experienced them. Forming doctrinal truth based on inexperience is error, and it is not uncommon to find entire groups of people rejecting the spiritual gifts because they have not experienced them.

- **I've seen ministers who use a combination of titles to describe their office (such as Prophet-Pastor or Apostle-Teacher). Is this a Biblical practice?**

In the New Testament, we do not see the mixing of offices or combining of such as we see today. There are three main reasons why this practice is popular today.

The first is because people are genuinely confused about their ministries, and don't know what office they are called to serve. It is not uncommon for one to hold gifts which may be beneficial to another office, but this does not mean they are called to function in that office. For example, apostles hold a prophetic gift in accordance with their calling, but this does not mean they are prophets in the sense of the prophetic office. We also have disordered teaching, which uses five-fold ministry terminology to describe different duties for the office. One common myth is that "apostles pastor." This gives people the impression that apostles are pastors with churches, just in a different sense. This is false, as apostles don't pastor, but serve as apostles, an office with a different function. As a result of such confusion and false teaching, we find ministers who claim to be apostles, but serve as traditional pastors of churches. Mixing offices and duties confuses those with a calling as to what they are to do and what it means to be called to a five-fold ministry office. Even though these individuals are genuinely responding to what they were taught and are often sincere in their ministry aspirations, such individuals are doctrinally misguided.

God gives us many gifts in accordance with our calling to perform our ministry duties. This means sometimes we will demonstrate certain gifts and abilities that may not obviously "fit" with our calling in five-fold ministry. If we truly examine the New Testament and five-fold ministry, we will see the all gifts we've been given fall perfectly into our roles as apostles, prophets, evangelists, pastors, and teachers. It is only when we try to narrowly define the offices or put a human spin on God's calling that the five-fold ministry is supplemented with human ideas and concepts. In this instance, educational correction is needed, because the confusion exists between gifts and offices.

The second reason why such a practice is popular ties into the first. There is also the attempt to conform callings to what is religiously comfortable and accepted by the mainline religious community. An apostle or prophet that can cover under the guise of a pastor will gain acceptance among religious communities, at least on the surface. Sometimes denominational ties, despite claims to overcome legalism, hold fast and make ministers think compromise is in order. All who know the Word know that such compromise is unacceptable.

I do not believe those who use titles like this are ill-intentioned; rather, they are misguided. They are attempting to execute ministry by the measure of worldly success it can reap. This is not always for personal glory, but because the individual does not understand another way to do things. While their motives may be good, the results will never be positive in the

Kingdom. We must never forget the fruits of ministry are not numbers, large churches, or big followings of people. The fruits of ministry are lives changed, people saved, and holy, committed followers of Jesus who do their best for the Lord every day.

The third reason why people mix offices is because they are attempting to describe every established purpose of their ministry in a title. Such seek to sound important and believe using many titles will sound better than using only using one. I am not hesitant to describe such as an ego-trip. Such are not misguided, but truly blinded by the lies of this world. Ministry is not about holding many titles, but being called of the Lord into His service.

There may very well be rare cases where an individual is in a situation and they need to function in more than one ministry gift at one time. In such an instance, the gifts should align with the work, and would also reduce one to the main, or proprietary gift, and the other as a ministry function. At some point in time, the functional gift would cease to be as prominent, because it is given for that instance. This, however, is rare, and that does not mean people should identify themselves as multiple things.

- **What is the difference between a gift and an office?**

Understanding the difference between having a gift and walking in an office are essential for success in ministry. The difference between the two comes about through discernment and solid understanding of spiritual gifts and offices.

Every single office of the five-fold also has gifts that are a part of those offices, but not exclusive to those offices. For example: an apostolic gift, a prophetic gift, an evangelistic gift, a pastoral gift, and a teaching gift. If we break these gifts down to a practical level, an apostolic gift is a gift of administration, a prophetic gift relates to conveying a divine message in any number of forms, an evangelistic gift is an ability to convey a message, a pastoral gift relates to love and care for others, and a teaching gift enables one to teach. Let us understand a few things about these gifts. If we understand the gifts of God in these ways, these gifts can apply in a secular setting as much as they apply in a spiritual one. For example, a principal has an administrative, or apostolic, gift. A guidance counselor has a prophetic gift. Someone who does announcements has an evangelistic gift. A mental health worker has a pastoral gift, and a teacher in any form has a teaching gift. Even though these people may not be called to function in the church office pertaining to these ministries, they still have been given gifts that benefit the five-fold and are of benefit to the work they do in their respective professions.

In the five-fold ministry, gifts operate much of the same way. An apostle can't be an apostle without an apostolic (administrative) gift. An apostle can, however, have other gifts present in different offices of the five-fold ministry, which serve to enhance the ministry they've been given. An apostle who works in their respective office may also be gifted prophetically, in order to enhance that office, or gifted evangelistically, to benefit the work of the Kingdom. This doesn't mean an apostle is also a prophet or also an evangelist. As the Apostle Paul spoke of himself as an apostle, preacher, and teacher of nations (2 Timothy 1:11), that does not mean he was not an apostle or was an Apostle-teacher – it simply means he was describing the duties and gifts of the apostolic office.

Simply put, a gift is something God gives to enhance and bless whatever it is He has given you to do. An office is a ministry execution given to God as its own separate gift – a gift of leadership purpose within the body.

- **What are the functions of the church?**

A function is a work of the church that relates to the function of the church but is not necessarily an office and is not necessarily held by an individual in the five-fold ministry. There are different types of functions, but to explain the role of the function as simply as possible, it is something given to an individual that is neither listed as a spiritual gift nor is necessarily an office to that individual. There are nine examples of functions:

- Preacher
- Missionary
- Dreamer/visionary
- Dream/vision interpreter
- Intercessor
- Watchman/gatekeeper
- Handmaiden/menservant
- Scribe
- Spiritual father/mother
- Church mother
- Mystic

There are also functions that relate to ministry, or the way a minister operates in their office. For example, a watchman or a seer would be a prophetic function. An intercessor who is also a prophet would be an example of a prophetic intercessor, with the intercession serving as a function to that office. If an individual is an apostle and they are operating strongly as a prophet because there is no prophet to assist them, the prophetic office, in this instance, is a function because it exists to assist or add to the apostolic. At the same time, someone can operate in a function without an office. Someone can be a preacher, a scribe, a visionary, a spiritual parent (in the sense of a spiritual mentor), or a church mother without being a five-fold minister.

- **Do five-fold ministry leaders need to receive education, such as college or seminary?**

Some teach that all one needs to have for successful ministry is a calling from God. Others teach God's anointing as sufficient for everything one may encounter in ministry. If we study the Word, this logic is flatly denied. Every apostle, prophet, evangelist, pastor, and teacher came to their callings with education, information, and solid understanding of the things of God. They were learned from educational knowledge received, God's revelations, and experiences they'd had. To dismiss education as unnecessary for ministry is completely unscriptural and unreasonable.

Every competent minister of the Gospel recognizes they must educate themselves and learn things to better proclaim the Word and operate ministry efficiently, according to the God's ways. We learn from working in both spiritual and secular worlds, and skills we acquire from many places are beneficial to Kingdom work. Opportunities for higher education, seminary education (given a seminary is in align with God's Word), and basic skills are always of asset to Christian ministers. Education is a help, not a hindrance, to the work of God!

So yes, five-fold ministry leaders need instruction. Whether that comes through a formal seminary or college, a training offered by a ministry or ministry institution, or through some other means, ministers need education.

- **Do gender distinctions exist in the five-fold ministry?**

The five-fold ministry is concrete proof that there is neither male nor female in Christ (Galatians 3:28). Through the mirrored purposes, roles, and callings among God's male and female ministers, we see proof of Galatians 3:28 in action. Female apostles, prophets, evangelists, pastors, and teachers do not have different duties from men who serve in the same offices.

- **Is the five-fold ministry structure a "ladder" by which one moves from a lower office to a higher one?**

Several years ago, I attended a conference where a main speaker said God was going to "promote" her to apostle. She was, at that time, a prophetess and very excited about her so-called "promotion." Nobody said much in response to her statement. I think all leaders present were rather surprised by her statement, and unsure of how to respond.

I've heard other musings similar to hers. A concept floating around out there has the apostle as the chief office, most prime to be called, and most important. Many believe if they are faithful in their existing five-fold ministry offices, God will promote them to a so-called "higher" office.

There are two basic flaws with such thinking. The first is

that someone can climb through the ranks of five-fold ministry. This nullifies the Biblical concept of a calling and gifting. We are either called by God to our ministries or we can change our calling and advance to the one we think most desirable. The second error is that the apostle's office is the highest rank within the church. The five-fold ministry is called to work together in unity, not in a sense of traditional religious hierarchy. While the apostolic office holds certain authorities and responsibilities that other offices do not, this does not make the apostolic office better than any other in the five-fold ministry.

There are people genuinely walking in the wrong office. I have met many, many ministers who are genuinely called by God, sincere in their ministerial efforts, but are misled as to which ministry God has called them. In such circumstances, it is the job of responsible ministers in the correct office to educate about the office they are called. Misled ministers need to get in touch with the truth about leadership and follow God's prompting unto the understanding of His calling.

Then there remain individuals like the one I spoke of earlier, who misjudge the ministry as a ladder of success. We must teach and correct such individuals as well as those affected by their ministries.

- **Have there been eras in history where one office of the five-fold is more prominent than others?**

If we understand history, there have been points in time where it would at least appear that certain offices of the five-fold were more prominent than others. The early church reveals the apostolic office as the most prevalent among mention. The revivals of the 1800s spawned a great interest in evangelism, and a number of people who claimed to be evangelists. The years surrounding the Protestant Reformation were times of great prophecy and evangelism. The prominence of these specific offices arose from the culture, time, and style of ministering present within the church in these eras. This does not mean, however, that the other offices of the five-fold were not present during these times. For example, if we look at the ministers of the 1800s, most of them classified themselves as evangelists. If we look at their work, however, they did far more than just evangelize. Many started and led churches, they worked in missions to establish other churches, and some oversaw entire denominations. Their work was not that of an evangelist, but that of other offices in the five-fold.

Even though it may appear, at least on the surface, that certain offices have been more prominent in some eras than others, the entire five-fold ministry is needed for the edification of the church in every era until Jesus returns. If one office seems to have the spotlight over others in a historical era, that can be due to our own misunderstandings of what it means to be in the office with the most prominence, it can be due to stereotyping of history and church historians, or it can just be due to the fact that we haven't dug deep enough in history to see the five-fold ministry working in that era.

Discussion, study and review questions:

- What have we seen throughout religious history? What do we not see very often? Why is the New Testament structure of ministry leadership revolutionary? What did and does the Kingdom of God offer?

- If we want to understand Christian leadership, what must we understand? What do many claim? Does this apply? Why or why not? Why is the five-fold ministry relevant for today?

- What has been given to everyone in the church, and why? What does this mean?

- In the case of church leadership, what offices are gifts? Who are they a gift to? In what ways do people reject these offices? Why is rejection of the offices wrong?

- What are the purposes of the five-fold ministry? Why can we not argue the validity of the five-fold ministry?

- What command does the church have? What is part of the reason for the immaturity in the church? What are some non-Biblical roles present in today's religions? Is it appropriate to elect church leaders? Why or why not? What happens when we eliminate or try to replace Scriptural offices with non-Scriptural ones? Why?

- How are the offices of the five-fold ministry to be executed? What is the purpose in the five-fold ministry? How is the church edified?

- What are the characteristics of the five-fold ministry in working together? What are some specific Biblical examples of the characteristics of the five-fold ministry benefiting ministry?

- What are some Old Testament types of the five-fold ministry? How do these types shadow what the five-fold ministry is to represent?

- Discuss and share some of the questions and answers found in the "Questions and Answers" section. What did you learn that you did not know about the five-fold ministry? What did you learn that changed your mind about an opinion you might have had prior about the ministry? How did learning about specific issues related to the five-fold ministry help you to grow in your understanding of ministry? The church? Your own relationship with God?

THE OFFICE OF THE APOSTLE

What encouragement the apostle holds out to us. O my friends, that we might leave all our pretensions, and come to the truth in our own hearts.
– Elias Hicks [1]

Of all New Testament offices, the office of the apostle is, by far, the most controversial. The controversy over the apostolic did not begin in modern times. If we study the office according to the New Testament, controversies existed over who could call themselves an apostle, even back then. Nowadays, the majority of churchgoers are far out of touch with this office and its vital function for the church. Years of improper teaching on the office of apostle has caused many to believe the office is unnecessary, unimportant, and irrelevant for our modern church. Too many are unaware that we can't have the church without apostles! Through the apostolic office, we find the foundational revelation of Christ on which the church is built. No other church ministry can provide this direct revelation, because God has given it to the apostle. With this revelation of Christ resurrected, it is the apostle's job to go forth and establish the necessary doctrinal, prophetic, structural, and corrective ministry. In doing so, the apostle establishes the means to build the church upon Christ Himself.

Text study

1 Timothy 2:1-7

Supplementary texts

Matthew 10:1-4, John 12:46-50, Acts 1:13-26, Acts 26:14-18, 1 Corinthians 4:1-2, Galatians 1:1 and 11, Ephesians 3:1-7, Hebrews 3:1.

Power verse

1 Timothy 2:7:

- *"Whereto I am ordained a preacher, and an apostle (I speak the truth in Christ, and lie not); a teacher of the Gentiles in faith and verity."*

- *"And for this purpose I was appointed a herald and an apostle—I am telling the truth, I am not lying—and a teacher of the true faith to the Gentiles."* (NIV)

- *"And of this matter I was appointed a preacher and an apostle (special messenger)--I am speaking the truth in Christ, I do not falsify [when I say this]--a teacher of the Gentiles in [the realm of] faith and truth."* (AMP)

- *"For this I was appointed a preacher and an apostle (I am telling the truth, I am not lying), a teacher of the Gentiles in faith and truth."* (ESV)

- *"For this I was appointed a preacher and apostle – I am telling the truth; I am not lying – and a teacher of the Gentiles in faith and truth."* (NASB)

- *"...In which I am set a preacher and an apostle. For I say truth, and I lie not, that am a teacher of heathen men in faith and in truth [Soothly I say truth in Christ Jesus, and I lie not, a teacher of heathen men in faith and truth]."* (WYC)

Power words

- **Ordained** – From the Greek word *"tithemi"* which means, "to set, put, place; to make; to set, fix, establish."[2]

- **Preacher** – From the Greek word *"kerux"* which means, "a herald or messenger vested with public authority, who conveyed the official messages of kings, magistrates, princes, military commanders, or who gave a public summons or demand, and performed various other duties. In the New Testament, God's ambassador, and the herald or proclaimer of the divine Word."[3]

- **Apostle** – From the Greek word *"apostolos"* which means, "a delegate, messenger, one sent forth with orders."[4]

- **Teacher** – From the Greek word *"didaskalos"* which means, "a teacher; in the New Testament one who teaches concerning the things of God, and the duties of man."[5]

- **Gentiles** – From the Greek word *"ethnos"* which means, "a multitude (whether or men or of beasts) associated or living together; a multitude of individuals of the same nature or genus; a race, nation, or people group; in the Old Testament, foreign people not worshipping the true God, pagans, Gentiles; Paul uses the term for Gentile Christians."[6] (compare to the English word, "ethnic").

Historical context

There was question about the apostolic office, even in the Apostle Paul's day. Questions as to the veracity of his apostolic calling are visible all throughout Paul's apostolic walk. As he was not one of the original twelve who walked with Jesus throughout His earthly ministry, some questioned whether or not Paul was really an apostle.

By virtue of the Apostle Paul's calling, we find new criteria for one called to be an apostle. These standards establish the apostolic office as we understand it, down to today. The Apostle Paul clarifies to Timothy (and any who might doubt of his calling) that an apostle's establishment comes from God alone and is proven through implementation of apostolic ministry and successful function of the apostolic office.

Notes on text

The office of apostle is an essential to the five-fold ministry. The Apostles Paul, Peter, John, and others proved this through their ministries. Those called to the office of apostle will follow in likekind, serving to teach, to administrate, work as an apostle, and hold ministry to the nations.

Power points

- The word "apostle" means "a delegate, an ambassador, a messenger with a special message, or one who is sent forth with orders."[7] The office is received by the grace of God. With that grace comes the power to represent Christ, as Christ was the first apostle sent forth with divine orders to represent God, the Father (John 12:46-50, Hebrews 3:1). The apostle serves as God's ambassador, specifically commanded by God to go forth with the message of the Gospel (Galatians 1:1). The apostle is a guardian of this message: sent to ensure those who proclaim the Gospel in any office do not stray from the Gospel message. Apostles are ministers and witnesses to the grace received in Him, the direct calling received from Him, and the faith learned through revelation of Christ (Acts 26:14-18).

- There are two sets of criteria for the apostolic office in the New Testament. The first set of criteria required apostles to have followed Christ throughout His earthly ministry and after the resurrection. These apostles were apostles of Jesus Christ, the Lamb of God. After Judas' suicide, this criteria served to elect Matthias, his replacement (Acts 1:13-26). The second set of criteria was established through call of the Apostle Paul. It is this standard which establishes criteria for the apostolic office unto this day. It is the calling for apostles of Jesus Christ, representing and heralding the new covenant. The criteria is as follows: one must be called of God to be an apostle, directly by Jesus Christ (1 Corinthians 1:9, Galatians 1:1); through that calling, an apostle of God must have an encounter with Christ as He is resurrected (Acts 26:14-18); from that revelation, an apostle comes to be taught by Jesus Christ (Romans 1:5, Galatians 1:11); be sent by Christ for the purposed work of The Gospel (Ephesians 3:1-7); and have a thorough knowledge of the Scriptures (2 Timothy 2:15). The ministry of the apostle is proven through teaching, preaching, and ministry work of the Gospel (Galatians 1:11, 1 Timothy 2:7). The calling of the apostle is confirmed by others in authority, and sealed in ordination (1 Timothy 2:7).

- The duties of the apostle include: guarding, teaching, and revealing the mysteries of Christ (the revelation of Christ, the foundation of the church) and remaining faithful with them (1 Corinthians 4:1-2); organizing, administrating, and working dutifully to establish the body (1 Corinthians 12:28); serve in the office of doctrinal establishment, correction and moral establishment and correction (Acts 2:42); train and educate church leaders (1 Corinthians 4:17, Philippians 2:22, 1 Timothy 1:18); operate in the gifts of the Spirit (Acts 5:12, 2 Corinthians 12:12); walk in prophetic offices and assess prophecy on a doctrinal level (1 Timothy 4:1-9, 2 Peter 1:12-21, 2 Peter 2:1-22); work as a preacher and teacher for the church and to mixed or unbelieving groups as well (1 Timothy 2:7, Acts 2:4-35, Acts 3:12-19), teach and baptize new members (Acts 2:36-43), pray for people to receive the gift of the Holy Ghost (Acts 8:14-17), establishing and commissioning deacons (Acts 6:1-7), and affirm others in the five-fold ministry to offices by the laying on of hands (1 Timothy 5:22, 2 Timothy 1:6, Hebrews 6:2). The church cannot be built upon a pastor. The apostle comes with the revelation of God for the right foundation and doctrine of the church (Ephesians 2:20, Ephesians 4:11).

- There are a number of people (over fifty) who we can say with accuracy served as apostles in the New Testament, both men and women: the original twelve (Matthew 10:1-3), Matthias (Acts 1:26), Paul (Acts 26:14-18), Mary Magdalene (Luke 24:10), Photini (John 4:1-30), Timothy (1 Thessalonians 1:1), Silvanus (1 Thessalonians 1:1), Barnabas (Acts 14:14), Junia (Romans 16:7), Andronicus (Romans 16:7), Apphia (Philemon 1:2) and Epaphroditus (Philippians 2:25), to name a few. There were others as well, such as those mentioned without name in 2 Corinthians 8:22-24 and the Seventy (or Seventy-Two, depending on translation) who were sent out in Luke 10:1-8.

- Many argue we do not need apostles today because we have the Bible. Without the apostle, people will continue to misuse the Bible and misinterpret it. It is the apostle that reveals the mysteries of God, designed to teach the Body of Christ (Ephesians 3:2-5).

Characteristics of the apostle

There are essential characteristics God gives to each apostle, enabling him or her to fulfill the apostolic call with full grace and dignity. In looking at some apostles, we can see these characteristics clearly.

- **The Apostle Peter, Acts 2:14-41:** The Apostle Peter displays a take-charge persona in the situation on Pentecost, essential to the apostolic office. When someone needed to stand up and speak, the Apostle Peter took the initiative. When something needs to get done, an apostle rises to the task. Apostles accept responsibility for their actions, their teaching, and the call of God on their lives. The Apostle Peter also displays amazing clarity and truth in his presentation of the Word. Apostles, with their intense heart for doctrine, are fully equipped by God to speak, write, and teach the Word. Even though some might have found the Apostle Peter to be harsh and punitive, he was able to stir conviction unto repentance in the people. Apostles must never forget to herald the basic call to repent and believe in Christ with conviction and power.

- **The Apostle Paul, 1 Corinthians 3-4**: The Apostles Paul and Peter had a lot in common. They both came from very staunch Jewish backgrounds and were well-versed in the law. We also know from historical records that they didn't always get along very well with one another. In viewing their dialogues, we can see they had similar personalities, which led to their personal conflicts. Apostles have strong personalities, and the strengths present to work the apostolic office do not always equate to an ability to get along well with others. For this reason, it is essential that apostles remain humble, focused in God, and maintain a strong balance between truth and integrity. Apostles must have the ability to solve problems, both their own and those pertaining to church ministry. While problem solving can be complicated as many do not desire to change a position, apostles must still have the ability. As a Christian leader, the apostle is constantly dealing with questions of doctrine, debate, and conflicts between individuals. We also see in the Apostle Paul the ability to examine a situation and develop necessary teaching for that situation. We know from reading further epistles in the New Testament that the Apostle Paul was not always perfect; he grew frustrated, angry, and hot tempered at times. We know from his writings that he pushed for and desired perfection, and sometimes advocated standards hard to meet. All apostles struggle with these same personality issues within themselves as well as in their interactions with others as they strive for, promote, and pursue a greater holiness and unity with God.

- **The Apostle James, James 2:1-25**: The Apostle James exemplifies the apostolic emphasis on doing rather than merely receiving. Apostles are participants in life. They respond to everything head-on, with enthusiasm and zeal. It is no accident an apostle was the one who commanded all believers to live the Word as doers, and not hearers only.

Apostles are involved in their faith, working with God and for God.

- **The Apostle John, 2 John 1-13:** The Apostle John truly displays the independent spirit at work in God's apostles. Their independence provides an essential component of objective detachment needed to assess problems, difficulties, and doctrinal questions. The Apostle John also shows us the depth of an apostle's love. It is truly the heart of an apostle to disciple others, displaying the love of Christ and heart of the Father. Apostles do not desire to see anyone depart into error, but will remain stubborn and intent on keeping all in the church walking in God's light.

Types of the apostolic office

- **Genesis 12:1-6** – *Abram, turned Abraham,* a type of the apostolic ministry. Abraham was the first individual called to the nations, beyond his immediate people. Told to depart from his immediate surroundings and venture into unknown territory, Abraham's call gives us an idea of the practical spirituality in being an apostle. He is a type of the New Covenant apostle, one with the vision and scope to go beyond the immediate religious world and comfortable spiritual confines into uncharted territories. As Abraham became the father of many in Spirit, so do apostles become the originators, leaders, and progenitors of those who hear the Gospel call.

- **Exodus 6:1-13:22** – *Moses,* a type of the apostolic ministry. Most of us revere Moses as a prophet and type of Christ. While this is true, Moses is also a type of the apostle. Moses was sent with God's message to Pharaoh and He was a leader of His people. He also received direct revelation of God, proving himself to be the original Kingdom leader. His personal insecurities, failures, frustrations, and inadequacies truly show being a leader isn't about being perfect, but about being obedient to God and led by Him.

- **Joshua 1:1-18** – *Joshua*, a type of the apostolic ministry. Joshua wasn't just the follow-up act to Moses. In his own right, his Kingdom leadership shows him to be a type of the apostle as well. By leading the Israelites into the Promised Land, Joshua dealt with the difficulties and joys of leadership. Directly receiving revelation from God, Joshua empowered the Israelites unto God's promise. Apostles do the same as Kingdom leaders.

- **Judges 4:4-16** – *Deborah*, a type of the female apostolic ministry. Deborah was a prophetess and judge, the only female judge mentioned in the Bible. Her role as military leader, disputer, and spiritual authority proves women competent, capable, and efficient leaders in all necessary areas of apostolic ministry. Deborah was a trailblazer, one who led the way for her nation rather than let it fall into despair. Her call is the call of an apostolic woman, fully equipped and prepared to lead the people of God in spiritually tumultuous and warring times.

- **Matthew 3:1-12, John 3:27-36** – *John the Baptist*, a type of the apostolic ministry. As John the Baptist lived under the law, he was a type, rather than a reality, of the apostolic office. His life reflected the apostolic ministry to come: he was directly called by God for his purpose, appointed to lead people unto Christ, and a powerful Kingdom preacher. His ministry was the preparation of the One to come, manifest with a strong emphasis on repentance, baptism, and changing one's ways. He was completely counter-culture, proclaiming a message out of step with the religious of his time and pointing the way unto truth. When apostles view the ministry of John the Baptist, they should see shades of themselves: out of step with religion, proclaiming the Kingdom, calling people to repent, baptizing, and pointing the way to Jesus Christ.

The historical apostle

In adding this section, I had to contemplate a few things. The first is the obvious understanding that many of these people were not identified as apostles, but as other offices, some of which were built on church traditions and not Biblical in nature. I also recognize that, in being these were historical figures, some of their understandings, culture, and social practices may or may not align with those that we have today. They are included here because the work they did truly aligns with the five-fold office, and we need to acknowledge their work as such.

- **Nina, Apostle and Enlightener to Georgia** (296-335) – Nina of Georgia knew from an early age that she was called to go and convert the hearts of the pagans in the nation of Georgia. She single-handedly converted the entire nation to Christianity, including the Tsar and his family, the Tsarina and her family, and much of the Georgian government. She worked without fame, independently and slowly. Nina was known as a powerful preacher of God's Word, a performer of miracles, and a powerful influence and model, even down to this very day in certain churches. Thanks to her, the Christian church was both established and built within Georgia.[8]

- **Lady Selina Hastings** (1707-1791) – Lady Selina Hastings was Founder of the Countess of Huntingdon's Connexion Society of Evangelical Churches, as well as a prominent Evangelical and Methodist revivalist. She served as Superintendent over her churches and chapels, of which over sixty-four were in existence. She also founded a minister's training college and is one of many in history who was expelled from the Church of England for her preaching.[9]

- **C.H. Mason** (1862-1961) – The founder of the Church of God in Christ, C.H. Mason grew up loving the things of God and pursuing spirituality. In pursuit of holiness and teaching holiness, Mason was expelled from his Baptist denomination only to discover the Azusa Street Revival and fully join Holiness with Pentecostal gifts and understanding. His church, the Church of God in Christ, now has well over six million members, making it the fourth largest denominational church body within the United States.[10]

- **William J. Seymour** (1870-1922) – The major founder of the Azusa Street Revival which launched the Pentecostal Movement, William J. Seymour is considered the founder of an entire movement that stretches down into church belief, even until today. A student of Charles Parham, Seymour experienced criticism in his beliefs, which led him to establish his own work in Los Angeles, California. The impact of his work has led to the founding of numerous denominations and changed the entire way the world looks at the gift of tongues.[11]

- **Elliot J. Deobe-Sheeks** (1872-1946) – A forgotten woman of history, Elliot Sheeks was a southern and Midwestern circuit rider. She was a charter member and co-founder of the New Testament Church of Christ, which then became the Holiness Church of Christ, and later, a member of the Church of the Nazarene. Not only did she plant churches, she also oversaw several of these congregations, and was one of only a few women in this time frame to receive ordination credentials. It has been said that, in her lifetime, she preached almost two hundred sermons and travelled over seven thousand miles in the year 1904 alone. Later in her life she served as a college professor at Bresee College.[12]

- **Charles Fox Parham** (1873-1929) – Along with William J. Seymour, considered to be one of the two major figures involved in the spread of Pentecostalism. Conducting services since the age of fifteen, Charles Parham was known for travelling work, doctrinal instruction, and founding Bethel Bible College. Despite questions about Parham's social beliefs, his work was among the first in the American religious scene to feature racial integration and the Pentecostal Spirit.[13]

Questions and answers

- **How can we know apostles exist today?**

    The calling to be an apostle is not contingent on time or

space. All throughout history, men and women have been called to serve God as apostles or types of apostles. Even though the individuals may not have been acknowledged as apostles, they did indeed fulfill the duties of an apostle of the Most High.

If we assess the office by criteria and calling, anyone in any age (save after the return of Christ) can be called to fulfill the office. The need for the apostle has not left the church.

- **If apostles are directly called by God, how can we know when someone is genuinely an apostle? Doesn't this mean just anyone can claim to be an apostle, and we won't know the difference?**

We recognize a true apostle by the fruits of their ministry (Matthew 7:16-20, Matthew 12:33, Matthew 21:43, Colossians 1:6). The ministry of a true apostle speaks for itself. The same is true for a false apostle. A false apostle's ministry is noted by its bad fruits, and likewise, it speaks for itself.

It is true that with the things of God (especially those involving a direct call) abuse exists. There is no doubt false apostles, prophets, evangelists, pastors, and teachers exist today. However, we cannot deny true ministers also exist who are genuinely called of God. We don't disregard the true because of the false. Instead, we stand back and measure ministries by their fruit.

We also consider that apostles must conform to the present system of ordination and licensing we recognize that the apostles of God must be recognized within the church as part of accountability and authority. Yes, there will always be some who insist a leader is this or that, or not legitimate based on someone's personal opinion. Regardless, a true apostle is acknowledged by God, the fruit of their ministry work, and by others in leadership within the Body of Christ.

- **Can apostles pastor?**

An examination of the New Testament shows us apostles were not pastors over churches. It is evident that while Peter,

John, and Paul worked in the apostolic work, establishing and overseeing churches as apostles, they did not themselves pastor those churches. While some argue the Apostle James was a pastor of the Jerusalem church, the Bible does not support this.

The fact that no apostle in the Bible served as a local church pastor must be relevant to apostles today. Many ministers today title themselves "apostle" and limit themselves to a pastoral role. While there is nothing unbiblical about an apostle establishing a church or overseeing a church and its leaders as an apostle (for training, leadership, and doctrinal purposes), there is something unbiblical about an apostle serving out a ministry as a full-time pastor.

The push for apostles to pastor roots itself in the structure of modern churches. For thousands of years, pastors were the main visible asset to churches. This concept reached its peak with the Shepherding Movement, spoken of earlier in this book. Now we have the rise of apostles in modern times who have heard about the relevance of the pastor through their entire Christian lives. Is it any wonder many believe ministry is about having a local church? We also have the modern-day over-emphasis on the local church to the detriment and ignorance of the universal church. The result of these theories combined gives the impression to modern ministers that serving as a local pastor is the only purposeful ministry experience.

The Bible does not indicate this to be true. These ways of thinking are detrimental to apostles, pastors, and church members reared in these concepts. The apostolic office is a different function and purpose than the pastoral office. While both may work together and benefit each from the other, apostles are not pastors! Yes, there may be a time while an individual performs a work as a function, but this does not change their call from God to the work of the apostle.

I receive many defensive arguments from individuals who claim to be apostles and pastors, all-in-one. My answer to them: let's examine all the criteria it takes to be an apostle. If at the end of every day you can say you've met all the apostolic criteria, and have dutifully studied the pastoral criteria and have time left over to meet all of that too...then more power to you. In my many years of ministry experience, I have never seen a dual ministry work well. The leader winds up burnt out and favors one aspect of ministry over the other, ending up frustrated. In the end, neither aspect of ministry is done well.

Let us not forget that the Apostle Paul, like all apostles, was to go wherever the Gospel had not been preached (Romans 15:14-22). The apostolic call is not limited to a local group or community, but goes beyond the local into uncharted territories, new regions, and diverse places.

- **What about apostles who have churches, worship centers, or training institutes?**

All apostles have ministries. The manifestation of these ministries may vary in application. Sometimes when an apostle speaks of "their church," they are referring to a church that they cover or oversee apostolically. They may be referring to a church that they already started, or one they are currently starting, with plans to install a pastor when someone has been trained and prepared. They may also be establishing a new church and serving a specific leadership role within that church for an expressed period of time. We do see in the New Testament evidence of the Apostle Paul visiting different churches to which he served as an apostle (1 Corinthians 4:18-21, Philippians 4:10-20). We also see him writing and instructing churches that we do not have evidence that he directly founded. He did not, however, pastor any of these churches. The same can be true for apostles today. Many apostles train other leaders through the use of their ministries. They may do this through services, classes, seminars, conferences, institutes, colleges, universities, educational programs, training, or weekly worship meeting centers. This does not make apostles pastors, but apostles executing their apostolic duties. There may be a time when an apostle has to establish a church and oversee it themselves, but this will only be for a time – not for years at a time. The true apostle will be called elsewhere.

- **Can a pastor cover or mentor an apostle?**

Many teach the apostolic office to be nothing more than a "big pastor." This is an outgrowth of larger-than-life concepts about the local church. Today people are encouraged and pushed to be a part of a local church, much to the exclusion of the universal church. In this thinking, the church becomes no larger than the immediate church community. As a result, the universal church becomes an extension of this little local community. In this same mindset, we see pastors who try to make their local churches universal ones, expanding out and out into new communities. These actions are not in alignment with the pastoral anointing (1 Peter 5:1-4). To many, the local church is all there is within the Christian realm.

There are many reasons why this thinking has taken hold in the church today. The primary reason rests in that most of us haven't grown up in a church with an intact five-fold ministry for multiple generations. A great purpose of apostles and prophets is to bridge the gap between the local church and the international body of believers. A second reason is the push for people to support the extravagant lifestyles of many pastors. While this is not always the case, we cannot deny many church leaders are in their positions for no other purpose but to control and manipulate people into supporting their wants. A third reason is because many genuinely want to worship and gather with other believers, as the Bible teaches (Hebrews 10:25). Such who do so are genuine in their hearts. Even though they are genuine, they have not received the right vision or teaching about the purpose of the local church, the pastor, the apostle, and the role that all play within the universal church.

This local and universal church confusion displays a powerful reason why we need the full functioning five-fold ministry. It also brings answers to whether or not pastors can mentor apostles. While I would never question a pastor can provide information or encouragement to an apostle, the pastoral office is not the same as the apostolic office. This difference creates an imbalance for ministerial mentoring. The apostolic office is a universal office, not a local one. In reverse, the pastor is not a universal office, but a local one. Apostles serve the church universally, going wherever they are sent. Even though an apostle may not work in every church in the world, they function to unite the church universal in doctrine, teaching, morals, education, and standards of leadership. Pastors work to care for a group or sometimes groups of local people, seeing to their spiritual needs and upholding doctrine and teaching established by the apostles and prophets. It is out of God's order for an apostle to be mentored and covered by a pastor because the office functions are different. Reversely, it is not inappropriate for a pastor to be covered by an apostle; that is a part of God's order.

- **What is a "Chief Apostle" and how does it differ from a regular apostle?**

It's a modern internet showcase to see people boasting titles such as "Chief Apostle," "Chiefest Apostle," and "Super Apostle." Once upon a time, it was a challenge and struggle for one who had the apostolic call on their life to accept it. Now we see people not only embracing such a call, but acclimating themselves to it in an arrogant fashion.

I've spent probably close to twenty years studying church history (of both the church itself and specific denominations). The designations of "Chief Apostle," "Chiefest Apostle," and "Super Apostle" are not found in the legitimate church of the New Testament, nor in the subsequent centuries of the church. Nobody legitimate was ever called these things – not even the Biblical apostles and prophets themselves. This tells us two things: first, that such a designation is unnecessary, even unbiblical; and second, the acceptance of such designations is a newer, modern-time phenomenon made to create specific designations within the offices of apostle and prophet.

I've heard numerous theories as to what these designations are supposed to mean. For example, many people argue that a

"Chief Apostle" is an apostle that covers either other leaders or other apostles. If we are going to be technical as to what apostles do, covering leaders is what an apostle does. Most apostles probably do cover other apostles at some point in their ministry – so the "Chief Apostle" designation is, therefore, unnecessary. The "Chiefest Apostle" designation is, likewise, completely absurd. The foundation for the title is a perversion of Mark 10:44: *"And whosoever of you will be the chiefest, shall be servant of all."* The Greek does not support the position that this refers to an apostolic designation, nor does Jesus designate anyone as a "Chiefest Apostle." The purpose of this verse was not to create a designation into a separate office. We know that Jesus would not have encouraged such designations as the apostles and disciples at this time already had issues with who was the greatest, and who was superior to whom, and doing such would have just created more competition. The purpose of this verse was encouraging people to service, not to designations boasting that one leader was servant of more people than someone else. The "Super Apostle" designation is, likewise, something someone made up to sound more like a hero in a comic strip than a legitimate office of the church.

These distinctions are bad simply because they create a division within the office of the apostle. Apostles are called to do what apostles do – and we need to stop trying to designate different capacities of service. The Word is explicitly clear about what apostles do, and if one has a hard time figuring it out, they should not refer to themselves as an apostle.

In 2 Corinthians 11:1-15, the Apostle Paul addresses the issues of these "Chief Apostles" and "Chiefest Apostles" with the following words: *"Would to God ye could bear with me a little in my folly: and indeed bear with me. For I am jealous over you with godly jealousy: for I have espoused you to one husband, that I may present you as a chaste virgin to Christ. But I fear, lest by any means, as the serpent beguiled Eve through his subtilty, so your minds should be corrupted from the simplicity that is in Christ. For if he that cometh preacheth another Jesus, whom we have not preached, or if ye receive another spirit, which ye have not received, or another gospel, which ye have not accepted, ye might well bear with him. For I suppose I was not a whit behind the very chiefest apostles. But though I be rude in speech, yet not in knowledge; but we have been thoroughly made manifest among you in all things. Have I committed an offence in abasing myself that ye might be exalted, because I have preached to you the gospel of God freely? I robbed other churches, taking wages of them, to do you service. And when I was present with you, and wanted, I was chargeable to no man: for that which was lacking to me the brethren which came from Macedonia supplied: and in all things I have kept myself from being burdensome unto you, and so will I keep myself. As the truth of Christ is in me, no man shall stop me of this boasting in the regions of Achaia. Wherefore? because I love you not? God knoweth. But what I do, that I will do, that I may cut off occasion from them which desire occasion; that wherein they glory, they may be found even as we. For such are false apostles, deceitful workers, transforming themselves into the apostles of Christ. And no marvel; for Satan himself is transformed into an angel of light. Therefore it is no great thing if his ministers also be transformed as the ministers of righteousness; whose end shall be according to their works."* In other words, the Apostle Paul was being sarcastic in his discourse here. People apparently used the terms "Chiefest Apostle" and "Chief Apostle" to appear to be something they weren't, even once upon a time. Note that the Apostle Paul himself identifies them as being false! They may look right, say all the right things, do all the right things at the right time, but underneath, they are completely false. Having to use such a designation is not a sign of a true leader, but a false one, because it shows they do not have a right understanding of the apostolic office. 2 Corinthians 12:11-15 goes on to clarify the position further: *"I am become a fool in glorying; ye have compelled me: for I ought to have been commended of you: for in nothing am I behind the very chiefest apostles, though I be nothing. Truly the signs of an apostle were wrought among you in all patience, in signs, and wonders, and mighty deeds. For what is it wherein ye were inferior to other churches, except it be that I myself was not burdensome to you? forgive me this wrong. Behold, the third time I am ready to come to you; and I will not be burdensome to you: for I seek not yours but you: for the children ought not to lay up for the parents, but the parents for the children. And I will very gladly spend and be spent for you; though the more abundantly I love you, the less I be loved."* Here the Apostle Paul goes on to clarify his own humility and willingly be the least of these stark-raving mad idiots – and be "just" an apostle, because God doesn't call people to these ridiculous designations within the apostolic office.

There is no such thing as a legitimate "Chief Apostle," "Chiefest Apostle," or "Super Apostle." God has given apostles, plain and simple – and if an apostle understands their office, they know such a designation is unnecessary.

- **In the study, you mention Junia as a female apostle. My text reads that she was of note among the apostles, not an apostle. How do you answer the lack of clarity in the text?**

The Junia issue has been debated for a while. There are heavy opponents against Junia and what she represents: a woman serving as an apostle. Opponents of Apostle Junia usually reject her only one reason – they don't believe a woman could ever be called to be an apostle.

The debate about Junia comes from Romans 16:7:

  o *"Salute Andronicus and Junia, my kinsmen, and my fellow-prisoners, who are of note among the apostles, who also were in Christ before me."*

- "Greet Andronicus and Junia, my fellow Jews who have been in prison with me. They are outstanding among the apostles, and they were in Christ before I was." (NIV)

- "Say hello to Andronicus and Junia, my relatives and my fellow prisoners. They are prominent among the apostles, and they were in Christ before me." (CEB)

- "Remember me to Andronicus and Junias, my tribal kinsmen and once my fellow prisoners. They are men held in high esteem among the apostles, who also were in Christ before I was." **(AMP)**

- "Salute Andronicus and Junias, my kindred, and my fellow-captives, who are of note among the apostles, who also have been in Christ before me." (YLT)

- "Greetings to Andronicus and Junia, my relatives, who were in prison with me. They are very important apostles. They were believers in Christ before I was." (NCV)

While modern adherents who want to embrace traditional understandings about women tend to make the passage complicated or obscure, the Greek reveals that it really is not.

- **Greet** – From the Greek word *"aspazomai"* which means, "to draw to one's self; to salute one, greet, bid welcome, wish well to; to receive joyfully, welcome."[14]

- **Andronicus** – From the Greek word *"Andronikos"* which means, "'man of victory;" a Jewish Christian and a kinsman of Paul."[15]

- **Junia** – From the Greek word *"Iounias"* which means *"'youthful;"* a Christian woman at Rome, mentioned by Paul as one of his kinsfolk and fellow prisoners"[16]

- **Kinsmen** – From the Greek word *"suggenes,"* which means, "of the same kin, akin to, related by blood; in a wider sense, of the same race, a fellow countryman"[17]

- **Fellow-prisoners** – From the Greek word *"sunaichmalotos,"* which means, "a fellow prisoner."[18]

- **Note among the apostles** – From three Greek words: *"episemos,"* which means, "having a mark on it, marked, stamped, coined; marked in a good sense, of note, illustrious; in a bad sense, notorious, infamous;"[19] *"en,"* which means, "in, on, at, by, with;"[20] and *"apostolos,"* which means, "a messenger, one sent on a mission, an apostle."[21]

- **Were in Christ** – From three Greek words: *"ginomai,"* which means, "to become, i.e. to come into existence, begin to be, receive being; to become, i.e. to come to pass, happen, of events; to arise, appear in history, come upon the stage, of men appearing in public; to be made, finished; of miracles, to be performed, wrought; to become, be made;"[22] *"en"* which means, "in, by, with etc.;"[23] and *"Christos"* which means, "'anointed" 1) Christ was the Messiah, the Son of God 2) anointed."[24]

- **Before me** – From two Greek words: *"pro,"* which means, "before,"[25] and *"emou"* which means, "me, my, mine, etc."[26]

The Greek text is clear as to the role of Andronicus and Junia as being of outstanding reputation among the apostles. Whether this is the twelve apostles they were of note among or other apostles is not really relevant; they were individuals who were in their respective apostolic offices and of renowned for their efforts. To say they "were in Christ before me" can have more than one meaning in the Greek. It could mean they were a) in Christ, as in Christians, b) in the anointing of the apostolic before Paul was, or c) both references in combination. They were not just, as we can see, people of good reputation, but people who were known for their apostolic work among their peers.

The reality of Junia as an apostle, thanks to thorough study of the Greek text, makes it clear that women as well as men are called to the apostolic office. It's not a convenient suggestion, but a powerful reality. Even though the Bible does not provide us with the descriptive experience that we have of apostles like Peter and Paul, the one verse of Romans 16:7 provides us with all we need to know about this powerful woman of God and her apostolic purpose.

- **My Bible cites your Junia as "Junias," a man. If Junia was a woman, why is Junias found in my Bible translation?**

History tells us Pope Boniface VIII made numerous papal decrees against the advance of women in the church. He began by establishing every nun to remain cloistered, unable to affect or influence the church or outside world in any way. Even though women defied his position, it quickly became church practice to suppress the advance of God's women. Latin copyists began altering the text around 1298, the same time Pope Boniface enacted his papal bull against women. [27]

- **What about Mary Magdalene?**

Books such as *The DaVinci Code* and *Holy Blood, Holy Grail* have sparked debate about Mary Magdalene and just who she was. While these books are intriguing in their content, they do not provide factual information about Mary Magdalene and her role in the early church.

Mary Magdalene is often called the "apostle to the apostles." She received this title because she was the first to witness the resurrected Christ. She was the first apostle of the New Covenant and the first female apostle after the resurrection of Jesus. She was given this office uniquely at the time of its reception. Because she was an apostle of the New Covenant before the time of Paul, Mary's role as an apostle was progressive and different. She was selected to herald the promise of the New Covenant back to the apostles of the Lamb. Until the calling of the Apostle Paul, her New Covenant apostolic calling remained hers alone. She is, therefore, both a type of the New Covenant apostolic office to come through every apostle since Paul, and its first reality.

It is for this reason that Mary Magdalene was also an apostle over the early church. Non-canonical early church documents establish and confirm her apostolic role as the first female apostle after the resurrection of Jesus.

- **Who was Apphia? I never heard of her before.**

Apphia was a first-century apostle, considered among the seventy sent out by Christ in Luke 10:1-23. She is only one of two women listed, according to Orthodox records, as being among the seventy apostles.[28] She is mentioned in Philemon as a sister in the faith.

- **Were there unnamed apostles in the Bible?**

Yes. 2 Corinthians 8:22-24 names "messengers of the churches." The Greek word *"apostolos,"* is translated as "messengers" incorrectly. The verse should read, "apostles of the churches." These apostles are unnamed servants of God, active as apostles over an unknown number of churches.

Discussion, study and review questions:

- What was question of even in the Apostle Paul's time? What can we see through the Apostle Paul's work? What does the Apostle Paul clarify?

- How do we have proof of the importance of the office of apostle? What will those called to this office do?

- What does the word "apostle" mean? How is the office received? What does the apostle serve as? What is the apostle guardian of? What are apostles a witness and a minister unto?

- How many sets of criteria exist for apostles? What did the first set of criteria require, and what was the purpose in this criteria? How was the second set of criteria established, and what purpose does this criteria serve to establish? Which standard is the standard today? What criteria exists to be an apostle?

- What do the duties of an apostle include? Can a church be built on a pastor? Why or why not?

- Who are some people who served as apostles in the New Testament? Did both men and women serve as apostles?

- Are people who argue that the office of apostle is no longer needed correct? Why or why not?

- What are the characteristics of the apostolic office? What are the strengths and weaknesses of apostles? How do these characteristics manifest to make them better apostles?

- What are some Old Testament types of the apostolic ministry? How do these types shadow what the apostolic office is to represent?

- In looking at the "Historical apostle" section, how were you able to see the office of the apostle differently than before? How does this change how you view leaders in history, even though they may not have been ever called an "apostle?" Who else can you think of in history who was an apostle, even if they were not acknowledged as such?

- Discuss and share some of the questions and answers found in the "Questions and Answers" section. What did you learn that you did not know about apostles and apostolic ministry? What did you learn that changed your mind about an opinion you might have had prior about apostolic ministry? How did learning about specific issues related to apostles and apostolic ministry help you to grow in your understanding of ministry? The church? Your own relationship with God?

Chapter Seven

THE OFFICE OF THE PROPHET

"Ages when custom is unsettled are necessarily ages of prophecy. The moralist cannot teach what is revealed; he must reveal what can be taught. He has to seek insight rather than to preach."
— *Walter Lippmann*[1]

The office of the prophet is both controversial and highly examined. Of all Biblical offices, it is the most studied, and often the least understood. Many know about prophets, but at the same time, confuse the office with other Biblical offices (and some non-Biblical ones as well). The role of the prophet as the spiritual discerner and guardian of the church has been long misunderstood, undervalued, and ignored to the detriment of the Body of Christ. As a powerful source of spiritual eyes and ears for the church, prophets speak the Words of God and herald His voice, that the will of God may be known among the people of God until the time when Jesus returns.

Text study

1 Corinthians 14:29-33

Supplementary texts:

Deuteronomy 18:15-22, 2 Kings 22:14-20, Isaiah 6:1-13, Jeremiah 1:1-10, Ezekiel 2:1-10, Acts 15:32-35, 1 Corinthians 14:1-4, Revelation 10:9-11.

Power verse

1 Corinthians 14:31-32:

- *"For ye may all prophesy one by one, that all may learn, and all may be comforted. And the spirits of the prophets are subject to the prophets."*

- *"For you can all prophesy in turn so that everyone may be instructed and encouraged. The spirits of prophets are subject to the control of prophets."* (NIV)

- *"For you can all prophesy one by one, so that all may learn and all may be exhorted; and the spirits of prophets are subject to prophets..."* (NASB)

- *"For ye can all prophesy one by one, that all may learn and all be encouraged. And spirits of prophets are subject to prophets."* (DARBY)

- *"For ye all can prophesy one by one, that all may learn, and all may be exhorted; and the spirits of the prophets are subject to the prophets..."* (ASV)

- *"For you can all prophesy one by one, so that everyone may learn and everyone may be encouraged. And the prophets' spirits are under the control of the prophets..."* (HCSB)

Power words

- **Prophesy** – From the Greek word *"propheteuo"* which means, "to prophesy, to be a prophet, speak forth by divine inspirations, to predict."[2]

- **Learn** – From the Greek word *"manthano"* which means, "to learn, be appraised."[3]

- **Comforted** – From the Greek word *"parakaleo"* which means, "to call to one's side, to call for, summon; to address, speak to (call to, call upon), which may be done in the way of exhortation, entreaty, comfort, instruction, etc."[4]

- **Spirits of the prophets** – From two Greek words: *"pnemua"* which means, "a movement of air (a gentle blast); the spirit, i.e., the vital principle by which the body is animated; a spirit, i.e., a simple essence devoid of all or at least all grosser matter, and possessed of the power of knowing, desiring, deciding, and acting; of God; the disposition which fills and governs the soul of any one;"[5] and *"prophetes"* which means, "in Greek writings, and interpreter of oracles or other hidden things; one who, moved by the Spirit of God and hence His organ or spokesman, solemnly declares to men what he has received by inspiration, especially concerning future events, and in particular such as relate to the cause and Kingdom of God and to human salvation; a poet (because poets were believed to sing under divine inspiration)."[6]

- **Subject** – From the Greek word *"hupotasso"* which means, "to arrange under, to subordinate; to subject, put in subjection; to subject oneself, obey; to submit to one's control; to yield to one's admonition or advice; to obey, be subject."[7]

Historical context

The office of the prophet is distinguishable from the gift of prophecy. In the Old Testament, the gift of prophecy was limited to those who walked in the prophetic office. In the New Testament, we see people receiving the Spirit and speaking prophetically without being prophets. This clear distinction is made because the office of prophet is raised up a part of the five-fold ministry, distinguishing it from the gift of prophecy. In an intense way we see the office of discernment heavy on a prophet's life, as prophecy is still discerned by the prophets – not the general body of believers or those who may receive a prophetic gift. Along with the apostle, the prophet forms the foundation of the church. Spiritual discernment is a part of the office of the prophet. It has always been the position of the prophet to stand in the place of discerning spirits, maintaining an atmosphere of spiritual order, and ensuring matters of self-control with the gift of prophecy active and alive.

Notes on text

The gift of prophecy is subject to the true office of the prophet. This means that when one receives the gift of prophecy or a prophetic word from God, the word we receive is confirmed by true prophets of God. It also means that maintaining spiritual order is the responsibility of the prophet. When individuals act out of turn spiritually in a meeting or spiritual gathering (failing to exercise self-control in their prophecies and spiritual words), it is the job of the prophet to halt the individual and correct any present error. Whenever we speak a public prophetic word for the church, that word is subject to the prophets' confirmation or disciplinary measure. While many question, mock, or even insult the office of prophet, the prophet holds a unique and powerful position as a spiritual guardian of God's church.

Power points

- There is a difference between a prophetic gift (gift of prophecy, giving a spiritual word) and the prophetic office as found in the five-fold ministry. Anyone in the body of Christ can receive the gift of prophecy and can prophecy; in fact, it is a much sought-after gift (1 Corinthians 14:1-4). The prophetic office is a specific walk with a specific calling from God. It has grace for the foundation and building up of the church body (Ephesians 2:19-21, Ephesians 4:11). The word "prophet" means one who speaks for God; a spokesman of God; an oracle of sacred or hidden things.[8] The purpose of the prophetic office is to ensure the church receives the message of God in this day and age and the revealing of the message for tomorrow (Amos 3:7). Prophets have many unique duties and gifts which pertain to their mystical and spiritual office. Their duties and gifts help to guard the body of Christ spiritually, with discernment (Ephesians 3:5).

- The office of prophet is found both in the Old and New Testaments, and the requirements for the prophetic office remain the same. Prophets must be called of God, and not by human beings. The prophetic office cannot be received by human appointment (Isaiah 6:1-13). A prophet must have a willing heart and tongue, must fully deliver the message God relays to him or her (Acts 15:32-35), have discernment to distinguish personal thoughts, perceptions, and opinions from received divine prophecy (Jonah 1:1-3), a heart of courage to speak God's will to whomever God sends them to speak (Jeremiah 1:1-10), and the ability to discern between spirits (1 John 4:1-3). The office of prophet is universal; prophets are not sent to serve in immediate locations alone, but are a gift to the universal body of believers. A prophet may be sent with the received message anywhere in the world (Jeremiah 1:10). The ministry of a prophet is proven by his or her words; if a prophet speaks what is true and his or her prophecies come true, they are a true prophet. If he or she proclaims and prophesies falsehood, he or she is a false prophet. False prophets should never be given heed (Deuteronomy 18:15-22).

- The duties of the prophet include: Speaking God's will to individuals, regions, nations, and the entire body of believers (Revelation 10:9-11); interpret current events in the light of Scriptural prophecy (Daniel 7:1-15); teach on prophetic matters, including the interpretation of Scriptural prophecy (1 Peter 1:10-12); discern spirits and prophetic words (1 Corinthians 12:10, 1 John 4:1-3); serve as a seer and visionary, and as interpreter of dreams, visions, signs and words of God to individuals (Hosea 12:10); be heralds of God's judgment and grace (Jeremiah 28:9, Jeremiah 44:4); function in intercessory prayer and praise and worship (2 Chronicles 32:20-23); serve to deliver messages to God's people from God Himself (2 Kings 22:14-20); serve as a discerner of character, morals, and actions among believers (Ezekiel 2:1-10); walk in the gifts of the Spirit, especially prophecy (1 Corinthians 14:1); provide warning of times and divine correction from God, telling the church what is to come (Ezekiel 4:9-16); and be aware of natural phenomena in the light of prophecy, especially aware of God's judgment manifest through nature (Joel 2:28-31). As the direct messenger of the Lord, the prophet provides an important foundation in the church (1 Corinthians 14:36-40).

- Many men and women in the Scriptures served in the office of prophet. They include Miriam (Exodus 15:20), Deborah (Judges 4:4-5), Samuel (1 Samuel 3:1-18), Isaiah (Isaiah 6:1-13), Isaiah's wife (Isaiah 8:3), Ezekiel (Ezekiel 2:1-10), Jeremiah (Jeremiah 1:1-10), Daniel (Daniel 2:25-26), Hosea (Hosea 1:1), Moses (Exodus 4:11), Aaron (Exodus 4:14-16), Obadiah (Obadiah 1:1), Micah (Micah 1:1), Jonah (Jonah 1:1-3). Zechariah (Zechariah 7:1-9), Zephaniah (Zephaniah 1:1), Malachi (Malachi 1:1), Huldah (2 Kings 22:14-20), Anna (Luke 2:36), and the four daughters of Philip (Acts 21:9).

- It is unscriptural to believe the prophetic era of God's people has ceased. If testimony of Jesus is the spirit of prophecy, all prophecy continues to point toward Christ (Revelation 19:10). Prophets remain an important and active component of faith today. We still need an office of mystical and spiritual discernment, intercession, and purpose in the body of Christ.

Characteristics of the prophet

There are essential characteristics God gives to each prophet, enabling him or her to fulfill the prophet's call with full grace and dignity. In looking at some prophets, we can see these characteristics clearly.

- **The Prophet Jeremiah, Jeremiah 3:6-25:** Jeremiah was an interesting individual. He was strong as a prophet, powerful in his presentation and his words, and marked by true conviction. Jeremiah was confident in God, trusting Him for everything, as he was a young prophet. Prophets have confidence in the message they proclaim. They are serious people, moved gravely by matters that others take lightly. They are broken in spirit to see people disobey God and harm one another. For this reason, Jeremiah's moniker as the "weeping prophet" truly displays the personality of a prophet. Prophets tend to be sad, moody, and melancholy. As prophets have their confidence in God alone, they may tend to see the negative, rather than the positive, in people. While these may make it difficult to interact with a prophet sometimes, the serious, intense personality of a prophet makes them perfect individuals to serve as oracles of God.

- **The Prophetess Anna, Luke 2:36-38:** Anna was both devout and intense. Constant in prayer, Anna displays the serious regard prophets have for prayer and intercession. The things of God are no amusement park to a prophet! Prophets are devoted to God, spiritual things, and regard intercession as a true duty. Anna also shows two very important aspects to prophets: their awareness and their seeking nature. Prophets know the things of God when they see them, and they are eager to share them with others.

- **The Four Daughters of Philip, Acts 21:8-9:** We know nothing about the four daughters of Philip, except for two key things: they walked in the prophetic and they were unmarried. Even though we know nothing else about their lives, the four daughters of Philip display a unique characteristic of prophets: eccentricity. As it was customary for first-century women to be married, it is notable the daughters of Philip are described as "unmarried." Just as these women tended toward a march off the beaten path, so do all prophets. Prophets don't follow conventional rules or fit into conventional stereotypes of societal norms.

Types of the prophetic ministry

The prophetic office was alive and well in the Old Testament. Since the office has not changed in its intent or purpose, the New Testament office of prophet is a continuation of the Old Testament office. The major difference between the Old and New Covenants is the reception of God's grace by all who will receive. This difference touches the prophetic office in one major way: the gift of prophecy is open to any whom God gifts with it, rather than prophecy limited to prophets alone. In the Old Testament, we see shadows of this promise to come, as well as shadows of New Covenant prophets. These prophetic shadows do not change the Old Covenant prophetic calling on the individuals mentioned, but shows even in their prophecy a pointing to the covenant of grace alive and well under Christ. In examining these types and shadows, we are not diminishing their unique call, but expanding the viewpoints of these truly anointed and special individuals.

- **1 Samuel 1:1-2:11, 18-21** – *Hannah*, a type of Mary, mother of Jesus. Before I began teaching on Hannah as a type of Mary, I had never heard any parallel between the two. In studying the life and experiences of Hannah, I couldn't believe no one ever taught the parallels between Hannah and Mary. Hannah and Mary both were, in their own right, prophetesses of God. They both became mothers by divine intervention. As they both birthed firstborn sons vital and essential to salvation history, they were not just mothers, but two women who spoke essential prophecies. Hannah was the first to prophesy the resurrection, and Mary spoke powerful words about the last days. Both women had to surrender their sons, one to the prophetic life and One to salvation. Hannah's life and experience shadows Mary's life and experience, and the essential message contained therein. Hannah and Mary's experiences provide all with empowerment, spiritual life, and prophetic words relevant for us today.

- **Malachi 4:5-6** – *Elijah*, a type of John the Baptist. The ministry of Elijah was powerful, prophetic, and important in its own right. His prophetic work also shadowed John the Baptist's presence and purpose. The essential ministry of Elijah was one of repentance, challenging idolaters and sinners to humble themselves before God and change their ways. John the Baptist's purpose was the same, as he called hearts to repentance and prepared the way of Jesus Christ. Just like Elijah, John was sought by government officials and unpopular with the enemies of his time. Heralding changing times and bringing forth promise, Elijah and John both point us to eternal truth and the saving message.

- **Isaiah 44:3-4** – *A shadow of the New Covenant spiritual outpouring.* The book of Isaiah gives many important words and prophecies about the last days. To the people of Isaiah's time, diverse people in God's Kingdom was quite foreign. Isaiah's prophecies give great detail of the many who would one day come to worship God in His Kingdom unity. The prophetic spiritual outpouring of all believers a part of this spiritual growth and development. Isaiah does not diminish the prophetic office or state it shall cease, but that the gift of prophecy shall be open to all spiritual believers. We find evidence of fulfillment in Romans 5:5: *"And hope does not disappoint us, because God has poured out His love into our hearts by the Holy Spirit, Whom He has given us."* (NIV)

- **Joel 2:28-32** – *A shadow of the New Covenant spiritual outpouring.* The book of Joel is often quoted because of its clearly stated promise: God's spiritual outpouring on all believers. Paralleling Isaiah 44:3-4, Joel further expands on the vision of spiritual outpouring, showing it to result in prophecy, dreams, signs, and visions. Joel promises the people of God shall prophesy and receive prophecy. Nowhere does it state the prophetic office shall cease, but instead, the gift of prophecy shall flourish.

The historical prophet

- **John Climacus** (c. 525-606) – A unique figure in Christian history of whose life we know very little about, John Climacus had a lasting impact on Christian spirituality. From what we do know of him, he spent many years studying the lives of other Christians, in the hopes to gain and develop a better understanding of Christian spirituality. He is considered one of the most learned among the early fathers in the faith. John Climacus' most infamous work is known as *Ladder of Divine Ascent*, which gives vivid imagery to the Christian's walk throughout their spiritual journey. By valuing asceticism, John Climacus illustrated each step as a rung on a ladder, with the individual starting at baptism and continuing all the way up to the most important of all virtues: love. Although his teachings are not as popular in the west, his writings are among the most popular among Eastern Orthodox churches.[9]

- **Joan of Arc** (1412-1431) – Joan of Arc was born in 1412 at Domremy, France. As a child and teen, Joan of Arc began experiencing visions. When she was just sixteen years old, she was urged through a vision to aid the Dauphin in capturing Rheims, as the French throne was threatened by Britain. By doing this, the French throne could be restored. In May 1428 she traveled to Vaucouleurs and told the captain about her visions and instructions. He disbelieved her, and sent her home. In January, 1429, she returned and this time, impressed the captain with her piety and commitment. He allowed her passage to the Dauphin at Chinon. She dressed in men's clothing for protection and had to be accompanied by six soldiers. Upon reaching the Dauphin's castle in February 1429, she was allowed to have an audience. Joan immediately picked Charles, the rightful heir of the French crown, out of the crowd, and informed him of her divine mission. For several weeks, Joan was subject to theological interrogation. Even though she was considered strange, they did believe she would be an asset in this persistent battle. She was furnished with a small army and on April 27, 1429, she set out for

Orleans, which had been captured by the English since October 1428. While the French distracted English troops, Joan entered into Orleans undistracted, buying supplies, and inspiring the French to step up to battle. She personally led the charge in several battles. Even when struck by an arrow, she quickly dressed her wound and returned to battle. The French won that victory, and the very next day, the English left Orleans. Over the next several weeks, Joan of Arc and the French commanders led the French into a series of victories in battle. On July 16, 1429, the army reached Reims, and the very next day, Charles VII was crowned king of France. Joan stood nearby holding an image of Christ in judgment. On September 8, 1429, King Charles VII, with Joan of Arc commanding, attacked Paris. Here she called on the Parisian citizens to surrender the city to the King of France. She was wounded, but despite such, she continued on until Charles ordered a succession of battle. The siege was unsuccessful. For the remainder of that year, she commanded several more campaigns, including the capture of the town of Saint-Pierre-le Moiter. In December of 1429, Charles VII ennobled Joan and her family.

In May 1430, the Burgundians laid siege to Compiegne. Joan went into town in the night to aid the defense. On May 23, 1430, while leading battle against the Burgundians, she was captured by them. She was sold to the English. In March, 1430, she went on trial before the ecclesiastical authorities on charges of heresy. According to her accusers, her most serious crime was her rejection of church authority in favor of direct revelation and inspiration from God. She refused to submit to the church, and her sentence was read May 24, 1430. They decreed her to be turned over to secular authorities and executed. Horrified by her pronouncement, she agreed to recant and was condemned to imprisonment. They demanded she put on women's attire. She conformed for a few days, but they found her in her cell later on dressed in male clothing. When questioned, she stated she'd been spiritually reproached for giving into the church against God's will. She was found to be a relapsed heretic and ordered to be handed over to secular officials on May 29, 1430. On May 30,

1430, at the age of nineteen years old, was burned at the stake for heresy at the Place du Vieux-Marche in Rouen. Before the pyre was lit, she requested a priest to hold a crucifix high enough for her to see and shout out prayers loud enough to be heard above the roar of the fire.

Ordered to put on women's clothes, she obeyed, but a few days later the judges went to her cell and found her dressed again in male attire. Questioned, she told them that St. Catherine and St. Margaret had reproached her for giving in to the church against their will. She was found to be a relapsed heretic and on May 29 ordered handed over to secular officials. On May 30, Joan, nineteen years old, was burned at the stake at the Place du Vieux-Marche in Rouen. Before the pyre was lit, she instructed a priest to hold high a crucifix for her to see and to shout out prayers loud enough to be heard above the roar of the flames.

To this day, Joan of Arc is regarded as an inspiration for the military, for women and girls, and for youth. Thanks to her work, she helped turn the Hundred Years War in favor of France. By 1453, King Charles VII reconquered all of France except for one area, which was relinquished from England in 1558. In 1920 the Roman Catholic Church recanted her heresy and she was recognized as a saint.[10]

- **Francis of Paola** (1416-1506) – The founder of the Order of Minimis, Francis of Paola grew up experiencing the miraculous, including healing. For much of his life, Francis spent his life devoted to prayer and miracles, especially coming from his prayers. In his day, he was in great demand, due to the accuracies of his prophecies and the incredible experiences which followed him throughout his life and ministry. Even though his order has never been the most popular one existing in the Catholic Church, Francis of Paola's prophetic impact was enough to be canonized as a saint in 1519.[11]

- **John of the Cross** (1542-1591) – John of the Cross was a Carmelite friar, priest, Spanish mystic, and doctor of the church. His work was also a part of major reformation needed within Catholic orders during that time; thus, he was highly opposed. His writings are not just considered spiritual masterpieces, but also, relevant works in the Spanish language. He is best known for *Spiritual Canticle* and *The Dark Night*, which spiritually details stages of depression and spiritual struggle within the Christian life. His third work, *Ascent of Mount Carmel*, details the varied miracles and ascetics required on the journey to seek perfect union with God. He has influenced other mystics, modern prophets, visionaries, activists, and pacifists throughout history, down to this present day.[12]

- **Jeanne Marie Bouvier de la Motte-Guyon** (1648-1717) – A leading figure in the Quietism Movement, Jeanne Marie Bouvier de la Motte-Guyon was a most interesting figure in visions, mysticism, and prophecy. Known for her writings, including *A Short And Easy Method Of Prayer*, she advocated staunch holiness, quietness, and was a proponent of grace rather than works in the avenue of salvation. She was a powerful teacher, with a number of students and followers, who continued to follow and assist her, even after she was imprisoned for contradicting Catholic doctrine. She was denounced as a heretic by the Catholic Church. Even though her writings are not the most popularly read, her works and thoughts continue to influence people, even today, who seek a deeper understanding of prayer and the Christian life.[13]

- **Fanny J. Crosby** (1820-1915) – An interesting example of the prophetic manifest through music, Fanny J. Crosby was author of more than nine thousand hymns, despite total blindness and the death of her son, while he was only an infant. Her hymns, such as *To God Be The Glory* and *Blessed Assurance* are so powerful, they are sung throughout Christian churches to this very day. She was also a public speaker, preacher, women's rights advocate, teacher, and poet, quite influential in her day, and renown by dignitaries and ministers. In 1975, she was inducted into the Gospel Music Hall of Fame, and she is also honored as a saint in the

Episcopalian Church, with a feast day on their liturgical calendar.[14]

Questions and answers

- **Is the prophetic function of the New Covenant prophet different from that of the Old Covenant prophet?**

No. The purpose of the prophet is to speak the words of God and discern spiritual things. That purpose of the office remains unchanged regardless of the covenant we are now living under. While the New Covenant has extended grace and prophetic gift to any believer receiving that gift, the office of the prophet still remains solid. The office is just as relevant, if not more so, than it was in the Old Testament era.

- **Why would the prophetic office be more relevant today?**

If the gift of prophecy extends beyond the prophetic office, there is more call for spiritual discernment and instruction on prophetic matters. It is not just a matter of determining false leaders, but false messages delivered from congregants or onlookers. There is a great need to test spirits. There is also an added need to understand prophecy, prophetic gifts, and the purpose of prophecy in the life of a believer. We need prophets today!

- **Can prophets pastor?**

The purpose of the prophetic office is to speak the words of God. This tends not to be an office to mollify people. It is also a purpose which oftentimes needs other offices to uphold its teachings and expound upon them. We see no evidence of prophets serving as pastors in the New Testament. The office is treated as a separate, respected entity with its own unique purpose.

One of the major reasons prophets are not called to serve as pastors lies in an underlying aspect to prophetic office. Prophets are called to be objective in their dealings with people.

Part of what makes prophecy revealing and God-ordained is the distance between a prophet and the people. A prophet is able to speak relevant words to an individual, group, or situation without knowing the specific situations present in those circumstances. Pastors are given a heart to be more directly involved with the people they serve and in the lives of their congregants. Pastors teach, guide, and care about people on a local level, while prophets speak for God and impact lives on a larger scale.

The primary duty of any five-fold minister is to attend to the calling they have from the Lord, not to try and create a new calling. This is true for every office of the five-fold ministry. For this reason, prophets are not called to serve as pastors. While a pastor may have a prophetic gift – and many often do, a prophet's office differs from a pastor's office.

- **How should the church handle false prophets?**

The modern approach to correction is to ignore problems, hoping they will go away and that "God will deal with them." God addresses false leadership through true leadership, not through hoping the false leaders will be spirited away. The responsibility for addressing false prophets goes to true apostles and prophets (Galatians 2:1-4).

To many, addressing false prophecy seems harsh and punitive. However, it is fully necessary for false teachers to be addressed and removed, if necessary, from the church to avoid division, schism, and error (1 John 4:1-7). The church must stand for something and must uphold God's truth. This means doing so, even when it seems unpopular.

- **Why does it seem there are so many false prophets today?**

The prophecy of false prophets is a part of the end times (Matthew 7:15, Matthew 24:11, Matthew 24:24, Mark 13:22, 2 Peter 2:1, 1 John 4:1). We can recognize the last days in our modern times based in part on the overabundance of false prophets. False prophets are a part of this age.

False prophets have the set goal of destroying the Body of Christ. Though they may not recognize their destructive actions, it is the underlying evil purpose in false prophets and false prophecy. When people encounter false teaching or prophecy, it creates doubt about what is true. This opens the door to move people away from the truth and into error. As we live in an age noted for its untruthfulness, we can see people turning to fables through false teaching and false ministers (2 Timothy 4:3).

- **Can false prophets perform miracles?**

If we study the Scriptures closely, believers and non-believers alike had the ability to do things judged miraculous. On judgment day, there will be people who claim to do great and wonderful things in the Name of Jesus. Jesus casts them out of His presence, stating He never knew them (Matthew 7:15-23). It is no accident this prophecy follows Jesus' warning of false prophets. Miracles alone are not a testimony that a ministry is true. A real ministry is measured by its teaching and the fruit it bears, and it is confirmed by signs and wonders. Signs and wonders by themselves are not proof of a true prophet. On the other hand, a prophet able to perform miracles is not necessarily a false prophet. We must use discernment and wisdom when assessing the fruits of ministry.

- **Do prophets have to be of a certain age?**

Prophets all throughout history have been both young and old. Jeremiah's prophetic calling specifically mentions his age, indicating he was a young man (Jeremiah 1:4-10). When God called Moses to visit Pharaoh, he was about the age of eighty. Anna, the prophetess present at the presentation of Christ, was a woman over eighty years old (Luke 2:36-38). The calling of a prophet is not contingent on age. An individual, however, who believes they are a prophet should still subject themselves to the necessary training and disciplines of the prophetic.

- **What is a school for prophets?**

A school for prophets is formal training in the prophetic office. Schools for prophets are is usually exclusive, open only to those functioning or called to function in the prophetic office. Those who apply for such schools must prove their calling in order to participate. They are heavy in examining prophecy, the lives of the prophets, the prophetic call, and duties of prophets. Another concept of a school for prophets is a gathering where prophets study and analyze prophecy all throughout history, including modern prophesies. Some are just training institutes with the goal of covering other ministries under the guise of prophetic education. The internet has popularized training for prophets, using correspondence and technological means. It is not uncommon to see prophetic schools advertised online. As many of these schools come under the vision of a ministry, many of them vary in requirements, teaching, and understanding.

The traditional understanding of a "school of the prophets" was equivalent to seminary or college training. Schools of the prophets included study of Biblical languages, Scripture, and essential educational functions such as mathematics, geography, and traditional philosophical rhetoric. Modern concepts do not mirror this notion, but do follow the same mentality: ministry leaders need education and receive it from those who are walking in ministry.

- **What is the difference between a prophet and a fortune-teller?**

In one sentence: a prophet is from God, a fortune-teller is not!

A prophet has a call from God to be the spokesperson for God. Such speaking comes forth by revelation, not divining methods. It is an awesome responsibility to walk in this office, as our study reveals. The prophet has numerous functions and duties that are beyond telling people what will happen to them in the future. The prophet stands with a spiritually relevant call that is beyond what we often see in the office today.

A fortune-teller uses different methods to foretell the

future. A fortune-teller or psychic may contact and consort with the dead, read palms, use tea leaves, read tarot cards, use crystals, or other methods to gain certain spiritual powers. Their goal is to tell people things that will happen in the future or answer their specific questions. Fortune-tellers are automatically limited, as they must use certain elements in order to manifest predictions or answers. While the industry generates high profit, psychics and fortune-tellers have an accuracy rating around ten percent. There are three reasons why the percentage is so low. The first reason is because psychics and fortune-tellers tend to read things about people from what they say, causing them to make reasonable guesses about people and what they want to know. As they read people very well, psychics and fortune-tellers are able to determine where people are going by what they say and how they respond to things. The second reason is because a fortune-teller, operating as an agent of Satan, will deceive people just enough to cause them confusion about what a fortune-teller has told them. The third reason is because Christians are not to look to such to learn about the future, but trust God on faith.

The fortune-teller does not speak by the power of God, but by deceptive means and Satanic purposes. A prophet's purpose is not to tell people what will happen to them, but speak for God to the people. A prophet delivers to God's people everything He desires them to know for their day and age. For this purpose, a prophet is never to set "up shop" and give words to people for monetary gain (Micah 3:11). This also applies as prophets should never establish their ministries requiring excessive gain or unreasonable measures to perform their purpose and duties as God's oracle.

- **What is a "Master Prophet?"**

Simply put, a "Master Prophet" is something someone made up. It is not a term found in the Bible, and nobody recalls seeing it before a few years ago. There is no such thing as a legitimate "Master Prophet." In keeping with what we discussed about designations in the apostolic, "Master Prophet" is a sign of a false prophet.

- **What is a seer?**

The Bible indicates that prophets were originally called "seers" (1 Samuel 9:9). Without complicating things, as many today try to do, a "seer" was someone who had the prophetic gift of dreams and visions. As this is a part of the prophetic, it is more correct to refer to someone as a prophet than a seer. The term itself is not found in the Bible after the book of Micah. If an individual has a gift of seeing as relates to the spiritual, a "seer" is a function of the prophetic office.

- **What is a mystic?**

A "mystic" is someone who has experience and knowledge of the supernatural. In terms of a Christian mystic, a mystic is kind of like a prophet-plus. The experience of the mystic encompasses more than just the immediate visual or auditory senses, and is a more complete, intense spiritual experience. One can be a mystic with the divine or a mystic in the arts of the demonic. This is a very general description, as the ins and outs of what defines the realms of mysticism are very complex in nature. Throughout history, many prophets have been described as "mystics" because of their intense relationship with the supernatural. Dreams, visions, inspirational writing, prophecies, and the miraculous can all be considered a part of mystical experience. This does not mean all mystical experience is good, nor does it mean every encounter one claims to have is prophetic – it is just a general designation for all supernatural experience, and that includes the realm of the prophetic.

- **What is the difference between the apostolic and prophetic offices?**

I have explained the apostolic and prophetic as being the same foundationally, but different in execution. The result is two offices that, ideally, are supposed to function together. The prophetic is more mystical and the apostolic is more administrative. Even though both do represent and speak on behalf of the revelation of God, the apostle and the prophet have different spiritual gifts which purpose the building up of the Body in their own unique design.

Discussion, study and review questions:

- How are the office of prophet and the gift of prophecy different?

- How is the gift of prophecy subject to the prophetic office?

- How does the prophetic office operate? How is this different than receiving a prophetic word? What does the word "prophet" mean?

- What are the requirements for the prophetic office?

- What are the duties of a prophet?

- Who has served as a prophet? Has the office been held by both men and women?

- Why is the prophetic office relevant today?

- What are the characteristics of the prophetic office? What are the strengths and weaknesses of prophets? How do these characteristics manifest to make them better prophets?

- What are some Old Testament types of the prophetic ministry? Who do these types mirror? How do these types shadow what the New Testament office is to represent? What types exist of the prophetic gift in the Old Testament?

- In looking at the "Historical prophet" section, how were you able to see the office of the apostle differently than before? How does this change how you view leaders in history, even though they may not have been ever called a "prophet?"

Who else can you think of in history who was an prophet, even if they were not acknowledged as such?

- Discuss and share some of the questions and answers found in the "Questions and Answers" section. What did you learn that you did not know about prophets and prophetic ministry? What did you learn that changed your mind about an opinion you might have had prior about prophetic ministry? How did learning about specific issues related to prophets and prophetic ministry help you to grow in your understanding of ministry? The church? Your own relationship with God?

Chapter Eight

THE OFFICE OF THE EVANGELIST

Give honor unto Luke Evangelist; for he it was (the aged legends say) who first taught Art to fold her hands and pray.
— *Dante Gabriel Rossetti* [1]

The office of evangelist holds one of the most important functions in the church. Unfortunately, evangelists are one of the most forgotten elements of modern church ministry. With a strong push to establish local churches, the office dedicated to proclaiming Christ, both to believer, distant believer (backslider) and non-believer, has gone ignored. Apostles and prophets bring stability and structure to the church, and the evangelist brings Christ's life-saving evangelism to the church. Evangelists help to avoid legalism, forgotten faith, and lukewarm countenance among the people of God. Through the evangelist, the promise of new life is continuously proclaimed, and never forgotten.

Text study

2 Timothy 4:1-5

Supplementary texts

Isaiah 61:1-3, Mark 1:1-5, Acts 8:4-40, Acts 21:8, Ephesians 4:11-16.

Power verse

2 Timothy 4:5:

- *"But watch thou in all things, endure afflictions, do the work of an evangelist, make full proof of thy ministry."*

- *"But you, keep your head in all situations, endure hardship, do the work of an evangelist, discharge all the duties of your ministry."* (NIV)

- *"But you, Timothy, must always be watching. Be patient in your troubles. Tell the good news. Do all the work God has given you to do."* (WE)

- *"As for you, be calm and cool and steady, accept and suffer unflinchingly every hardship, do the work of an evangelist, fully perform all the duties of your ministry."* (AMP)

- *"But you should keep a clear mind in every situation. Don't be afraid of suffering for the Lord. Work at telling others the Good News, and fully carry out the ministry God has given you."* (NLT)

- *"But thou, be sober in all things, bear evils, do [the] work of an evangelist, fill up the full measure of thy ministry."* (DARBY)

Power words

- **Watch** – From the Greek word *"nepho,"* which means, "to be sober, to be calm and collected in spirit; to be temperate, dispassionate, circumspect."[2]

- **Endure afflictions** – From the Greek word *"kakopatheo,"* which means, "to suffer (endure) evils (hardships, troubles); to be afflicted."[3]

- **Evangelist** – From the Greek word *"euaggelistes"* which means, "a bringer of good tidings, an evangelist; the name given to the New Testament heralds of salvation through Christ who are not apostles."[4]

- **Full proof** – From the Greek word *"plerophoreo"* which means, "to bear or bring full, to make full."[5]

- **Ministry** – From the Greek word *"diakonia"* which means, "service, ministering, especially of those who execute the commands of others; of those who by the command of God proclaim and promote religion among men; the ministration of those who render to others the offices of Christian affection, especially those who help meet need by either collecting or distributing of charities; the office of deacon in the church; the service of those who prepare and present food."[6]

Historical context

Even though Timothy was not an evangelist, Paul called him to do the work of an evangelist as part of Timothy's apostolic duties. This call was as a part of Timothy's already established work in the Kingdom. In so doing, this tells us much about the office of evangelist and what an evangelist does. Paul presents the work of an evangelist as an answer to people's objections about Timothy's ministry, and make full proof of his ministry.

Objections to Timothy's ministry were all age-related. History cites Timothy as a young man, working as an apostle under the age of thirty. As traditional religion required leaders to spend years in teaching and training, a twenty-something apostle turned more than a few heads. It was essential Timothy bore fruit in his apostolic ministry. Paul advised Timothy to establish his ministry by doing the work of an evangelist: proclaiming and bearing Christ in his ministry work. By following Paul's commands, Timothy was able to make full proof of his ministry.

Notes on text

The word "evangelist" is found in the New Testament three times. The example presented in 2 Timothy 4:5 speaks of doing the work of the evangelist. It was not spoken to an evangelist directly, but to another apostle. In this vain, Timothy was to learn more of the evangelistic office through his ministry work. In doing so, we can draw Timothy was then able to teach evangelists about their ministry purpose. For us to understand the work and ministry of an evangelist, we must do three things: Look to the word "evangelist," the commands of ministry present in 2 Timothy 4:5, and look at the work of the only evangelist mentioned by name (Philip) in the New Testament.

Power points

- The office of evangelist is different than the general Christian command to bear and witness the Gospel. All Christians have the command to tell others the good news (Isaiah 61:1-3), while the evangelist moves in God's grace to bear and witness of Christ through ministry. The word "evangelist" means one who brings good news, good tidings, and more specifically, the whole of good news through the Gospel[7] (Acts 8:5). Strong's Exhaustive Concordance of the Bible makes a point to say evangelists are not apostles, clearly establishing the office has its own role and purpose.[8] Evangelists are endowed with God's special grace to carry the message of the good news about Christ to the world, especially to the nonbeliever (Acts 8:5-6).

- The office of the evangelist is unique to the New Testament. The evangelist's central purpose is to tell of Christ. We do not read in the New Testament about a specific way the evangelist is called (i.e., by a dream or direct call of God). The requirements to be an evangelist are: an ability to reach out to the nonbeliever and believer alike, knowing where to go for the harvest of souls (Acts 8:26-29), recognize preaching Christ as the primary duty of an evangelist (Acts 8:5); provide concrete proof of Jesus Christ as God's Son and Messiah (Acts 8:27-35); proclaim the Gospel successfully (Acts 8:37); present maturity and balance in faith (Ephesians 4:11-16); present a willingness to work with other ministries, especially apostles and prophets (Acts 8:13-25); have the ability to teach crowds and one-on-one (Acts 8:5-6, Acts 8:27-30); and have a deep concern for those who do not know the Lord (Acts 8:5-6). Evangelists are not a stationary office. Evangelists hold the command to go forth with the Word, not remain fixed in a local church. The purpose and preaching of an evangelist are different from a pastor, prophet, or apostle. Unlike apostles and prophets, evangelists are independent but accountable for what they teach in their ministries because they do not have the direct revelatory teaching from the Lord that apostles and prophets have. Evangelists must study with apostles and prophets to be thoroughly equipped for their ministry (2 Timothy 4:5).

- The duties of the evangelist include: teaching and preaching for nonbelievers (Acts 8:5-6); itinerant work, requiring travelling from location to location (Acts 8:40); awaken all (believer and nonbeliever) backslidden and lost in sin, and convict to repentance, bringing about the fruit of salvation (Mark 1:1-5); baptize new members, emphasizing the importance and the heart of baptism (Acts 8:38-39); teach on water baptism (Acts 8:12); teach on the life and work of Christ, both in the Old and New Testaments (Acts 8:30-37); work in the area of basic apologetics, being able to answer questions about faith and offer pragmatic answers (Acts 8:34-35); bring joy to others from the fruit of repentance (Acts 8:8); assist and cooperate with others in ministry (Acts 8:13-

25); train the church in matters of evangelism and witnessing (2 Timothy 4:5); operate in the gifts of the Spirit, especially healing (Acts 8:6-8); and operate ministry for the purpose of charity to the poor and less fortunate (2 Timothy 4:5).

- The New Testament records one by name as an evangelist: Philip (Acts 21:8). We recognize through historical writings and non-canonical works that others served as evangelists, men and women alike.

- Some argue the office of evangelist has ceased. In place of the evangelistic office, such believe every believer must now take on the office. How can this stand if there is no one to train believers in the ways of evangelism? We must recognize the call to proclaim the Gospel to every creature calls for anointed and equipped individuals to perform this evangelistic duty and train the church to do so as well (Isaiah 61:1-3).

Characteristics of the evangelist

There are essential characteristics God gives to each evangelist, enabling him or her to fulfill the evangelist's call with full grace and dignity. In looking at an evangelist, we can see these characteristics clearly.

- **The Evangelist Philip, Acts 8:4-40:** Philip is the only evangelist recorded in the New Testament, yet he is a powerful example of the necessary characteristics given to evangelists. We could describe the evangelist as having a restless spirit. Evangelists are called to go, living in a constant state of travelling for the Gospel. They enjoy adventure, new places, and meeting new people. The evangelist is called to be social, engaging with people. Evangelists must be able to speak with power and engage others in discussion about essential matters. They must be prepared to answer questions and give solid answers. Evangelists are eager to speak, quick to offer support, and eloquent in presentation. They are fast learners, quick to pick up essential details and matters pertaining to the essentials of faith. Evangelists are fiercely independent, yet balance their love of people with a true need to be independent and seek out the lost.

Types of the evangelistic office

- **The book of Isaiah** – *The prophet Isaiah*, a type of the evangelistic ministry. Isaiah was a powerful prophet. His ministry bore a special Messianic stamp, making it unique among Old Testament prophetic ministries. Isaiah did not just foresee events in his prophecies, but a clear picture of the person, character, life, and nature of Jesus Christ. Isaiah's prophecies cover everything of the Messiah's life, including His birth, life, death, and second coming. Isaiah proves the Messiah is the very heart and soul of salvation, history, and life. It is no accident Philip the evangelist explained passages from Isaiah to the eunuch.

- **The book of Jonah** – *The prophet Jonah*, a type of the evangelistic ministry. Jonah received a task from the Lord he could have lived without. He was called to travel and warn the nation of Nineveh about God's coming wrath if they refused to repent. Jonah's response? Guided by a heart full of racism, Jonah fled God's command because he desired the destruction of Nineveh's people. Jonah's flee from God didn't last long, however. After spending three days and three nights in the belly of a large fish, Jonah gets his act together, spreads the message of repentance to Nineveh, and the people change their ways. Even after this, Jonah's attitude does not seem to improve. He is sullen and downcast because God's mercy triumphed over judgment. In Jonah, we can see a powerful type of believing evangelists reaching out to non-believers in the hope of their repentance and salvation. Evangelists don't get to choose where they go, but must be obedient to the Lord. We also see the evangelistic spirit of overcoming personal biases and bigotries to reach out to the lost. Instead of being angry over saved souls, the evangelist is called to rejoice in God's great and merciful work, never standing in judgment.

- **The book of Hosea** – *The prophet Hosea*, a type of the evangelistic ministry. Hosea was a prophet with a unique call: God asked him to personally live the situation of fallen Israel. Hosea's marriage to Gomer, a prostitute, literally mirrored the spiritual reality of Israel chasing foreign gods and abandoning the one true God. Hosea's children signified Israel's abandonment of God and God's response in declaring them no longer His people. However, we find a powerful promise of restoration and hope in the heart of Hosea: a group of people would repent and return to the Lord, abandoning false ways, and be accepted as God's people. Hosea's ministry was purposed to bring about repentance and conversion through proclamation and illustration. Through the call of Christ, evangelists too bring about repentance by proclaiming the Word and illustrating it through clarity. The heart of Hosea: repentance and God's love for His people, which they receive when they come to Him, is a central theme of evangelistic ministry.

The historical evangelist

- **Dominica of Constantinople** (c. fifth century) – A woman on a mission, Dominica of Constantinople immediately entered a women's monastery after baptism, but refused to remain isolated. She went about, healing the sick, performing miracles, and walking in authority over the natural elements. Due to her witness, many came to know the Lord and investigate more about the spiritual realm. Today she is revered as a saint in both Roman Catholic and Orthodox traditions, although she is seldom studied and acknowledged.[9]

- **Anthony of Padua** (1195-1231) – A priest and Franciscan friar, Anthony of Padua was best known for his extensive work in preaching and teaching. In starting out, Anthony originally protested, but the quality of his preaching went on to leave a deep and lasting impression in those who would hear. Throughout his life, despite efforts to work in education, his most powerful gift was that of a preacher, with the ability to convict, convince, and impact those who heard. His preaching was hailed as the "jewel case of the Bible" and he produced a collection of his sermons before his death at thirty-six years of age. He was canonized a saint in the Roman Catholic Church in 1232, and declared a Doctor of the Church in 1946.[10]

- **The Beguines** (thirteenth and fourteenth centuries) – The Beguines were active, non-cloistered communities of women who were not nuns. In contrast to the Catholic leaders of the time, they were very involved with common men and women. These women were powerful preachers, unbound by cloisters, rules, and controlling authorities, travelling in varied places, and supporting themselves through artisan and crafting work. They worked despite disapproval and condemnation (they were deemed heretical) from the Catholic Church.[11]

- **The Lollards** (1382-1430) – The Lollards were a group of poor, itinerant men and women who labored hard to preach the Gospel. Most were followers of John Wycliffe, a prominent figure in the English reformation. In contrast to the Catholic Church which believes itself to be the only true church, viewing church as a corporate entity, the Lollards believed in the "Church of the Saved." They believed the church was a universal, invisible entity of believers worldwide, not just one group. They faced strong opposition for their beliefs and preaching, and many were burned at the stake.[12]

- **Jarena Lee** (1783-?) – A woman who grew to love the Lord, Jarena Lee had no formal spiritual training in her youth. She was the first woman authorized to preach within the African Methodist Episcopal Church by the founder of the denomination. Although her ordination was initially put off, her preaching was so convincing and convicting, she was ordained eight years after her initial request. She began preaching throughout the United States and Canada in 1820, even among slave states. Her words were bold and converted many souls.[13]

- **William Ashley "Billy" Sunday** (1862-1935) – Billy Sunday was a famous American baseball player who later converted to Christianity. After his conversion, he became a well-known evangelist in the early 1900s. He was known for a practical, down-to-earth style and his energetic delivery. He worked in public campaigns through the largest cities, pulpit preaching, and attracted large crows. His crowds, in fact, were the largest assembled prior to sound equipment. Thanks to the work of his wife, his ministry was grown and developed, and he was able to reach even more people through revival circuits than before. Despite heartache at the end of his life, Billy Sunday's ministerial work speaks of the testament of true evangelism.[14]

Questions and answers

- **Aren't all Christians evangelists?**

All Christians are called to evangelize. All Christians have the duty of proclaiming the Gospel of Christ to others through their words and actions. This general command is different from being called to be an evangelist. The evangelist's very ministry is to bear Christ, teach Christ, reveal Christ to the non-believer, and bring a greater revelation of Christ to the believer. It is a ministry bringing not just testimony, but proof of Christ as the Savior of mankind. The office is central to letting others know about Jesus, Who Jesus is, and what He did for the world. Evangelists help to train and equip all Christians to be better witnesses of the Gospel and lead others to Christ through witness and testimony.

- **If there is only one named evangelist in the Bible, is the office relevant?**

There are no specific examples of pastors in the New Testament, so by this logic, the office of pastor has questionable relevance! Now we all know pastors are relevant to the Body of Christ, so why would such logic reason for evangelists? Just because the Bible limits the number of evangelists we see by name doesn't mean we know any less about the office versus having many examples. The singular example of Philip truly exemplifies the fullness of the evangelistic office and its purpose.

The New Testament was not written as an autobiography or biography. Its purpose is not to provide explicit detail of every person who filled a five-fold ministry office. In recognizing the New Testament as the model for church faith and practice in every subsequent generation, we don't need to read the experiences of every single apostle, prophet, evangelist, pastor, and teacher alive back then. What we must do is focus on the information, details, experiences, and examples provided. In the case of an evangelist, Philip provides perfect detail and clarity on evangelists and what they do.

- **What is the central heart of the evangelist's ministry?**

The heart of an evangelist's call is to find and prove Christ as the center of all things. The evangelist's position is to draw out Christ, both in an evangelical sense and in a Scriptural sense. The evangelist truly shows people Christ is the center of the Scriptures, history, and life itself.

- **How are evangelists trained?**

First, the evangelist receives their ministry gift to go forth and share the Gospel in the way God has called them to from God. Evangelists are trained for their work by apostles and prophets. They receive the revelation given to apostles and prophets. They then go forth with the revelation, preaching Christ, the Word. As we can see from Philip's example in Acts 8, evangelists must be well-trained and competent to preach Christ, as they expound Him in the Word of God and as the Word of God.

- **Are evangelists tied to a "home church?"**

Home church is another term for a local church. This remains the same concept spoken of earlier, with the local church regarded as the ultimate in church understanding. Evangelists must be under the guidance and covering of apostles and prophets. This is the deposit for Christ's revelation to evangelists. Evangelists are required to have apostolic or prophetic covering (or both), but not pastoral covering. While it is of great benefit for evangelists to work with local communities to train in evangelism, evangelists are called to be mobile and work wherever they are sent for the Gospel.

- **Why do evangelists have the authority to baptize?**

Evangelists are commissioned by apostles and prophets, and thus have authority to baptize. As evangelists preach Christ and call unto repentance, there is a necessity for evangelists to baptize people into Christ for the remission of sins as part of their ministry work.

- **Is the church evangelical (based on evangelists) or apostolic (based on apostles)?**

We understand the term "evangelical" in the sense as defined by the Evangelical Movement of the 1800s. The Evangelical Movement emphasizes the need for every believer to tell others about the work of Jesus Christ. It also emphasizes the need for all to know of the Lord on a personal level. This movement roots itself in revivals and, therefore, revival mentality. Such thinking is truly evangelical in every sense of the word. It is about the heart of the evangelist, to proclaim the Gospel and bring all to salvation.

Because most of us grew up in a circumstance where we were taught to think evangelical, we often believe an apostolic church (based on the five-fold ministry and the foundation of apostles and prophets) is a contradiction to every believer's command to let others know about Christ. What we don't recognize is an evangelical movement as founded upon the evangelist and the evangelist's attitude is not the way of the New Testament church. The New Testament church was evangelical, but it was evangelical because it was apostolic. The apostles were the first ones sent with the revelation of Christ resurrected. They were the first to tell others of what God had done through Jesus Christ. The office of an evangelist followed thanks to the revelation received from the apostles. As everyone followed God's order, the church was successful in its evangelical efforts. There is no contradiction between evangelical and apostolic if done according to the order of the New Testament.

Discussion, study and review questions:

- Was Timothy an evangelist? Why did Paul call him to do the work of an evangelist? What does this tell us?

- How many times is the word "evangelist" found in the Bible? How do we come to an understanding of what an evangelist does?

- How does the office of evangelist differ from the basic Christian call to evangelize? What does the word "evangelist" mean? What grace does the evangelist have?

- Why is the office of evangelist unique to the New Testament? Is there a specific description of the evangelist's call in the New Testament? What are the requirements to be an evangelist? How is the evangelist's office different from that of apostle and prophet?

- What are the duties of an evangelist?

- Who is recorded in the Bible as an evangelist? How do we find that other people, both men and women, served as evangelists?

- Why is the office of evangelist relevant today?

- What are the characteristics of the evangelistic office? What are the strengths and weaknesses of evangelists? How do these characteristics manifest to make them better evangelists?
- What are some Old Testament types of the evangelistic ministry? How do these types shadow what the evangelistic office is to represent?

- In looking at the "Historical evangelist" section, how were you able to see the office of the evangelist differently than before? How does this change how you view leaders in history, even though they may not have been ever called an "evangelist?" Who else can you think of in history who was an evangelist, even if they were not acknowledged as such?

- Discuss and share some of the questions and answers found in the "Questions and Answers" section. What did you learn that you did not know about evangelists and evangelistic ministry? What did you learn that changed your mind about an opinion you might have had prior about evangelistic ministry? How did learning about specific issues related to evangelists and evangelistic ministry help you to grow in your understanding of ministry? The church? Your own relationship with God?

Chapter Nine

THE OFFICE OF THE PASTOR

It's interesting to note that all revolutionary literature was written by pastors. These guys were involved in a revolution against the mightiest power that the world had ever seen.
– Randall Terry[1]

The pastoral office is the most universally recognized Christian ministry. At the same time, the pastoral office is also the most misinterpreted ministry representation. Many believe a personal pastor is mandatory, thinking the offices of pastor and teacher are the only five-fold ministry offices left. The ramifications of this thinking are far and wide. Some think everyone must be subject to a pastor. Others think everyone in ministry needs to be a pastor. Some think only men can pastor. Some believe pastors can never leave the churches they serve. Some believe they can never leave the authority of the singular pastor over their church. These misguided extremes have left the church with misconceptions and questions about the office of the pastor.

As with all things, the extreme concepts about pastors find their solution in balance. The pastor may not be the end-all, be-all ministry office many seek, but pastors serve a vital and important function for the church and five-fold ministry. To find answers about the pastoral office, we must study the Word. It is time to fully reinstate the pastoral role in the church, according to God's precepts, once and for all!

Text study

Jeremiah 3:15-16

Supplementary texts

Psalm 23:1-6, Jeremiah 10:19-25, Jeremiah 12:10-17, Jeremiah 17:13-27, Jeremiah 23:1-4, Matthew 18:15-17, Acts 16:14-15, Acts 18:18-28, Ephesians 4:11.

Power verse

Jeremiah 3:15:

- *"And I will give you pastors according to Mine heart, which shall feed you with knowledge and understanding."*

- *"Then I will give you shepherds after My own heart, who will feed you on knowledge and understanding."* (NASB)

- *"Then I will give you shepherds after My own heart, who will lead you with knowledge and understanding."* (NIV)

- *"I will appoint shepherds with whom I'm pleased, and they will lead you with knowledge and understanding."* (CEB)

- *"And I will give you shepherds after My own heart, who will feed you with knowledge and understanding."* (ESV)

- *"And I will give you shepherds after My own heart, who will guide you with knowledge and understanding."* (NLT)

Power words

- **Give** – From the Hebrew word *"nathan"* which means, "to feed, to tend a flock, to keep sheep."[2]

- **Pastors** – From the Hebrew word *"ra'ah"* which means, "to pasture, tend, graze, feed; to associate with, be a friend of (meaning probable); to be a special friend."[3]

- **Mine Heart** – From the Hebrew word *"leb"* which means, "inner man, mind, will, heart, understanding."[4]

- **Feed** – From the Hebrew word *"ra'ah"* which means, "to pasture, tend, graze, feed; to associate with, be a friend of (meaning probable); to be a special friend."[5]

- **Knowledge** – From the Hebrew word *"de'ah"* which means, "knowledge (of God)."[6]

- **Understanding** - From the Hebrew word *"sakal"* which means, "to be prudent, be circumspect, wisely understand, prosper; to lay crosswise, cross (hands)."[7]

Historical context

Jeremiah was most definitely an Old Testament prophet with shadows and shades as a type of the New Testament pastor. Jeremiah's call, vision, and work centered around the lost people of Israel, who functioned without truth and guidance. If we truly understand Jeremiah's writings, the people were lost because they did not have the right leadership in their lives. As a result, Jeremiah prophesied a time to come when the people would be rightly led by shepherds (pastors) selected and given by God Himself. The comparison of the pastor to a shepherd is both historical and illustrative – likening the pastor to a shepherd gives us an idea of how people saw the call, and also helps us to see the way a shepherd cares for and tends the flock they are given as the way pastors are called to lead God's people.

Notes on text

Until Jesus returns, there will be people who seek to exploit and mislead the people of God. That's why the people of God who are called to pastor are compared to shepherds. Calling a pastor a "shepherd" speaks both of his or her call and work and the people they are called to lead. A shepherd must be patient with sheep, who tend to be stubborn, ignorant, and self-destructive. The shepherd's heart is one of love and concern, care and tending, and feeding and provision. If God provides pastors after His own heart, this means that the pastor's heart is inclined for his or her people, as God's heart is inclined towards us, His people. It is the pastor's job to lead with knowledge and understanding, requiring the pastor to have that, as well. When we have pastors who lead according to God's heart, the need for law fades, because truth and reality reigns in the hearts of God's people.

Power points

- The word "pastor" is found only one time in the New Testament: in Ephesians 4:11. We do see the word "pastor" present in the Old Testament, especially in the book of Jeremiah (Jeremiah 3:15-16). Because the word is only used one time in the New Testament, the office is commonly confused with the offices of elder, overseer, or bishop. These offices, in fact, are not the pastoral office. These different terms represent different purposes, ranks, and work within a church, and do represent different leadership roles. The different terms refer to different work (bishops, elders, and deacons are all appointment ministries, ministries established to be "helps" to the five-fold), although in many instances, they do overlap. The Scriptures suggest elders oversaw the responsibilities of a congregation, a pastor was the "shepherd" of the people, attending to their various spiritual needs, and a bishop may have overseen more than one church or held a senior position as an overseer. The Word does not indicate how many pastors a church should have, but we can recognize that a church may have pastors function to oversee different church ministries. Examples include youth ministry pastors, women's ministry pastors, men's ministry pastors, and so on. The primary grace of the pastoral office is caring for God's people, meeting their spiritual needs (Jeremiah 3:15-16). Pastors are called to have a heart for the people they serve, as they meet spiritual needs in love and purpose (Psalm 23:1-6). They are not the foundation of a church, as are the apostles and prophets (Ephesians 2:20). Therefore, you cannot build a church on the foundation of a pastor or many pastors – that is not a part of God's order. Therefore, not being the supreme authority, the pastor learns of the truth of the Word through the apostles and prophets.

- As a shepherd tends to one flock, a pastor is called to pastor a local church community. This is different from apostles and prophets, who instruct and establish the foundations of the church through leadership (Ephesians 2:20), and evangelists, who build up the church by reaching those who need to learn more of the Lord or develop a deeper walk with Him (Acts 8:26-40). It is the pastor's job to care for the people, walking after God's own heart. The Bible indicates pastors are called by God for this purpose: to provide knowledge and understanding to the people (Jeremiah 3:15-16).

- If we look carefully at the teachings of Jeremiah, we learn much about what the pastor is called to do by the prophetic admonishments that are given. Pastors are called to be agents of unity, uniting the flock rather than causing it to scatter. Rather than be destroyers of the vineyard, pastors help care for and tend it. Instead of bringing to desolation, pastors are called to bring forth life and restoration. Pastors are also called to have a powerful heart of compassion and love toward those they lead (Jeremiah 12:10-17). Pastors are not called to be brutish, nor abusive in their leadership (Jeremiah 10:19-25).

- Pastoring is the only office of the five-fold that mentions the prosperity of the people in a repeated way. As the Scriptures tell us to prosper, even as our souls prosper (3 John 2), so the pastor is called to be an agent of prosperity, fruitfulness and increase (Psalm 23:5-6). This is because as a shepherd tends the flock, they work so none are lost and the flock increases in number. This means a healthy congregation reflects spiritual health and health in every area of their lives, thus leading to a blessed and prosperous living (Jeremiah 23:1-4).

- The duties of the pastor include: Love and care for the flock of God (Jeremiah 3:15-16); spiritually feed the flock of God through teaching (Jeremiah 17:13-27); teach and instruct in the ways of God, that they may be clear (Acts 18:18-28); lead in ways of righteousness and knowledge (Jeremiah 3:15-16); work in the ministry of restoration (Psalm 23:3); encourage (Psalm 23:3-6); handle matters of local church discipline and mediation (Matthew 18:15-17); assist the apostles and prophets upon their visit to a local assembly (Acts 16:14-15); refute falsehood and false leadership (Jeremiah 17:13-27; Jeremiah 23:1-4); and walk in the gifts of the Spirit (Romans 12:6-8).

- No individual is named as pastor in the New Testament. Some denominations teach Titus and Timothy were bishops or pastors because of the pastoral instruction in the Apostle Paul's letters to them. Some refer to 1 and 2 Timothy and Titus as "pastoral epistles" for this reason. The Bible cites Timothy as an apostle, and not a pastor (Philippians 1:1). Titus' role to appoint elders in Crete most likely indicates an apostolic office, rather than a pastoral one (Titus 1:5). The fact that pastoral issues are addressed in these letters indicates they needed address within the church. It does not indicate the men who received these letters were pastors or bishops themselves. As we know Timothy was an apostle, it is reasonable to suggest he trained and installed pastors and needed to know the criteria of the office. What we do find via thorough studies are several references to individuals who most likely were pastors, based on the information we have of them – and all of them were women. These include Priscilla (Acts 18:1, 18-28; Romans 16:3, 1 Corinthians 16:19, 2 Timothy 4:19), Chloe (1 Corinthians 1:11), Lydia (Acts 16:14-15), and Nympha (Colossians 4:15. As we have evidence from the New Testament that women were included as pastors and we can see that women were deacons, it is reasonable to assume that women served in all offices of oversight, as well (1 Timothy 3:8-13).

- While there is no modern debate about the pastoral office, it is misunderstood. The Biblical standards for pastors must stand for Kingdom success (1 Peter 5:1-10, 1 Timothy 3:17, Titus 1:6-16).

Characteristics of the pastor

There are essential characteristics God gives to each pastor, enabling him or her to fulfill the pastoral call with full grace and dignity. In looking at some aspects of a pastor's call, we can see these characteristics clearly.

- **The call to shepherd, Jeremiah 3:15-16:** The word "pastor" literally means "shepherd." This means a pastor is given a heart to act as a shepherd to the people of God's flock. Pastors are called to sacrifice, often putting others before themselves. They demonstrate a great love for people, and an ability to teach, lead, and correct in a heart of love. Pastors are given the important gift of patience and long-suffering. They are able to withstand much and give much at the same time, teaching and training the whole time. With such patience, pastors are fully prepared to nurture individuals from spiritual infancy to spiritual maturity. As shepherds, pastors walk in compassion, having a true heart to help others. Pastors do not do their work out of greed, but out of love for the flock of God. With such an intense call, some pastors may become controlling, dominating, and angry, over-emphasizing one aspect of pastoral ministry rather than another. Remembering the heart of a shepherd is essential to serving as a successful pastor.

- **An honorable man or woman, Jeremiah 10:19-25:** Pastors are called to be men and women of honor and order, not brutish or abusive. Pastors uphold these precepts in their professional and personal lives. As people of honor and order, pastors are called to maintain a balance between their ministries and their homes. Family life cannot be neglected due to the call to pastor, nor can the call to pastor be neglected due to family life. Pastors are called to find that balance and handle both with honor and dignity. Pastors are called to exude dignity in their character. They present and teach matters with strength and clarity, and are able to explain things when there is question. Pastors are people of honesty, both being honest and expecting honesty in return. Pastors are also visibly noted for living without question and without blame, not exuding character in contradiction to the essence of pastoral honor. The biggest challenge a pastor faces is the ability to walk in the necessary honor of the office. Under the pressure, many pastors fall into sin. Remaining in balance is the true key to remaining honorable in ministry.

Types of the pastoral ministry

- **Genesis 29:10** – *Rachel as a shepherdess*, a type of the female pastoral ministry. There are a lot of people who question whether or not a woman can pastor. These people do not understand the Scriptures, nor the types and shadows that pre-date the pastorate involving women. Rachel was a shepherdess; in fact, her name means "ewe" or "sheep." Her responsibilities mirrored that of a male shepherd, and she was called to uphold these responsibilities in excellence. As the shepherd over her father's flock, she was a type and shadow of women who would serve God as pastors in the new covenant.

- **Psalm 23:1-6** – *The shepherd*, a type of the pastoral ministry. Shepherding was a common occupation in Bible times. For this reason, using the shepherd as a pastoral type would have been recognized and understood by the people. The intense care, love, time, and effort a shepherd took with his sheep shows us the love a pastor should have for God's people.

- **The book of Jeremiah** – *The prophet Jeremiah*, a type of the pastoral ministry. No one questions the incredible prophetic ministry of Jeremiah. If we look at Jeremiah's ministry closely, we can see Jeremiah as a pastoral shadow. Jeremiah had a "shepherd's heart," a true burden for God's people. The sins of the people grieved this great leader to the point of sorrow. He had a heart for correction and instruction, and was effective in his methods. We also see Jeremiah's deep burden for God-appointed and corrective leadership among the people of God.

- **The book of Amos** – *The prophet Amos*, a type of the pastoral ministry. Amos was an Old Testament prophet. Rather than having a prophetic lineage, Amos was a shepherd. His powerful prophecies show the importance of pastoral integrity and last days instruction. Amos' prophecies are about calamity and order at the same time: when disaster or persecution may come, the people of God are to find His order and follow His guidelines. Amos teaches a need for consistent doctrine, agreement with the precepts of God, and standards of justice.

The historical pastor

- **Gaiana of Armenia** (Third century A.D.) – The abbess of a monastery in Asia Minor, Gaiana of Armenia worked tirelessly to teach a young girl named Rhipsime how to live a holy life devoted to prayer. When the Emperor Diocletian saw Rhipsime, he desired to marry her. Upon her refusal, he threatened her with kidnapping and torture. She still declined. She was killed as a martyr for her position. Her witness was so strong that Gaiana, her pastor, and another woman were also martyred for the faith. According to legend, the men who tortured and killed these women lived out the rest of their lives as wild beasts, having the wrath of God come upon them.[8]

- **Anthony the Abbot** (251-356) – Seeking solace and monastic life, Anthony the Abbot retreated to the desert, but found his solace interrupted by numerous admirers and followers. He had a gift of healing and strongly urged followers to live lives based on the Gospel. He had so many disciples, they had to establish two monasteries. Later he left monastic life for a period to encourage and lead those under the persecution of Maximinus. He was dearly loved, and long-respected as a leader of many seeking counsel and guidance.[9]

- **Bernard of Clairvaux** (1090-1153) – At age twenty-two, Bernard of Clairvaux feared the influences of the world and retreated to the monastery along with four of his brothers and twenty-five friends. He went on to found and lead the monastery at Clairvaux, which had over seven hundred monks and over a hundred other houses. Through his work, he went on to revise the Cistercian rule and order. As a firm believer in the command to lead a holy life, Bernard instilled this value in all he led through spiritual guidance and purpose. He was canonized in 1170 and later declared a Doctor of the Church.[10]

- **Andrew Murray** (1828-1917) – Andrew Murray was born the son of a Dutch Reformed Church missionary in Graaff Reinet, South Africa. After attending college in Scotland and the Netherlands, Andrew and his brother became members of Het Reveil, a revival movement opposed to rationalism. He was ordained by the Dutch Reformed Church in 1848, and returned to South Africa. He pastored churches throughout South Africa, and a major figure in the South African Revival of 1860. Among his other notable works was as one of the founders of the South African General Mission, and his work as a prolific writer. An author whose works still hold relevance today, Andrew Murray wrote over two hundred books.[11]

- **Catherine Booth** (1829-1890) – As a child, Catherine Booth overcame illness and was deeply inspired by faith. By the time she was twelve, she had read the entire Bible eight times. She grew up to become the "Mother of the Salvation Army," wife of Salvation Army founder William Booth. By no means was she in a lesser position than her husband: she was known for holding meetings for converts, and worked extensively with alcoholics. She was a female speaker and preacher, and was active in youth, children's, and adult ministries. She was responsible for many organizational and doctrinal adjustments made, especially as the Salvation Army started to grow. Her final sermon was delivered before twenty-five thousand people. Even though she is not as well known today, her work as a pastor is legendary and relevant to leaders in every subsequent generation.[12]

- **Agnes White Diffee** (1886-1970) – Saved and sanctified by the age of fifteen, Agnes White Diffee was hesitant to answer God's call to ministry. By the time she was sixteen, she was the youngest revivalist in the United States. Despite this fact, Agnes refused to answer God's call on her life, blaming her disobedience on the fact that she was a woman. After avoiding her call for a number of years, she developed arthritis, which she believed came as a result of her disobedience to God. She was ordained a pastor in 1919, and her first church grew to over one thousand members. She went on to serve as pastor in several other churches and also served on the Board of Regents for Nazarene College.[13]

Questions and answers

- **Are you saying pastors are not as important as apostles or prophets?**

No, not at all. Pastors are not unimportant in any sense. Pastors have their own unique and upstanding purpose within the Body of Christ. The purpose pastors serve must be celebrated for what it is. Most denominations and independent churches are not following God's established purpose for pastoral leadership. God never exalted the pastor above the apostle or prophet. All offices work together as each office follows its unique ministry calling. If we assign purposes or gifts to offices not purposed for them or exalt one office over another, we will never come to a place of respect, upholding the offices as God designed them to function.

- **Are pastors limited to only working within their immediate congregations?**

No. The pastor is not subject to spend an entire lifetime working within the immediate four-square walls of a local church. Pastors are free to attend or preach at other conferences, or host conferences and bring in other ministers to those events. Pastors should be encouraging in the work of mobilizing evangelistic outreaches among the congregations and involved in community services. They should also be active in Christian education. Pastors are free to travel, preach, and proclaim the Gospel if they do not have congregations. If they are in a position to install another pastor while they are in transit, they also have the option of mobility if they have a congregation.

These freedoms do not mean pastors can do whatever they please. The role of the pastor is to be a local authority, one that works dutifully with people on a local level. The pastor's role is not limitless, nor is it universal. Pastors have authority in a local setting over those sent to that local realm. While a pastor may be respected as a pastor in another setting, they do not have the same authority there that they do in their local congregations. Likewise, pastors have their first and immediate responsibility to their local congregations and the souls present there. It is not befitting, nor appropriate, for a pastor to besmirch their immediate duties without seeing to it that someone else meets the needs for those congregations.

Pastors cannot expect to build churches without the apostle (Ephesians 2:20). Apostles build churches; pastors love people and care for the people sent to those churches. It is the pastor's sacred duty to instill and teach on the revelation given to apostles and prophets. It is the pastor's job to expound on the revelation of Christ given through the evangelist. The pastor's job is not menial, nor irrelevant. The pastor performs an extremely important function within the five-fold ministry and for the church body.

- **If there is no apostle present over a specific church, does that mean the pastor fills in for the apostle?**

No. If there is no apostle serving as an apostle over a congregation, it is the pastor's duty to pray and be led to an apostle to oversee the congregation as part of their apostolic ministry. Pastors are never apostles, and apostles are never pastors!

- **If a pastor is in error, who corrects him or her?**

The job of correcting a pastor in error lies with apostles and prophets. If an apostle or prophet is not aware of the circumstance, it is appropriate for them to be notified.

- **Can an apostle correct any pastor in error?**

In theory, any apostle has the authority to correct any pastor they see in error. It is not, however, always appropriate to exercise such authority, nor is it customary.

We recognize the church is built upon relationship: relationship with God through Christ, relationship among leaders, relationship among followers and leaders, and general relationships among the body of believers. As the church is relationship-based, those in leadership have the opportunity to educate others as they help to develop them spiritually. The same is true within leadership: apostles and prophets grow and develop pastors as they build relationships with them.

Ideally, apostles should correct those they oversee in ministry, having a leadership relationship with the pastor or other leader who needs correction. That is a part of apostolic relationship, and it is essential to being a solid apostle of the Lord. If an apostle feels unable to do this, they must step back and evaluate their position in ministry and relationship with the leader who needs correction. If they are unable to do so, such apostles must step aside and allow another apostle to handle this matter.

Sometimes God does send objective, impersonal, and nonrelational leadership into the lives of errant leadership for the purpose of correction. Sometimes being a mentor with another renders one unable to be objective when it comes to certain correctional issues. There are also cases when those who have a leadership relationship feel unable to step back and handle the matter due to lack of education or personal perspectives. Then there are circumstances where leader receiving the correction acknowledges the leadership of the correcting party, but the correction is rooted in personal dispute or opinion.

Learning how to accept correction is an important part of being a leader, whatever ministry a leader may have. It is equally important to recognize when someone is unreasonable, overstepping boundaries, or speaking inappropriately. We must guard what God has for us. Recognizing when people seek our ministry and personal best versus when they seek control is essential to ministry discernment. Through relationship and the Spirit, leaders come to know which situations merit correction, which situations merit distance, and which situations demand corrective objectivity or acceptance.

- **How many pastors does a church need?**

The New Testament does not offer a specific number of pastors required for a church. It does indicate a plurality may have existed in each New Testament church, and we can draw a plurality should exist in today's church. Pastoral need can be addressed on the number of ministries a church has or needs, and how many people attend the church on a regular basis. Matching the church's ministries, numbers, and needs with the necessary number of pastors is essential to a solid, functioning church. Working with an apostle to install appropriate leaders and establish appropriate ministries is the way this task is successfully accomplished.

Discussion, study and review questions:

- What New Testament office was Jeremiah a type of? What did Jeremiah's call, function, and work center around? Why were the Israelites lost? What time did Jeremiah prophesy? Why is the pastor compared to a shepherd?

- In what ways are pastors compared to shepherds? What does it mean if pastors are provided after God's own heart? What is the pastor's job? What happens when we have pastors who lead according to God's heart?

- How many times is the word "pastor" found in the New Testament? Where is it found in the Old Testament? Because of this, what terms are commonly confused with the pastoral office? What do these different terms refer to? How many pastors should a church have? What are some examples of pastoral ministries? What are pastors called to have? Are pastors the foundation of the church? Why or why not? How do pastors learn the truth of the Word?

- What is a pastor called to do? How is this different from the work of the apostle, prophet, and evangelist? What is the pastor's job? What purpose are pastors called by God for?

- What is the pastor called to do?

- Why is prosperity specifically mentioned in connection with the pastoral office?

- What are the duties of a pastor?

- Are any pastors named in the New Testament? Do those who believe Timothy and Titus served as pastors have evidence to support their beliefs? What can we draw from the Word about women serving in the pastoral office?

- Is the role of pastor of debate? Why or why not? Instead of debating the pastoral role, what do we need to learn and examine about it? Why?

- What are the characteristics of the pastoral office? What are the strengths and weaknesses of pastors? How do these characteristics manifest to make them better pastors?

- What are some Old Testament types of the pastoral ministry? How do these types shadow what the pastoral office is to represent?

- In looking at the "Historical pastor" section, how were you able to see the office of the pastor differently than before? How does this change how you view leaders in history, even though they may not have been ever called a "pastor?" Who else can you think of in history who was a pastor, even if they were not acknowledged as such?

- Discuss and share some of the questions and answers found in the "Questions and Answers" section. What did you learn that you did not know about pastors and pastoral ministry? What did you learn that changed your mind about an opinion you might have had prior about pastoral ministry? How did learning about specific issues related to pastors and pastoral ministry help you to grow in your understanding of ministry? The church? Your own relationship with God?

Chapter Ten

THE OFFICE OF THE TEACHER

A good teacher is like a candle – it consumes itself to light the way for others.
– Unknown[1]

Who was your favorite teacher when you were in school? Most of us can remember a teacher or teachers who had a profound impact on our learning experience. The same is true of the office of teacher in the church. Even though it is largely forgotten today, the office of teacher was once regarded as one of the essential aspects of Christian ministry. Teaching is primary to making informed and spiritually empowered disciples. Through teachers, believers are equipped, not just for personal belief, but to stand as witnesses of the Christian life.

Those who oppose modern Christianity often accuse the church of lacking solid apologetics, teaching, and substance. Naysayers claim the church is built on emotion rather than substantial evidence or proof for its faith. While it is tempting to blow off the opposition, they are revealing something to us about the modern church. The church needs teachers! We cannot ignore the teaching office or minimize it if it's not entertaining. A strong teaching office represents the church, guards it against error, instructs it for edification, and defends it against those who want to tear Christianity apart. As teachers serve such a vital function, we can never ignore or underestimate the relevance in the church's teaching ministry.

Text study

Romans 12:4-8

Supplementary texts

Exodus 18:19-20, Isaiah 30:20-21, 1 Corinthians 12:27-31, Titus 2:1-15, Hebrews 5:11-14, James 3:1-18.

Power verse

Romans 12:6,7:

- *"Having then gifts differing according to the grace that is given to us...Or ministry, let us wait on our ministering; or he that teacheth, on teaching."*

- *"We have different gifts, according to the grace given us... If it is serving, let him serve; if it is teaching, let him teach..."* (NIV)

- *"We all have different gifts, each of which came because of the grace God gave us... Anyone who has the gift of serving should serve. Anyone who has the gift of teaching should teach."* (NCV)

- *"According to the grace given to us, we have different gifts... if service, in service; if teaching, in teaching..."* (HCSB)

- *"Having gifts (faculties, talents, qualities) that differ according to the grace given us, let us use them... [He whose gift is] practical service, let him give himself to serving; he who teaches, to his teaching..."* (AMP)

- *"We have different gifts because God has blessed us in different ways... If a person can help others, he must help others. If a person can teach, he must teach."* (WE)

Power words

- **Gifts** – From the Greek word *"charisma"* which means, "a favor with which one receives without any merit of his own; the gift of divine grace; the gift of faith, knowledge, holiness, virtue; the economy of divine grace, by which the pardon of sin and eternal salvation is appointed to sinners in consideration of the merits of Christ laid hold of by faith; grace or gifts denoting extraordinary powers, distinguishing certain Christians and enabling them to serve the church of Christ, the reception of which is due to the power of divine grace operating on their souls by the Holy Spirit." conviction of the truth of anything, belief; in the, faithfulness."[2]

- **Grace** – From the Greek word *"charis"* which means, "grace; good will, loving-kindness, favor; what is due to grace; thanks (for benefits, services, favors), recompense, reward."[3]

- **Teacheth** – From the Greek word *"didasko"* which means, "to teach; to teach one."[4]

- **Teaching** – From the Greek word *"didaskalia"* which means, "teaching, instruction; teaching."[5]

Historical context

Ancient cultures held great regard for teachers and experts in thought or a specific area of study. Both Greek and Roman societies were notorious for great debates and schools showcasing the methods of their greatest thinkers and philosophers. It was no shock to the ancients to have teachers as part of the five-fold ministry, responsible for teaching and instructing others. Early Christian teachers were often personal sponsors to new converts, teaching them in essential matters of the faith. Teachers also taught individuals and groups in the church on all different levels of faith and ages.

Notes on text

Teaching is identified as a gift of God's grace. Throughout the Old and New Testaments, we see teaching as a venue to pass on faith to new converts and future generations. Teaching also serves to enhance and grow believers, educating and empowering them. If one is called to teach, then one must teach! A teacher who teaches recognizes God's grace at work within that individual for His purpose.

Power points

- Like the gift of prophecy, one can have a gift of teaching without holding the office of office of teacher (Ephesians 4:11, 1 Corinthians 12:27-31). One such example was the Apostle Paul, who described himself as a teacher as part of his apostolic office (2 Timothy 1:11). The role of teacher carries over from the Old Testament, as does the office of prophet (Exodus 18:19-20). Throughout the Old Testament, we see a clear command for the people of God to be taught by God's teachers in the essential matters of belief and faith (Isaiah 30:20-21). Even though all the offices of the five-fold ministry involve teaching, the specific office of teacher acknowledges the grace of teaching to individuals who teach, but do not serve in administrative church leadership (1 Corinthians 12:27-31).

- The New Testament does not list specific criteria to be a teacher. This is because the duties of a teacher would have been understood from the Old Testament understanding as well as cultural beliefs about teachers. We can draw on criteria for the teaching office from different places within the Scriptures: Have been thoroughly taught, including basic and advanced doctrinal matters (one who has not moved to advanced teaching is not qualified for teaching) (Hebrews 5:11-13); be well-skilled within the Scriptures and bring about maturity in faith (Hebrews 5:13-14); be sound in speech that cannot be condemned or contradicted (Titus 2:8); show forth a pattern of good works that align with Scriptural teaching

(Titus 2:7, James 3:15-18); not be blasphemers of God's Word (Titus 2:8); and bring forth wisdom from words (James 3:13-14). Teachers can teach non-believers or believing adults (Deuteronomy 4:1-6), children (Deuteronomy 4:9-10), youth (2 Timothy 2:22), men (Titus 2:6), and women (Titus 2:4-7).

- In James 3, the church is warned against approaching the teaching office lightly. Those who teach are in danger of greater condemnation for teaching falsehoods (James 3:1). We also see an eloquent and informative dialogue on the tongue and the importance of taming the tongue (James 3:2-12). It is especially important that teachers, who use their mouths for the teaching of God's glory, do not use their words lightly. We see in James 3 the importance of being consistent in speech, and it is important for teachers to refrain from blessing and cursing from their same words (James 3:2-12).

- The duties of a teacher include: Teaching the Word (Hebrews 5:13-14): showing forth good works (Titus 2:7); show the way in which believers should walk (Exodus 18:20); walk in the gifts of the Spirit, especially teaching (Romans 12:6-7); and teaching on conduct and other essential matters of faith (James 3:13-18).

- Although no individual is named as a teacher in the New Testament, the office of teacher was clearly held by both men and women (Mark 12:14, Titus 2:1-15).

- Many conjoin the offices of pastor and teacher, believing they form a singular office. The Greek language of Ephesians 4:11 does not recognize this unity. If we conjoin the offices, we do not see the office of teacher upheld in its proper context. Teachers comprise an important function in the body that should be valued rather than dismissed. Paul lists the office of teaching as third in importance (1 Corinthians 12:27-31).

Characteristics of the teacher

There are essential characteristics God gives to each teacher, enabling him or her to fulfill the teacher's call with full grace and dignity. In looking at some examples of teachers, we can see these characteristics clearly.

- **Careful and deliberate in ministry, James 3:1-12:** Teachers are careful people. As most teachers have studied their subjects extensively (sometimes for years), teachers are careful to insure they deliver accurate information. Teachers are self-conscious, insomuch as they desire to examine what they believe and what they speak. They pay attention to detail, and can be very particular about various matters. The end of such work adds up to perseverance present in detail. Such a detail-oriented nature can extend into other areas of life, and it can be enhancing or excessive.

- **A powerful voice, James 3:1-12**: Teachers are powerful voices to the world on essential matters. They have a great power of influence. The voice of a teacher has the power to help or harm and influence others both positively and negatively. Teachers are interested in educating others, working with others, and presenting information. They can grow frustrated when the information they present is rejected or misunderstood. As a result, teachers must be careful about their word usage, their speech, and how they use their influence. God-given gifts must never be used in anger. Teachers need to master the arts of silence, speech, and stepping aside for experience.

- **A wise voice, James 3:13-18:** Teachers must be a people of wisdom, individuals whom others seek because of their great wisdom. To avoid losing people, teachers must maintain a balance between offering wisdom and speaking too much. Knowing when to speak and when not to speak are vital aspects of wise teaching.

Types of the teaching ministry

Just like the prophetic office, the teaching office was alive and well in the Old Testament. While the intent or purpose has not changed, the heart of a New Testament teacher's message is not the law, but Christ, doctrine, and life in the Spirit. The division between grace and the law makes the offices different. In the Old Testament, we see shadows of the teaching office to come.

- **Exodus 18:13-26** – *Moses' assistant judges/elders*, a type of the teaching ministry. Moses' calling was not in any way minor. He led the people of Israel in every conceivable way: he was their physical leader, in their departure from Egypt; he was their spiritual leader, on matters pertaining to faith; he was their moral leader, guiding them on moral issues; and he was their legal adviser, handling disputes and interpreting the law on a case-by-case basis. Anyone would become exhausted in the face of such a demanding schedule. Jethro, Moses' father-in-law, offered him a comprehensive plan to alleviate some of his workload: select capable, God-fearing men for training in the law and establish them as judges for the people. Moses would then handle the cases of great question and take matters directly to God. These judges served as a type of teacher. They were the first group of educators established for the people to handle practical spiritual and legal matters. Appointed by a type of apostle, these teachers demonstrate the deposit of God's revelation for the church: the apostle receives His direct revelation, the apostle teaches other leaders in the church, and the teachers teach that revelatory deposit.

- **Ezra 7:1-10:44** – *Ezra*, a type of the teaching ministry. Ezra was a scribe and priest specifically described as a teacher. The combination of his priestly office, scribal work, and teaching gift shows how well spiritual education can come through anointed writing and teaching. We also see the relevance of historical documentation of events and organization among God's people. Ezra was one well-versed in the ways of God, having discernment on spiritual matters. He was able to point out error according to God's precepts and teach on it, why it was wrong, and expound the issue to a point of understanding among God's people. This directs to the necessity of a well-educated, strong teaching office.

- **The book of Proverbs** – *The wisdom and wise sayings of Proverbs*, a type of the teaching ministry. Sometimes we forget the value in wise sayings, no matter how short they are. Proverbs makes wisdom teachable and practical, applicable to everyday life. The duty to make truth understandable, easy to relate, and practical is a powerful anointing any teacher of God will have upon his or her life.

- **The book of Ecclesiastes** – *The philosopher/preacher/teacher of Ecclesiastes*, a type of the teaching ministry. The book of Ecclesiastes doesn't get its just do. This valuable book instructs not just in wisdom, but in a powerful process by which a teacher discerns truth. Answering deep and profound questions about life, spirituality, human behavior, purpose and faith are a part of standing as a teacher in the church. Teachers aren't just teachers, they are also people who study, think, and ponder issues that pertain to the people of God.

- **Isaiah 30:20-21** – *The visible teachers of Isaiah 30:20*, a type of the teaching ministry. Isaiah prophesies to a people fallen in idolatry of a time when teachers would be accessible, rather than hidden. These New Covenant teachers would proclaim the Word, standing with right teaching at every turn.

The historical teacher

- **Lucian of Antioch** (mid-third century-312) – A man who studied Scripture under Macarius at Edessa, Lucian of Antioch was an extremely well-known early teacher of the church. He was a hermit for a period of time, ordained, and a spiritual director who went on to found a school of theology in Antioch. From his school came numerous individuals deemed heretical by the church, including Arius. Even though it appears he might have been excommunicated for a time, he was eventually reinstituted again. He also had a serious interest in the preservation and translation of the Bible, insisting copyists made the most accurate copies possible while editing errors found in older copies. His translation of the Bible was known as the Lucian Recension, and was used both by churches and Jerome in his work on the Vulgate. He was arrested under the Diocletian persecutions and spent nine years in prison, and experienced a time without food or water while in there. He was killed by sword in 312.[6]

- **Angelus of Furci** (1246-1327) – An Augustinian hermit known for his powerful teaching. He was also a learned preacher, whose knowledge went before him. In understanding and knowing his calling, he refused to be made a bishop three times. Now that is someone who stood up in his calling! He was beatified in 1888.[7]

- **Jean-Baptiste de la Salle** (1651-1719) – A priest, educational reformer, and founder of the Institute of the Brothers of Christian Schools, Jean-Baptist de la Salle is founder of educational teaching methods still in place within education today. He received his tonsure very young and his education young by most standards, even today. He became involved with education as an effort to establish a school for the poor in his hometown, and this went on to become the focus for his vocation. He abandoned his position as Canon, left his home, and moved in with the teachers. This became the foundation of the Institute of the Brothers of Christian Schools, which was an entirely lay order. His work was the first to train teachers for their work, and develop students (while teaching them in their native language) in areas of technology, language, science, and art. His teachers were well-prepared, students were well-educated, and parents were readily involved. He was canonized in 1900, and declared the Patron Saint of Teachers in 1950.[8]

- **Susanna Wesley** (1669-1742) – The mother of Charles and John Wesley, Susanna Wesley was called "the Mother of Methodism" due to her powerful impact on her sons. She lived through spousal abandonment, watching her house burn down to the ground twice, financial hardship, and numerous other oppositions. It was her strong faith conviction that led her to educate all of her children at home, both in the contemporary curriculums and spiritual education, as well. She started a home church which neighbors and others began to attend, eventually numbering over two hundred people in attendance. She wrote extended commentaries for her children's education, such as the Lord's Prayer, the Apostle's Creed, and the Ten Commandments. Even though she does not get her "just do" in religious and women's history, Susanna Wesley was, most definitely, the foundation of several Christian denominations existing today.[9]

- **Elizabeth Ann Bayley Seton** (1774-1821) – A wife and mother of four, Elizabeth Ann Seton worked in charity work until her husband's death. Right after he died, she started an academy for girls (as was customary for women of social standing in her day). She ran into intense anti-religious sentiments due to her beliefs, and began seeking help to establish a school that would not only educate girls practically, but in her faith, as well. With the help of Sulpicians, she established St. Joseph's Academy and Free School for girls. She established a religious order devoted to teaching and is credited with founding the first free Catholic school in the United States. She was canonized in 1975.[10]

- **Henriette Feller** (1800-1868) – A Christian missionary who moved from Switzerland to France simply for ministry, Henriette Feller wound up working in Quebec, which was, at the time, a French province. Sometime around 1835, she started a church, later destroyed by fire and despite threats from angry mobs. She worked on, despite the difficulties she encountered. In 1854 she opened the Institut Feller at Longueuil to educate girls; in 1840, they expanded the school to include boys, as well. In 1855, the school formally incorporated as the Evangelical Society of Grande-Linge. It is now hailed as the oldest French Protestant Church in Canada. Henriette also helped found the Societe Missionaire Franco-

Canadiene (the French Canadian Missionary Society). Prior to World War II, her work was the foundation for several French-speaking Baptist ministers. Her school closed in 1967, and is now a museum and historical site.[11]

Questions and answers

- **Why are teachers so vital to the church?**

I am of the opinion that most in church have the ability to get up in a congregation of believers and preach on a subject. Under the function of the Holy Ghost, there are many who can speak by the Spirit and deliver a message. This doesn't mean all the messages will be of great substance, but that they will move the people who hear the messages, at least on a basic level.

Most are able to accomplish this because they have seen others in the church do the same thing. They know what moves the congregation, what gets people excited, what makes people want to hear more, and what kind of messages flow with the status quo of fever-pitch excitement in a service. For this reason, anyone can model the style of anyone else and stir up a congregation with an emotionally-charged message, whether it contains substance, or not.

Most enjoy messages that encourage, and enjoy the emotionality of messages that bring about a stir within. Many like to jump out of their seats and say things like "Amen!" and "Hallelujah!" because they are so excited about the content of the message. There is definitely a place for this, but, truth be told, most do not learn much from such enthusiastic preaching. They may be stirred, they may walk away with some thoughts, but emotionalism does not make for a great educator. If the church receives too much emotionality in its faith, the church will not grow as it should or understand faith as it needs to be effective in the Christian life.

This is the boundary of teaching in the church. While anyone may be able to stir up a group, not everyone can teach cohesively, effectively, and powerfully. Teaching is more than just stirring people up; it is delivering an essential message on an essential topic and delivering it in a way that people understand the message.

There comes a time in every believer's life when it's time to sit down, stop shouting, and listen to the Word and learn from it. If someone is jumping out of their seats over a message and talking over the minister in enthusiasm, they can't hear what is being said and cannot discipline accordingly. While I think it's great to encourage a speaker in agreement with their message, we better be sure we know what is being taught before stating agreement! The only way we know what is spoken is if we listen and discipline ourselves toward study on that topic.

Teaching is the substance of the church and its message. Enthusiasm is great, but the discipline of the church lies in its teaching and accepting its message. Many accept Christianity to the shouting point, but begin to protest, ignore, or defend valid teaching because the disciplined life isn't always entertaining or fun. We need strong teachers because living, accepting, and hearing strong teaching separates those who are serious about God and will go the whole way with Him from those who just want a "get out of hell free" card.

- **Can teachers preach?**

Certainly. A teacher who is gifted to preach should do so, and convey their teaching through that means. Teachers should not just limit themselves to preaching, though. They should teach in any way God has graced for them.

- **Since all five-fold ministry offices require some form of teaching, how do you distinguish the teaching office from the other ministries?**

The major difference between a teaching gift, necessary for other offices of the five-fold ministry, and the teaching office, is authority. The teaching office is its own non-administrative authority. Teachers are responsible and have authority solely over what they teach and how they teach what God has given them. Other offices of the five-fold ministry are responsible for their teaching, and have authorities in other areas such as leadership, leadership over leaders, discipline and doctrinal correction, congregations, and church establishment.

- **Would a person who teaches Sunday school be considered a teacher?**

Yes. Any ministerial function involving teaching without administrative or structural authority falls in the category of teaching.

- **Can teachers work beyond an immediate congregation?**

Yes. Teachers can travel, teach, preach, write, and teach on a university or academic level. These are just some of the great things teachers can do to benefit the Body of Christ. Teachers are accountable to other ministers (especially apostles, churches and pastors). It is especially important teachers are connected to a congregation or ministry for additional learning and revelation.

Discussion, study and review questions

- How did ancient cultures regard teachers? How does this respect the office of teacher in the five-fold ministry? What do we know about teachers in the early church from history?

- How is teaching identified? Why was teaching important in the Scriptures? If one is called to teach, what should they do?

- How is the office of teacher like that of prophet and evangelist? Who is an example of this? Where does the role of teacher carry over from?

- What do we see about teachers in the Old Testament? How is the office of teacher unique?

- Is there specific New Testament criteria to be a teacher? How do we gather criteria to teach? What is the criteria to be a teacher?

- Why are people warned against taking the teaching office lightly? What important dialogue follows as a warning to teachers, and why? What importance do we see in James 3?

- What are the duties of a teacher?

- Is anyone named as a teacher in the New Testament office of teacher? Did men and women hold this office?

- Why is it wrong to conjoin the offices of pastor and teacher? Why are teachers important?

- What are the characteristics of the teaching office? What are the strengths and weaknesses of teachers? How do these characteristics manifest to make them better teachers?

- What are some Old Testament types of the teaching ministry? How do these types shadow what the teaching office is to represent?

- In looking at the "Historical teacher" section, how were you able to see the office of the teacher differently than before? How does this change how you view of leaders in history, even though they may not have been ever called a "teacher?" Who else can you think of in history who was a teacher, even if they were not acknowledged as such?

- Discuss and share some of the questions and answers found in the "Questions and Answers" section. What did you learn that you did not know about teachers and teaching ministry? What did you learn that changed your mind about an opinion you might have had prior about teaching ministry? How did learning about specific issues related to teachers and teaching ministry help you to grow in your understanding of ministry? The church? Your own relationship with God?

Section 3

THE APPOINTMENTS OF BISHOP, ELDER, AND DEACON

Chapter Eleven

DEACONS: AN APPOINTMENT OF SERVICE

Scripture specifically designates as deacons those whom the church has appointed to distribute alms and take care of the poor, and serve as stewards of the common chest for the poor...Here, then, is the kind of deacons the apostolic church had, and which we, after their example should have.
– John Calvin[1]

We don't hear much teaching on the purpose and role of deacons today. We often see extremes in diaconate role. Some denominations give deacons full control over congregations, pastors, finances, and administration, while others restrict deacons to mere figureheads. In such extreme examples, the church does not recognize deacons are not signposts of the past, nor do they control the function of Christian ministry.

In contrast, we do hear a great deal today about a modern church role known as the armor bearer. This often tends to represent an extreme of ministry whereby five-fold ministry leaders enslave others as personal servants. While some armor bearers operate in prayer and general ministry assistance, a great many more serve their leaders twenty-four hours a day, seven days a week, on both personal and ministerial matters. Some clean their leader's houses, watch their leader's children, prepare meals for their leader and his or her family, dress their leader, and travel with their leader – all at the armor bearer's personal expense.

The church has displaced deacons, and added armor bearers. There is clear confusion in both roles and extremes all around. While God calls us to service, does He call people to serve ministers personally, without pay or recognition? Is the armor bearer mentioned in the New Testament? How can diaconate service be restored in the church, and the role of the armor bearer be rightly understood?

The answer lies in one place: we must review the deacon, and understand the purpose in the diaconate office, as deacons are called for church service.

Text study

1 Timothy 3:8-13

Supplementary texts

Judges 9:50-54, 1 Samuel 14:4-11, Acts 6:1-15, Philippians 1:1-2.

Power verse

1 Timothy 3:10:

- *"And let these also first be proved; then let them use the office of a deacon, being found blameless."*

- *"They must first be tested; and then if there is nothing against them, let them serve as deacons."* (NIV)

- *"And let them also be tested first; then let them serve as deacons if they prove themselves blameless."* (ESV)

- *"Try these men first. Then let them help the church people if they have done nothing wrong."* (WE)

- *"Test them first. Then let them serve as deacons if you find nothing wrong in them."* (CEV)

Power words

- **First** – From the Greek word *"proton"* which means, "first in time or place; first in rank; first, at the first."[2]

- **Proved** – From the Greek word *"dokimazo"* which means, "to test, examine, prove, scrutinize (to see whether a thing is genuine or not), as metals; to recognize as genuine after examination, to approve, deem worthy."[3]

- **Office of the Deacon** – From the Greek word *"diakoneo"* which means, "to be a servant, attendant, domestic, to serve, wait upon."[4]

- **Blameless** – From the Greek word *"anegkletos"* which means, "that cannot be called into to account, unreproveable, unaccused, blameless."[5]

Historical context:

Ancient societies and many modern third-world cultures would be baffled by modern systems of welfare. They would be confounded that the system is sometimes abused by otherwise able-bodied people who do not work and are supported by those who do work. Even in cases of hardship, all classes of ancient society worked, with the exception of those who inherited a large sum of money. If one could not pay off a debt, they were sold into slavery and forced to work off their debt. Even those selected for service by the king were often considered slaves or servants, not of equal rank with the king or his officials. The concept of voluntary service to God within the Kingdom – one specifically selected for general service – would have been unique and confusing to ancient society. This is why the Scriptures provide both criteria and description to us on the diaconate role and its importance in the Kingdom.

Notes on text:

The New Testament establishes the deacon's role as one of service.

Those who serve as deacons are to conduct themselves as Kingdom servants, working through stewardship to build and edify the Kingdom. Despite modern confusion about deacons and their function, the Scriptures are clear on their purpose, expectation, and function of service.

Power points:

- The word "deacon" literally means "attendant" or "servant"[6]. From this definition, we recognize the deacon is a steward of God and servant to the Kingdom of God. The Bible depicts deacons as assisting apostles (Acts 6:1-5) and pastors (Philippians 1:1-2). While not a part of the five-fold ministry, the office of the deacon developed in response to the need of a church administration specifically devoted to meeting the needs of church members, especially those in a state of lack. While inappropriate for apostles to leave the work of the Word (their service to the Kingdom) to wait on tables and raise additional money to help those in need, the diaconate office was established to serve this purpose and meet the needs of those in the church (Acts 6:1-5). We also learn from Stephen's experience deacons operate in signs and miracles (Acts 6:8).

- We could define the diaconate as a practical "helps" ministry for the church. Their purpose is assisting running and church ministries which involve serving others and seeing to their practical needs (Matthew 25:34-40). Deacons are not commissioned by pastors, but by apostles for their duties. They are established in their ministry by the apostles (Acts 6:6). It is also obvious from Acts 6 that deacons serve in Christian ministry as well. In the first establishment of deacons, they were appointed to assist apostles in practical ministry so apostles can focus on apostolic work. Deacons assist apostles and pastors. By extension, they can assist the entire five-fold.

- Deacons are selected for this act of service, appointed for work in the ministry of stewardship. They are to be of honest report, full of the Holy Ghost, and operate in wisdom. Deacons are ordained by apostles for this task (Acts 6:1-7).

- In order to be a deacon, one must be serious, not prone to doublespeak, not prone to drinking, not greedy or into ministry for money, holding to the mystery of faith (revealed by the apostles) in pure conscience (1 Timothy 3:8-9). Women are spoken of here, also as deaconesses, and advised to seriousness, not given to slander, sober, and faithful in all things (1 Timothy 3:8-10). Deacons must be married to only one spouse at a time, able to manage a household well, and good stewards within their own households. The training of a deacon within the home is training for good stewardship and service within the Kingdom of God (1 Timothy 3:11-13). The diaconate ministry is not to run a church, nor is it one where deacons attend to private needs of five-fold ministers. Rather, the deacon is a ministry of stewardship for the entire Body of Christ.

- Many in today's church believe the office of armor bearer is appropriate for New Testament five-fold ministers. The office of the armor bearer was a political military position in Old Testament times. The word is found no more than ten times in the Old Testament, in only a few verses in Judges and 1 Samuel. The armor bearer served to carry the armor and act as a steward for the king and those in the king's camp during battle. They would carry armor, prepare food, and tend to medical needs, as necessary. In some cases, the armor bearer would take the life of the warrior if the warrior was mortally wounded or there was question of disgrace (Judges 9:50-54). The relationship between an armor bearer and a leader was very strong, as we can see in the case of Jonathan and his armor bearer (1 Samuel 14:4-11).

- The word "armor bearer" is not found in the New Testament and there is no evidence to bespeak five-fold ministry leadership employed armor bearers in service. The armor bearer, however, is a type of the deacon, and the important heart of service in the ministry of stewardship necessary in

God's Kingdom. It is no longer a personal office, but one for the Body of Christ.

- The New Testament names eight deacons by name: Stephen, Philip, Prochorus, Nicanor, Timon, Parmenas, Nicolas (Acts 6:5) and Phoebe (Romans 16:1). It was Stephen, a deacon of the church, who was later stoned for his witness (Acts 6:8-15).

- While many believe deacons serve on church boards or to regulate the church, or exist to make executive decisions about who shall pastor or lead a congregation. In reality, this is untrue. Deacons serve a relevant aspect in service to the Body of Christ and seeing every need met, bridging different gifts within the Body and different aspects of service. As Phoebe was commended, so too were all in the church commanded to be of assistance to her as necessary, reminding all of the necessity of service in the Body (Romans 16:1).

Characteristics of the deacon

There are essential characteristics God gives to each individual called to deacon's ministry, enabling him or her to fulfill the teacher's call with full grace and dignity. In looking at some examples of deacons in action, we can see these characteristics clearly.

- **The seven chosen deacons, Acts 6:1-7:** Deacons must be uniquely aware of the needs and issues of others, especially the needs present by members of the Body of Christ. A deacon cannot see a need and desire to simply turn their heads aside, wanting to pretend it does not exist. Deacons are hard-working individuals, as the seven chosen were. They worked in their jobs, recognizing their work was present to profit the Kingdom. For this reason, deacons must be equipped, prepared, and strong to work for the Kingdom of God. A deacon's service profits the Kingdom financially as well as through stewardship of resources and finances, thus deacons must be Kingdom givers. Deacons must be of good report, full of faith and the Holy Spirit so their service can never be questioned or condemned. A spirit of true obedience, both to God and true godly leaders, is observed in a deacon. Deacons are also individuals with a willing spirit, willing to go as far as needed for Kingdom service. A deacon is also interested in representing and spreading the Gospel.

- **Deacon Stephen, Acts 6:8-7:60**: In Stephen's experience, we see him full of grace and power. One can't be of Kingdom service without God's grace and power at work in his or her life. Stephen was also known for his distinct and definitive personality. Being of stewardship, deacons are no-nonsense people. There is no question to the serious nature of need and the immediacy to meet needs, and this is not taken lightly. Deacons are defenders of Kingdom stewardship and service, recognizing the call to serve as good stewards of God's gifts, and are quick to stand in defense of anyone who tries to compromise the true purpose of God's Kingdom service. Deacons are able to speak eloquently and comprehensively by the Holy Spirit's wisdom. They are called to be knowledgeable in the Word as they understand the faith service to which they have been called. Knowing the balance between faith and works, Deacons have the unique ability to rebuke religious nonsense and legalism, blocking people from true repentance. Deacons display their total trust and faith in God.

- **Deaconess Phoebe, Romans 16:1-2**: Deacons do a commendable work. They are truly worthy of acceptance among those they serve, and should never be condemned. Eager to serve, deacons need not be abused or mistreated in the church. As they remind all people to serve, deacons should be assisted in their work and the church body should be eager to assist a deacon. Deacons may take excessive responsibility upon themselves, and need reminding about boundaries, limits, and personal rest. In true style with the office, deacons are a great help to church leaders.

Types of the deacon's ministry

The diaconate ministry is unique to the New Testament. Its call to service, however, is echoed through those who were of service to leaders in Old Testament times. The armor bearer of the Old Testament is a type of diaconate service in the New Testament. With all things revealed the new covenant, we recognize the deacon's office does not serve for a personal purpose, but to bless the entire Kingdom of God.

- **Judges 9:50-54** – *Abimelech's armor bearer*, a type of the deacon's ministry. Abimelech's armor bearer was asked to do something many of us today would consider unthinkable: he was asked to take his leader's life...and he did it. Abimelech's armor bearer saved his leader from reproach, as deacons do by seeing practical needs are met among the house of God. Rather than allow the Kingdom to go into disrepute, deacons stand up and see needs are met that cannot be met by ministry leaders without having to abandon ministry. Stepping up to the plate, the armor bearer uses action to defend the honor and dignity of his leader. The same is true in the church: the armor bearer steps up with action and defends the honor and dignity of Christian ministry and God's Kingdom.

- **1 Samuel 14:4-11** – *Jonathan's armor bearer*, a type of the deacon's ministry. Jonathan's armor bearer reveals the true heart of such service. Just as armor bearers displayed complete trust in their leaders, so do deacons display that trust in God, knowing their service is needed in His church. Deacons have a heart to obey and total faith, just as an armor bearer did.

- **1 Samuel 16:14-23** – *David as Saul's armor bearer*, a type of the deacon's ministry. Sometimes we forget how powerful service can be in a Kingdom, especially God's Kingdom. David's service as an armor bearer shows us service leads to divine promotion, not just with people, but with God. Through such service, the Holy Spirit flows through the individual – especially a deacon – to meet any and every need present.

The historical deacon

- **Lawrence of Rome (225-258)** – Little is known about Lawrence's life, although it is believed he was born in Spain. He was one of seven deacons commissioned to serve over ancient Rome, even though he was young upon his appointment. After the death of his leader, corruption in the church demanded financial assets turned over to the government, to which he rose up and saw as much of the church's assets distributed among the poor and suffering as was possible. He was martyred due to his actions, which were seen as political subvergence.[7]

- **Vincent of Saragossa (d. 304)** – As with most early martyrs, there is little known about Vincent's life. He served as deacon of Valerius of Saragossa, the bishop of that city. He was imprisoned for his faith and tortured, but was successful in converting those who put him in prison. Given the option to be released from jail if he would burn the Scriptures, he refused.[8]

- **Poplia (4th century AD)** – Think women can't be deacons? Think again! History is full of women who served as deacons in both traditional and non-traditional settings. Poplia lived in Antioch during the fourth century. During her marriage, she had a son who later went on to work as a member of the clergy. After the death of her husband, she became a deacon. As part of the historical diaconate, Poplia operated women's ministry, serving in the needs and spiritual work of the women of the church. She later became a martyr as a result of her Christian belief and position.[9]

- **Marthana (400-417)** – This is a story of a woman who clearly didn't live very long, but who was relevant enough to receive mention in Egeria's Pilgrimage to the Holy Sepulchre. Marthana was a deaconess in Jerusalem, mentioned because her entire way of life was known to everyone in the east. In addition to working in her work of diaconate service, she also oversaw monastic women in Jerusalem.[10]

- **Sigolena of Arles (736-769)** –Sigolena of Arles' husband died after ten years of marriage. Even though her parents tried to convince her to pursue another marital relationship, Sigolena sought out a life devoted to the Lord. She was commissioned in a simple rite to the diaconate and later pursued the monastic life as well.[11]

- **The Basque Sorera, Sorora, or Freila (5th to 16th Centuries AD)** – A little-known tradition of ancient France and Spain, these women served in the role of deaconess without being called such. They operated the same exact works, including women's ministry instruction, baptismal assistance, care for the sick, poor, and needy, assisting pastors and ministers, arranging funerals, and supervising the work of the church during services. These women had unique criteria: they had to be at least forty years old, celibate, and remain connected to a consistent parish house or monastery. In their later centuries of existence, they did additional work, including care for the church building.[12]

Questions and answers

- **Were deacons appointed in congregations?**

Yes. Deacons were appointed in congregations, along with pastors (Philippians 1:1, 1 Timothy 3:8-13). It is clear from this role of service that deacons did not just serve as assistants to apostles, but pastors as well. Deacons also served the extensive social needs of the local church, making sure provision was in order for those who were in need.

- **How do deacons assist pastors?**

Pastors deal with the challenge of overseeing congregations. Many today, as probably did in the first century, also maintain work to support their families and their Kingdom purpose. Such is overwhelming to any pastor, let alone trying to maintain financial and practical purposes for the needs of the congregation. In the same way deacons assisted apostles, so do deacons assist pastors: they ensure the practical needs of the congregation are met so pastors can focus on pastoral ministry.

- **Do deacons assist other members of the five-fold ministry?**

As deacons were first appointed by apostles, it is very clear to me that the work of the deacon goes beyond that of the local pastor. There is more than one function to that of the diaconate. Because deacons fill a role of service, they are available to the five-fold and the general body of believers for that purpose.

- **Why are the criteria to be a deacon almost identical to those of an elder?**

Both elders and deacons work with church members in an up-close and personal way. While elders work closely to meet spiritual needs, deacons work to meet practical needs. Such close contact with congregation members demands both elders and deacons stand of high moral caliber, seeing their personal lives enhance their ministry, rather than causing reproach.

- **Would deacons serve in areas of ministry assistance beyond congregational needs?**

Deacons remind the church of the call to serve. Deacons are not the only people called to service in a church. The deacon's ministry does not just serve to meet the needs of people, but to alert the general Body of Christ to the needs present in the Body. Deacons can assist and serve any way they are called, and also encourage others in the church to service as well.

- **Are armor bearers part of the modern church?**

The diaconate exists to be of service, thus I consider the role of the armor bearer as we understand it today to fall under the category of the diaconate. The role that an armor bearer fills as an assistant to a leader (both spiritually and in service) is simply a different form of service, though just as valid and important as any other aspect of service a deacon may fill.

- **What can deacons teach the church?**

Service is a call for everyone in the Kingdom of God. Every person who is a part of the Body of Christ has a call to do something good or relevant for someone else. Matters of spiritual warfare, intercession, prayer, assistance in time of need, edification, care, service during meetings, and general service are not limited to one specific office within the church. We are all created for service! No matter what one's position is in the church, everyone is called to be in support and encouragement to their leaders and to be of service therein.

Discussion, study and review questions:

- How did ancient societies regard slavery and serving others? Why would people be confused about the role of the deacon in the church?

- What does the New Testament establish the diaconate as? Why is certain conduct required of deacons? Is the Word of God clear about the deacon's role?

- What does the word "deacon" mean? What does the deacon do? Who did deacons assist? What function did deacons serve? Why was the diaconate established?

- Are deacons elected or selected? What are they appointed for work for? What type of character should deacons have? Who ordains (affirms) deacons?

- What is the criteria to be a deacon and a deaconess? Why were deacons to manage their own households well? Who is the office of deacon for?

- What is an armor bearer? What function did they serve?

- Should armor bearers be used by New Testament leaders? Why or why not? What is the armor bearer a type of? What do we learn in this type?

- Who were the deacons named in the New Testament?

- What functions do deacons have today? Is this a correct application of the job of a deacon? Why or why not? What important function do deacons play among congregations?

- What are the characteristics of the diaconate ministry? What are the strengths and weaknesses of deacons? How do these characteristics manifest to make them better deacons?

- What are some Old Testament types of the diaconate ministry? How do these types shadow what the diaconate ministry is to represent?

- In looking at the "Historical deacon" section, how were you able to see the appointment of the deacon differently than before? How does this change how you view of deacons in history, even though they may not have been ever called a "deacon?" Who else can you think of in history who was a deacon, even if they were not acknowledged as such?

- Discuss and share some of the questions and answers found in the "Questions and Answers" section. What did you learn that you did not know about deacons and deacon's ministry? What did you learn that changed your mind about an opinion you might have had prior about deacon's ministry? How did learning about specific issues related to deacons and deacon's ministry help you to grow in your understanding of ministry?

The church? Your own relationship with God?

Chapter Twelve

BISHOPS AND ELDERS

It is the special duties of [the bishops] to be concerned about others, not themselves. ... He must be attentive and diligent, even though all others be slothful and careless. Were he inattentive and unfaithful, the official duties of all the others would likewise be badly executed.
– Martin Luther[1]

What is a bishop? What is an elder? Many churches and denominations believe these are titles appropriate for pastors – but are they correct? Even though most denominations accept bishops and elders in some form or another, the appointments are universally misunderstood. Many mistake these works for pastoral offices in one form or another, or use the understandings of these offices as a reason to misunderstand the pastoral calling.

Bishops and elders provide an essential function for the church, and an invaluable role as they assist the work of the five-fold ministry. Upholding these offices as the appointments they are help us to gain a greater respect for their work. It also helps us to better understand the important role demonstrated in the work of oversight and helps ministry.

Text study

1 Peter 5:1-10

Supplementary texts

Acts 20:17-31, 1 Timothy 3:1-7, 1 Timothy 5:17-18, Titus 1:6-16, Titus 2:1-8, James 5:14-15, 2 Peter 2:19-25, Revelation 5:5-14.

Power verse

1 Peter 5:2:

- *"Feed the flock of God which is among you, taking the oversight willingly; not filthy lucre, but of a ready mind."*

- *"I urge you then to see that your "flock of God" is properly fed and cared for. Accept the responsibility of looking after them willingly and not because you feel you can't get out of it, doing your work not for what you can make, but because you are really concerned for their well-being."* (PHILLIPS)

- *"Tend (nurture, guard, guide, and fold) the flock of God that is [your responsibility], not by coercion or constraint, but willingly; not dishonorably motivated by the advantages and profits [belonging to the office], but eagerly and cheerfully..."* (AMP)

- *"Care for the flock that God has entrusted to you. Watch over it willingly, not grudgingly—not for what you will get out of it, but because you are eager to serve God."* (NLT)

- *"Feed ye the flock of God, that is among you, and purvey ye, not as constrained, but willfully, by God [purveying not constrainingly, but willfully, after God]; not for love of foul winning, but willfully..."* (WYC)

- *"Tend the flock of God which is among you, exercising the oversight, not of constraint, but willingly, according to the will of God; nor yet for filthy lucre, but of a ready mind."* (ASV)

Power words

- **Feed** – From the Greek word *"poimaino"* which means, "to feed, to tend a flock, to keep sheep."[2]

- **Flock** – From the Greek word *"poimnion"* which means, "a flock (especially) of sheep; a group of Christ's disciples; bodies of (Christian) churches presided over by elders."[3]

- **Oversight** – From the Greek word *"episkopeo"* which means, "to look upon, inspect, oversee, look after, care for."[4]

- **Willingly** – From the Greek word *"hekousios"* which means, "voluntarily, willingly, of one's own accord."[5]

- **Filthy lucre** – From the Greek word *"aischrokerdos"* which means, "eagerness for base gain."[6]

- **Ready mind** - From the Greek word *"prothumos"* which means, "willingly, with alacrity."[7]

Historical context

1 Peter 5 gives us insight into ethical conduct expected of appointments related to oversight, which are bishops and elders. The first century was an intense time for thought and perspectives on systems of thought. It was not uncommon for people to join certain philosophies or schools of thought to excel in the field for the end goal of making a net profit. Even in the New Testament we can see some regarding the work of God as a money-making enterprise. It

was not acceptable to view the work of God for profit then, and it remains unacceptable today. The attitude of a bishop and an elder must be carefully checked, measured, and examined. These attitudes are to be standard for appointments in every age. Elders were also reminded to work with others. The church cannot be built upon disconnection. To assist in the equipping of the church, bishops and elders must cooperate with other ministers rather than trying to steal or lord control over church members.

Notes on text

False doctrine and modern error have led today's local church leaders into confusing concepts of ministry purpose. Modern churches reflect bishops and elders with roles misunderstood and misapplied. The elder is to be an individual of high conduct, both professionally and personally. Elders are called to be examples, not dictators. They must center themselves on loving the people of God, not on financial gain or profit. An elder should be excited about the work of God, performing all tasks of their ministry with anticipation and eagerness. Much of today's bishopric and eldership can benefit from intensive study about the purpose, integrity, ethics, and conduct established for leadership.

Power points:

- In the New Testament, the appointments of elder, overseer, and bishop were helps ministries to the five-fold ministry (1 Timothy 3:1, 1 Peter 5:1, Acts 20:28). The term "bishop" was added to the King James Version to support the Anglican Communion, and, in reality, is used in place of "overseer" (thereby making an overseer and a bishop the same thing). The different terms refer to different leadership responsibilities and situations. For example, an overseer/bishop may have overseen a specific aspect of a church or ministry, or may have dealt as an overseer in more than one church. It is also possible a bishop held a senior position of oversight, while an elder oversaw more local church responsibilities. Bishops might also have been assigned to oversee a local leader (pastor, teacher, or an evangelist's ministry), while an elder may have seen to more local duties related to congregations. Different leadership terms also might have reflected the size of a community's worship center and the needs present there. Terminology was also used to indicate rank. Elders probably held a longer status in position and duties than younger leaders, and the younger leaders were accountable to older ones (Peter 5:5). The New Testament indicates churches require more than one elder for their function according to New Testament guidelines (Titus 1:5). The primary grace of the bishop's office is caring for God's people, meeting their spiritual needs (1 Peter 5:2-3). The Scriptures describe the bishop's appointment as a "good work" (1 Timothy 3:1). Bishops are also called to have a heart for the people they serve (Acts 20:28-29).

- Bishops, elders, and deacons represent an appointment. This means they are appointed, or assigned for such work. It is different from a five-fold ministry calling in that an appointment is desired and sought by the individual (1 Timothy 3:1) and then the individual is appointed, or assigned to that office by an apostle. These works of oversight and service help assist leaders in their work, in the completion of Kingdom purpose. Apostles, as ones who are sent, cannot be everywhere at once. Bishops and elders ensure that things are carried out according to directive, and proper teaching comes forth in every ministry (1 Timothy 5:17-18). Bishops and elders also ensure good communication between ministers, ministries, churches, and leadership (Acts 20:28-29). This reminds us of the importance in helps ministries. They are not belittling offices, but relevant important appointments in the Body of Christ.

- The term "elder" is used three different ways in the Bible. The first way is to indicate someone is of an older age than someone else (Luke 15:15, Romans 9:12, 1 Timothy 5:1-2). The second way is to indicate a superior in ministry, as in one who is of a higher office than another (Exodus 19:7, Joel 2:16, 1 Timothy 5:19). The third way is to refer to the "elders of the church," as in individuals who serve as overseers over a local congregation (Acts 25:15, 1 Timothy 5:17, Titus 1:5). It is the third definition we will be examining in our look at the appointments of bishop and elder.

- The appointments of bishop and elder specify personal and professional conduct for those who operate therein. The personal conduct for a bishop includes: live blameless (1 Timothy 3:2, Titus 1:6); have only one spouse (i.e., not polygamous) (1 Timothy 3:2, Titus 1:6); be a steward of God (Titus 1:7); the parent of faithful children not given to extraordinary and having the household in order (1 Timothy 3:4-5, Titus 1:7); not given to selfishness or self-will (Titus 1:7); not easily angered (1 Timothy 3:2, Titus 1:7); not a drunkard (1 Timothy 3:3, Titus 1:7); not abusive (1 Timothy 3:3, Titus 1:7); not seeking personal gain (1 Timothy 3:3, Titus 1:7); be hospitable (Titus 1:8); loving those who are good (Titus 1:8); sober (1 Timothy 3:2, Titus 1:8); just (Titus 1:8); holy (Titus 1:8); and temperate (Titus 1:8). One unique requirement is a bishop cannot be a new believer, as a new believer may become prideful and bring disgrace to the appointment (1 Timothy 3:6). The listed professional conduct required: Holds fast to the Word that has been taught (Titus 1:9); have the ability to refute false doctrine and teachers (Titus 1:9, 14); protect the flock entrusted to their care (Acts 20:17-31); and be able to teach (1 Timothy 3:2).

- The personal conduct for an elder includes: working willingly, not by constraint (1 Peter 5:2); not greedy (1 Peter 5:2); ready and eager for work (1 Peter 5:2); not controlling (1 Peter 5:3); an example to the congregation (1 Peter 5:3); humble (1 Peter 5:5-6); sober and vigilant (1 Peter 5:8); and steadfast in faith (1 Peter 5:9).

- The duties of a bishop include: Refute false doctrine and teachers (Titus 1:9-16); oversee the local churches of God (Acts 20:28); pray (Acts 20:36); walk in the gifts of the Spirit (Romans 12:6-8); protect the flock (Acts 20:28-29); and provide for the flock of God (Acts 20:34-35).

- The duties of an elder include: Love and care for the flock of God (1 Peter 5:2); teach and preach to the people of God, ensuring they receive right teaching (1 Timothy 5:17-18); assist apostles in doctrinal examinations to return and provide true teaching to the churches (Acts 15:6); serve as a godly example in the church (1 Peter 5:1-2); pray for the sick (James 5:14-15); and walk in the gifts of the Spirit (Romans 12:6-8). The elder must likewise never forget his or her duty to worship the Lord, as elders are specifically mentioned around the throne of God in Revelation (Revelation 5:5-14).

- The New Testament does not give names of individuals who were elders or bishops, although it is reasonable to assume that in the Apostle Paul's many commendations to leaders in his letters, some were bishops or elders. There may be a number of reasons why bishops and elders are not specifically named in the New Testament. The first possible reason is because as appointments, the individuals were not in the offices permanently. The second reason may be due to the fact that bishops and elders do not operate their own ministries, but rather, are working to assist other ministries; therefore, the focus is on the ministry, rather than the bishop or elder working therein. The third option is that the bishops and elders were so numerous in locations, there were too many of them to list. Whatever the reason was, we know bishops and elders did exist, and are relevant for ministry today.

- There is question in the minds of many as to whether or not a woman can be a bishop or elder, due to the wording used in passages pertaining to bishops and elders. As it is specifically mentioned in connection with wives (1 Timothy 3:2, Titus 1:6), many assume this means women cannot be bishops or elders. If we step back and consider this logically, it would not make sense that women can fill every office of the five-fold ministry and serve as deacons, but not as bishops or elders. Why would a woman have the power to install a bishop as an apostle, but not have the power to install a woman to oversee that aspect of ministry? The fact that it is clear women served as deacons makes it clear that women may indeed be called to serve as a bishop over a women's ministry, a church ministry, or other ministry, and as an elder of the church. The specific nature of men in these passages is due to the ancient society's influences, and the clear understanding that more men probably served as bishops and elders than women did. There are many passages that are gender-specific in the Bible, but we understand through revelation that these passages include women as well as men and do not omit individuals (Psalm 82:6, Matthew 5:9, Romans 8:19, Romans 9:26, Galatians 3:26, Galatians 4:6, Hebrews 2:10). It is also clear that Titus 2:1-8, often translated as being "older women," refers not to women in age, but is actually the Greek word for female elders. In other words, the women elders were admonished to teach both women and men in the church about the right way to live. We need to have that same kind of clarity and understanding as we apply such here, as well.

- While there is no modern debate about the appointments of bishop and elder, these works within the Kingdom are clearly misunderstood, as this study clarified. It is essential the church of today understands the works of bishop and elder, and acknowledges and honors them for such as they are.

Characteristics of bishops and elders

The Bible specifies more personal criteria for bishops and elders than it does for individuals in the five-fold ministry. The reason for this is simple: If one desires this appointment, they must reflect the necessary vision and attitudes to produce fruit within the work. If we look clearly at some of these various criteria, we can understand better why each one of them is important to the appointment of bishops and elders.

- **Above reproach, 1 Timothy 3:2, Titus 1:7 (bishops):** The word "reproach" means "to find fault with." If someone is reproachable, that means there are things people can say that prove someone has poor character. The numerous characteristic traits mentioned in 1 Timothy 3:1-7 all relate to being above reproach: blameless, vigilant, sober, of good behavior, not given to wine, not a striker, not greedy, patient, not a brawler and not a thief. All of these traits refer to character. If a bishop were to be involved in overseeing an aspect of ministry relating to finances, for example, and was given to greed or theft, this would cause question as to the reputation of the ministry. If a bishop has a reputation for domestic violence, this would generate a reputation for the ministry in question. Ministers need to be very cautious about who they place in positions of leadership and supervision within their churches, simply because the reputation of their people becomes their own reputation very quickly.

- **Given to hospitality, 1 Timothy 3:2, Titus 1:8 (bishops)**: Hospitality was an earnestly sought-out gift in ancient times. The way one handled strangers and guests within their house was the foundation to their reputation within society. The reason a bishop must be given to hospitality relates to their ministry of oversight. If a bishop is overseeing an aspect of ministry, they must be service-minded. A bishop needs to be willing to serve both the leader who has appointed them for service and the people who may be affected by that ministry. No leader wants to appoint someone with a nasty attitude to a ministry pertaining to oversight.

- **Ruling well their own house, 1 Timothy 3:4, Titus 1:6 (bishops)** – Over the past twenty years, it has become more and more commonplace to see people distracted on the job. You see people on their cell phones during working hours and trying to track their families' activities while trying to work. It's not uncommon to see workers leave early for varied family functions or because a crisis is going on with a relative. The same is true in today's church. It seems like every time you talk to a minister, they are having a family situation of one sort or another. It is completely understandable that things come up here and there from time to time, but consistent states of crisis shows an inability to manage matters at home. It also shows one will be unable to dutifully oversee an assignment, due to distractions.

- **Worthy of double honor, 1 Timothy 5:17-18 (elders)** – Being worthy of double honor means being so noteworthy and excellent in the work assigned, one goes above and beyond the call of duty into an area that is worthy of double excellency. An elder is called to go above and beyond, making that extra effort in all situations to do the best possible job required.

- **Willingness, 1 Peter 5:2 (elders)** – Being an elder should be an honor, not something done by force. All that goes along with being an elder should also be regarded as an honor. An elder needs to be willing because, as working in an appointment, the leader cannot have to stand over the elder and force them to do the required work of an elder. Someone who has to be forced to do something is not an asset to a ministry.

- **Not greedy, 1 Peter 5:2 (elders)** – In paralleling what was said above about a bishop, an elder can't be greedy because this causes financial issues and questionable reputation within a ministry situation. An elder cannot extort members for money, nor steal.

- **Not controlling, but examples, 1 Peter 5:3 (elders)** – Being a leader is challenging, especially when the job of a leader is to constantly assist and oversee people on a local level. You see the same issues, problems, and complications time and time again, often growing frustrated. It is tempting for a leader to become controlling, especially when the answer to a problem seems obvious. The Word does not call leaders to become hostile or intolerant, but rather, to be examples of what they believe and teach.

- **Humility, 1 Peter 5:5-6 (elders)** – It's impossible to work with someone who refuses to be humble. Pride makes it impossible to discuss matters with a leader and follow through on tasks. It also makes it impossible to be a servant. As elders work in service, both to their leaders and their congregations, they must operate in a spirit of true humility to accomplish every task.

Types of bishops and elders

- **Genesis 39:4-5** – *Joseph*, a type of the bishopric. We've heard the story of Joseph applied many different ways: overcoming, faith, endurance, patience, and trusting God to give us more than we started with. Joseph is also a powerful type of a bishop. He was made an overseer of the house of Potiphar and later an overseer of the entire nation of Egypt. God's blessing for Joseph was in a helps ministry leadership capacity, proving a bishop's appointment is not of lesser importance than those in the five-fold.

- **Exodus 3:16-18, 12:21** – *The Israelite elders*, a type of the New Testament elders. The elders of Israel were tribal or clan heads established for the purpose of governmental representation. The elders represented a certain number of people in each tribe and brought forth the disputes of the people to Moses, Joshua, or other leader. They also brought back responses to disputes and issues, and had the responsibility of implementing the necessary order. In paralleling the elders of the New Testament, they had similar responsibilities: bring forth dispute to apostles, bring back teaching and assessments, maintain order, and teach the people.

- **Exodus 24:14** – *Aaron*, a type of the bishopric. Aaron's call must have been a challenge. Since he wasn't Moses, he wasn't the main leader of the people, but was a leader appointed to help oversee and assist Moses in his ministry. Aaron was, therefore, a type of the bishop, as his work pertained to assistance of an apostolic type and overseeing of the people.

- **Ezra 6:14** – *The elders of the Jews*, a type of the New Testament elders. The elders mentioned in Ezra were active, working group who attended to necessary matters pertinent to both the Kingdom and the city. The Word specifies these elders were appointed in every city, just as those in the New Testament are appointed in every congregation. Elders must be actively involved with their local congregations, understanding the circumstances, involved in the work, and meeting spiritual needs as they arise.

- **Nehemiah 11:9-22** – *Joel son of Zichri, Zabdiel, and Uzzi*, types of the bishopric. These men were appointed as overseers over ministry work and practical work, seeing to the proper execution thereof.

The historical bishop and elder

- **Grapte (c. 148)** – The Shepherd of Hermas, an apocryphal account of a vision that was, at points in history, considered canonical, stipulates that two copies of the writing shall be made and one given to Clement and one to Grapte. Clement, a male bishop, represented the male population of the clergy; Grapte, a female bishop, or overseer, represented the female population of the clergy. Not only does this show the importance of the document, it also shows the important role women played in the early church.[8]

- **Electa (2nd century AD)** – We know almost nothing about Electa, except that Clement of Alexandria identified her as the "Elect Lady" of 2 John. She was believed to be an overseer of women, all of whom were virgins and living a life of chastity, devout to the work of ministry. Most historians agree 2 John was written to a church, but the fact that it was addressed to "Elect Lady" is very important, because it does indicate that a woman served as a leader somehow in connection with that community. Whether or not Clement's connection to this specific woman, women, and writing of John is factual is unknown, but it does prove that women held authority, especially in the capacity of overseeing, in the early church.[9]

- **Francis Asbury (1745-1816)** – Francis Asbury was one of the first two bishops appointed to serve over the Methodist Episcopal Church in the United States. His life was devoted to ministry, and he travelled as an early circuit rider, over thousands of miles to oversee congregations and believers on the American frontier. Starting out as a travelling preacher, Francis Asbury spent over forty-five years doing the work of a minister and overseer. He is also notable for founding several schools.[10]

- **Elders and Eldresses (1747- 20th century)** – The United Society of Believers in Christ's Second Appearing, more commonly known as the Shakers, held a complete belief in the equality of men and women. As a result, two men and two women held the position of elders at the headquarters, Mount Lebanon Shaker Society. They also governed via pairs of elders and eldresses at all their Shaker communities found throughout the United States. The elders within the Shaker communities handled both spiritual and natural matters.[11]

- **Marjorie Swank Matthews (1916-1986)** – Marjorie Matthews served as an American bishop of the United Methodist Church from 1980-1984. She first served as an elder, beginning in 1965. She was the first woman bishop of the United Methodist Church and the second female District Superintendent.[12]

- **United Presbyterian Church in the USA** – An organization that has been appointing both women and men in the church since the 1930s. Since 1978, this church has included a provision in its constitution that both men and women be elected as both elders and deacons in each congregation.[13]

Questions and answers

- **Can a bishop be divorced?**

The Biblical criteria for bishops sates they should have only one spouse (1 Timothy 3:2, Titus 1:6). The words, "having only one spouse," have been used all sorts of ways. Most often, this stipulation is used to justify the exclusion of divorced men and women from ministry. It also is used to make divorced individuals feel unqualified for ministry due to their marital dissolution. The Apostle Paul was not addressing divorce or the reasons why people get divorced in these passages. The passages do not say a leader can have only one spouse for all time. If this passage were a matter of saying leaders can only have one spouse forever, widowed individuals who go on to remarry would also be unqualified for ministry. As we know there is no Biblical prohibition on remarriage after death, this passage is not a statement on divorce and remarriage. This verse is a direct prohibition on polygamy and polyandry. Both customs were common in New Testament times, and pagan religious leaders often lived under polygamous and polyandry relationships. Prostitution was also common as an understanding for religious rites. Bishops may not be married to, living with, or engaging with more than one spouse at a time. Bishops must uphold marriage while they are married, and not commit adultery, host secret households, or carry on in unbecoming conduct with multiple intimate relationships. By extension, we can understand this to be a guideline relevant to all church leadership, both five-fold ministry and all appointment workers, as well.

- **Can women or single men serve as bishops and elders?**

In my book, *Ministry School Boot Camp: Training For Helps Ministries, Appointments, And Beyond*, I write the following:

This is perhaps the most controversial piece of the puzzle, which is given in the context of the bishopric. Many read the Bible's words about a bishop "being the husband of one wife" means it excludes single men and women from the bishopric. Is this indeed the case?

There are numerous statements in the Bible that are delivered in what is known as neuter tense – or masculine tense, which is implied to include women. When the Bible speaks of "Sons of God," nobody reads that to exclude women. Even though it is a gender-specific statement, we do not think it is impossible for women to become a part of the Kingdom of God.

We tend to selectively apply gender-specific wording as we see fit. The issue of the bishopric is one such example. With the bishopric, one is "overseeing" something – they are fulfilling an assigned duty within a ministerial capacity. Anyone who is responsible for something is "overseeing" it – and, thus, we recognize a woman's ability to oversee matters. This same logic applies to the bishopric, and to all helps ministries, in general. The language is not excluding women – it was, most likely addressing a marital issue present in that day and age, which we shall speak of momentarily.

The criteria for bishops and deacons wives were almost the same as for the men, indicating the women held a certain equal status within the community.

The specific nature of this statement is not just about men and women – if we take it so literally, it also excludes singles from serving in the bishopric. The issue was not one of whether or not a bishop was female or not or whether a bishop was single – it was a question as to whether or not a man who was a bishop could be married to multiple women. The prohibition here is on polygamy, or being married to more than one woman at a time. This practice was common in both Greek and Roman culture. Women and single people taking multiple husbands was not an issue; thus, it was not addressed. The Apostle Paul was affirming the exclusivity of marriage between a man and a woman, not the exclusivity of the bishopric to only married men. If someone desires to serve in the bishopric and they are married, they must have only one spouse, at a time. This means if one is divorced and remarried, they must be legally divorced before they can remarry; if one is widowed, they may also be remarried; if one is single, they may serve as a bishop; and if one is a woman, they may also serve, given they are not living a polyamorous lifestyle.

In short – we have to stop using the Bible conveniently to uphold cultural biases and recognize the context behind language usage. Women are not prohibited from serving in any office of the five-fold ministry, nor of serving in the offices of helps. The same is true for single men.

- **Can an individual have an appointment to bishop or elder and be in the five-fold ministry?**

Because there are different ways to understand the concepts and work of "bishops" and "elders," it is possible to extend the understanding to include work of the five-fold ministry. For example, The Apostle Peter refers to himself as an "elder" in 1 Peter 5:1. This doesn't mean he was no longer an apostle, but it does mean that as part of his work, he worked in cooperation with elders and oversaw their work. In being an example, he too did the work of an elder. If we truly understand a bishop as an overseer, anyone with a ministry technically "oversees" that work. There is one major difference, however, between the five-fold ministry and the appointments of bishops and elders. A bishop or elder is appointed for their work by a minister in the five-fold. It is an assignment given to specifically do something. This is different from a ministry calling, which is for life and irrevocable. A bishop and elder will, at some point, reach the end of their service in that role, while a five-fold minister will continue therein. Even though certain understandings of the words can be understood to include the duties of both, appointments are different from ministry callings. Yes, an individual in the five-fold may hold an office of appointment, especially considering the work they do in the ministry.

- **Why is the language the same for a bishop, elder and pastor if they are not one office?**

The language for the works of bishop, elder, and pastor are similar because they are all offices of oversight, or offices by which someone or something is governed by someone else. When assessing the offices of bishop, elder, and pastor, they all have many things in common. All of them relate to people, and all of them relate to responsibilities that extend to ministries and local churches. This means that, by the nature of their work, they do work that is, at times, alike. This calls for understanding. It is easy to read something in English and assume, because of similar words, that something is the same, when it is not. Just because offices and appointments have duties that are alike does not make them one and the same.

- **Why are pastors of churches sometimes called bishops or elders?**

Pastors of churches are sometimes called bishops or elders due to the beliefs of their denominations. Many denominations are in error about the nature of bishops, elders, and pastors. There is any number of reasons for this error. Many denominations emerged in different times and eras, where understanding about such matters was muddled. Some are carrying on the traditions of their ancestors in the faith without considering the accuracy of them. Some have been blinded by denominations that say the three works are all one office, even though they are not. Such groups need to be taught the truth on these matters, and receive that truth so they can better understand God's system and principles relating to order in church.

- **What is an archbishop?**

An archbishop is a designation within the bishop's work. It signifies a higher status than a bishop. This designation is unbiblical by its nature (there is no such thing as an archbishop in the New Testament), although very common. It is seen in the Roman Catholic, Orthodox Catholic, Anglican, Episcopalian, Methodist, and assorted Pentecostal denominations with ties to liturgical religious denominations.

Discussion, study and review questions:

- What are appointments related to oversight? What insight does 1 Peter 5 give into these appointments? What concepts were prevalent in the first century? What was not uncommon? Is it acceptable to view the work of God as a means for financial gain? What attitudes are the standard of appointments in every age? Why are elders reminded to work with others? What must elders and bishops do to assist in the equipping of the church?

- What things have led local leaders into error? What kind of person should an elder be? What should an elder be excited about? What can today's bishops and elders benefit from?

- In the New Testament, what were the appointments of bishop, elder, and deacon? Where does the term "bishop" come from? What do these different terms refer to? For example, what might a bishop have done? What might an elder have done? What else might these varied terms represented? What is the primary grace of the bishop's office? How do the scriptures describe the bishop's appointment? What are bishops called to have?

- What do bishops, deacons, and elders represent? What does this mean? How is this different from a five-fold ministry calling? How do these works of oversight assist the five-fold ministry? How do bishops and elders insure good communication between leaders and communities? How does this validate the relevance and importance of helps ministries?

- How is the term "elder" used in the Bible? In terms of an appointment, how is the word "elder" used?

- What is the required personal conduct for a bishop?

- What is the required personal conduct for an elder?

- What are the duties of a bishop?

- What are the duties of an elder?

- Are any bishops or elders named in the New Testament? What are some of the reasons why this may be?

- Can women serve as bishops and elders? Why is there a question about this issue? What is most logical and reasonable in approach on this issue? Why is the language of the New Testament worded as it is in these passages? How can we understand them, and what does this mean for women in these appointments?

- Why is it important the church of today understand the appointments of bishop and elder?

- What are some Old Testament types of the bishopric and elder's appointment? How do these types shadow what the appointments of bishops and elders are to represent?

- In looking at the "Historical elders and bishops" section, how were you able to see these appointments differently than before? How does this change how you view of elders and bishops in history? Who else can you think of in history who were elders and bishops, even if they were not acknowledged as such?

- Discuss and share some of the questions and answers found in the "Questions and Answers" section. What did you learn that you did not know about bishops and elders? What did you learn that changed your mind about an opinion you might have had prior about the appointments of bishops and elders? How did learning about specific issues related to bishops and elders help you to grow in your understanding of ministry? The church? Your own relationship with God?

Section 4

MINISTRY AND CHURCH ORDER

Chapter Thirteen

DISCUSSING PROPER UNDERSTANDINGS OF CHRISTIAN MINISTRY WITH OTHERS

> Engage in conversation with intelligent people, and let the Law of the Most High be the topic of your discussions.
> – Sirach 9:15 (GNT)

An increasing number of Christians are turning attention toward the relevance of the five-fold ministry and order within ministerial offices and appointments. Dialogue is great because it gets people thinking, facilitates important discussion, and starts the process toward God's change. As the church takes an interest in its leadership and who its leaders will be, more will begin looking to the Scriptures about these matters. It is a time of encouragement and challenge on the topic of church leadership.

With the grace of dialogue also comes opposition. We must prepare ourselves, as agents of change, for the difficult as well as the encouraging. Many traditional religious leaders have set themselves aside from Christian leadership order and principles, establishing many arguments to justify their positions. Many famous names (some of whom are considered scholars) are vehemently against the idea of a restored five-fold ministry, and provide plenty of arguments. How do we talk to people like this or influenced by this?

Today's evangelistic emphasis is on testimony and giving testimony. The church is trained to tell others what Jesus has done for them, in the belief this alone is sufficient to reach others for Christ. There is nothing wrong with giving testimony, and within church structure, such definitely has its place. However, not all evangelism boils down to telling someone about what Jesus has done in your life. There are plenty of people in this world who don't care what Jesus has done in your life, and don't want to hear about it. Personal effects and experiences don't rock a doctrinal core. Many want to see evidence of claims rather than just hear about personal experience.

The ecumenical and interfaith movements of the twentieth century have not helped Christian understanding of doctrine and belief, either. Both movements push to set aside doctrinal differences and focus on core aspects of belief, most of which are personal. Order and authority are deemphasized, as they often create conflict. As concepts of Christianity become more personalized and watered down, many believers don't have the first clue of what their faith is really about. Because everything is so personalized, we do not know how to share or discuss doctrinal realization. The church today does not know or understand the art of discussion, especially on important matters. Shying away from controversy does not help us learn how to discuss important and essential matters, because it does not give us the opportunity to be taught. As a result, today's church does not know because it has not been taught.

In order to discuss matters of faith (especially matters of doctrine and order) we must be prepared for the various situations that may arise. We live in a church that is extremely forum-driven, or centered on people's personal concepts of faith and opinions about what is true, appropriate, or doctrinally correct. Their ideas may or may not line up with Scripture, and are often a mix of Scriptural and unscriptural ideas. This combination makes for frustrating debate and disrespectful believers. Most believe it is their divine right to voice any opinion they may have about any subject. The restoration of true Christian ministry, both in conduct and order, is especially threatening to this viewpoint: it erodes the notion that everyone gets to decide what they think is true. As a result, people are very quick to voice their thoughts about Christian ministry and whether or not they will accept such authority in their lives. A discussion on Christian leadership can quickly turn into a fever-pitched argument with a forum-driven church member or leader.

People hold very fixed concepts and beliefs when it comes to religion. Legalism implants itself in the minds of adherents to the point of unreasonable defensiveness on topics threatening to the mindset. Legalistic people read things a certain way, interpret matters a certain way, and believe in a certain way because as they stand by the letter of their man-made law, they can retain an unchanging stance. One is correct to state this is bondage; however, it is a comfortable bondage for many. Legalism provides a complete four-walled approach to belief, providing everything anyone will ever need to know in the basics of their belief, which never expands or grows with time.

Legalism provides self-righteousness, self-centeredness, and the belief that one is always right, whether or not they are. The result of legalism resembles that of the Pharisees, those who believe they have diligently studied something to the end of every answer when they miss what is most obvious. As dialogue on the relevance of the five-fold ministry begins to challenge traditional legalistic concepts, ideas, and mindsets, more so-called experts will rise to uphold traditional concepts of ministry and church. Their motive is the desire to maintain their control and unchallenged positions.

In defensive argument, legalism shifts the argument, making it personal rather than topical. They question the minister: "Why do you think you have the right to minister?" "Who gave you the right to call yourself an apostle?" "Who do you think you are as a woman, challenging men?" "How can you call yourself a prophet?" "Who are you to make such lofty claims?" Such an attitude can't be overcome by answering their questions as they are worded. Nothing anyone says or does, no matter how convincing, will change their position. Reducing the argument to a personal level makes it one of opinion instead of truth. That is the inherent goal in the debate: make the argument personal, argue one's claims and experience, and deflate the issue to one of opinion.

It is not impossible to talk to these people. To do so, we must reassess our purpose and motives. We are not going to win everyone over with our arguments. Sometimes we must walk away from the Pharisees, as Jesus did; leaving them speechless rather than verbose. Jesus was an effective evangelist because He knew to whom He was speaking. Jesus did not speak to the Pharisees like He spoke to the Samaritan woman at the well or the crippled man by the pool. We too must begin to examine our evangelism methods and learn how we can better reach people by knowing who they are and how to address them.

How do we discuss Christian ministry in a way that will reach people? What we must seek to do is present the power of the ministry itself than our opinions of it. This can be challenging, especially when we are passionate about the Word and the way it has transformed our perspectives and viewpoints. Here are some important guidelines for talking about the five-fold ministry in a way that will make people think, rather than argue:

- **Reassess your purpose** – We often go into discussion with the intent to voice our viewpoint. There is nothing wrong with this in theory, but…how well is this concept working for you? Are you able to bring about transformation to people, or does it become a matter of you say, they say? If we are going to witness effectively on doctrinal matters, we need to change our purpose in speaking. Before speaking, we need to establish our purpose in mind: this is not about my opinion, but presenting truth. Whether or not someone agrees is up to them, but the purpose is to present truth rather than voice opinion.

- **Inform yourself** – We are speaking on faith and the things of God. Too often we believe this reduces the discussion to speech from our hearts rather than our heads. It is true we don't understand everything about faith. Faith is not about logistics, rules, and memorization. On the other hand, doctrine is something we must seek to know and understand if we are to believe it fully and present it to others. We can't just stand back and label things as mysterious, unknowable, or unfathomable to those who don't believe. We also can't say we believe in something such as the five-fold ministry and appointments and then not even understand it from a Biblical perspective. If we leave holes in our theories, those who seek to contradict the Word will find those holes and rip them open. Get informed! Study about Christian ministry, hear teaching on it, be around leaders who uphold it, and don't just believe in it, know it!

- **Don't expect change to happen overnight** – I love the idea of instant conversion: people who immediately see the error of their ways and change to God's ways in a split-second. I also recognize this is the exception to conversion rather than the rule. For most people, conversion is a process of turning from one's own way to God's way. Belief is an essential aspect to this process, as individuals shift from upholding their opinions to upholding God's Word. It's a blessed process, a glorious process...and with some, a slow process. Sometimes we don't see the results we seek, seeing resistance and defensiveness instead. We must remember that in all we do, we are sowing seeds, seeking to bring about change and repentance, even if we don't' see it. Every opportunity we have is an opportunity to sow a seed. Sow seeds and trust God for the rest.

- **Be clear** – Muddled, confusing messages with an overabundance of references, information, and opinions are inappropriate when discussing the things of God. God has made discussion of the five-fold ministry very easy and clear to follow. We don't need a lot of extra definitions or sidebar conversation. Allow the Word to be clear and speak for itself.

- **Distinguish genuine inquiries from argumentation** – Sometimes people come to us under the guise of asking a question with the intent to argue. Even though the argument may come in the form of a question, a strong and dominating opinion is found in its contents. They work by seeking to rile defensive emotions and strong feelings within about the topic at hand. Avoid arguments of this nature because nothing beneficial comes out of them. When someone genuinely is seeking, it is important to present information; but when someone is just looking to badger, offend, or put someone in their perceived place, it is better to leave it alone.

- **Avoid the game, "a verse for a verse"** – "A verse for a verse" is argument dialogue where someone presents a Bible verse contradicting an opposing viewpoint and upholding theirs…and then you provide a Bible verse contradicting their viewpoint and upholding yours…and then they provide one…and you provide one…and so on. This never-ending technique is not meant to change minds or ask questions, but to create a doubtful debate about what the Word teaches. The Word can't uphold cessationalism and the five-fold ministry at the same time, no matter how many verses are shown which seem to indicate so. The Bible is not a series of unconnected verses, but the living Word of God designed to be read in a whole context. Before the verse presented there is another verse; after it there is another verse; and there are chapters and books also a part of the context in which we must understand the Word. Presenting a verse for this or that argumentatively does not prove either viewpoint. It proves people need to study the Word under inspired leaders and gain a contextual viewpoint of all God has to say on a doctrinal issue.

- **Experience is great…but it's not enough** – I would love to tell you all that we live in a world where you can say "God called me" and that is enough to legitimize your ministry work. Unfortunately, it doesn't work like that. Personal experience is essential for us to have because it validates the faith and facts behind our work. Personal experience, however, is not the faith and facts of ministry. We need to have more of an answer to our ministry offices, appointments, and work than "God called me for it." People need to see the Word in action, history, context, and understanding to our work. This legitimizes it far more than just making a claim that can't be backed up without the Word.

- **Don't make it personal** – It's difficult to discuss these matters with friends, relatives, and people we have known for a long time. To people who knew us "back then," we will forever be who we were "back then." Presenting new ideas doesn't always go over real well with people who are stuck in a relationship boundary that no longer exists. It can hurt when we are confronted with contradictory attitudes or offensive behavior by loved ones, especially when we want to see them receive God's truth. Don't let this debate reduce you to personal picking, bringing up things that happened ages ago, or offenses for personal feelings. If you can't stick to the witness at hand, it is better to let the discussion rest and be handled by someone else at another point in time.

- **Respect the offices in your own walk** – It doesn't make sense to say the offices of apostle, prophet, evangelist, pastor, and teacher are relevant and then not respect such leadership. It doesn't make sense to say you believe in appointments and then confuse the work of bishops, elders, and deacons. Upholding respect for Christian ministry is a great conversation starter because the living witness challenges conventional religious concepts. Believing in God's form for leadership may mean changing the church you attend, disassociating with a denomination, or leaving behind old ways of thinking. We must remember that there is no price too great for truth, and if God leads us into truth, we must also depart error.

- **Be of service** – Many believe Christian ministry is used as an excuse to demean, enslave, or mistreat others. They have drawn these conclusions from observing certain behaviors, both from leaders and followers, where people are excessively demanding or subservient. Don't forget the basic call to service present in Christianity, whether a Christian minister or not. How we are of service determines our leadership training for service, and our understanding of what it means to be a part of God's Kingdom.

Chapter Fourteen

THE FORUM-DRIVEN CHURCH

'I know your deeds, that you are neither cold nor hot; I wish that you were cold or hot. So because you are lukewarm, and neither hot nor cold, I will spit you out of My mouth. Because you say, "I am rich, and have become wealthy, and have need of nothing," and you do not know that you are wretched and miserable and poor and blind and naked, ¹⁸ I advise you to buy from Me gold refined by fire so that you may become rich, and white garments so that you may clothe yourself, and that the shame of your nakedness will not be revealed; and eye salve to anoint your eyes so that you may see. Those whom I love, I reprove and discipline; therefore be zealous and repent.
– Revelation 3:15-19 (NASB)

One of my most vivid life memories is me, standing in my seventh grade homeroom, toe-to-toe with a girl we could call my "archenemy." We never got along, not from day one. She was the total opposite of everything I was. She liked to snuggle up to authority; I couldn't stand the authority in the school I attended. She excelled at everything she was supposed to excel; I so excelled at nothing. She paid attention in church; I talked to my boyfriend and let the song books bang in their holders. When it came to topical issues of the day, we agreed on nothing: not politics, not social issues, not even how to get a project done. She represented one extreme, and I the other. On this particular day of my recall, we were arguing about a political topic of the times. Even though we weren't even old enough to vote, we both took extreme interest in current events and were somewhat knowledgeable of the subjects we spoke. There we stood, debating back and forth, hot and heavy and infuriated through it. Both of us were completely determined to make the other see the point of view we were coming from, and couldn't get why we couldn't change the mind of the other. It was quite a scene: other kids started watching us, sitting around with mouths agape as the argument escalated. Somehow our debate ended because it had to, but I know had we had all day to stand there and argue, we would have.

It was incredible, unspeakable, and yet...pointless. For such a notorious debate, would any of you be surprised to learn our endless debating had absolutely no end? Neither one of us changed our viewpoints. We did not walk away with any sense of respect for the other's perspective, and we certainly didn't find we had any common ground. The President of the United States didn't hear about our debate and think he should call us in to enhance public policy. It didn't endear our fellow classmates to us; if anything, I think a lot of them walked away thinking we just liked to argue (and I can't say they were wrong in that assessment!). Our teachers weren't even interested in the fact that we could put up a debate and argument with the best of them. Out of all that energy spent debating, yelling, fighting, and putting up a good front, none of it accomplished...anything.

I remember this incident because it reminds me a lot of trends I am noting as an apostle in today's church. I've been a Christian since 1999, an apostle for a good portion of those fifteen years, and over the period of time I have worked in ministry (seventeen years now), I have seen a number of changes occur within Christianity. I remember the pastor was regarded as the ultimate in those early days of my faith, to the point where many were out of control in their offices. There were reports of pastors who told people who to marry in their churches, what offices they were to walk in and what gifts they could exercise in the church. We never heard about apostles and seldom, if ever, about prophets. While congregants might have had opinions, they seldom voiced them. What people used to do after church was go out and gossip about the pastor and other people present and voice their opinions in a lesser-stated way. While some churches were noted for an electoral structure, the majority of churches had no say in who their leaders were, how their leaders operated, or in any way in what their leaders did. When I received my call to be an apostle, it was a big deal; I was thought to be usurping authority already in place. As there was a great push toward the local church and people being in local churches, apostles were thought to be a problem, rather than a solution. It was a different world, and in many ways, a radically different church back then. The way the church functioned, structured, and operated was very different than the way it does today.

Not all the changes to the church have been bad. The dictator-like states some pastors had running in their churches were cause for alarm, and definitely cause for reform. A church without the five-fold ministry is a church missing vital aspects of its leadership. Pastors need to know their place in the structure of ministry as much as other offices need to know as well. Church members likewise can't feel oppressed and downgraded, as if they are less important than their leaders. We need to recognize that church is not just a buzz term for local congregants, and see the bigger picture of ministry as a whole. Yet with all these positive changes, we need to step back and address a modern phenomenon in Christianity today: the forum-driven church.

The forum-driven church reminds me in many ways of the debate I had in junior high which I spoke of at the beginning of this article. Its major mark is that everyone has an opinion - everyone voices that opinion - and nobody gains anything from the endless voicing of opinions. The concept is that every member has a relationship with God and is therefore entitled to voice their opinions, no matter how irrelevant or inappropriate voicing those opinions may be. It is not uncommon to see the exact opposite of what was seen years ago: church members openly interrupt and argue with church leaders during sermons or lessons they disagree with; members with no training and no vision seek to usurp authority from seasoned and well-intentioned leaders; and church leadership is selected based on who likes who the best. It is difficult for ministers to develop a strong following because people stick around until the second they start to disagree with something. Internet forums have become a popular way for the forum-driven church to accelerate: people bicker, fight, debate, and argue with no end in sight over issues that are either already settled or totally irrelevant. A blog written by a church member not in leadership is given the exact same weight and consideration as one written by an apostle or prophet. Even though we may not want to face this reality, the more forum-driven the church becomes, the more divided it becomes as well. With so many opinions, so much focus on issues that don't really matter, and so many useless debates, many think the church is nothing more than a loud and disagreeable think tank. This is not the way God designed the church to be!

Just like the forum-driven fad of today, the first century too was a place of debate, thought, and universal contribution to situations. Philosophical schools existed in the pursuit of thought, the art of debate, and the method of rhetoric. Democracies and republics brought personal opinion and values to the realm of politics. This attitude, however, of completely open-ended discussion and boundary-less opinions, did not have place in the church. Titus 3:9 advises: *"But avoid foolish controversies and genealogies and arguments and quarrels about the law, because these are unprofitable and useless."* (NIV) This passage clearly cautions us against the dangerous world where everyone's opinions, thoughts, and perspectives are given the same amount of consideration. Where are the boundaries of opinion and debate? The New Testament gives us good model and structure to go by when it comes to matters of opinions, debates, and settling issues:

- **When it comes to matters of leadership, doctrinal debate or clarity, and moral issues which pertain to faith, it is the duty of leadership to assess and clarify** - The issues are to be handled by church leadership, namely apostles and pastors (Acts 15:1-21). Pastors are present not for debating purposes, but to receive the revelatory teaching of the apostles back to their congregations and select individuals fit to relay word of the council (Acts 15:22-35). Apostles and prophets are the foundation of the church, with Christ as cornerstone (Ephesians 2:20). Apostles are vested with a divine revelation of Christ, special and unique to the office, and it is the job of the apostle to reveal the mysteries of God as result of that revelation (1 Corinthians 4:1-2). If a matter does not seem clear in the Scriptures, it is the duty of the leadership to make it clear. It is not for the church body to vote, debate, or decide on their own as to what is true theologically and doctrinally. Truth is not a debate up for discussion! This is not an affront on the gifts of individual members of the body; this is not to say that the gifts of the individual church member not in the five-fold ministry are irrelevant; but the purpose of spiritual gifts within the church is not to establish or clarify doctrinal issues. It is likewise totally inappropriate for a church member or visitor to openly stand up or argue with a minister while they are preaching or teaching as church meetings are not a public debate forum. If there is question about a matter, it may be brought to the leader after the meeting has concluded (Acts 15:2, Acts 15:6).

- **Christians of all callings, offices, and with all gifts need to avoid needless debates** - How can we identify a "needless debate?" Needless debate is anything that does not lead to life, but instead, leads to division and argument (Titus 3:3-8). The Bible is clear on many different issues. At the same time, God's Word is amazingly silent on many issues which pertain to personal morals and ethics. This means if the Word is silent, we too are to be silent (1 Corinthians 10:23-33, Romans 14:1-23). While it is perfectly acceptable to have a personal opinion or to research or study issues, it is also important to keep non-essential issues out of church debate, statements of faith, witness to non-believers, and doctrine. Discussing these issues back and forth with no merit bears no fruit, especially because these issues grow to divide and conquer the body for no sustainable reason. Opinion can't be the guiding force of why we go to a church, follow a ministry, or support ministry leadership; we must be there, follow, and support because it reflects the truth of God (2 Corinthians 3:1-6).

- **It is not the position of church members to voice their opinions about everything because, when it comes to the essential matters of faith, they are not up for debate (1 Corinthians 2:12-16)** - It is irrelevant what any of us may think about what is true; it is our job to transform to God's precepts rather than enforce and debate our own.

- **Ministry is not by election, but by divine appointment** - Church leadership is not up for debate, and is not discovered through the election of leaders (Ephesians 4:11-17). God appoints and calls leadership, and the ministries of leaders are confirmed by their ministries and upholding of Scriptural standards (2 Corinthians 4:1-12). If there is a question of ungodly leadership, members are to bring the issues unto the church leadership for disciplinary action. If one is unsatisfied with the outcome, there is always the option to find another ministry or church more in alignment with God's Word. The answer is NOT to discuss the issues, but to see that they are addressed as debating, discussing, or voting on the issues won't solve them.

Everyone is called to participate in the church. We can see from the call to be a part of the body (1 Corinthians 12:1-31) that every member has a participatory role in church. We learn, however, that not everyone is called to the same role, and we certainly can establish that everyone participating in church leadership is unscriptural. As we understand the church to operate by spiritual gifts - and different gifts at that - it is unreasonable to allow people without a gift for leadership to stand in a decision or forum-participatory role when it comes to leadership matters in the church. In a forum-driven world, the entire church body must remember that God is of order, and not confusion (1 Corinthians 14:33). This means that there will be times when everyone is called to refrain from voicing an opinion, sharing a thought, or expressing a perspective. Let's be reminded of Ecclesiastes 3:7: *"There is a time to be silent and a time to speak."* (NIV) May we never forget the time to be silent comes before the time to speak.

Chapter Fifteen

ONE UNIVERSAL CHURCH: THE CHURCH BEYOND THE LOCAL COMMUNITY

I myself have been made a minister of this same Gospel, and though it is true at this moment that I am suffering on behalf of you who have heard the Gospel, yet I am far from sorry about it. Indeed, I am glad, because it gives me a chance to complete in my own sufferings something of the untold pains for which Christ suffers on behalf of his body, the Church. For I am a minister of the Church by divine commission, a commission granted to me for your benefit and for a special purpose: that I might fully declare God's Word—that sacred mystery which up to now has been hidden in every age and every generation, but which is now as clear as daylight to those who love God. They are those to whom God has planned to give a vision of the full wonder and splendour of his secret plan for the sons of men. And the secret is simply this: Christ in you! Yes, Christ in you bringing with Him the hope of all glorious things to come.
– Colossians 1:24-27 (PHILIPPS)

One thing anyone within Christianity has heard a lot about is the "local church." Most of us were told, at some point in time, that we need to find ourselves a local church and set ourselves up there - staying there consistently, under the same pastor or leader, in order to receive what we need from God. Some individuals go to the vast extreme to discourage anyone and everyone from ever leaving that church, no matter what error or wrong may occur there; and we also see the extremes of people being told they have to go to a local church and "settle" on one, even though they may disagree on part of what is taught doctrinally. We also have the experience that people are often so into the concept of a local church that they forget about the bigger church picture, failing to realize Christians are found all over the world, not just in a local community within the United States. I've personally experienced the testimony of many who found themselves so wounded by an immediate local church that they lost all sight of faith in Christ and the bigger Christian picture - and simply abandoned Christianity all together. Others see the displays of some churches as an opportunity to mock and defame Christ because the representation of such religiosity is so poor that one can't help but believe something has to be wrong.

The struggle between that which is local and that which is universal

These varied responses about the local church tell us two things about it. The first is that the local church has the opportunity to represent Christianity in a powerful way to those who are immediately impacted by its presence. The second is that the local church, while receiving many such opportunities to represent Christianity, has to represent that balance as both local and universal. This balancing act of presenting both a universal faith and response to both universal and immediate need is a delicate one, and not to be taken lightly. It is why, as Christians, we must take a serious look at the local church and examine its place within the universal body of Christ rather than seeing the universal church as a larger extension of the local community.

There is no doubt that the local church has always made up an important aspect of Christianity. As the church began to grow, history shows a struggle between the expanding church and the local church. We can see from church history that when universal control is implemented upon the local body, the local church becomes nothing more than a mouthpiece for religious politicians. When a small oligarchy emerged to battle over the entire worldwide church, the first thing that notably disappeared was the five-fold ministry. One of the most powerful purposes held for apostles, prophets, and evangelists alike is to remind local churches of the universality of the body. As these three offices have traditionally served itinerantly, we can clearly see the relevance they would play to constantly remind the local communities and churches they visited about the fact that there is more to recognize, do, and believe than what just may be immediately taught by local authorities. The apostle, prophet, and evangelist certainly did not and do not operate to lord control or intimidate others - but they do hold a powerful relevance to bridge the universal and local churches together. A notable absence of these offices in history should awaken us and make us all aware of the great importance in the fully-functioning five-fold ministry. It also reminds local leaders that they indeed are not the end of the line as ultimate authorities, and do likewise have to be accountable for what they teach beyond themselves.

Yet in modern times where the universal body is sometimes denounced, we see problems emerge that display the exact opposites of those created when the local church is ignored. One of the greatest emerging problems of the past fifty or so years has reared itself in the form of controlling local leaders. Numerous reports exist showing forth local leadership which takes upon itself the right to tell people who to marry, what gifts they may or may not walk in within the church, what jobs they can take, how many children they can have, and threaten church members with hellfire or disobedience to God if they decide to leave the church or disregard the dictates of the leaders. In my own life, I have experienced more local leaders like this than not; and it has been my own experience that these leaders are often one of the biggest oppositions to the modern rise in apostles today. I don't question there are many sincere local church leaders who genuinely seek the best for their congregations and lead as tender shepherds; but we likewise can't pretend that individuals do not exist who are out there, giving local church a bad name. It is such leaders who create the thousands of victims of spiritual abuse walking around among us today; people who have grown so scarred by their images of defective leadership that they find themselves unable to face God in a personal and life-changing way.

Another common problem we see is the over-emphasis of the local church in which members lose sight of everyone else. We have reduced persecution to a trite expression uttered when someone at work doesn't want to attend church with us and completely forgot that people still intensely suffer for their faith. Somewhere in the world right now, as you read this, there is a man, woman, or child dying for their faith in Christ. In many countries in this world, someone can risk losing their job, their housing, their children, and their very life because they are a Christian. There are believers everywhere in the world - and there are Christian apostles, prophets, and evangelists laboring for the Gospel in other cities, countries, and territories beyond a local church for the pursuit of the Gospel. Such workers can never be forgotten, even when somebody attends a local church.

There is also the issue of local churches which try to be universal on their own, with a pastor or leader that tries to fill the role of the five-fold ministry in one man or woman. In so doing, the church often becomes about reaching more people without meeting their needs. It is possible for a local church to be so impersonal and distant that the church can become totally void of teaching substance. There are many churches today which pride themselves in such; they claim to be about reaching non-believers, yet ignore the needs of developing and growing Christians to walk as the mature sons and daughters of God. The local church has the job to respond to the immediate needs of its community - including spiritual needs. This means that there is something for everyone in the church at any stage of spiritual growth; those who are new believers are not ignored and neither are those who have been walking with the Lord for a long time.

It is also a frequent problem that local churches provide nothing but, as they would say, "teaching" to the community. The church definitely has a spiritual call, which cannot be ignored; but the local church can neither deny its call by Jesus to meet the practical needs of those who are hurting (Matthew 25:31-46). This balance is achieved by recognizing that by meeting practical needs we open the door to meet spiritual needs; even Jesus Himself used common, ordinary means of practical means to meet and illustrate spiritual needs (Luke 9:14-17).

Why the church is universal

According to the *Merriam-Webster Online Dictionary*, the word "universal" means: *"1: including or covering all or a whole collectively or distributively without limit or exception; especially : available equitably to all members of a society 2 a: present or occurring everywhere b: existent or operative* *everywhere or under all conditions 3 a: embracing a major part or the greatest portion (as of humankind) b: comprehensively broad and versatile 4 a: affirming or denying something of all members of a class or of all values of a variable b: denoting every member of a class 5: adapted or adjustable to meet varied requirements (as of use, shape, or size) < a universal gear cutter>."[1]*

It is important to understand how the church fits into the definition of universal in order to recognize it is not merely a local body, but a universal one. How is the church universal?

- The body of Christ is universal because Christ died not just for the immediate handful of believers who followed Him through His earthly ministry, but for every person in the world who might come to repent and believe in Him (John 3:16). The church is not just for a certain ethnicity, group, or organization, but is open to everybody; it is not exclusive. Universality emphasizes inclusivity; an over-emphasis on locality emphasizes exclusivity.

- The church exists everywhere because the New Testament tells us the Kingdom of God is within us and among us (Luke 17:21). We are the building of God, and the temple of the Holy Spirit (1 Corinthians 3:9, 16). Anywhere there is a believer, there is the church. The church exists under all sorts of conditions, situations, and cultures worldwide; and it is still the church, with the same God operating in believers (Ephesians 4:6). We can believe in what is true despite our cultural, language, or societal differences.

- The church is universal because it is not based on economic status. Anyone from any class, category, or income status can believe in Christ and is equal in the sight of Christ (James 2:1-12).

- The church challenges traditional notions of sexism and racism. It is religion which builds these walls solid, but God truly reveals there is neither male nor female, slave nor free, Jew or Gentile, but a true oneness among believers who have died to themselves and risen to life in Him (Galatians 3:26-

29).

Thus the church is universal because it is the one new humanity born in Christ. It is a Kingdom, not a mere earthly society; and it shall never end. And what we must recognize is that the local church does indeed have a place in the universal body of Christ; however, the universal body is not the extension of the local church. The local church is a small, immediate body of the larger body of believers. It is a type, or reflection, of that larger glory which we can recognize transcends cultures, languages, and barriers through the eternal Spirit of God.

Purposes of the local church in light of universality

- **The church operates to function for meeting** - The Scriptures tell us not to forsake the assembling of ourselves together (Hebrews 10:25). Understanding the church to be the "called out" ones recognizes we must do something now that we are called out. The local church functions for believers to gather together, meet, fellowship, worship, pray, praise, and learn. It is a powerful forum for learning and teaching. The local church, however, does not have to be a group that formally meets on Sundays in a building and promptly ends at 12 PM. Communities in the New Testament met a wide variety of needs; we see communities that met in homes (Romans 16:5), local groups that seemed to have assembled in buildings specifically for the churches (Romans 16:16), and individuals who were even taught by individuals in their own homes (Acts 18:26). Fellowship in the New Testament likewise went far beyond a Sunday morning meeting; the church of Acts seems to have met daily and engaged in the sharing of communion, breaking bread in the form of meals, sharing items, and giving in collections (Acts 2:42-47).

- **The local church, as the universal church, should have** *"all things in common"* (Acts 2:44) - The biggest facets in religion today are the obvious disagreements of men (2 Timothy 2:14). Denomination after denomination rises up with the intent to establish rules or regulations which disagree with someone else's rules or regulations. One thing we often do not see when examining the history of such disagreements is a turning to God's Word for the answers. More often than not, what we find instead are history's mistakes where the opinions of men are passed off as the Word of God (Matthew 15:1-9). Having "all things in common" does not mean we have to agree about everything; the Word doesn't require us to hold to the same politics, have the same world views about current events, or even the same opinions about most social customs; but it does require that we all adhere to certain beliefs: one body, one Spirit, one hope, one Lord, one faith, one baptism, one God and Father of us all (Ephesians 4:4-6). We learn as we continue in Ephesians 4 that these essential teachings and proper understanding of them are held through God-inspired and ordained leadership in the five-fold ministry (Ephesians 4:7-16). This means there are going to be a lot of times where we have to put aside the non-essential and grow out of the notion that church is getting people to agree with us. Church is not a political forum to push candidates or agendas. It is about introducing people to Christ!

- **Attending or fellowshipping with a local church is not a matter of choosing the "church of your choice"** - Years ago at the end of Billy Graham crusades, it was advised that those who prayed the sinner's prayer should join the "church of your choice." What we must realize is that belonging to church - both local and universal - is not about us! While we do belong by our choice, we must follow where God leads us and seek to uphold, grow, and develop a greater sense of God's truth as we do so. God commands us to be where we are spiritually fed and supported on the foundation of the apostles and prophets (Ephesians 2:19-22). We are also commanded to turn aside from false teachers and not simply attend somewhere because the teaching appeals to us on a fleshly level (1 Timothy 4:1-5). If a church does not meet this criteria, it is not where God would have us to be. Attending a church can't be about going to be popular, following wherever seems to be the most crowded, liking the pretty music, or showing off our church clothes. A church that is no more than superficially deep in this sense is truly not the church of Christ and is not for true followers to attend.

- **The local church is to grow** - Local churches that seem more like an unwelcoming family reunion (the pastor's wife plays the organ, the pastor's son takes the collection, the pastor's cousins teach Sunday school, etc.) than an environment where anyone is welcome are not reflecting the growth that is to take place within the church. Local churches aren't supposed to be topping out at a certain membership roster and then ceasing to grow. I certainly acknowledge the challenges churches face today and the competitions of secular events; but the New Testament era also had its own entertainments and competitions which the first century churches faced, fought, and won. We aren't facing something new and revolutionary today. How does the church grow? Acts 16:5: "So the churches were strengthened in the faith and grew daily in numbers." (NIV) The churches must be strengthened in faith to grow in numbers! The answer isn't to turn everything into a seeker-friendly hot spot; it is to strengthen the faith of the church. This takes the participation of every member!

- **The local church functions by the gifts of the Spirit** - Every member mature and operational in the Spirit must be free to walk in their gifts within the command of order and peace in the churches. Church isn't a free-for-all, but at the same time, it is a participation of every member (1 Corinthians 12:1-30) because every member is a part of the body of Christ and given necessary gifts for the building up of the church.

- **The local church is to serve as the hands and feet of Christ to the community** - Never forget the opportunity to witness the Gospel not just through evangelism and teaching but also through feeding the hungry, providing drink to the thirsty, clothing the naked, visiting the sick and imprisoned, and meeting other necessary practical needs of those in the community (Matthew 25:31-46). Such provides an important grounding because it makes spiritual teaching practical, real, and applicable.

- **The local church provides a springing forth for community evangelism** - A lot of churches teach evangelism to be about handing out tracts. I don't remember handing out tracts in the New Testament, and I have yet to meet anyone who came to know Christ through a tract. Tracts can be great informational resources and teaching materials; but we can't ever forget that the most powerful witness is found through the lives, actions, and testimonies of church members who are living the Christian call to be "little Christs" to everyone they meet (Romans 1:16-17, Colossians 1:9-14). The local church is the training center to equip Christians to be this difference.

- **The local church exists to provide Christians in every city, nation, and part of this world with practical assistance to spiritual and life issues** - In life, we encounter situations that call for advice, guidance, and support. The local church is there to provide this to its members - to give guidance, assistance, teaching, counseling, and support in every situation (Matthew 16:13-19, Matthew 18:15-17, James 5:13-16).

Apostles, prophets, evangelists, pastors, and teachers

I am not going to take a lot of time in this article to discuss the specific duties of each office of the five-fold ministry, as that can be found earlier in this book. What I will look at here briefly is the relation of these three offices to the local church and how they do indeed impact those on the local level.

As I stated earlier, the offices of apostles, prophets, and evangelists are all universal. Each of these three offices serves a greater purpose than can be accomplished by staying in one local community. The apostle, serving not just for administration but also doctrinal formation, correction of local church abuses, witness and evangelism to believer and non-believer alike, and serving as one sent with the direct revelation of Christ (Acts 26:14-18) creates an important office to not just correct but present the importance of the universal church to each local congregation or community one visits. The apostle likewise should not feel unable to correct issues or abuses committed by local clergy, and should never, ever be condemned when such correction occurs (1 Timothy 4:6-11). While there is no question that the apostolic authority is not autocratic, it is indeed by relationship; and when one is acknowledged as an apostle, the authority one has as an apostle is to be respected. The New Testament does serve examples, however, of individuals who clearly did not accept apostolic authority who were also called out for their disobedience - clearly recognizing that the apostolic office extends beyond those who do or do not accept one's apostolic calling (2 Peter 2:1-12). Prophets also show forth universal prophecy, prayer, praise, intercession, and prophetic interpretation to local congregations in addition to whatever may be received for the immediate body (Jeremiah 1:1-10). Evangelists proclaim the Gospel - and are often instrumental in causing additions to a local church (Acts 8:26-35). Pastors oversee local congregations as shepherds; but we must recognize the Bible prompts for more than one pastor in a congregation (1 Peter 5:1-4). This can take the form through pastors overseeing different aspects of the ministry (women's ministry, men's ministry, youth ministry, etc.); however, it is obvious that it takes more than one person to oversee a congregation. The role of teacher also can't be undermined; it is important that teachers work to educate all aspects of the church in any way which God has anointed them (Hebrews 5:13-14).

Conclusion: what is needed?

The bottom line of the division between the local and universal church is one of control between leadership. Local pastors and leaders do not want to feel subject to universal leadership, especially when centuries of abuses have incurred at the hands of individuals who sought universal control. Yet in pursuit to avoid a universal control, too many local church leaders have in turn become the monsters they sought to avoid. It is understandable that a local church leader with many years invested in a congregation may be inclined to resist the changes of an apostle or the prophetic words of a prophet; however, that doesn't mean it is acceptable to reject such to maintain absolute control. The local church can only get better by letting in the universal church and its ministerial representatives.

The local church and universal church are called not to co-exist, but to be one with the other. There is still a division in the hearts and minds of many, a competition, if you will, between the local church and the universal church. The local church is a miniature version of the universal one body which exists in Christ. They are not to be antithetical, nor are they to become problematic to the other. A local church which divides itself from the universal body has need of either education among its leaders or removal from their positions until they learn God's plan for the local church. It is only when the local church begins to connect itself again with a universal understanding that the true oneness God intends for us - that we be one as Christ and the Father are one - begins to emerge and we find ourselves able to proclaim the Gospel to the nations as Christ's original command to us becomes a possibility once again (Mark 16:15-20).

Section 4 study, discussion, and review questions

- After reading, what suggestions and ways are there to discuss ministry form and proper ministry form with others? What ideas do you have of your own?

- What issues exist in the church from being forum-driven? What do leaders need to do? What do people who are a part of church need to do?

- Why is there a struggle between the local church and the universal church? Why is the church universal? What purposes do the local church bodies play in the universal church?

Section 5

THOUGHTS FOR CHRISTIAN LEADERS

Chapter Sixteen

THINGS MINISTERS SHOULD CONSIDER BEFORE GETTING MARRIED

But I am saying this more as a matter of permission and concession, not as a command or regulation. I wish that all men were like I myself am [in this matter of self-control]. But each has his own special gift from God, one of this kind and one of another.
– 1 Corinthians 7:6-7 (AMP)

It's a fact of life: most people get married. From a very young age, we are primed to anticipate that day when the two become one...or something like that. We hear a lot about that, but all throughout history, men and women have been fighting – and striving – to find the vision between individuality and togetherness. If we study history and modern culture carefully, it becomes clear this balance has not always been easily achieved or well-executed. From the very beginning, the dynamic between men and women has been full of passions, intimacies, love, and marriage, and understanding these dynamics help us to understand the reason marriage is frequently rocky and tumultuous: because the relationship between men and women has questions and intensities not easily answered with rhetoric or clichés.

Marriage is often minimalized, and yet exalted, by today's

church. This creates a bit of a "marital inflation" by which Christians expect marriage to work itself out to be one thing, but often is something else entirely. It doesn't help that those who speak the most on marriage often have the most marital difficulties. Whether living in misery, having all sorts of private problems, or more serious issues ranging from spousal abuse to neglect, church leaders are not exempt from martial trials.

Whether they admit it or not, most ministers have marital difficulties. Some of this comes from ministers not properly understanding about marriage themselves and carrying over distorted religious notions into their marital relationships. It doesn't help that the sexism of the world often affects how people translate the Bible, giving a starkly patriarchal approach to Christian marriage rather than seeking to understand God's vision for marriage.

This book is not about marriage, so I won't be delving deeply into the issue of marriage itself. I will say God's purpose for marriage is to provide a "type" between the love that is to exist between Christ and the church. This sounds simple enough, but the reality behind it is deep and takes a lifetime of two serious and committed people to bring this type to pass. This makes the relationship ministers have with their spouses all the more relevant and serious. It also means ministers must approach marriage seriously, with a practical and level-headed approach.

Most ministers approach both marriage and ministry without a proper understanding of the commitment both will require. Combining the two with improper perspective leads to heartache and divorce later on, and can lead to ministry complications, as well. If Christian ministers of every sort want to find the balance they need, they need to consider some major points when approaching marriage and ministry.

I am not seeking to degrade marriage or talk ministers out of being married. It is my hope that by considering some of these essential points, ministers may make better choices in their personal relationships that will enhance their ministries as well. In doing so, ministers can be better witnesses of God's type present in marriage.

- **Ministry is more than just a job; it is a way of life** – Ministry is not just "another job." Being in ministry affects the lists of personal "dos" and "don'ts" an individual has and pursues. It also effects the way an individual spends their time, money, and interests one has. Ministry is an entire approach to humanity, the church, and the human condition, demanding an individual be of service as a human being. Such a way of living requires boundaries in a marriage that may not be easy for a minister to find. The demands between ministry and personal lives can pull a minister one way or the other, causing misunderstanding. It is essential a married minister find that balance between the two, and a mate who understands the balance won't always swing toward marriage and family.

- **Why do you want to get married?** – This may sound like a stupid question, but it is something that needs to be asked by a minister of God. There are many reasons why people want to get married. Some of those reasons are good, some are bad. If a minister thinks they have to get married because it's the "next thing to do," due to pressures, implications, or indications by others, or because someone else thinks it's what right for them, getting married will follow with disaster. If the decision is made because a minister thinks marriage will provide a balance in life, that should also be approached with caution. Most ministers marry because they desire both natural and spiritual things: they want the spouse, the home, the comforts, the sex, the children; and they want to pursue the things of God at the same time. There is nothing wrong with wanting to have these things, but that doesn't nullify the fact that there are choices involved in choosing both. Stepping back and assessing one's motives for marriage makes it easier to see the pros and cons and examine what each individual minister can do for themselves. Both marriage and ministry are commitments that must be taken seriously, and figuring out where priorities lie with each can be answered in the "why" a minister desires marriage.

- **Where is the faith of your mate?** – The Bible talks about the "unequal yoke" (2 Corinthians 6:14) and why it is a bad idea. Its most obvious context is between a believer and a non-believer: a believer marrying someone who is a non-believer creates an imbalance and inequality in the relationship. It can apply in another context, too: the context of a couple where one has a strong faith and one has a weak faith. In ministry, this type of imbalance causes misunderstanding. The husband or wife of a minister does not need to be in ministry themselves, but they do need to be strong in their faith and right with the Lord. This helps a mate to be understanding about the call on a minister's life and enhances their own identity as they develop their own calling in Christ.

- **Does your mate have the image you desire to convey as a minister of the Lord?** – I know we're not supposed to say it, but ministry is largely image-based. People perceive ministry in a certain way based on the presentation of the minister over that ministry. This presentation extends to the way in which a minister carries themselves as well as how those in his or her life carry themselves. It isn't so much about having a certain profession or amount of money as it is about attitude, appearance, speech, and support. If you're with someone who can't ever make time to hear you preach, make the effort to have lunch with you and another couple in ministry, can't control their vulgar tongue in public, or just generally finds themselves totally disinterested in your life and work, they aren't the right image for you as a minister. Remember: someone's consideration of your work could very well come down to the person they see you out to dinner with or your photos of you and them on an internet social networking site.

- **Can you balance a professional AND a personal life?** – An overwhelming number of people answer yes to this question while their lives scream a resounding no. Anyone with serious pursuits in life must recognize the challenge this balance poses, especially in ministry. Ministry doesn't always fit into the nine-to-five workday standard. Ministers often work at least one day per weekend, sometimes all day and then in evenings as well, and are constantly faced with emergencies and phone calls at all hours of the day. Ministry can change a social life, and a social life can cause dilemmas for the minister. Ministers are frequently burnt out and stressed out due to the pull of both. This means a minister must devise "mental" space, personal time, individual time away from ministry work, for refreshing and balance. It's not always well-achieved, nor perfect, but a good minister knows the importance in being a good human being as foundational to being an effective minister.

- **It is essential to maintain individual needs, both in life and in spiritual development.** – Couples where one or both parties are ministers go at marriage with the idea to eliminate the individual and individual needs. This does more harm than good and leads to two very angry people in a relationship. God doesn't call us to marry someone and lose our identity as human beings, forsaking all aspects of our former selves. When married, either as ministers or one person as a minister, both people will have individual needs that may differ from the other partner. It's essential that, if both are in ministry, neither partner attempts to cover the other, and each pursue a different covering to formulate their needs and vision. If one is not in ministry, the decision for the one in ministry to cover the other needs to be considered based on the calling of the minister and the direction of their ministry. It's also important that the spouse of a minister who is not in ministry has support beyond their spouse to help when they are unavailable due to ministry. It's essential both have friends to talk to, to encourage, and to support where they are as they pursue their calling as people.

- **Have realistic expectations** – Sometimes ministry demands more hours in a day than is convenient for a marriage and family life. Sometimes a lack of time causes misunderstanding between people. A minister of God is not Superman. Expecting too much of yourself – or having a partner that expects too much of you – is a drain on a relationship and places an unnecessary burden on your ministerial call. It is not possible to be all things at once to everyone in your life.

Having a realistic outlook on what you can do as a minister versus trying to take on too many things at once.

- **Can the two of you fit jointly into your visions?** – It's easy to maintain a vision when it just involves one person...but much more difficult to maintain two visions and be supportive of both while having the responsibility as the visionary of one of them. Marriage is not just the exchange of rings; it's also the support of each other's visions, even if they are different from one another. Sometimes it's not possible for a man or woman of God to support another's pursuits. For example, if you want to do the things of God and the other person wants to pursue the bar scene or wants to spend all their time on something that's not of God, it's not possible to fit a minister into that vision. A person who wants to pursue a life of leisure won't fit in well with a person who wants to spend their lives in ministerial service. A selfish person is a bad match for a minister. What interests people and what drives them to be successful in life are essential to figuring out the long-term "vision" compatibility of a minister's marriage or relationship.

- **Communicate about the sacrifice of the natural and the spiritual.** – It's great to think marrying a minister is this holy pursuit, but with that holy pursuit comes many sacrifices to the flesh by default. The majority of ministers today invest large portions of their income to make their ministries work. This means not only will a minister not always be able to fully contribute to the household, they may actually drain financial resources from it. Ministers don't always have a lot of leisure time, and spend much of their personal time tired to the point of being uninterested in social activities. Some ministers are called to spend extensive time on the road. Then there are the deeper issues: some ministers, especially women, are not always called to pursue family life in the form of having children due to the difficult impossibility between obeying God and building the Kingdom and having to raise children. It is essential the minister is aware of the sacrifices they are required to make to pursue their ministerial call, and communicate those to a potential mate.

- **Handling temptations** – We don't like to think of ministry as a temptation pit, but there are a lot of temptations that exist when someone is in ministry. Sometimes church doubles as a gigantic pick-up scene. With ministers often having a status in the eyes of others somewhere between a rock star and a demigod, there is no shortage of men and women eager to involve themselves with a minister…whether they or that minister is married or not. Being away from a mate and surrounded by ready, willing, and available people can cause obvious temptation. Even when temptation is averted, the suggestion of it can be difficult for a partner to handle. When marriages are difficult or partners seem distant, the temptation always remains to find someone else, as having God or ministry in common is a very powerful thing for people to have. As long as ministry is about people, there will forever be temptations for hookups and inappropriate relationships. A minister must be able to withstand temptation, especially when married. If making that kind of commitment really isn't your thing…it's important to consider the serious commitment of marriage.

- **Consider the process of natural and spiritual maturity** – Maturity happens as it comes. In my own life, a guy who might have seemed like a good choice at one point may not have seemed like such a great choice only a few months later. It astounds me the number of people who make radical, life-altering choices on the basis of who seems like a good choice right then and there. When planning for marriage, we must receive the Lord's wisdom foresight to expect and anticipate for the maturity we will undergo in the natural and in the spiritual. We will change, we will mature, we will grow, and sometimes that means our outlook on things will change. In selecting a mate, a minister needs to have a partner who will support the maturity of God in their lives and ministries and continue to support their vision, while the minister is able to support that of their mate as well.

- **Be prepared for when two lives collide** – Marriage of any sort involves the collision of planning and events at one point in time or another. With ministry, collision can be more frequent and more intense. Ministry, not always operating during normal hours, can cause a mate to be unavailable for certain events and functions. It can cause difficulties when trying to share a vehicle or during periods of travel. The inevitable discussions about support, time commitments, and spending time together in general can turn ugly quickly. This requires level-headed practicality, the ability to divide time as well as possible, and empathy and understanding on both sides of the discussion. Don't just think these things will work themselves out themselves – be prepared to work them out!

- **There will be high times and low times** – Ministry is a difficult walk. There are periods where things go great, and often longer periods where they don't go so great. Most ministers struggle with discouragement and depression, and feel badly when things don't go the way they would like them to go. Living with a minister means encouraging them in the vision God gave them even when things don't look good. Ministers need to find mates supportive of their difficulties during these times, not just a mate who wants to be there when things seem favorable and good.

Chapter Seventeen

TEN REALITIES OF MINISTRY YOU NEED TO EMBRACE TO RUN YOUR RACE

But I make no account of [my] life [as] dear to myself, so that I finish my course, and the ministry which I have received of the Lord Jesus, to testify the glad tidings of the grace of God.
– Acts 20:24 (DARBY)

It's no secret that when I started out in ministry many years ago, I didn't have the first clue of what I was doing. I knew little about ministry, how it operated, or that it had a day-to-day function. What I did know about ministry and its protocols and functions quickly changed within a few years of starting ministry work – and would go on to change again and again as different standards and concepts of what it means to be a minister continue to change in today's world. Nowadays I hear every demand, from first-class tickets to limousines, to five-star hotels and restaurants, to ten armor bearers established for "service!" Then we have the extremes of ministers who refuse to ask for anything, even travel expenses, because they believe they don't have the right to request anything. Both extremes reveal a deeply confused concept of ministry, but expose something deeper: the fact that many have no idea of the realities of ministry and the complications that ensue as a result.

It seems today as if everyone in the world thinks they are called to ministry, sigh. I use the term "thinks" because statistics cite an overwhelming majority of those who think they are called into ministry won't last more than two to three years. How do those of us make it who are truly called? We embrace the Apostle Paul's words in 1 Corinthians 9:24-27: *"Do you not know that in a race all the runners run, but only one gets the prize? Run in such a way as to get the prize. Everyone who competes in the games goes into strict training. They do it to get a crown that will not last; but we do it to get a crown that will last forever. Therefore I do not run like a man running aimlessly; I do not fight like a man beating the air. No, I beat my body and make it my slave so that after I have preached to others, I myself will not be disqualified for the prize."* (NIV) The Apostle Paul makes it clear that the point is not whether or not we come in first place, but that we stick with the training, discipline, and run to finish, that we may receive the crown of life to win forever.

How do ministers run this race if they have no idea of the realities of ministry? Here are ten realities of ministry, keys for preparedness and expectation, that can help you run that race, if you are truly called to ministry.

1) Ministry does not get easier with time

I've heard a lot of ministers say, "Ministry gets easier with time." I beg to differ. Not only is this a lie, it causes true confusion and deception about the ministry office. Ministry is not a work that ever becomes easier. While it is true that we may move out of older difficulties, we are only moving in to newer ones. The bigger a ministry gets, the more responsibility comes with it. The more opportunities for ministry appear, the more choices and decisions have to be made. The more money a ministry acquires, the more business sense a leader must have. Ministry is still a business, albeit, it is Kingdom business. Just as with any business, increase demands more attention to detail and precision.

Ministry calling and spiritual life do not ever get easier, either. Ministers must constantly face spiritual battle, issues with people who do not understand, harassment, worries, and fears, all that must be confronted and addressed with the Word of God and prayer.

Just because a larger ministry seems to have it all does not mean all they seem to have does not come at a price.

2) The majority of people you find so insightful and relevant right now won't seem that way two to three years from now

It's a sad but true fact: as we grow in God, everyone we know doesn't always grow with us. What may seem great, fantastic, even anointed today may not seem that way in the future because our perspective changes with our level of revelation. I once knew a woman for several years who, at first, intrigued me. She seemed so disciplined and structured, and seemed so successful at what she did. I figured her to be anointed because people seemed to respond to her in a way they did not respond to me. I was so taken with her! Now she just strikes me as a controlling, dominating woman. What caused this shift? Years of having her tell me what to do, order me around, criticize me, and put me down, with absolutely no right to do so, and seeing the reality of her ministry circumstances greatly changed my opinion. Some of what seemed deep now seems…different. There are many, many other circumstances I could also draw upon that are similar inasmuch as that the people don't seem the same several years into the future. If we knew now what we will know then, our perspectives on some of the people in our lives would be radically different.

3) Not having enough money is not your problem

No one wants to hear the truth about this one, but it is truth, nonetheless. I don't know when the drive for money became ministry's underlying motive, but I am so tired of hearing people tell me they don't have enough money to be in ministry or to obey God. God knows your circumstances and He knows what you can do when He tells you to do something! More money equals more responsibility and more people having to oversee finances, be involved with your money, and more hassle as you worry about who you can trust and who you can't. Whatever happened to being creative and clever in ministry? You don't have a lot of money? Be creative! Find ways to make your money go far and work with what you have instead of trying to get more. If you can't handle and work with the little amount you have, what makes you think God should give you more?

4) God gives homework – and you're not going to always like the assignments!

Obedience – now there's a big word we don't like to hear in sermons today! You want to be in ministry? You better be prepared to do some things you aren't going to like, or enjoy, or want to do. If God asks it of you, you better do it! If not, you can get a big, fat zero on your assignment and have to repeat the entire course over again. Ministry is a stewardship, an entrusting, something God gives us to do – not something where we tell God what we want to do and He does whatever we say. Just like when we were in school and we had to take a variety of subjects to be well-rounded people, some of what God assigns to us we will like, and some of it we will not. He is establishing us as well-rounded ministers, competent and prepared to go forth with the New Covenant and be all things to all people. It's just another reminder that we are to be about God, and God's work is not all about you.

5) Ministry is more than entertaining sermons and fancy titles

I meet too many people who come bearing the word "apostle" in front of their names, as if it is nothing more than an empty title, who get up in the pulpit and do nothing but scream and cry for two hours. It's grown to really bother me – no wonder the church is totally confused about the five-fold ministry and what each office does! Screaming, crying, and being entertaining are not in the list of apostle's duties (or any other office of the five-fold). Anyone can get up in a pulpit and scream and cry, running around using a ministry calling as a title. Not everyone can truly walk the day-in and day-out requirements of being an apostle, prophet, evangelist, pastor, or teacher. Ministry is not made in the pulpit. It is made in the everyday lives, conducts, encounters, and commitments we make to follow through on our missions from God. Can't return a phone call you prompted someone to make? Don't come and tell me you're an apostle (or anything else, for that matter)!

6) Ministers must know the Word, not just quote from the Bible

There are very well-known preachers who get on television every week and read a long list of Bible verses from a teleprompter that (supposedly) prove the point they are trying to make about the current news headlines. While some are very well-known for this style of presentation, does such a style actually prove he knows God's Word and what it truly teaches? Any one of us can look up a subject in a concordance and quote a long list of Bible verses that are on that subject. But truly understanding God's Word – beyond words on a page into an area of depth, history, practicality, and understandability – is the true command of anyone who proclaims God's Word. We need to not just prattle off a verse for everything, we must truly know the Bible. This also means we must know the Bible beyond personal or private revelation into a realm that is understandable, teachable, and embraceable by many, rather than just a few.

7) You will face opposition

When I was around ten or eleven years old, I was playing Barbies with my friend from down the street when she decided she was going to do some decorating on my dollhouse – without my permission. She took whatever it was she wanted to put in the dollhouse and proceeded to do so, and I wasn't going to have it. We had a big fight: when I told her no, she said yes, made me the whole problem, and stormed out of my playroom and went home. We didn't talk for several weeks. Even though we are (supposedly) all grown up and more mature, we're going to have an awful lot of people who want to decorate our ministries in one way or another....and we simply can't have it. People who contact us to argue about doctrine (the issue of women in ministry, spiritual gifts, denominational struggles, etc.) really don't want to talk or expand themselves, but want to change our minds, perceiving we have stepped out of a controllable area. The same is true with areas of critique, protesters, those who become difficult or out of line, and those who use the public arena to draw attention to their own beliefs are striving for control, opposing the work of the Kingdom to bring the focus to themselves and what they do.

Not everyone is going to like what we do, not everyone is going to like us. It can't crush us. We have to have a thicker hide, not falling into pieces every time someone calls us a bad word or tells us off spiritually. If setting the boundary means someone storms home and doesn't talk to us for awhile (or again), then that's the way it's going to be.

8) Ministry choices are not easy

I think we expect the ministry experience to be easier than it really is. We think God is going to send an angel on our shoulder to make all our decisions and speak Bible verses in our ears so we know what to do in any given situation. The choices we face in ministry are not always easy. Despite conventional notions, we can't have it all, and some of the decisions we make in the pursuit of personal lives, ministry careers, and deeper anointing all at once will mean someone or something along the way gets hurt, offended, cut out of the picture, or has to wait for later. When it comes to decisions about ministry direction, advice can be great, but the ultimate one who must be accountable for the decision is you, the minister. Challenges, quandaries, and difficult circumstances must be accepted as a part of ministry life if you are to make it as a minister.

9) We will tell the story how we've overcome...and we will understand it better by and by

The words to the chorus of the song, *When the Morning Comes*, are as follows:

> *By and by, when the morning comes,*
> *All the saints of God are gathering home.*
> *We will tell the story how we've overcome*
> *We will understand it better by and by.*[1]

While the song is undeniably about life after the Second Coming of Christ, there is something true about its lyrics for life this side of heaven as well. In ministry, we don't understand a lot of what we go through when we go through it. We don't understand why God has us do certain things, walk through certain trials, or have certain experiences. Many never understand what they go through because they never get beyond their experiences, but simply keep repeating mistakes and choices that cause them to go through the same problems over and over again. As overcomers, God calls His ministers to reach the point of "by and by," where they can stand back, having overcome their difficulties and trials. Even though it seems hard to get through, we have to reach the point of "by and by" to have our circumstances make sense. In the world, they say hindsight is 20/20. Our spiritual hindsight is in the "by and by."

10) Ministry life won't always be what you hoped it to become

An old friend of mine who was also in ministry told me once of a woman under her ministry who believed she too was called to be an apostle. She had it all planned out: she was going to have a nanny and travel with a professional hairdresser. To this woman, this is what being an apostle is about – despite the fact that she has watched both my friend and myself for years in ministry. While both my old friend and I know this woman will never have what she wants, her aspirations give us a good laugh when we are having a bad day. Her aspirations also reveal a common problem about ministry: we overestimate ministry life. People who aren't in ministry think ministers walk around on a cloud, wearing white, singing the *Hallelujah Chorus* all day. Many think ministers have no problems, challenges, or difficulties because "God takes care of them." These delusions of ministry life have flooded over to ministers themselves, who enter ministry with warped concepts about bills, money, payments, preaching engagements, travel, ministry response, and the like. Just like everyone else, every minister has their days when they wonder what their life would have been like had they done something else with it and fight discouragement, despair, depression, and stress. Not every minister likes every aspect of what they do in ministry; in fact, I would venture most ministers dislike something about what they are called to do. While it may not be the calling itself, there are plenty of things tagged on to having a calling that can prove difficult or unpleasant. Anyone who indicates anything else is lying or not in ministry deep enough to experience the true sacrifice every minister must experience.

Chapter Eighteen

IDENTIFYING JUDAS

While He was still speaking, Judas, one of the Twelve, arrived. With him was a large crowd armed with swords and clubs, sent from the chief priests and the elders of the people. Now the betrayer had arranged a signal with them: "The one I kiss is the man; arrest Him." Going at once to Jesus, Judas said, "Greetings, Rabbi!" and kissed Him. Jesus replied, "Friend, do what you came for."
– Matthew 26:47-50 (NIV)

In the movie *Jesus Christ Superstar*, we find the opening scene to the movie slated from Judas' narration. Judas is portrayed in a very specific light: as being one who, believing in the message of Jesus, was thoroughly afraid for himself and his own motives and interests. He was afraid that following Jesus would lead to uprising, further problems for the Israelites, and that, to put it bluntly...it would create more trouble than it was worth. Something in this portrayal of Judas clicked when I saw it: Judas wasn't willing to pay the cost to go all the way if that was asked of him. He wanted to be around to benefit, but not to pay the price. He wanted to be a part of the Kingdom to advance, not to advance it, if advancing it meant too high of a cost to himself.

Seeing Judas through this perspective gave me new thought about Judas, who is a Biblical figure I have thought much about over the years. The endless debates have come and gone about Judas, his purpose, what he was to do, what would have happened had he done something different, and the like. A lot has been written about Judas over the course of history. Judas and his actions are so well-known, they have come to be used in casual society. We call someone, especially a close friend, who betrays us a "Judas." Some people talk about a "Judas spirit." Often we try to give a new perspective to Judas and slant the issue to try and focus on who we are with Judas and how what Judas does helps us...but the viewpoint is still all about us and where we are going in the long run. We aren't identifying Judas and knowing how we respond to that kind of figure in our lives. As a result, we mistake Judas for something other than what he or she is and becomes in our lives. We are so busy trying to fight off people who seem to publically disagree with them and note that they step up and do such that we let Judas slip in and among, right under our noses, until Judas does what he has come to do and then deal with that aftermath. In that aftermath, sometimes we allow Judas to destroy us in the immediate, rather than holding on to look at the long-term.

We live in a very emotionally-charged church that takes betrayal of any sort as a personal attack. We worry about so much in today's church: we fear scandal (whether warranted or not), bad reputation, gossip, and the tarnishing of our image...whether or not that image is who we really are. We know that we do not fight flesh and blood, but the way Judas plays, it often feels like we start fighting people. It's hard to see the bigger picture when dealing with Judas, but it is something we must do. We need to identify and know how Judas works so we can recognize what we are really dealing with behind the scenes. In the bigger picture, Judas is a particularly pathetic character. Judas was bound up by so many things in his life, he viewed Kingdom service as yet another way to advance himself. In that bondage, he betrayed the Lord Himself, only counting his own personal gain. This is the basic map and prototype of Judas: it is an individual who lives so caught up with themselves, everyone and everything is about them. In the case of a Judas, they operate their endless cycles of need, want, and narcissism by using the Kingdom. They walk among those rightly called. They look the part; they seem ample and able to handle important duties and responsibilities; they sound the part. On the surface, nobody would ever be able to tell the difference between a Judas and a rightly called leader. They are designed to complement and blend in right up to the highest positions of Kingdom authority. It isn't until the cost becomes greater than sought that a true Judas starts to come out...and then they begin to operate in the spirit of sabotage. Judas attempts to sabotage anything and everything that challenges, drives, or pushes them and reveals their true nature. And, on the surface...it seems as if they did it without cost, and without any sort of prompting.

It's time we identify Judas...so we know how to handle Judas. We all have one. Many of us will have more than one during the course of our ministries, but all of us get at least one. We just aren't handling Judas correctly because we haven't been taught rightly on this topic...but we must alert ourselves as to what the right thing to do is so that when Judas arises, their betrayal leads our ministries to bring forth more redemptive work rather than killing us off.

Let's start by identifying what Judas is not, so we can better see Judas in a better way: A Judas is not someone who falls out of favor with us or someone who we grow to disagree with over time. All of us have worked with people who were with us for a time and who supported us for a time. That individual may have grown to become a powerful force in our lives - maybe someone even with influence or a trusted support or companion - but something occurred toward the end that caused a parting of ways. This is just a human process, whether good or bad, and in the spiritual side of it, sometimes people aren't designed to walk all the way with us. You may have words with this individual, they may talk about you behind your back, they may even seem to, in one form or another, "betray" you, but this doesn't make them Judas; it just means that a time has come and it's time to part ways because they aren't prepared, nor equipped, to go with you to the next phase of the journey. Likewise, Judas is not someone who just sins against us or the work of God in our lives. Let's never forget that the Apostle Peter also committed a sin against the Lord by denying Him three times, and that none of the apostles were able to stay awake and watch and pray with the Lord (Matthew 26:31-46). They too wronged the Lord, but they were not Judas, and what they did against the Lord was not counted the same as what Judas did.

That having been said, let's look at what and who Judas is.

- **Judas isn't about you or the work of God within you or even assisting the Kingdom vision....Judas is about**

himself or herself - We have no dialogue between Judas and the Pharisees in the Bible. In his self-centered state, I don't think Judas gave much consideration about what would happen to Jesus. The same is true about any Judas. While they appear to be in the right place at the right time and offering the right help, they aren't actually about the help: they are about how helping can advance themselves. It won't look like it because the purpose is to blend in and look like a very helpful and eager version of everyone else.

- **Judas 'tags along'** - My former leader once pointed out to me that we have a call for every apostle in the Bible...except for Judas. We have no incident where Judas was called by Jesus to leave behind his life and follow Christ. This tells us something very important about Judas: he wasn't called, but he started following and came along and was numbered as a part of the others (Matthew 10:1-4, Acts 1:15-26). He was self-appointed and gave himself his own anointing, because we have no indication that Christ ever gave it to him. As leaders, we need to be very wary of people who seem so eager to be a part of things but we can't pinpoint a call upon them. Style can be mimicked; imitation can be apparent; but the anointing can't be faked! All we seem to know about Judas is he looked like, walked like, talked like, behaved like, and seemed like everyone else. In other words, Judas knows how to mimic the call. Judas knows how to blend in and appear to be a part of...when he or she is only among. For this reason, we have to be extraordinarily careful about Judas' operation. Judas can be anybody that attaches themselves to our lives and our call (they just have to know about the call and seem interested in it) - it can be someone who we know intimately, someone we desire to know intimately, someone who is under or over our ministry, or someone who seems to be a part of it. They seem interested on a level that speaks to a leader, especially a leader with need of assistance or following. Before we know it, they are setting themselves up in our lives and ministries.

- **Something "just doesn't feel right" about Judas** - Ever have those people who keep trying to tell us something about themselves or present themselves in a certain way...and we just have that little gnawing that is telling us something isn't right about them? I'm not talking about judgment, I am talking about a genuine realization of something that we just can't identify or put our finger on because we don't know them well enough in the natural to know something just isn't right about them. I knew of a woman who is a leader who I had that feeling about from the beginning. She claimed to want to be my friend, but something always stopped me from taking her into my confidence. Something just didn't feel right with her, something felt uncomfortable about her and her claims, both in her own leadership and how she wanted to interact with me. Why? It turned out she was sent to be a Judas.

- **Judas wants to go beyond the pulpit - and you know it's a bad idea** - All of us have our support systems. We know and recognize there are different types of support. There are people I am on a first-name basis with, who I love dearly, and who I will continue to stand with through until the end. There are people who I cover in ministry who I also love dearly and know God will continue to work in their lives and raise them up for His purpose, and I am honored to be a part of that process. Then there are those I work with and respect in the ministry on a ministerial level, love them, support them, and stand with them. Then there is the rest of them: those who want to snuggle up to me...just enough to get close enough, but not be a part of...and I refuse to let them. We see these boundaries present within the Bible as well: the Twelve had a certain relationship the Seventy did not have, and that while they had it amongst themselves, they did not have it among the general church body. As the Twelve walked and worked together, their lives went beyond preaching and pulpit work. They travelled together, ate together, slept in close quarters together, prayed together, had their daily routines together, and worked together. We can see that interaction in their manners one to another: at times, they acted like children (John 21:20-23) and even had competitions and jealousies of one another (Matthew 20:20-27, Matthew 10:35-45). We don't see Judas participating in this kind of interaction with the other eleven apostles. When we do see Judas speaking up, it is usually in criticism (John 12:1-8). Judas wanted to be around just enough to get what would benefit him, without becoming a part of it. Why? At some point in time, Judas probably would have used what he saw against the others. Judases are always gathering up what they can in just enough proportion to use it to their benefit. For this reason, if there is only one thing I can say to the church that you will hear, hear this: be very careful of who you take into your confidence and, even then, what you say and how you word things...because Judas is very eager to get the dirt on you that you would never expose in the pulpit.

- **Judas appears to be your friend, at least by the standards of outsiders** - Most of you know I am Italian, and that means my entire life I have had non-Italians joke with me about the "kiss of death." The Mafia's kiss of death (where one close to the other kisses them as a sign that is the person to be killed) is a play on Judas' kiss to Jesus in the garden (Matthew 26:45-56) by which the enemy identified Jesus and was able to take him to death. Judas was one that nobody would have suspected because the kiss itself was disguised as a kiss among friends - a common greeting in ancient and some modern cultures. The kiss was a cultural sign of friendship and thus it made it most appropriate to be used as a weapon. To everyone but Judas, Jesus by His revelation, and the guards, Judas appeared to be Jesus' friend because Judas' action gave that impression. This is how Judas operates today as well: others may view you and your Judas as being close friends, close in ministry, or at the very least, respectable acquaintances. They may refer to you as a friend or in some other way, indicate a love or care for you, and even promote you as such before others...all the while trying to use you unto your demise.

- **Judas "conspires" with your enemies** - We all just want to pretend that everything in the Kingdom is sunshine and roses, and that we don't deal with people who are our enemies. The truth is that we do have enemies, even those who claim to be Kingdom. Yes, they are most likely operations of the enemy, and yes, we know that we love our enemies, but that doesn't mean we trust them. When someone is close enough to know who your enemies are, and identify them, and still fraternize with them...it's time to be careful. I know that we don't always get along with others and that we shouldn't expect people to just stop talking to other people because we don't want to talk to them anymore (making allowances for revelation, understanding, perspective, and personality differences), but we need to beware the forming of exceedingly friendly alliances when someone knows how we were treated by someone else. I know of a woman who knew how I was treated by a former leader and created an alliance with her anyway - knowing fully well who she was and what she had done - and are we really surprised to discover this woman was a Judas to me? Yes, we have different experiences with people, yes, not everyone gets along...but yes, there is the call for loyalty in the Spiritual realm and we are called to beware those who are clearly aligning with those who come against God's Kingdom leaders. If someone acknowledges you are of God and then aligns with someone they know is not of God...something is wrong.

- **Judas does not ascribe to the order which he is called** - In re-echoing the fact that we have no call of Judas, coupling the fact that Judas likes to cozy up to people to extract information from them, we have the bottom line of both: Judas does not ascribe to order. Even though it may appear that he did, it is only an appearance because he was able to mimic style and manner to blend in with the others. Thus we can recognize a Judas does what everyone else does and may even seem to do it with the right attitude - but they aren't really doing it because it is what God is asking of them. Within, they have an unspoken spirit of rebellion just waiting to come out. In those days when the Twelve were coming together and learning about ministry, they were learning about order and mutual submission to one to another. They were also learning about the headship of our Lord and about having a right relationship with Him. Both were important and both present an essential balance needed to be apostles in any time within the church. Judas was always on the outskirts of that: he wasn't a real participant in the development...he was just always there, seeming to do his part. A Judas defies order in one form or another, often using the personal information they have either extracted or think they have extracted (they may in reality know nothing at all but think they know something and will run with it until it becomes some semblance of accurate). In modern times, Judas will use whatever means available to them to defy order: they will abuse the pulpit you so respectfully allow them to use, the conference you invited them to speak at, the internet, their blog, Facebook, Twitter, word of mouth, or their own venues. They usually have a darkened history that they slant and do not speak much about where they have done the same to others, especially those who have served as their leaders and have tried to instruct them. Their history is one of a defiance of order and a disgrace of other ministers.

- **Judas likes money** - To the point of being good with it - and yet all about it - many have questioned about Judas' role as treasurer. If he wasn't really an apostle - if he was just an imposter - why did Jesus allow him to be treasurer? Because he was good at it, and doing such was prophetic to his ultimate betrayal and demise. You don't have to be a true leader of God to be good with money - in fact, we can see that many in the world are far better with money than those in the church. Judas' love of money made him trustworthy with it...but it also made him greedy with it (John 12:1-8), thinking it was his and he got to have an opinion about the expense of things. A Judas is all about money in one form or another. They may give you large amounts of it for the "work" but then they start telling you what to do with it. You hear how much money "they" gave you and why they think "you" are mishandling it. Then they start to get stingy or withhold from the offering. Truth be told, they are most likely so good at handling money they have many things financially order in their own lives and it may even seem like we should imitate them...but their financial blessing eventually becomes their financial downfall. Judas betrayed Jesus because he loved money. The Pharisees and Sadducees waved the right amount of money under his nose and he threw his Lord over for the amount laid before him (Matthew 26:14-16). At some point we know Judas had his regrets because he tried to reverse the process and return the money, but this doesn't change the fact that the leaders knew how to get to Judas. They knew because they had been watching and knew his embrace of money. The same is true with Judas today. They want to advance in ministry because they want the money. They see the Kingdom as the advance to their own materialism.

- **We know that Judas will betray in advance** - Judas' actions were not a surprise to Jesus. Jesus knew that Judas was going to betray him all along. That's why Judas wasn't ever privy to the very important counsel and spiritual revelations that Peter, James, and John were allowed to behold and witness. God always gives us a revelation about who Judas is among us somewhere along the way...and we are usually told to leave them to themselves. We watch and we know and we assess every move, every action, everything that seems to be coming to pass...and God requires us to let it happen...even though we know and feel the inevitable. God has us let our Judas' do what they came to do and leave it at that. If someone surprises you with a betrayal, they aren't your Judas.

- **Judas represents a specific type of betrayal** - The greater purpose of Judas (which a Judas does not recognize) is to work to bring about a necessary sacrifice within a leader's individual self, work, and ministry to bring forth a greater victory. Judas' betrayal works with an intent to kill a spiritual vision that they, within their own disorder, perceive to be getting out of control or out of their own perspective of a boundary line. Judas' mind operates by such that they may actually wish harm on us to stop the process, only to feel they went too far later. They seek to destroy what God has set forth. Yet in the process of their actions, they actually further our ministry because what they do brings about the necessary sacrifice to advance the work. Judas comes along with his or her own agenda, yet God uses Judas to bring about His agenda in our work and lives. That is the end of a Judas process with us...but not the end of Judas within and among himself or herself.

- **Judas moves themselves unto destruction** - I've often said that the spirits of Judas and Jezebel operate very closely together. They both have a similar purpose. Judas and Jezebel both have issues with order, seek to usurp something that just isn't theirs, seem to have the air of confidence and authority, operate with the goal of destroying the work of God unto death...but Judas and Jezebel have two very different endings. Jezebel must be cast out, while Judas destroys himself or herself (Matthew 27:3-5). I believe that Judas was so busy thinking of himself, he didn't consider how his actions would affect Jesus. Because he couldn't see the long-term picture, he felt a sense of loss and guilt unto death. Judas' suicide speaks that he didn't consider the real ramifications of his actions. Judas today does the same: they try to kill God's leader, whether it's through destroying the vision, the work, or the leader themselves in some way...but don't consider the ramifications of such. Every Judas, in the end, commits a suicide of sorts: they wind up out of the ministry and without much of the things they might have sought after in their lives. Who they are comes back to them and they have to face that, in one form or the other, and they are unable to do so. Judas is, simply put, his or her own worst enemy because they bring about their own demise.

Those who are true ministers will deal with a Judas. Whether or not Judas kills us is up to us. When it comes to Judas, this is what I have to say: One of us will be left standing at the end of the day...and it's not going to be you. To those of you who are true, I thank you and love you. To those who are Judas...you may think you won on Friday...but Sunday is only a few days away!

Section 5 study, discussion, and review questions

- What are some things ministers should consider before getting married, and why?

- What are some realistic aspects of ministry we need to embrace in order to run and operate successful ways in ministry?

- How can we identify Judas?

Section 6

Covering

THE THINGS I WISH PEOPLE WOULD RECOGNIZE ABOUT COVERING

Remember your leaders who have spoken God's word to you. As you carefully observe the outcome of their lives, imitate their faith.
– Hebrews 13:7 (HCSB)

Once upon a time, I had a vehement discussion with an individual I covered for over a year. I spent time with her, listened to her, helped her, taught her, and cared about her. As her covering, it was my deepest desire to see her develop in ministry. The Lord gifted her, yet she would not settle down within herself and focus on His calling. She was always all over the place, running here and there, undisciplined and disordered. I worked hard with her in a loving way to try and bring her to the realization she needed, but she just wouldn't play by the rules. In this state, I could never have her minister for me - gifts or not. When I confronted her, her answer to me was, if I was really her covering, I'd be calling to see how she was and I would know she was busy with her own ministry assignments.

This wasn't her first complaint. Prior it was she didn't like what I was teaching on and felt it was negative. Before that, it was that she didn't think I was doing something right. Now her complaint is that because I confronted her about not participating with us, that leaders don't have the right to act like we "own people." Opinions, opinions, opinions!

It is times like this when I hate covering people. We live in a world immersed with self-esteem and concepts about self-worth, and the church now thinks a gift entitles them to be mouthy, rude, disrespectful, and in the pulpit all at once. It's obvious she didn't realize she didn't have a ministry yet. She had the gifts and potential, but she didn't have the necessary structure and order. I couldn't place her in a position of ministry because she wasn't ready to handle it. At that point in time, her place was not in the pulpit, it was in the pew, learning the disciplines and ins and outs of ministry. She wasn't a leader yet and didn't yet have the ability to be one. That is something developed with time, and yet she didn't want to deal with that development. She wanted to be all that, and some, and I was expected to sway with her as she blew toward the next thing she felt was her "ministry."

One of my former friends, who was also an apostle, told me of her old-school leader who, years ago, used to tell people - "You and your gifts, sit down. You may be anointed, but you're nasty." He recognized order within ministry and the disciplining of the self to be an asset to the body of Christ. In a different time and place, the disciplines of leadership seemed to mean more. Nowadays people mouth off in disrespect to their leaders, holding nothing back, bringing ancient history up, and find another leader who will allow them to do whatever it is they feel they want to do. People throw tantrums, act in all sorts of denial and irresponsibility, and truly expect us to just sit back and not say anything about it. Sigh.

I've had good and bad leaders in my life. I am so appreciative of the covering I now have, but that wasn't always the case. I have submitted and been faithful to good and bad leaders alike, trusting God to lead me out of a situation when it was time. I've had leaders make unreasonable demands, reasonable demands, ask too much of me, take up all my time, and lord abuse and control over me. There have been lots of days when I knew I was more advanced in an area than my leader was, but because I wasn't advanced in other areas, it was my job to keep my mouth shut and learn. Now that I am the leader, I remember so many of those days so well - but find such vastly different results in the responses of the people I cover. Many seem to be so busy thinking they are wonderful, they fail to realize covering is just as difficult as being covered. It's a balance that takes time and effort. Now there's a lot out there on being a good covering, but not much about how to be good to your covering. It's not unquestioning obedience, but basic respect and consideration. There are so many things I wish people who are covered would realize about their covering, about the process, and about the purpose in covering.

We should never be covering people to meet our own unmet needs or to meet other people's unmet needs. This isn't about taking the place of a deceased or absent caregiver; it's about training for the Kingdom and empowering those under us for that purpose. It's not an easy or enviable process, and I know that in covering, there is growth, pain, and discipline that must come forth. That having been said, we all need to remember a few things when covered about our covering and the process they are working for our good within us.

- **We've been there** - I didn't roll out of bed one morning and wake up where I am now in ministry. What I did do is spend a number of years walking through problems and working things out. I have spent every minute, of every year, learning, growing, and developing the things I needed to in order to be where I am in ministry. I know what it's like to be under a leader who doesn't feel you are ready yet, when you feel you are ready. At the time, I thought they were wrong. Now in hindsight, I don't think they were. Whatever their reason for not allowing me to do whatever it was I wanted to do, I wasn't allowed to do it because God knew I wasn't ready for it. I've dealt with the frustration, the pain of having to face myself and the choices I've made, the difficulty in healing hurts and wounds, confronting my life, and confronting who I was. I still deal with things, still go through revelations and areas that need improvement, and I know all too well how difficult it is to realize a leader doesn't think we are right for something or ready for something. Any good covering has walked the walk they now lead someone through and knows the pain in the process.

- **The accountability we seek to instill within you is only the beginning** - Every one of us in the church should have someone to whom we are accountable to. Some people call it a covering, some people call it a leader, and some people call the person by their first name. It doesn't matter what you call the person - all of us are accountable to someone. Accountability to a leader is key to learning and developing the different areas of accountability we face as leaders. Being a leader means you are accountable to everyone who hears your words, to other leaders in different events, to different people for different projects, and yes, accountable to God. When issues come up with a reasonable leader, don't dodge your responsibility because that just proves you aren't ready for greater leadership and greater accountability; it shows you need to sit down and shut up some more.

- **We don't ask a lot of you** - I have met some coverings who really do ask a lot of the people they cover: everything from doing the leader's housework to putting on shoes and babysitting kids. I can honestly say I have found this to be the exception and not the rule, which does give me some restored hope in today's leadership. Unless you're being asked to be a virtual slave or do something truly immoral or inappropriate, it is not a lot for your leader to expect you to be present at a meeting, a teleconference call, a worship service, or get yourself together and be present for something. If your leader has called you to be there, that is your ministry assignment for that time, not something else. While there are exceptions to this, of course, like having to work, or preach, or something of that nature, your leader is not asking too much of you to expect you to show up and behave like an adult. If a meeting is called and your presence is expected, it is because you are not only needed there, but because you also need to gain something from being there. Don't act like every time a leader needs you to do something that you're being sent to the gas chamber in a concentration camp. If you can't make a meeting over and over again, that is showing you don't follow through on commitments, and aren't ready to be a leader. Also: don't be late. I know we sometimes have circumstances that cause us to be later than we would like, and sometimes we just don't make it on time, but don't think showing up late repeatedly counts as being committed because it shows disrespect.

- **We aren't good leaders if we don't correct** - If something is going on, a good leader has to bring it to your attention. It is a sign of a bad leader to just let things slide all the time. This means we won't always be tickling your ears and making you feel good emotionally. Sometimes it means you will just get a kick in the pants as gently as we can give it to you. Good parents discipline their children. Good spiritual parents/coverings also discipline those under them, knowing it is for their own good. Also consider the fact that if a leader is correcting you on something, this probably isn't the first time the issue has come up, nor is it the first issue that has come up. We try to give you the benefit of the doubt and allow you the space to work things out on your own, so by the time we say something in correction, the issue isn't something you haven't had a chance to work out on your own.

- **We enjoy correction as much as you do...in other words, not at all** - While a good covering recognizes discipline is necessary, I have yet to meet a dedicated, concerned, caring covering who enjoys correcting those they cover. With the current situation in the church being tantrums, finding new people, and never talking things out or being responsible, most coverings know speaking up about a situation will cause those they cover to leave their covering and find someone who doesn't speak up so much. Then we have the avenue that people being so rude and mouthy these days means the person they have invested time, love, and teaching in will not only speak rudely or lash out at them, but will badmouth them to others as well. Correction is probably needed now more than ever, and coverings are afraid to correct because they don't know the outcome. Want to make the process easier on you both? Listen and keep yourself in check, and realize your covering is just as uncomfortable with the process as you are.

- **We don't set up regulations because we want to control you** - The people under my ministry have certain regulations they must follow to remain under the ministry covering. These regulations aren't there because I want to control anyone. On the contrary, covering isn't my favorite part of ministry as I have found most people I've covered to be a huge and tremendous headache. While everyone hasn't been a problem, I have found a lot of the people I've covered to be uncommitted, difficult, and so enamored with their gifts, they don't have room enough in their hearts or heads to actually develop ministry discipline. I'm not real tolerant of temper tantrums and mudslinging, not to mention the expectation that I am available to them 24/7 only to have them throw any requirements I have for covering back up in my face. The regulations are in place so I can help those I cover develop into what God has placed within them. The process and regulations are more work for me, not less - and I don't benefit in the least from them. The same is true for your covering - the instructions and directives are put into place, not because they want to control your ministry, but because they want to help you to actually have one.

- **If you're not ready to minister...we can't let you** - I venture maybe one-third of all people who claim to be called to leadership really are. Some people are strongly anointed for leadership, and some just are not. Some people are on the path to being leaders or public ministers, and some just are not. I think we all need to step back and consider our own purpose to the Body and recognize it may not be to be in control and have power. The person who considers this is our covering. They may be seeing something in us that we don't see or are unopened to recognize from the Lord. While a person under a covering may see the glory side of ministry, the covering intimately knows the work behind the public side of ministry. They know better whether you are displaying the ability to handle the deep and intense downs and responsibilities of ministry than you are. Just because you aren't able to do it now doesn't mean you will never be able to do it, but it does mean that a covering has the responsibility to prohibit you from ministering on account of their accountability before the souls that will hear you and before God....plus, if you step out and do something before you are ready, you can incur consequences you are unable to handle.

- **You are either in order...or you are not** - Order is kind of like being pregnant: you either are pregnant or you are not pregnant; there is no being "a little pregnant." Either you are in order or not in order - you can't be a "little in order." Coming into God's order is a process, and I recognize it doesn't happen all at once. Order is also a condition of the heart. A good leader can tell when you are working toward order, and when you are just being mouthy, rude, or insubordinate. If you are out of order and we call you on it, you're out of order. We raise the issue out of concern for whatever is to come or where such disorder will take you. FYI: how you treat your covering, how you speak to your covering, and the attitude you have toward your covering are clear displays of your level of order.

- **We don't have time to call you all the time** - My former friend in ministry who I mentioned earlier has also noted a major shift in covering over the years. In days gone by, a covering paid for everything in someone's ministry; now those who are under a covering dump all over that covering. Both extremes are incorrect, but display the intense expectations those who are covered by someone have of their covering. I've gotten everything, from texts at two in the morning from people expecting me to get up and talk to them, to people who expect me to pay for everything they need and be their garbage cans, to those who think covering means I use them in all my events without question or investigation. Most often I find people want me to meet their emotional needs, listen to their problems and talk them through it all...day after day after day. I don't have time to call every day and hear about the same issues you didn't resolve from yesterday. Coverings are in ministry; they have multiple administrations, lives, and issues to deal with. While we intend to be there for you as best we can, we can't be there to hold your hand through every little problem and trial you encounter. Never forget that you are supposed to be growing in God, and that means you don't need so much hand-holding all the time.

- **You are not the only person we cover** - Most people who cover someone also cover several other people at one time. I question a leader with thousands of "spiritual children," but most coverings work hard to maintain the balance between a reasonable number of people under their covering and other ministry duties. While your problems, issues, thoughts, feelings, challenges, difficulties, etc. are the most relevant things in your life, they are probably issues that your covering has seen before not once or twice, but over and over again. Your covering has the foresight to recognize you will either get over your issues or you won't, and that these things you think are really relevant...in actuality...are not that relevant. We are not here to be all about you and your issues; we are here to develop your ministry and help you grow to be all God has appointed for you to be. You are a part of the ministry we have, but you are not all of it.

- **We don't need to hear all the details of your private life** - There are some things I just don't wonder about people. I do not picture people having sex, I don't need to know about whose bedroom you sleep in, and I don't want to know about all your familial struggles. I am here to help you grow, so if talking about something will help that process, great; but I don't need to know all the gory details. Telling a covering too much crosses a line and makes it hard for that covering to make proper leadership decisions as pertain to you and your walk. Sometimes we know you just need to talk; sometimes you want to talk too much. If a covering cuts you off, don't think it's because they don't care about what you have to say;

they are just trying to maintain a certain objectivity in their walk with you.

- **Speak to us and about us with some respect** - I believe a good covering becomes a friend to those they cover, with certain limitations. A covering can be a friend in that they are someone you can talk to, someone who wants to help you develop your work, someone you can trust in your life to be for your good. Some people spend a lot of time with their coverings; others do not. There are limits to that friendship, however. Your covering is still an authority in your life, and is called to discipline and correct. There are certain ways in which a covering should never be addressed. A covering's work, accomplishments, and achievements should be respected, not scoffed at. A covering should never be talked about behind their back. Just because you don't get your way about something doesn't mean you have the right to speak to a covering however you please. This confirms the covering is correct in whatever they said and you are an immature baby. If you want to be elevated, treat your leader with respect. Personally I elevate nobody who acts like a big baby. I don't have time for people who tell me how gifted they are for leadership, but act like spoiled children.

- **You take a lot of my time, whether you think so or not - and you don't give me back much for it** - Most of the people I know in ministry have a hard time wrangling tithes and offerings out of the people they cover. Considering the fact that coverings often extend extensive help to those they cover in conversation, counseling, consultation, intervention, teaching, study, private assistance, and help their coverings develop in other areas of their lives, including business or writing, the amount of money someone gives to their covering is meager and insulting when measured with what they receive. Even though you may not think you take up that much of your covering's time, you probably take up more than you consider - especially if you count the time they spend working on teaching, preaching, and lessons as part of teaching you receive. The offering you send every now and then when you've committed to help your leader every week is not very much at all, in this light. Considering this, a thank you, a note or gesture of appreciation, and an apology when you've behaved badly instead of mouthy disrespect all go a very long way in the eyes and relationship one has with their leader.

- **Please...don't tell me what you think about "ministry leaders"** - Most of us who have been in ministry more than a few years - let's say ten years or more - have seen more leaders come and go than we have seen come and stay. It is our sincere prayer that, if you are called to leadership, you won't become one of these fly-by-night leaders. Yes, we all know there are bad leaders out there, but calling you on something you are doing wrong doesn't make us one of them. I am sure you have lots of opinions about leadership, what everyone is doing wrong, and how you can make it all better because you are the only one who has it right...but to be honest, your covering really doesn't want to hear it. I had plenty of opinions about what everyone did wrong in days gone by and now in many circumstances, I find myself understanding their positions. It's not easy to be a leader, and until you have been one as long as your leader...keep your opinions to yourself.

- **We are of far more benefit to you than you are to us** - Don't go thinking about all you do for your leader when you aren't even doing anything for them. Money is great, but it only goes so far, and it's often considered to be an unspoken string. Just because you send your leader money doesn't mean they owe you. You are giving to God through that ministry so you're just doing what you're supposed to be doing. Nobody owes you a thing. You take time, energy, teaching, training, and a whole lot of patience out of your leader. Stop thinking you own them because you sent them an offering at some point in time. Believe me, the way ministry is today and with the expense of things, your offering was gone to cover something to help continue the work of God a long time ago.

- **Don't compare us to your former covering** - One of the biggest misconceptions in today's church is that all covering is alike. Apostolic covering is different than pastoral covering because it has a different purpose. The way I cover as an apostle is markedly different from the way someone who is a pastor will cover someone. Why is this? As an apostle, I am working with future or current leaders rather than new believers or people who do not have a call to church leadership. The people I cover have different needs than a new Christian or a person not called to ministry leadership. Don't tell me how you wish I would do this or that like someone else. You're not under them now, which means you don't need what they had in your life anymore. If this is where God has called you to be, suck it up and accept the new level of accountability, discipline, and responsibility so you can move up higher in Him!

Your covering is not your enemy. If something is really and genuinely wrong, it's time to move on; but your covering is not in the wrong because they don't entertain you when you're not in the right.

Chapter Twenty

MORE THINGS I WISH PEOPLE WOULD RECOGNIZE ABOUT COVERING

Obey your leaders and submit to them, for they keep watch over your souls as those who will give an account, so that they can do this with joy and not with grief, for that would be unprofitable for you.
– Hebrews 13:17 (HCSB)

When I wrote the blog, *The Things I Wish People would Recognize About Covering*, I had no idea it would become as universal as it did. I had no idea people would send it to the people they covered, I would get called by people to teach on this subject, and that I would continue to receive the same consistent word I had from anyone who knew about the situation which the blog inspired: stand my ground. The more we all discussed, conversed, and shared about this issue, the more I realized how important it is that we start to balance the two issues more. We hear so much today about leaders and being in good leadership. Whether it's because of our own histories or because we truly want to take people at their word, I've noticed that we automatically blame a leader for where someone is in their walk. As one who has spent numerous years in ministry and a good number of years as a believer, I have had my share of all sorts of leaders: good, bad, and indifferent. I have seen leaders who were just not anointed for leadership, and it was obvious. At the same time, they were unwilling to let go of the prestige of their positions. Some of them are still around from years ago, buy most of them are not. It takes some staying power to remain in ministry year after year after year, dealing with the same issues in people over and over again. It takes a lot to be a leader, and the one consistent thing I am noting from the response from my blog and from those who responded is the resounding realization that people who are not in active leadership don't understand just how much responsibility leadership is. Everyone thinks they can do it better, be better, handle it better, but the statistics say otherwise. All those people who think they know better than God and have no intention to ascribe to God's order don't wind up making it in ministry long-term.

Sometimes it's not the leader's fault. We need to stop automatically blaming leaders for where people are. Sometimes people are hard-hearted, stubborn, difficult, and proud. It was not Moses' fault the people of Israel decided he was gone and they would create a golden idol in his absence. Moses had walked with them for years to the point where he got angry and frustrated because of them. He desired to lead them to a place where they needed to be. In his own frustration, he lost sight of why he was working so hard with them. It grieves me to see leaders who take so much responsibility for where those they cover are that they begin to lose sight of God. Yes, there are bad leaders. Yes, there are leaders who manipulate and control, and hurt people because that's why they do what they do. Yes, there are problems among leaders in the church. These facts, however, are not an excuse to manipulate yourself around God's order. Find a leader who is not a problem, and start showing your leader who is not a problem how much you appreciate who they are in your life.

I received some negative feedback my work, *The Things I Wish People Would Recognize About Covering*: that it wasn't of God because it wasn't "loving" and then there was my favorite one: that when God gives us a revelation, we should keep it to ourselves - we shouldn't share it. I don't have time for this nonsense. Anyone who has read it knows it wasn't unloving, and I don't know why any one of us would get a revelation from God so we could not share it. This just proves to me how needed that post was - because it's obvious the individuals responded due to their own lack of order. What these people don't realize, because they don't bother to ask or consider, is how difficult it was in my own life to come to a place of accepting leadership and covering. I have experienced bad leadership: leaders who couldn't handle basic questions, who told me to go to another church, who misused and abused me, who were discouraging and negative no matter what I did. I came out of the Catholic Church, which treats its man-made leaders as if they were gods. I watched abuses of power, ministers run off with their secretaries, and so-called leaders get arrested for inappropriate relationships with children. I wanted no part in that. What I didn't understand at the time is that that was not God's order, either. People could tell me it was order, but it wasn't. It was hard for me to accept God's order and structure within my own life, and within my own ministry. God wouldn't move me up until I did, and without getting into all the long-winded details of this aspect of my testimony, God didn't start to move me into positions of authority and leadership until I accepted those things as just as necessary for me as for others. For me to come on here and post about order and covering would have been unheard of ten years ago - but God moved in my life. God operates by certain principles, and leadership is one of them. It is only because of God's intervention that I can teach on this topic today.

In speaking about covering, I speak from years of experience learning the ins and outs of order and disorder. I know order by the Spirit when I see it, and I know disorder when I see it as well. In knowing order, we know God. In seeing disorder, we meet the enemy. The battle present in today's church as pertains to covering and covered is a part of the long-term struggle between good and evil. People want their own way. They want what they have to be enough, and don't want to have to answer for it to anyone. They want to be anointed and that be sufficient. In terms of building ministry, long-term, it's just not.

I realize in writing these things about covering and being covered the serious gap we have in today's church. We don't understand what covering is and how we are to be covered. Good coverings are afraid to cover well because they don't want to see their ministries destroyed by vindictive, angry, heard-hearted people. This is a dialogue we need to open up, and open up wide. We need to understand what it means to be someone's leader and what it means to have someone as our leader. A relationship needs to exist there.

We need to abandon the concept of covering just to get by in ministry and say that someone covers us. We need to hear God's deeper call to us to follow Him and honor one another. It is time to stop being all about ourselves and our own personal ministries and come to a greater understanding of what it means to be the church, connected to one another, and making both disciples and leaders to spread the Kingdom of God far and wide. If we would only get over our petty selfishness, our egotistical tirades, and our own delusions of grandeur, maybe we can see God's gift present to all of us in leadership and in accountability.

The Lord has continued to speak, and reveal to me about this issue...not just for myself, but for all of us...and in that spirit...here are more things I wish people would recognize about covering:

- **Don't "name drop"** - Sometimes we are in events or we are asked by others who our covering is. That is different from what I am talking about here. In those circumstances, people are connecting us to our leaders and seeking a validation for our ministries. On the inverse, I've met a lot of people in ministry who are covered by someone, not because they recognize God has drawn them to that person, but because they want to advance their own ministries through the person that covers them. In many cases, I've seen it work...sort of. The person may get a preaching engagement out of the deal, but the minister in question gets found out when word gets back to their leader. What I wind up seeing are very, very angry coverings, who are angry for good reason. Your covering has most likely spent many years developing and growing their ministry to reach a point where, at least in certain circles, their name represents a standard of excellence. Trying to claim that for yourself when you haven't done the work is insulting. Most coverings will recommend those under their ministries when the individuals in question display a certain level of excellence in their own ministries, but I'm not going to lie - it may take a while. How long it takes depends on you. In the Bible, one's name represented the fullness of who they were, what they stood for, and what they had. If we apply this to ministry, name dropping is a disrespect to everything a leader stands for.

- **Presentation is everything** - Nobody would show up to a meeting with Donald Trump dressed in ripped jeans, an old T-shirt, and smelling like they hadn't bathed since Jesus walked on earth. We get this makes a bad presentation in the world - so why do we present ourselves to our Kingdom leaders like this? If you want to "advance," for lack of a better term, in the Kingdom, it's best you present yourself like you do. I'm not talking about wearing robes or thousand-dollar designer suits, but I am talking about being neat and clean, being hygienic, not being greedy or overstaying one's welcome somewhere, not eating someone out of house and home - or buying the most expensive thing on the menu, and dressing for Kingdom business - suits, dresses, neat pantsuits, nice shoes, nothing too casual or that says "I'm ready for a weekend off!" If you are working on some sort of community project that demands a casual dress, that's different from what I am talking about here. If you look like you're ready for a weekend off in pulpit ministry or other areas of ministry presentation, you're covering is going to give you an extended leave of absence so you can take that "weekend off."

- **If you want to do greater things, be responsible with the little things** - We all know - You're the next big thing, you've got a mega-ministry coming your way, you're going to publish three thousand books, you're going to drive a Bentley, you're going to get everything right that the rest of us have all wrong, you're going to be on TV - yadda, yadda, yadda. I tell you, the ego of today's church needs to put some ice on it so it can de-swell. Too many people have placed themselves as worthy of having mega ministries when they can't even go and check a ministry post office box faithfully once or twice per week, or get on the phone once or twice per month for a conference call. Everyone who has ever covered someone else realizes how menial you think the responsibilities you are given to complete are, and every one of us also recognizes you think you are worthy of much, much more. We also realize that ministry is not about what happens in the pulpit, it's about keeping faithful no matter how menial or minute the issue seems to be...and you still think so highly of yourself, you probably don't have this revelation just yet. The Bible teaches us the little foxes spoil the vine. It was a friend of mine who is also an apostle who pointed out to me that this is not just a negative statement - it is also telling us that little things make a difference. If little things can trip us up, little things can also make a huge and powerful impact. All those people on TV - whether we agree with what they teach or not - got there because they were attentive to little things. If you are, as you believe, going to be in mega ministry, you better start paying attention to small things. Before we hit big crowds, we work with smaller ones, perfecting details, and yes, even handle little insignificant tasks...and we are just as faithful to God's details now as we believe we would be then.

- **You are all about your gifts, but your covering is interested in your fruit** - It's exciting to recognize the anointing on one's life. It's exciting to be developing in the spiritual things of God. One thing you will begin to find out about your anointing: if you don't get the necessary discipline and order in your life, having an anointing will still cost you a dollar to get on the bus. What I mean by that is simple - just because you're anointed doesn't mean you are going to achieve what you want to in your ministry. It's a great thing to be gifted, but it is more important we do something with that gift. The Lord's powerful words to the twelve: telling them not to rejoice that demons are subject to them, but rather, that their names were written in heaven, gives us powerful perspective on this topic. Your covering knows you are gifted and anointed and, at the same time, they want to see you make the gifts you have fruitful to the Lord. It's a process to make a tree bear fruit: there is planting, years of growing, pruning, watering, fertilizing, testing, and shaping to make a tree produce fruit. It's great to have an anointing, but your covering is more interested in your ability to walk in that covering versus watching your gifts go without purpose.

- **We are validating your ministry, not the other way around** - Ministry is made by relationship, especially the relationship between covering and those covered. Your covering puts their ministry name and reputation on the line to serve as your covering, especially if they see something within you but you aren't to a place of maturity yet. I've covered people who really thought they were doing me a favor by "allowing" me to cover them - insert obvious joke here. It's a great thing to train people for leadership, but believe me - your covering is doing far more for you than you are doing for them. Their teaching, love, caring, and concern helps bless you and grow you. To your leader, you are work. It's a work of love, but it still requires work. Don't overestimate your relevance. If you break from a leader without God's direction, your ministry won't go anywhere. Your leader will most likely go on, with or without you.

- **We love to edify you...so give us a reason to do so** - Bad leaders who never encourage people but are always negative have given every leader a bad name every time they have to correct something. I love to encourage the people I cover. I love to build up what you are doing right. So do most coverings. Most coverings like to look back at those they cover and really know the people under them are doing their best and living as God has commanded them. What we don't realize within Bible teaching is that edification is not unconditional. If you are doing something wrong, we can't build that up in you, because then you will be confused about the truth and we will be responsible for it. If you are doing something wrong, we have to bring it up at some point in time. If you don't want to be corrected...don't do things wrong. If you want to be edified, do the right things...problem solved!

- **You're not untouchable** - I am so sick of hearing "Touch not mine anointed! Touch not mine anointed!" anytime anything at all comes up. That is an example of misquoting the Word for selfish purposes. Every time I see it, I shake my head, realizing how disordered the church has become. Nowadays people don't even tolerate being asked a simple question or having a discussion about something without becoming irate and defensive. This is how I look at it: if you are so anointed, then I shouldn't have to be touching what you do all the time because it shouldn't all be so wrong. If any one of us is doing something in error, we are all become very touchable. That's just a Kingdom fact. The purpose of having a covering isn't to be a person who enables everything and complicit in sin, wrongdoing, or error. If we come to you with something, take it like a grown-up. Don't revert and hide behind gifts because that isn't why you have them. If you use your gifts like that, you will lose them. Also, don't be so defensive; that just lets your leader know that something is indeed wrong and that you are not in the right.

- **We have our bad days, too - you just never hear about them** - Once someone I covered told me if I was really her covering, I would have been checking up on her constantly. She was angry because I told her she would not be attending our event at my cost if she couldn't participate with us at mandatory meetings. I knew she was just blowing the meetings off because she was angry that her participation in the event had been notably diminished due to her immaturity and her rude behavior toward me. What she didn't know is that I was planning the event myself - when she was supposed to be the conference administrator - while she ran around in her bad mood - and was also dealing with chronic back pain, a dislocated shoulder, the death of my husband's grandfather, personal illness and other problems, stress, other ministry activities, and eight other people to attend to and cover. Despite all this, I was as available to her as I always am; she just wanted to be chased down because she was being childish. She might have never seen the personal pain and discomfort I was in, but that didn't change the fact that it was there. It wouldn't have matter had she known, however, because when she found out about some of it, she blew it off as if I never said it. I can say on behalf of most coverings: we don't like to dump our problems on you. We don't like to make you think we aren't there for you or can't be there for you because of something that is going on in our lives. Your covering doesn't use their personal problems as an excuse to escape ministry responsibilities, and neither should you. Yes, we have our bad days and our bad times - which makes it all the more relevant you don't storm off in a bad and nasty mood every time you don't get what you feel like you deserve from your leader. Instead of expecting your leader to make the overture, give them a call or note every now and then to be an encouragement and to ask how they are. Don't just contact them because you want guidance or feel you need something. Keep your leader covered in prayer and refrain from childishness because you just assume what you always see on the surface is how things really are.

- **Good leaders are also good followers** - I know it's cliché, but it's the truth: we learn how to be good leaders by being good followers to those who are in leadership over us. In following, we learn what to do and what not to do; what people who are led need in their lives; how to reveal truth in a powerful way; and how to see God work things in our lives because we ascribe to Him. All of us must work our way through God's timing and be faithful to all He has put in place. Want to be a better leader? Be a better follower first, and watch God work!

- **Be courteous** - Your gifts and anointing do not entitle you to be rude. I understand you may be angry at times, but it's not your place to mouth off to your covering or to others about your covering. Coverings should not be spoken to or of like casual friends; they should be spoken to like teachers, leaders, and guides in your life. Don't use casual slang, fowl or coarse language, or be rude in your presentation. If you wouldn't speak to your boss in a certain way, you shouldn't be speaking to your covering in that way, either.

- **We do not think we "own you"** - In my own personal opinion, this is the sorriest excuse I have ever heard for insubordination toward a leader - and yet I hear it over, and over, and over again. If you know something is expected of you, then do it. Your covering shouldn't have to twist your arm to get you to cooperate, only to be accused of thinking they own you and are becoming cult-like. That doesn't work with me and I'll tell you where it's at real quick if you want to go down that road, as I actually have training in cults and cult criteria. Until I require you to memorize the whole Bible, move to an isolated compound in the middle of nowhere, give me all your money, drink cyanide-laced Kool-Aid, kill yourself to chase after a comet, dress exactly like the person sitting next to you, and sacrifice your children at my feet - I don't want to hear it. You aren't being controlled when you are expected to be present for a meeting, at a service, or meet certain criteria to participate in an event. Your leader is here to help you - but they can't do it if you don't cooperate. If you don't want to, that's fine, then be mature and honest about it - don't make accusations that you don't know anything about.

- **Don't get involved when we discipline someone else under the covering** - I've not only heard of it, I've also experienced it myself: someone is so angry about the fact that they were addressed, they go and tell someone else, the whole time knowing that person is going to come and try and "correct" the covering...indirectly defending the person who feels they were wronged. If you want to remain in good standing with your covering, be direct about things that are going on and if you have a question about something, ask them. Good coverings don't discuss the people under their ministries with one another, unless there are circumstances which require the covering to literally step in and intervene between two people. Don't think you have the whole story when you only have half of it, and think you have the right to question leadership decisions. This only causes your leader to think that you're not ready to lead anyone, anywhere! Gossip doesn't just hurt others - when you listen to it and then try to defend it, it hurts you, too.

- **You're covering knows you - and doesn't appreciate it when you try to manipulate them** - I know when someone is trying to get me to do what they want me to do. I also hate that spirit. Just because you come on all meek, quiet, and humble doesn't mean we don't see through all that. Coverings don't operate on the "mama's boy/daddy's girl" kind of system where you can wrap your leader around your little finger and get whatever you want by flattery, deceit, or the right words at the right time. A good leader checks that spirit of Jezebel quickly, wastes no time with it, and will not only be extra-cautious the next time, but will also not give you the same consideration they might have had you behaved more uprightly.

- **We're not psychics, but we do know when something's wrong** - We don't know every detail of your life and what you are doing every second of your day. When you say you are busy, that may very well be true. That's not real descriptive to describe what's going on; most people are busy. Even though we are not psychics, we do know when we aren't sensing something as right by the Spirit - whether you are busy or not. Most coverings know when they are being lied to. They also know the signs of someone being upset about something and not being direct about the issue: lack of attendance or presence, lack of communication, etc., especially if this behavior occurs after something obviously happened. Don't use the "busy" excuse with a leader; if something is wrong, be direct. Lying to a leader only creates more problems and the situation where ultimatums often come into play: either get it together or get out.

- **Be fully disclosing about matters** - Ever deal with one of those people who tells you about a situation, only to leave out fifteen relevant details that change how they look in the situation? Being honest with your leader about things that happen is the best way to display your accountability toward them. When a leader finds out someone has been deceitful...edification does not happen.

As the Lord continues to reveal more to me on covering, I will continue to write as His apostle, that the dialogue may continue, and we may all grow in our understanding of leadership in today's church.

Chapter Twenty-One

THE THINGS I WISH COVERINGS KNEW ABOUT COVERING

Look! I made him a witness to the peoples, a leader and a commander for the peoples.
– Isaiah 55:4 (LEB)

My two most infamous writings are both about covering: *The Things I Wish People Knew About Covering* and *More Things I Wish People Knew About Covering*. Initially, it was a surprise to me that these two notes took off like they did. In hindsight, I understand why they were so popular: they touched on a universal topic. The issue of covering is a controversial one, and yet an important one, in today's church. The reason why it is so common and important is because on both ends, we are seeing people totally out of control. We are quick to point out out-of-control leaders and, on the other hand, out-of-control individuals under a ministry. Seeing extremes means that we must take heart to understand what covering and being covered is about in a deeper way.

Recent experiences have caused me to step back and think more about covering. When I say "recent," I am recalling events that have happened within this past year as pertains to those I cover and the result of those events. In my day, I feel as if I have seen every childish temper tantrum in the book by people who supposedly have a "calling." I've been lectured on how anointed they are, how they see things in people I don't, and if I don't do it their way, they just won't participate anymore. I won't get into the depth of witchcraft I am seeing: that will be for another note. What I am realizing is the opposite of order is not simply disorder, it is witchcraft. It is believing one's self to be above any semblance of order, therefore disordered, but believing one has the power to decide that they do not need to be subject to God's order. Therein lies the essence of power and control: it is Satan's "I will" statements, believing they can do better than God. No matter what they may claim to believe about God, they are not subject to God in their own lives. They have not learned submission to Him and do not know how to be sensitive to the Holy Spirit's leading in their lives. As a result, they carry what some call a "bastard spirit." In order to become sons and daughters, we must know order, which breeds maturity.

It is the covering's job to work toward this maturity. This is a difficult task in our modern church, where people gather leaders to themselves who tickle their ears and entertain them, right in accordance with the prophecies of this time. In an earlier work of mine, titled, *Decency and Order*, I pointed out the modern-day phenomenon that people pick leaders who deliberately tickle where they are rather than challenging them...or at least they think will not challenge them. In other words, what they are working is a manipulation of God's system: they look like they are in order, when they in actuality are not in order. They are working witchcraft and trying to look all holy and saintly in the process. And today's coverings don't know what to make of it. I think in some ways, coverings today are grossly unprepared for the level of spiritual warfare that comes simply from agreeing to be somebody's leader. We expect it from the nasty woman who doesn't like us, we expect warfare from the man who doesn't think we should be where we are, but in other places...we miss it. Sometimes the witchcraft and demonic activity that touches us the closest is that which comes from our so-called spiritual sons and daughters. As a result, a covering needs to guard themselves spiritually, and refrain from breaking faith with all God has called them to be and do.

I want to say that this is not a post about bad coverings or debating things about covering. We all know about bad leadership, about what to look for, what to say, and how to handle it. What I am attempting to do here is help good coverings guard themselves spiritually from people who intend to do them harm by getting close to them in the spiritual realm. Here we are looking at the practical aspects of covering that, in some way, may defy our logic and thinking about these matters. We've been trained to love and give until we have nothing left...and now too many coverings literally have nothing left. They risk their reputations, health, well-being, and even their ministries to cover people who need to be cut off quickly and cleanly. Here are some ways for coverings to maintain discernment in the process, and realize spiritual parenthood is not for the faint of heart.

- **Operate an unspoken "trial period"** - When someone comes to me for covering, we "feel" things out for the first four-to-six weeks. I don't explain it like that to them, but use that time frame to watch them for a few weeks before I allow them to start formal training with me. How they behave during this period is very tell-tale to how they will be later on. If I notice things within them that will cause harm to my ministry or its reputation, or they don't seem as if they will be a good fit with the ministry I operate, they are usually politely and quietly informed of this. Not every leader is right for every person, and some people just aren't to a place where any covering will be right for them. If they are already failing to meet up with established requirements and already making a ruckus, they are dismissed before either one of us has become too involved.

- **You're not their "pal"** - I have met two extremes in covering, and have yet to find a lot of balance between the two. One extreme is the "best pal:" they go shopping, lunching, to social events, to movies, and do everything together. The other extreme is the covering who won't even let you eat at the same table with them. I think, as with all things, the truth lies somewhere in the middle. A covering is a friend in the same concept that God is our friend: it is a friend but, at the same time, is an authority and carries responsibility. A covering should make themselves available to those they cover for discussion and issues, and the person should feel comfortable going to their covering. There are limits and boundaries to this, however. A covering should not be treated like a girlfriend or guy friend. They should never be "paling" around with those they cover. Above all, a covering needs to maintain their position as having authority and exercising that authority as applicable. Years ago a pastor over a church I attended used to say that if he was invited, he'd go fishing with you because he wanted to go fishing, but you still needed to remember he was your pastor. I think this is an interesting comparison, so I am going to use it as the model for what I am talking about here. Don't be using the people you cover as your buddies. It's fine to relate how events and things went, it's fine to talk about stuff, I'll even say it's fine to go out to lunch once in a while, or to have fun or talk...but don't let them forget who God has appointed you to be in their life. It is not fine to treat covering like a gigantic trip to the mall.

- **You can't make personal choices for them** - One of the most frustrating things to me about covering is watching those I cover fall into certain behaviors or paths that I know will be destructive for them. It can be as simple as watching them cut people out of their lives, knowing they are in the wrong by doing so, or watching them take more drastic actions, such as with their well-being or relationships. I remember going to a person I used to cover with a situation such as this: she had someone in her life who was a friend, who she tried to cover, and when the woman made a personal choice she disagreed with, the woman I covered decided she wanted to cut her off. I did everything I could to encourage this woman I used to cover that she shouldn't cut her off - but it didn't matter, she did what she wanted anyway. If we release ourselves from trying to intervene in this way - we are releasing ourselves from a lot of stress and heartache. It's the same as when a natural child brings home a date we don't like - unless some sort of impending harm is coming their way, it's our place to back off and let them work these personal matters out for themselves. In the same way, the reverse is true: they do not get a say about your personal choices, friends, acquaintances, etc., either.

- **Don't believe everything they tell you about their past leaders** - Spiritual witchcraft is clever from the start. How these people get you is by coming to you with some sort of crazy horror story that appalls every sense of leadership a good leader holds dear and claims for their own. Then you are so shocked from what you hear that you start addressing the leadership issues rather than the reason why those things came up. They manipulate us by shocking us and detract from the real issue at hand - which should be, "Why were you told that?" or "Why did they handle things like that?" Even in asking those matters, we may not find totally honest answers - but we can tell a lot about them from how they answer when they are put on the spot. Leaders, I am the first to acknowledge both good and bad leaders are out there - but we need to respect the leadership decisions made by other leaders until we have concrete evidence to the contrary. Evidence to the contrary isn't a dramatic story told by someone who wants us to become their leader now.

- **Beware flattery** - Leaders today face a tough job. It's difficult to get people to tithe, to encourage, to even say "thank you" most of the time. We work long hours as jacks of all our trades and then face personal lives that often have their own difficulties and challenges. A covering that is trying to manipulate you will come to you with flattery. They'll do everything everyone else doesn't, then some: all the time, all over you, thanking you, mentioning you by name, recommending you to all their friends, and trying to draw you further and further into a world that they can orchestrate via control. I don't want to make leaders feel like they need to be suspicious of every compliment, honor, or dignity move those under them make, because they don't. What I am talking about are the ones who are always doing it, every time you turn around, without any cause or warrant. Not only are they doing it, they are doing it publically, in front of others, and to be noticed and get noticed.

- **Don't be bullied** - People who are covered today know that they can get whatever they want in the "buffet church." They can have a little dessert over here, a whole lot of whipped cream, a cup of soda, and a pile of candy rather than meat, potatoes, milk, and vegetables. They know if their leader doesn't do what they want, they can find a leader somehow, some way, somewhere, who will do what they want. So they bully their leaders: if the leader doesn't do what they want, they won't do something. If the leader doesn't handle things the way they want, they won't be covered anymore. Leaders give into this time and time again because they don't want to watch people leave their covering, for whatever the reason may be. All giving in to this kind of behavior does is lets someone know all your weaknesses and weak areas - and exactly what buttons to push, when and where, to get what they want. Giving in once means they will expect you to give in again...and again...and again.

- **Watch control and manipulation** - Akin to bullying is control and manipulation. Don't allow someone you cover to come and tell you what's wrong with all your friends, what's wrong with your group or ministry, or somehow offer to help you 'fix' some of these problems. Be sure to sit back and watch how those you cover interact not just with you, but with one another. Are they always trying to pick a fight? Do they overstep boundaries of order in other ways in their lives? Do they understand there is a time and a place for things? Do they operate in a sense of self-control? Do they know their own positioning within order? Do they have to have the last word all the time? No matter how they interact with you, how they interact with others is also key to how they will handle being under you as their covering.

- **Their anointing and sixty-five cents will get them on the bus** - It's easy to be enamored with someone who is very gifted and anointed, or even someone who has the potential to make their gifts and calling very great with the right training. It's easy to want to promote that anointing and place it above the problems in character you may be seeing as a leader. What we need to keep in mind in all things is this: being anointed is great. Having a calling is great. Being gifted is great. If we don't align ourselves with God's order, the gifts, anointings, and callings we see in someone will go to waste. I have seen some of the most anointed people fall by the wayside because they won't get their acts together. Don't be bewitched by gifts or anointing - because they are empty without substance.

- **Beware subtle attempts to rebuke you** - Some of the people we cover can be the most vicious...and we won't even see it coming because they spew their venom in the form of a question or the form of an opinion. "Well Apostle, don't you think...?" or "I would do this...." or my favorite, "This is what you should do..." Excuse me? I don't recall asking for an opinion! This is a rebuke in disguise: it's a subtle way someone under your covering is trying to usurp authority and get in their own form of control within your work. If you ask, that's one thing; if it is unsolicited, it is something else entirely different.

- **Beware those who seek to make an ally out of you** - Then there are those who come to you requesting covering who walk in the spirit of division. They come and very much cotton to you as their leader. They seem to be all about you and about learning from you and how important you are to them...until you start to notice things. They start criticizing other people you work with...they find something wrong with your friends....they start criticizing others under your ministry...and it's all done in the name of "God put us together so I have to be careful about myself." Hmmmm....suddenly the people you've worked with forever aren't good enough for your "spiritual child" and you should get rid of all of them and just pioneer it with a bad spirit...never and not in any uncertain terms! This individual isn't looking for a covering, they are looking for an ally: they want their leader to endorse them and attempt to isolate them from everyone who might suggest to the leader that they are behaving in a manner that requires disciplinary action. When this happens, mark those that cause division. Don't leave your friends, ministry acquaintances, advisers, and those you've worked with forever. Either that individual can keep their mouth shut or can grow up. If they can't, they can find a new covering.

- **Don't tell them everything you notice...at least not right away** - My mother used to say to me, "Just because I don't say anything doesn't mean I don't know what's going on." I never understood what she meant by this until I started covering people. As coverings, we want to show people things and fix it right away. What we need to do instead is sit back and watch for a bit before we bring something to someone. It is possible that a misunderstanding can come about, or that we misread something - and beyond that, it's possible that we can identify the root of a problem much better and with much more accuracy if we have all the information. Don't talk about everything all the time, run tale-bearing...wait for God's timing and His handling of every situation.

- **Enforce your guidelines** - Sometimes I wonder why we go through the trouble to establish guidelines when we don't enforce them. If you have requirements that people must follow to be covered by you, enforce them. If they don't follow them, they can stop being under your covering or they can face certain disciplinary options. Stop letting these people run your leadership. They can measure up or they can leave.

- **Know those who labor among you** - We use this verse to mean a lot of things, and we usually use it to justify knowing anything and everything we want to know about a minister's private life. This is not the context of the passage. We are commanded to know those who labor among us - know their strengths and weaknesses, who they are, and what spirit they operate by. We need to recognize things when we see them and stop pretending they aren't there. We need to know when someone is for us, against us, and how to tell the difference.

This is true for those under our ministries as it is for those we submit to in leadership as well.

- **Remain in order** - It can be difficult for a leader to remain within God's order and observing God's principles for handling various situations when we get so angry, we are ready to set someone that we cover on fire. I've had times where all I wanted to do was send someone a letter using every curse word in the book - but that was me in the flesh, not God. I've learned to wait on God's timing when that happens, and wait for His order to manifest. As leaders, we too have to remain in God's order, timing, and tone when things arise. If something is questionable, we seek out wise counsel or we take it before the Lord, or both. If it just doesn't feel like the right time to do something, we wait it out until it is. In the meantime and handling the situation, we do all things decently and in order.

- **Know when it's time to disassociate** - We, as leaders, fear disassociation. We think dismissing someone from ministry or disfellowshipping them will cause us dissatisfaction with God, with others, or a bad reputation. We fear that disassociation will make us hypocrites because we talk all the time about unity. We can't keep people around because we fear they will harm us by disassociation. The Bible itself upholds there are people we should dismiss from the ministry, there are people we should not unite with, and people we should break a unity from for our own spiritual well-being. If someone is going too far, behaving badly, causing disunity and disruption, or somehow acting unseemly - especially after they have had the proper time and counsel to order themselves with the disciplines of God - it's time to address the behavior, wish them well, and keep on moving. Holding onto someone like this only hurts your unity with the genuine Body of believers.

Covering is a process. Being covered is a process. Walking in decency and order means being agents of decency and order...in all that we do...and not fearing the call to walk in the godly disciplines of the

Lord.

Chapter Twenty-Two

COVERING: AN ASSIGNMENT OF LOVE

If I speak in the tongues of men and of angels, but have not love, I am only a resounding gong or a clanging cymbal. If I have the gift of prophecy and can fathom all mysteries and all knowledge, and if I have a faith that can move mountains, but have not love, I am nothing. If I give all I possess to the poor and surrender my body to the flames, but have not love, I gain nothing.
– 1 Corinthians 13:1-3 (NIV)

During a recent phone call and then being on a conference call with specific words of prayer spoken over me, I realized for the first time ever that covering is an assignment. It is more than just something that we do to look good in ministry or something that we do to impress people: it is a true drawing (which I have already described covering as, for many years) between the covering and the individual who is covered. Such a relationship comes about by revelation, as God brings the two together for His purpose and His edification. God assigns people for us to cover. He entrusts them to us and, as a covering does, we work in that walk of 'perfect love' that covers a multitude of sins (1 Peter 1:22). As a covering, we are called to walk in prayer, in intercession, in true love, and in true concern and care for those we cover.

I have written extensively on covering over the years: the good, the bad, the ugly, the indifferent, and the organizational. For the most part, most of what I've written is about the way that we should handle those we cover and the proper conduct for those that we cover. Today I am writing a little differently, because I am writing on the heart of the covering. We can't cover as we need to if we don't love those that we cover, and if we don't have the proper heart for it. I have met many, many gifted apostles, prophets, and pastors who were brilliant with scholarship, brilliant in instruction and revelation from the Word, even great with vision and organization. They are often sincere people who may be equipped from God...but they are missing something. They have difficulty covering others, either operating as tyrants, or with a constant rotational flow of people under them because they can't keep covering people. I myself was covered by someone like this for awhile. She was brilliant in the information, brilliant in the scholarship of the apostolic, but terrible with the people, myself included. A former leader even warned me about my this woman - but at the time, I didn't listen because I was trying very hard to be fair and unbiased...big mistake (but that is neither here nor there anymore). There are so many who I see, even now, like this in the church: they are gifted, even anointed...but missing something essential in their walk, because instead of loving those they cover, they treat everyone as a taskmaster.

I have covered people in my ministry since 2004. Learning how to cover as an apostle has been an interesting process in my life. When I started out covering, I didn't understand what covering was. I made many mistakes over the years and organized, reorganized, and reworked what I was doing many times over to bring it into understanding of the office and the revelation at hand. In the past eight years, I've seen people come and go. The first person I ever covered is still under the covering of this ministry, several years later. I've had to dismiss several people from my covering over time. Some people just became distant and I never heard from them again. My dirty little secret for a long time with covering was that I simply hated it. It was a chore, a bother, the people were difficult and disobedient, a stress factor, and often a nuisance. One of the women I used to cover became such a problem, I used to avoid answering the phone because she called everyday - sometimes two or three times per day - with personal issues to discuss, people to gossip and complain about, and a defiant, nasty attitude. I tried to work with her, I tried to act with grace - I was an incredibly tolerant and patient leader with her -

until the time came when she saw fit to simply stop talking to me and never return a phone call again. There were the ones who appeared to be everything someone studying with a leader should be - everything from calling me "Godmommy" (which please, those who are currently covered by me - don't do!) to claiming revelation and purpose - only to turn on me with a venomous spatter and see fit to disgrace me with vile and slander. Then we had the ones who just never seemed to get it together, no matter what I did - equally frustrating and challenging. Watching those who covered others was also difficult, especially when I would try to guide and correct their leadership skills, to no avail.

For a long time I thought I was just not graced to work with people as their leader on the level of covering. Given the above examples, I am sure you can see why. I am not the world's most patient person, and I don't tolerate a lot of nonsense. I don't like seeing people's gifts go to waste as they spend time pursuing endless nonsense, and I seriously dislike watching people mistreat others. I wrote guidelines, revised the guidelines, revised them again a few months later, and kept trying to find the perfect avenue for dealing with covering. It seemed like no matter what I did, people were seeking to take advantage of me, or seeking to get by with a free ride, thinking they wouldn't be disciplined when they behaved in an improper manner.

Then, one day, things began to change. The first thing that changed is I looked around and realized a large number of the people I was working with as their covering were no longer with me. I didn't lose everybody, but the majority of them were gone. For the first time in years, I was able to sigh and step back. The other thing that started to happen is I was able to start looking at covering differently. I never called it an "assignment," but I saw the drawing, and the heart that God gave me for certain people. I didn't realize it was for covering, at the time. I never went to anyone and told them they were supposed to be my covering (I never have and never will - I let God reveal to those who are to be covered and then we talk about it when they are ready). I just did what God asked me to do. I interceded for people in my life, some of them, for many years. I was on my face in prayer as they went through their trials. I cried with them, I supported them, I talked them through it, I gave them advice. I gave them the Word, both *Logos* and *Rhema*. I grieved as I watched many of them mistreated by bad leaders and people who were just trying to take advantage of them. I stood by through their situations, be they spousal abuse, unemployment, divorce, issues with their children, issues with their call, and the like, as they took their first steps into the true calling God had for them. I encouraged them and spoke to them whatever God gave for me to speak. I was there when they needed me, and backed off when it wasn't my place to speak up. I did, and continue to do, for them what my apostle did with me during the years that I spent under someone she knew, in the long run, wasn't going to be good for me, because she saw the former leader as a leader.

Many of these people are now a part of the work, covered by me, however they may describe that (as we all know people use different terms to describe leadership in their lives). They are now covered upfront, where everyone can see, but the real work of the covering began when God placed them on my heart. I am realizing that the relationship God gives to a covering is about more than being acknowledged as someone's leader. It is just as much about what we go through with and for those we cover that is never spoken about. It's about the true love that we have for these people and our willingness to stand with them and see them through, even if we aren't ever called their "covering" on the surface. I don't hate covering anymore. It might have taken me a long time, but God revealed to me that the reason I disliked covering is because I kept trying to cover people who I was not assigned to lead. I kept trying to forge something that was not placed there by God. While I certainly loved and cared about those that I covered, I didn't love and care about them as one who was called to cover them, in the way I needed to for the relationship to develop in them and in me. I learn as much from those I cover as I do now from anywhere else, and realize that in Christ, the leader not only brings something to the student, but the student to the leader, as well.

We can be brilliant minds in the apostolic, in the Bible, in scholarship. We can be the best preachers you've ever seen. We can take the world by storm with our fancy words and ways. If we don't have love, we are just a lot of noise, and we have no right to call ourselves anyone's covering or leader. It is definitely something that develops as God works within us through our own experiences with our leaders and with those who follow our work who are often difficult. It is something that is either within us, or it is not. We will never get there if we think of covering as a have-to chore that must get done or something whereby we require people to follow us so we can have large throngs of people under our ministries. Somehow, when God draws the people to us and places that true love within us for them, it all works out right. The regulations don't seem so important; everyone just does what they are supposed to do, even without asking. The work gets done, because both covering and the one covered are ready for work and ready to help, one to another. Accountability doesn't seem so difficult, because no one is judging anyone else. Everyone is ready and willing to work, and a trust exists that doesn't if a leader is busy trying to cover up for the fact that love is not there. Covering is not a system; it's not a dictatorship; it's a relationship that God entrusts us with, to develop and grow His leaders and His people into all they are destined to become. It's an assignment He gives us - one where the heart we have for those we cover (the Holy Spirit working within us) guides us in correction, education, and empowerment.

The sooner we recognize this...the sooner we will get to a place of understanding on leadership...and the Kingdom of God can turn the world upside down, everywhere one of God's servants steps down.

Chapter Twenty-Three

BECOMING ALL THINGS TO ALL PEOPLE

The LORD hath appeared of old unto me, saying, Yea, I have loved thee with an everlasting love: therefore with lovingkindness have I drawn thee.
– Jeremiah 31:3

When I started out in ministry almost twenty years ago, I was still Catholic. I also wasn't a very nice person. I was sociable, but judgmental. By my nature, I am serious and intense to the point of being grave. I like to think, to figure, to analyze. Yes, that is part of what makes me a good apostle - but at the time, I was so out of balance, I wasn't much good to anybody. After I was born again, I was still much of the same way: serious, austere, judgmental, perhaps even argumentative at times. Much of my conversion to the faith of the Lord came about through my intellect rather than my emotions, and so I figured everyone reasoned that way. I thought I would make such incredible arguments, people would have to want to become Christian. That means I spent a lot of time fighting with people over this doctrine or that, insistent I was right, and damning people to hell who dared to disagree with me. After all, I had Bible verses! I had answers for everything! They were just ignorant. I lived frustrated and angry...because I knew I had to be right.

One day God spoke to me, clear as day: "Lee Ann, people aren't saved because they agree with you. They are saved because of their relationship with Me."

I cried for three days. I couldn't believe God would speak to me like that. Here I was, trying to be in the ministry He said I was supposed to be in, and He tells me I am doing it all wrong. Part of me was mad at God. Another part of me was mad at everyone else, because I figured if they would have just cooperated, God wouldn't be having this conversation with me. The other part of me was mad because I didn't want to think I was wrong about something.

In hindsight, God was beginning to teach me an important principle: He was teaching me the foundations to becoming all things to all people. This first realization was my first break with the law I'd lived by my whole life, and my tears were just as much about that as they were about the chastisement I was experiencing. I was born again, but I lived by the law. I lived according to strict outward codes of so-called holiness and adhered to the doctrines of men. I struggled with my identity as a woman. I struggled in my relationships. I struggled with my leaders and I struggled within myself. I didn't like who I was, because I didn't know who I was in Christ. I didn't understand who God was calling me to be, or who He was asking me to be. I didn't understand, and I was struggling...because I like to understand. I was hardened, thinking holiness meant I had to be hard, unfeeling, uncaring, and uncompassionate.

Over the next several years, God dealt with me about myself, and about the concepts we hold so dear in the church because we simply do not want to let go. I experienced different religious services. I lobbied for women's issues, and dealt with politics. I sat with the women who contemplated abortion or who felt they had no other option at some point in time. I worked with and alongside the gay community, educating about HIV/AIDS because the church didn't want to touch it. I moderated the discussions about sex among women who were afraid to talk about it to anyone, even their husbands. I sat in the room with client after client, having to ask personal questions about their intimate lives, while doing HIV testing to assess risk. I saw a side of divorce that we don't consider in the church, as many push against divorce, thereby pushing the agenda of bad marriage. I worked with women inmates and women in halfway houses. I did literacy training. I held the hand of the woman who struggled with infertility. I watched the battered woman go back to her abuser, even becoming that battered woman multiple times throughout my adult life. I talked to the soldier with PTSD so severe, he couldn't talk about what he saw in combat, now nearly thirty years later. Over the years, I have watched people struggle, seeking, and hoping for answers, waiting for someone to come along who would not judge them, but instead, would reach out their hand and provide them with the love and support they need.

One day, while on the phone with someone who openly lives a life many in the church would disapprove of, I silently asked God why I was having this conversation. He said to me, "I am teaching you to become all things to all people." I didn't see the power in this statement at the time, but I see it now. God was quoting His Word: *"Though I am free and belong to no man, I make myself a slave to everyone, to win as many as possible. To the Jews I became like a Jew, to win the Jews. To those under the law I became like one under the law (though I myself am not under the law), so as to win those under the law. To those not having the law I became like one not having the law (though I am not free from God's law but am under Christ's law), so as to win those not having the law. To the weak I became weak, to win the weak. I have become all things to all men so that by all possible means I might save some. I do all this for the sake of the gospel, that I may share in its blessings."* (1 Corinthians 9:19-23, NIV)

The experiences I have had, in advocacy, education, and ministry, have taught me powerfully on God's precept of reconciliation and restoration. Apostles especially are called to act as ministers of reconciliation. We cannot operate in this ministry if we are so hung up on a hardened concept of faith that we can't reach out to everyone. God was teaching me, and continues to teach me, how I can reach out to people so that they might become reconciled to God, wherever they may be on that issue in their lives. This is a work that is for the sake of the Gospel - it is not contrary to it. Loving people doesn't mean we believe everything they do is right. It doesn't change what God has called sin, nor does it minimize it. What it does do is helps people to know that everything they have done does not have to be the end for them. It also helps us to consider our own selves and what God has brought us from, causing us to be humble instead of arrogant, using holiness as an excuse to abuse others. So much rhetoric in today's church condemns people for things that we ourselves are just as guilty of, only in different ways. Maybe you did not have an abortion in your day or you never struggled with same sex attraction, but I will venture you did gossip about someone, killing their reputation, and that you have united yourself to something idolatrous at some point, thereby creating an unholy union. If I say that, people say "Well, apostle, you don't understand what I went through." That's true - and you don't know what someone else went through, so stop judging them. Throwing the book at people over a few rhetorical issues isn't getting us anywhere. It is not a witness, and it is not productive. It is not becoming all things to all men - becoming a servant - becoming a solution instead of a problem - it is a deterrent to the Word.

Holiness is not a judgment: it is an assessment of ourselves. We talk about it all the time because the church wants to see an exterior of what it used to be. We can't be that now because the exterior never was. Throughout history, those leading the church and those in the church have struggled with the same issues we see today. Some of the biggest names in church history had the worst struggles with drug addiction, adultery, sleeping around, family issues, and the like. Some of them overcame those issues, but many of them did not. There are those in history who would find some of the modern concepts of holiness absurd and ridiculous. God is calling us to get real and get it together so we can help someone out, to become all things to all people. Stop the nonsense, stop imposing our perspectives on others, stop the "right fight," and start being productive. Holiness puts the burden on us - not on everyone else - to do what we know is right. It raises our standard, not the standards of the secular world or government. Instead of looking at everyone else, holiness stands to make us examine ourselves and the areas where we do not measure up in the pursuit that we will seek out God and walk with Him all the more.

We are holding on to stubborn pride in today's church and it is hurting our ability to minister and reach out. I understand a desire to stand for principle and to uphold holiness, but I also see the Word of God as a collection of divine precepts that encourage us to find a middle ground on its presented issues. Holiness, compassion, and love are not opposites. On the contrary, if we are living according to holiness, we will live in love. If we get so obsessed with holiness that it's all we think about, we get so hung up on rules and regulations that we lose sight of why God calls us to be a set apart people in this world. Too much preoccupation with holiness leads to self-righteousness, which leads us straight into rules, which leads us straight into legalism. Too much preoccupation with misguided love leads us into absurdities and abhorrent doctrines. We need to find the balance between the two: between love and holiness, compassion and principle. Holiness shows people the way, while love draws to the truth. In holiness we live as God calls, and in love, we become what we need to become to draw them to God's truth.

I will allow nothing to stop me from reaching out in the Gospel. If I am in a legalistic setting, I will wear a long skirt, I will put on a wig, I won't wear make-up, I will use the King James Version of the Bible, I won't wear pants, I won't talk pop culture in my message, I'll sing the old songs of the church, and I will make sure my secular ring tone does not go off in the church building. If I am in a setting where people need love, I will not let the fact that someone had an abortion or a pregnancy out of wedlock, is gay, is HIV positive, is or has been in prison, is a battered woman, or has a struggle in their lives stop me from reaching out to them in love. I will be what is needed at that moment, in that time, to that person, that human being created in God's image despite the course their lives, actions, and ways may have taken them. If they need a hug, they will get a hug. If they need a listening ear, they will get a listening ear. If they need a solution to their situation, I will be their solution. I will be all things to all people. It doesn't mean I agree with them, or will do the things that they do - but it does mean that I will not let a fear of compromise stop me from being the only living epistle these people may ever know. It's not compromise to live in God's love. It's just becoming all things to all people, that I may save some. People, let's get past our issues, so we can help people resolve theirs.

Chapter Twenty-Four

A GUIDE TO INTERNATIONAL COVERING: COVERING PEOPLE OVERSEAS

So the churches were being strengthened in the faith and were growing in number every day.
– Acts 16:5 (LEB)

More often than not, when people "hang out" a ministry shingle, the first people they hear from are those who are overseas. This is especially prevalent as the internet has made international ministry a tangible facet to ministry life. Initially it seems exciting and complimentary to be contacted by foreign ministries. Over time, it becomes more commonplace, especially as more and more foreign ministries contact with very specific desires in mind. Initial communications seem reticent and receiving...then start the requests for this, that and something else: money, Bibles, equipment, etc. Maybe they want to be "your ministry representative" in their country. If the minister meets these requests...in come more...and more. If the minister denies a request, communications become scarce. Then the cycle begins again with another foreign ministry, also desiring similar, if not the same things...and so on...and so forth...in what can feel like a frustrating and unsuccessful cycle.

Covering internationally is difficult for one reason: because you can't immediately jet off to that country and see the situation of the ministry. You may not be able to communicate via telephone on a regular basis due to high calling costs. You don't know what is true from what is not true, and much of what goes on goes on by trust. There can be communication difficulties if that person does not speak English. People in other countries may need a different type of Christian education than those in the United States, if for no other reason than they have been exposed to 'mixed' systems of belief that incorporate Christian and pagan ideas.

Covering internationally takes God's grace and extensive planning. It is different than covering others in the United States (which is where I am from, so that is the platform I am writing this from) or from an immediate nation where you may live. In order to successfully cover those you can't jump in the car and see in a few hours, here are a few keys to bringing forth solid covering and instruction that can help people all over the world.

Before I begin, I want to say the following: I am certainly not implying that every minister overseas lies about their circumstance or is somehow untrustworthy. I know many ministers who work internationally and are awesome men and women of God. They are trustworthy, capable, and powerful in the Word. Let's not forget one thing, however: they aren't soliciting ministers in the United States for things. We cannot ignore the fact that scams do exist. They exist in the United States as much as they do anywhere else. The difference, however, is that because we live in the United States, it is easier to figure out when something is wrong, because we are here. When dealing internationally, we have to be more careful. That having been said, let's look at our points.

- **Investigate, investigate, investigate!** - Just because you get an email telling you a long story about dire conditions, orphans, widows, and poverty doesn't mean those conditions actually exist. People exaggerate - they know how to tell a great story to illicit a certain response. This is especially true when it comes to Christians. Poverty, injustice, and mistreatment all tug at our heartstrings so we start paying attention with our emotions rather than our sound judgment and God's Spirit witnessing within. Don't just trust everything you are told. Investigate into foreign ministries. Check them out online, do a search on the email address they send emails from, look in the 'to' box on the email and see just how many other ministries they hit up, investigate into websites, do searches for the ministry name, and more. Check into the region they claim they are from and the conditions that exist there. Be wise as serpents, and innocent as doves.

- **Know the countries that contact you** - It's easy to think you know about India, Nigeria, Pakistan, or Egypt based on stereotypes and concepts you've heard from various sources. It's a lot harder to step back in discernment and truly discover the situations that exist in those nations. Not everyone in Nigeria is a "scammer." Not everyone in India lives in poverty. Not everyone in Pakistan lives under intense persecution. Simple research can introduce you to economics, politics, languages, and more that can help your interaction with someone in a certain country, what they may indeed be facing, and give better discernment when it comes to things they may come and tell you which may or may not be true. If you are called to interact with a certain nation by God's command, consider learning one of the native languages to that nation. For example, I know I am called to the European continent, the Middle East, and Latin America - so I am learning various languages that can help me communicate with people in the nations found in those areas. Doing so shows respect, and also helps clarify potential language barriers.

- **Ask for paperwork** - In the United States, we have a non-profit process known as 501 (c)(3) tax exemption. This means that, according to the Internal Revenue Service, a ministry organization is considered "charitable" and people can give to that organization without the money being taxed. Even though they don't call it "non-profit," most countries worldwide have a system by which a ministry organization is considered "charitable" and, therefore, legally allowed to collect donations. Do ask for copies of their filed paperwork and legal tax exemptions/charitable status. If they don't have this status, ask why. Odds are good that if they don't have it, the organization has somehow been considered 'subversive' for reasons other than religion. Don't accept the answer that they are being persecuted because they are Christian - because this is most likely untrue on a governmental level.

- **Have guidelines they must abide by - and show forth in signature** - It's essential that, when covering people, we have guidelines for them to follow. These guidelines should reflect Bible leadership and plain, old-fashioned common sense. It is especially important that those who are covered internationally have guidelines are required to follow - and that those requirements be upheld. They aren't a forum for *Let's Make A Deal*. If the guidelines require tithing, then they have to tithe - it doesn't matter how poor they think they are, they are still required to give. If they want to be covered but don't want to tithe, then they can't be covered. If they want to be covered but don't want to participate in the regular meetings, then they can't be covered. If they want to be covered but don't want to write the monthly reports, then they can't be covered. It needs to be that simple. Giving in on guidelines they just don't feel they can or want to meet shows that you, as their leader, can be manipulated and pushed around if they play the right buttons. This needs to be avoided - most certainly - especially given the next point.

- **Foreigners may have very fixed concepts about things that may need changing** - I'll never forget the day a man from Pakistan sent me a message on Facebook: "You come to my country!" My response? "Oh no, I not come to your country!" This is an example of a difference in cultural approach between nations. Other countries are not the United States - especially those in non-western nations. They have different social interactions, different concepts about men and women, different ideas about money, about ways money should be distributed, about giving, and about doctrinal concepts. The point on 'doctrinal concepts' is extremely important when covering. On initial examination, many of them sound Christian - they seem to know how to use the Bible and they seem to understand basics of doctrine and talk of Jesus. Upon closer examination, however, other issues may come to light that will need address. They may be mixing different Christian beliefs with ancestral worship, paganism, or occult practices, engaged with secret societies, or taking in so-called Biblical teaching from any number of sources accessible to them (Mormons, Jehovah's Witnesses, etc.). If you are to correct their incorrect understandings, it is essential that they understand your role in their life. They need to understand about the five-fold ministry and what you, as an apostle, prophet, etc., do in their life and ministry. They need to realize that you are an authority to them - and that they must speak with you in a certain manner, holding forth respect and courtesy, and do not have the right to undermine you or lie to you. If they do not feel that they can handle this system of respect, they should politely be informed that they would be better served elsewhere.

- **Don't be bullied** - Many ministries overseas that are seeking American covering are interested in what the American ministry can do for them. This means they can be demanding with time, impatient with the minister at hand, expect instant responses, and expect hours and hours of instruction, free materials, and yes, even money - all at the drop of a hat. This spirit needs to be checked with a foreign minister just as much as we would check it with an American counterpart. Foreign ministers need to realize they are not the only people covered by that person, that they are not mind-readers and don't know when a situation is up if they are not told as such, and that respect, decency, and order are all essential in their interaction with you, as their leader.

- **Do not agree to sponsor anything - not schooling, education, etc. through direct or alternative sources** - We have covering all wrong. It is not the job of a covering to financially sponsor everyone they cover. When covering, you are giving your time, your teaching, your materials, your instruction, etc. to them - and it is their job to give tithes and offerings to you. That's God's system, not the other way around. When it comes to foreigners, many foreigners are professional beggars - they know how to sound pathetic to get money. This pattern of begging needs to end in covering. A covering is not meant to meet every need an organization has, that's not a covering, it's a sponsor - and, while we are at it, a covering is under no obligation to meet personal financial needs, such as schooling or education. This is also a well-known international scam by which Americans have lost thousands upon millions of dollars. Make it explicitly clear that you are not covering them in their financial needs. Do not become a bank.

- **Expect them to make tithes and offerings** - Everyone in the Kingdom is required to bring forth tithes and offerings into God's house. Many foreigners believe that because they help widows or orphans, they don't have to tithe. Some believe they don't have to tithe or give offerings because they themselves feel they are too poor to give - and, therefore, feel somebody should be giving to them. Then there are those who still believe that tithing means giving to orphans and widows, because they have never had anyone properly explain Malachi 3 to them. Foreigners - especially those who feel they are too poor to give or believe they are "needy" need to understand about giving. Nobody is exempt from giving to God and bringing forth tithes and offerings to leaders. Teach them about giving, tithing, offerings, and the importance of giving - not just receiving.

- **They have more money than they indicate** - Did you ever wonder why all those emails you receive from overseas are always the same? It's because foreign ministers pay top dollar to "professional letter writers" to write those letters for them. All of them have computer access, cell phones, and most have vehicles. Do not believe the stereotyped lies that tell us all foreigners are poor, walking around, riding donkeys and camels. Yes, there are some who are "that poor," but they aren't soliciting you on the internet because they have no electricity, no access to internet cafes, and can't afford a professional letter-writer. Putting stuff together in this way helps keep us from being deceived in a big way later on.

- **Send no money, books, Bibles, items, etc. to people directly without proper evidence that there is a material issue to be solved** - An email or written request isn't enough evidence. Known scams exist by which people solicit Americans for free Bibles and then take those Bibles they receive for free and sell them on the black market - therefore using your free Bible to extort a seeking believer. There are many ministries overseas that lie about financial situations and take the money and profit off it for personal gain. If you truly feel led to give overseas, you don't have to give to an individual. Many organizations, such as Heifer International, Samaritan's Purse, and the International Bible Society work to provide Bibles, education, and goods to people in need in other nations. There is no need to provide personal transactions. If you are going on a mission trip to one of these nations, and you can personally distribute the items yourself, that's also a great way to get materials into the hands of those who need them. If someone insists they need materials in the meantime, tell them to contact the Bible Society in their respective nation or download some information for free materials in their countries online.

- **Do not allow poverty concepts to interfere with principles** - Let me say something that may sound cold, but I truly just mean it to be honest: being poor isn't new. People in foreign countries who cry poverty aren't experiencing something that hasn't been felt since the beginning of time. Is it something that is fun or fair, no, it's not - but it's not new and innovative, either. They should not be marketing themselves as such for that reason, like poverty is something that changes basic Gospel and Christian principle. Teach them how to rise above poverty - by sowing into the Kingdom and learning how to handle their money - not by giving them a handout. You can send them money and in another month they will want more money because they haven't learned God's principles of sowing and reaping.

Instead of being drawn in by poverty claims, make sure they learn Biblical principles that pertain to finances.

- **Require them to communicate with you on a regular basis** - This is perhaps one of the most powerful ways international coverings falter: at first, you hear from the ministry you are covering all the time. They are solicitous and charming, and seem to be in constant contact. Then, as time goes on...you hear from them less and less. The communication fades because the foreign minister either has gotten what they want or has figured out they aren't getting it. Just as we require communication with American ministers, so too foreign ministers must be held to regular communication with their leader. Do not allow expense to be an excuse to get out of the meetings. Schedule regular times to talk and discuss ministry matters. Skype, Yahoo, MSN, even Facebook IM are all free and accessible to foreign ministries - so non-communication is never an option.

- **Require their presence at meeting times** - Group meetings by which everyone international (and even possibly national) are called upon to gather for a conference call or Skypecast are essential. If time is a problem, have "regional" or "time zone" meeting for each group, timed so they can all be online. These meetings should be teaching or instructionally-based and should serve to get people together for instructional purposes - not social or recreational ones. Encourage the people on the conference to pray for one another, meet together, and share in joys and concerns.

- **Do not allow them to become extensions or "representatives" of your ministry** - You are covering their ministry, not absorbing them into yours. The reason foreign ministries always seem so eager to do this is because they believe having an American name or claiming to be a representative of an American ministry will further their own career in their country. In these instances, most of these ministers take the certificate issued and name of your ministry - not to mention your name - and run with them. Make it clear that being in ministry means they are developing the vision God has given to them - and that you are here to help them develop that vision. Also make clear that the needs and circumstances which exist where they are different from where you are, which means they need to rise to address the educational, spiritual, and practical needs which exist there. They need to have their own ministry identity, ministry paperwork, and ministry name.

- **Don't allow them to be covered by more than one ministry** - Once upon a time, a ministry came to me for covering, which I agreed to do on the spot, because I didn't handle things with a lot of discernment in those days. I learned a few days after the fact that, despite my acceptance of them, they went to a friend of mine for covering, as well. Foreign ministries will go from person to person, ministry to ministry, gleaning what they want here and there, to try and get money, acceptance, extension, etc. from whoever will give it. If someone wants to be covered by your ministry, make it clear they may not be covered by another ministry, nor may they receive money from another ministry via solicitation.

- **Do not go to their country for free, and do not sponsor or pay for them to come over here** - If God calls you on missions, go wherever God sends you. Do not go overseas because someone wants you to, and do not put up the money or sponsorship to bring someone over here - especially if you don't know them very well. This is just good, plain common sense. God doesn't ask us to "rescue" people from the difficulties of this life - He encourages us to teach and edify them in His Kingdom principles so they can experience a better life, no matter where they may be.

- **Don't overlook the basics of Christian doctrine in instruction** - Don't assume that because a minister from another country claims to be in ministry or claims to have gone to a foreign Bible college or ministry school that they know everything there is to know about ministry. Don't overlook the basics of Christian doctrine, including the five-fold ministry, nature of God, Jesus, the Holy Spirit, baptism in the Spirit, spiritual gifts, baptism in water, communion, salvation, atonement, sanctification, holiness, order, church and Kingdom government, etc. Do your job as a leader and make sure they have a sure foundation to grow upon for ministry.

Chapter Twenty-Five

LEADERS TO BEWARE AND AVOID

Just as Jannes and Jambres opposed Moses, so these men also oppose the truth, men corrupted in mind and disqualified regarding the faith. But they will not get very far, for their folly will be plain to all, as was that of those two men.
– 2 Timothy 3:8-9 (ESV)

We all know the essence of accountability and how important it is for us to have leaders in our lives that point us toward the calling God has bestowed upon us. If you follow my posts, you will note I've done several on covering: things we need to do when we are covered, as well as things coverings need to do. It's a balancing act that has challenges and complications on both ends and requires a partnership and growth for both coverer and covered to become all they can be.

It can be difficult to find the right balance needed in leaders today. The reason for this is because so many different concepts of leadership exist, and the process of selecting a leader thereby becomes confusing. Many people errantly are drawn under leadership that can be bad for them. A leader may come along and seem great in some ways, promising in some, and even powerful in others, but something gnaws at us telling us something isn't ringing true. There are some leaders that we just shouldn't attach ourselves to because they aren't going to benefit us in any way, shape, or form - and inversely, we can't benefit them. The list below of leaders to beware applies to both being covered and to covering, and are just good signs to avoid in general, whether in a leadership, follower, friendship, or ministerial alliance capacity.

- **The Prissy Preacher** - We've all met them. The preacher who just has to fly first class, has to have an entourage follow them everywhere to make sure they're "taken care of," has to have their water temperature "just right" or they will spit it out or make a fuss, has to spend one hundred dollars on their dinner...and then doesn't even give in the offering. This is the "Prissy Preacher," the minister who has to have everything "just so" or just can't do ministry. The problem with prissy preachers is that people accommodate them. If we step back and truly examine preachers who behave like this, they often aren't that great at ministry; there are lots of other people without so many requirements who will do a better job. They get their positions and reputation in ministry because of who their parents are or who their leaders are. They throw tantrums, start arguments, and get their own way through a childlike intimidation. When they don't get their own way, they start lecturing on "integrity." Let's define integrity, shall we? It means not acting like a spoiled, prissy child.

- **The Chatty Cathy** - In today's church, people seem to need to talk, a lot, about everything. I am not one to throw stones here - I know how difficult it can be to get people to listen and that means when we are going through things, we talk to those who will listen. We need to be selective about what we share and to whom, however. I've known coverings who reveal all their personal details to those they cover - and this is totally and completely inappropriate. The people we cover aren't sounding boards for our emotional or life situations. On the inverse, I've covered people who delve into very personal and inappropriate details with me because they simply "want to talk." People who talk too much - too often - and about too many things need to be avoided because you better believe gossip is a rampant issue with these types. If they talk so freely about others and themselves - you better believe you aren't getting the full story about them and they won't hesitate to talk about what they know of you (or feel they know of you) when you're not within earshot. It's fine to talk to friends, it's fine to talk to co-workers in ministry - but as an apostle I heard recently speak, "Talk to an equal - or a superior - not a subordinate."

- **The Solicitous Shyster** - Everyone needs to beware connecting to a leader who comes and tells you they "want" to be your covering or that God has "revealed" to them that they are to be your covering. Covering is a drawing between the leader and the person under them. It is a positioning for power, purpose, and destiny. It is not something where one person gets a revelation and then has to convince the other person of it. Covering is not a con-job. It's not convincing someone you are a leader that is worthy of covering them: it is being a worthy leader, and that speaking for itself. When someone is a good leader, they don't need to solicit people to be under their covering. Beware the leader who makes all sorts of advances on you to be under them - they are up to no good and they know it!

- **The Used Car Salesman** - A used car salesman will say anything, do anything, lie, cheat, or steal to sell you a lemon of a vehicle. The used car salesman as a leader is someone who will do anything to make you think they are the greatest leader in the world, and at any cost. You can have the world, and then some...if you will only come under their leadership. They promise to pay for things in your ministry, help you out, do this, that or something else...and it's all a big lie as they sell you themselves: one big lemon of a leader. These are leaders who are into making themselves look good - they will polish up nicely, present perfectly, and even say and do all the right things...but underneath, there is nothing there. I know it's tempting to jump head-first into a situation where a leader promises to do things left, right, and sideways. It's a big temptation to come under a leader who promises to pay for various items, give you opportunities, or someone who just seems well-connected and acts interested in what you are doing. Just remember: underneath all that shiny polish is one big lemon you don't want to entertain at the end of the day.

- **The Sperm Donor** - I use this term to be funny....but also to make an illustration. When a man donates to a sperm bank, his sample or samples can be used to impregnate any number of women. He may not know how many and may not know who they are, but he knows he has "spawned" any number of children - with no relationship with them whatsoever. Ever meet one of those people who insists they cover hundreds or thousands of people? Odds are good, this person is using the term very loosely. They may have some sort of association or institute by which people are offered some kind of education, but they have no knowledge of those people, don't talk with them, couldn't recognize them from a hole in the wall, and don't even know who any of them are. Beware these people who may sound really famous, but are just empty ministers who are terrible leaders. Their claims are a lot bigger than their fruit...which becomes obvious when you consider it is not possible to cover hundreds and thousands of people. It is possible to have that many people follow or interested in a ministry, but it is not possible to be the covering for and truly impact that many people in a covering context.

- **The Crisis Creator** - All of us in ministry encounter problems. We all have difficulties, crisis, and things we face because ministry is a hard walk. Then there are those who seem to have crisis...after crisis....after crisis...with no end in sight. People who constantly attack disaster don't understand warfare. They don't know how to fight the enemy and overcome victorious, which means they are constantly in situations to be attacked. The avoidance of crisis comes about through discernment, which they clearly lack. These people can easily become spiritually and emotionally draining because they constantly need something from those around them. This is especially true because they tend to lose support systems because they are always 'going through' something and people long become tired of dealing with them and their issues. When someone is in crisis after crisis after crisis, they thrive on the attention of misfortune and don't have any intention of developing true warfare strategy to get where they need to go to be victorious in ministry. People like this create crisis and stress for others, and should be avoided for this reason.

- **The Drama Driver** - Akin to the crisis creator is the drama driver. The drama driver too thrives on crisis after crisis. The difference between the two is that the drama driver seeks to create drama in the lives of everyone around them - not just for themselves. They thrive on the division chaos creates and takes every possible opportunity to seem like the answer to every problem. They do not have a legitimate call and seem to be unable to minister or offer their gifts without creating a crisis. Ministries can't handle constant drama. In order to maintain a sense of decency and order, every good minister knows the importance in maintaining a sense of peace. Drama drivers can't handle peace because it doesn't give them the opportunity to rise up and appear more competent than everyone else. The drama driver creates the situation then becomes critical and judgmental about the way others handle it - because, naturally, nobody can handle it better than they can! Well, of course not - the drama driver created it so they know exactly what to do to fix it! Manipulation, manipulation, manipulation!

- **The Parasite** - Parasites survive and thrive by feeding off their host. A ministry parasite does the same thing: they feed, thrive, and survive by feeding off the host of a good minister or ministry. In actuality, they may have little to no direction for their work, no purpose in ministry, and no real ministerial call, to speak of. They operate by usurping the anointing of those around them. They seem small, but they are mighty, and have this way of reproducing themselves until they destroy whatever is in their wake.

- **The Lazy Daisy** - Remember being assigned to a group project in school? Remember the kid you hated being assigned to work with because you always wound up doing all the work and they always wound up taking all the credit? Well, these are those kids we worked with back then all grown up. Maybe grown up is the wrong term: they are bigger, not grown up. Excuses abound with the leader who is just, simply put, lazy. They don't ever follow through on what they said they would do. They are just so busy (doing nothing), they aren't able to complete their promises. Lazy ministers often expect other people to do their work for them and "piggy back" on the anointing of those who are ready, willing, and able to work. The problem with lazy ministers is that, well, they are lazy. They don't pull their own weight but are the first to take the credit when something is noteworthy or praised. When working with others, everyone should bring their own part, their own gift, their own participation, and we should work together. Lazy leaders who are afraid to work or get their hands dirty are leaders who don't deserve to participate in the first place.

- **"Doesn't Work And Play Well With Others"** - Remember Kindergarten? We got marks for certain things: coloring inside the lines, staying in our place in line, cutting on the straight line, and working and playing well with others. The ministers I am talking about weren't the ones who worked and played well with others - they got the mark on their report card that said, "Runs with scissors." As much as all of us hate it, ministry is largely about our ability to interact with others. We can be the best preachers in the world, the most prolific leaders and teachers, but if we can't interact with others in a dignified and gracious manner, we are not going to get very far in ministry. We need to be able to handle basic interactions without a ton of aggression, throwing a fit, bursting into tears whenever someone doesn't like us, or second-guessing every comment geared in our direction. Not everyone in the church is going to get along with everyone else - it's a simple and true fact. We aren't going to like everyone, and everyone isn't going to like us. The problem is when someone is consistently at odds with everyone they seem to come in contact with. Beware people who just seem to be against everyone because it won't take much for them to become against you, too.

- **The Big Baby** - It's amazing to me how immature some leaders are. Gone are the days when they steal toys when no one else is looking, throw temper tantrums because they don't want to go to bed early, and pout because they don't like what's served for dinner. Now these ministerial big babies steal anointings, ideas and gifts, throw temper tantrums because somebody puts them in their place, and pouts because nobody thinks they are as fantastic as they perceive themselves to be. Big babies are always getting angry, their feelings hurt, offended, wounded, and feel perpetually "picked on." They cannot take correction or stand in the face of trial because they simply do not have the ability to handle it. Not much fun to be around or much fun to cover, big babies disgrace the ministerial office with their childish nonsense, reasoning, and misappropriated behavior. Correction to such a person causes them to pout and retaliate in some immature way. It's always somebody else with them - they accept no responsibility. Being around a big baby is exhausting - not to mention, can be discrediting.

- **The Disorganized Disgrace** - I am the first one to admit I am not the world's neatest person. I am, however, a person who is very organized despite not being neat. I am able to finish what I start and maintain projects and information. When dealing with the issue of disorganization, we need to be careful not to mistake neatness for organization - because the two are very different. A disorganized disgrace is someone who can't keep up with the basics of ministry. They are forever falling behind, misplacing things, and unable to complete basic tasks because they just do not apply themselves to ministry. In essence, a disorganized minister has issues with order in general: they may take issue with authority within the five-fold, dislike titles, carry issues of rebellion against authority and behave in manners of disobedience, and, most especially, take issue with God's order. Disorganized ministries don't get much done.

They talk a lot, have a lot of hypothetical events, tell people about this, that or something else, but nothing ever comes out of their talk. This is different than sharing a vision that takes some time to come to pass: the point is that all they do is talk about things but don't display the needed discipline to bring anything to pass. Disorganized disgraces are tiresome to work with: they are argumentative, disordered, and don't want to hear anything they don't want to deal with. Their lives operate on a chaos that cannot be considered legitimate ministry.

- **The Suffocating Lid** - Some people don't have a covering - they have a lid. The lid stifles every idea, thought, and vision they have. They are all about control: controlling the vision, controlling the person, dominating their lives. They confuse order with abuse and obedience with control. Nothing is good enough, right enough, or correct enough for these leaders. These ministers don't build up leaders in the Kingdom, they build them in their own image. Abusive leaders are stifling leaders. They are stifling as friends, as coverings as associates because everything has to be their way all the time. They mistreat those in their lives in the struggle and mighty dominance for control. Everything is about their vision, their ministry, assisting them. Nobody is ever ready, in their mind's eye view, to do anything that is not all about their service. This is not order, it's witchcraft! From a suffocating lid...run!

Chapter Twenty-Six

SIX TYPES OF PEOPLE EVERY LEADER NEEDS IN THEIR LIVES AND MINISTRIES

But it should not be that way with you. Whoever wants to be your leader must be your servant.
– Matthew 20:26 (ERV)

It's been said that it's lonely at the top. I can vouch to this myself. I have been in leadership for many, many years (more than I care to remember) and I can honestly say that as ministry has changed, as I have receive more authority and responsibility as pertains to ministry, and as I have changed as a person and a minister, the more exclusive the circle around you becomes. This isn't because ministry is some sort of luxury yacht. It is simply because the more we do, the fewer people are who are qualified to give advice or assistance where they are. There is nothing wrong with where anyone is (unless they are there out of disobedience), but we need to stop acting like everyone and everything in the Kingdom is exactly the same and functioning on the same level. Nobody is better than anyone else, nobody is "God's favorite," but we are not all appointed to have the same function as everyone else. Some people are called to be leaders, and their job in the Kingdom is different than those who are not called to be leaders, and that's it. Even among leaders we find different callings and purposes, and that means not all leaders are the same, either. In keeping with our spiritual call to maturity, we need to recognize that being a leader is an extraordinarily difficult task in our church today. People are frustrating, problems are rampant, and it often feels like you are drowning in a sea of crazy people. Even the leader with the best people in the world (which I do have!!!) has someone who rebels, disobeys, or causes them constant headaches. In a church where you barely make ends meet and have a hard time preparing or planning for life – let alone events or the ministry's future – we all need to know that people are there for us.

Just like it takes a village to raise a child, it also takes the support of many people to encourage a good leader. Good leaders might be born with the gifts to lead, but their ministry abilities are developed within them as they have the right people to educate and encourage them in their work. Here we are going to look at people every leader needs in their life – and why these people are so important.

1. A qualified leader/covering

"If you desire wisdom with all your heart, you will know what good leadership is." (Wisdom of Solomon 6:20, CEB)

One of my biggest mistakes as a minister earlier on in my walk was assuming that having a leader who barely handled her ministry well and was not pursuing it properly was a suitable covering for me because she offered to do it. At the time, she was someone who handed me papers and let me go on my merry way. I was more established than she was in ministry (I had almost eleven years to her four) and had a much larger scope in what I was doing than she did. Was I qualified to have the paperwork she issued – yes, I was. But that didn't change the fact that I was more qualified to be her leader than she was to be mine. This became more and more relevant as time went on and she failed to conduct herself as she should, both as a minister and as my covering.

On the few occasions I needed her to be there for me, she was never able to do so. There was always a reason, a situation, a problem or just a general attitude of not caring for what I was going through. She was not able to advise me properly and, on more than one occasion, she attacked me and my integrity wrongly in defense of her own inadequacies instead of rising up and seeing what was going on. What was going on was she was not able to understand what I was going through because she herself was not called to nor operating in ministry on the same level.

What I did not realize at the time was that when I needed her to be there for me, she was not able to do so because she didn't have the competency for it. She might have been a great leader for someone else who was not as experienced nor operating at the level of ministry I was, but she was not adequate for me.

We need to, first of all, address the fact that leaders need other leaders. We need someone in our lives and involved in our ministries that is objective and who is there to help us in our ministry process. It does not mean they need to be perfect, that they need to have our same level of education or our same exact ministry experiences, that their ministries need to be exactly like ours, or that we need to hold them to impossible standards by which to live. I do not subscribe to the belief that it is acceptable for leaders to operate ministry without being accountable themselves to another leader or organization. We learn how to be accountable as leaders first to our own leaders. I do believe every leader's needs are different, and that a good, qualified leader recognizes and ascribes to meet the unique needs that we have in ministry. We also need a leader who can help to guide us as we do what we are called to do in ministry. It's great to have friends, but a leader's purpose is to be more than just our friend or more than just somebody who backs us up because they like us as a person. A leader's job is to help discern things spiritually and provide the guidance and direction needed as we walk into all God has for us to become.

When we talk about a "qualified leader," we are talking about someone who is both legally licensed and ordained to practice ministry and has enough ministry experience and their ministry reflects the claims they make about ministry and that they are not afraid to implement the necessary structure and discipline to make ministry work. Yes, we are all figuring things out and trying to see what works best for us at times, but a qualified minister knows that balance between purpose and has the ability and fruit to exemplify the office to which they claim to be called.

We also need to recognize that one of the most important things you can do for your covering is, as Apostle Yolanda Davis puts it –

"cover" your leader. Leaders are human beings who are subject to people's judgments, attacks, and attitudes, and leaders should be covered by your prayers, your integrity when someone tries to attack them, and the defense of their right to a personal life and privacy, without the scrutiny of others.

2. People you cover

"Follow my example, just like I follow Christ's." (1 Corinthians 11:1, CEB)

If you are an apostle or pastor, the people you cover should take the form of five-fold ministry leaders (apostle, prophet, evangelist, pastor, and teacher) and appointments (bishops, elders, and deacons) for apostles and laity (non-ordained members) and appointments (elders and deacons) for pastors. Prophets should be covering other prophets and training them in the work of the prophetic. Evangelists are not a covering office, as neither are teachers. If you are in the office of apostle, pastor, or prophet, you should be covering people. If your ministry is new or restructuring and you are just starting out or reorganizing, then you should be working with your covering to get the necessary structure, education, and design in place to provide for those you will cover. I do feel, however, that it needs to be said – if you have no people – and you are not starting out or restructuring – you don't have a ministry.

3. Friends

"There are persons for companionship, but then there are friends who are more loyal than family." (Proverbs 18:24, CEB)

I am the first one who can say that I have covered friends in my life and even do right now and we have an awesome time, without conflict or issue. Even if you are covering people who are your friends, you still need people who you don't cover – who are not in any way under or a part of your ministry – to be your friends. The reason for this is simple: sometimes we just need people we can be ourselves with, to encourage and be encouraged by, and to share with.

Leaders have the notorious role of "being there" for everyone they cover. They fill many roles in people's lives: the spiritual director, the mentor, the confidant, the counselor, the teacher, the disciplinarian, the comforter, the exhorter, the encourager...and this is often just to start. We are not considering the many roles leaders still play in their private lives, be they husband or wife, daughter or son, relative, or parent, each with their own unique set of responsibilities and demands. Even under the best of circumstances, leaders get tired of filling all these roles without receiving much in return. It's great to say, "Jesus did it," but leaders are not Jesus. We are not divine, we are people, and as people, we too need to know that we can trust others and can just have fun at times without having to worry about meeting the needs of many people.

We, as leaders, also tend to see the worst of humanity in our jobs. We not only hear and see the effects of betrayal on others as part of our work, we also experience it ourselves. People get angry, venomous, jealous, and lash out at leaders who did nothing but see to their needs and care for them. It is easy to assume the world is a dark, evil place, and nobody is to be trusted. If we adopt this mentality, ministry quickly becomes a personal and emotional burden. For this reason, we need to have people in our lives who are trustworthy and empowering to help balance out the negatives we often encounter in our ministries.

Friendship is something that takes many forms. Just like there is not just one way to be a leader, there is also not just one way to be someone's friend. The most important part of this equation is that the relationship is based on trust and is equal in giving (i.e., when you need someone to be there for you, they are there, just as when they need you to be there for them, you are). Friends should be able to share and speak openly without judgment or criticism. Friends should also be available to have fun, a source of encouragement and people who can balance out that need when you just need a break from the rigors of ministry life.

I am not of the belief that every minister has to be married (neither male nor female) or that every minister should pursue such romantic avenues if they do not feel called to do so. I do believe, however, that every minister should have a "personal life" – one that is not all about ministry, all the time – and friends can provide that essential balance, even when one is single. In the balance of being human beings, we still need to enjoy things – go out to dinner every now and then, go shopping, watch a movie, enjoy a good meal at home, go to the movies – or even just hang out and talk with someone or a group that is encouraging and trustworthy.

4. Mentors/advisory counsel

"How beautiful is wisdom in the aged and thought and counsel in those who are respectable!" (Sirach 25:5, CEB)

The role of the mentor or adviser (in addition to your covering) is different than that of the covering. A mentor or adviser is someone who is of the same profession, calling, or work as you who is older and/or more experienced in the same work you are doing. The basic role of the mentor or adviser is to advise or encourage on specific issues that arise as you work to build up what you are doing based on the experiences of the mentors and advisers, present through their advice.

Mentors and advisers are very useful when it comes to creating corporate boards for ministers (required for every 501(c)(3) organization and every state incorporated body), for creating separate spheres of advice and mentoring from your board (as is the case within my ministry) and are also useful when changes and other issues come up as pertains to the field or aspect of ministry you are specifying within. A mentor or advisory council does not have a disciplinary role within a ministry body (such as a covering does), nor do they have the right to license or ordain behind a covering's back, or to undermine the work of the covering in your ministry. Mentors and advisers are often not as involved as a covering is with our work, they do provide the important role of encouragement and information on necessary work and subject matter as it comes up.

5. Ministry elders

"The next day Moses sat as a judge for the people, while the people stood around Moses from morning until evening. When Moses' father-in-law saw all that he was doing for the people, he said, "What's this that you are doing for the people? Why do you sit alone, while all the people are standing around you from

morning until evening?" Moses said to his father-in-law, "Because the people come to me to inquire of God. When a conflict arises between them, they come to me and I judge between the two of them. I also teach them God's regulations and instructions." Moses' father-in-law said to him, "What you are doing isn't good. You will end up totally wearing yourself out, both you and these people who are with you. The work is too difficult for you. You can't do it alone. Now listen to me and let me give you some advice. And may God be with you! Your role should be to represent the people before God. You should bring their disputes before God yourself. Explain the regulations and instructions to them. Let them know the way they are supposed to go and the things they are supposed to do. But you should also look among all the people for capable persons who respect God. They should be trustworthy and not corrupt. Set these persons over the people as officers of groups of thousands, hundreds, fifties, and tens. Let them sit as judges for the people at all times. They should bring every major dispute to you, but they should decide all of the minor cases themselves. This will be much easier for you, and they will share your load. If you do this and God directs you, then you will be able to endure. And all these people will be able to go back to their homes much happier." Moses listened to his father-in-law's suggestions and did everything that he had said. Moses chose capable persons from all Israel and set them as leaders over the people, as officers over groups of thousands, hundreds, fifties, and tens. They acted as judges for the people at all times. They would refer the hard cases to Moses, but all of the minor cases they decided themselves. Then Moses said good-bye to his father-in-law, and Jethro went back to his own country." (Exodus 18:13-27, CEB)

I am using the term "elders" here to refer to those individuals who have been with your ministry a long time and have proven they are competent and purposed to work alongside you in positions of authority within your ministry. When operating a ministry, especially an apostolic ministry (where the ministers you cover are frequently out of state or otherwise far away), every leader needs people to assist with state, regional, or national work on a regular basis. For example: someone in my ministry who lives in Texas can be in Louisiana a lot faster than I can be in the case of an emergency. If someone comes to the ministry and I am not sure as to whether or not they should join with our organization, it is the elders who are able to come together, pray, and discuss and advise on the matter. When disciplinary matters arise, the elders help stand as witnesses and also assist in disciplinary measures. Whether you call it a prelate system, an elder system, they are your board members, or just have people in your ministry that you trust administrative matters with that you do not give to everyone, your group of ministry elders help in the leadership jurisdiction of your work.

6. Financially responsible and reliable contributors

"Feasts are made for laughter, wine cheers the living, and money answers everything." (Ecclesiastes 10:19, CEB)

We tend to over-spiritualize things in church today because we don't want to address the fact that people are not only not doing right by the ministers of God, they are downright shameful in their attempts to get out of giving. Being a shepherd in the Old and New Testaments was a job, not a volunteer project. Shepherds didn't hang out with the sheep because they believed in animal rights; they did it because they were compensated and made a living from it. I don't know why we expect modern "shepherds" (leaders) to do ministry now as a volunteer project, and then blow off the difficulties of such in the process. It's simple to say "God will provide," but if person after person keeps saying that without giving, it's obvious they do not understand that God provides through their giving. Hearing "God will make it happen" when your light bill needs to get paid, your phone is about to get shut off, you are facing eviction, or you can't go to the store doesn't just sound hallow and shallow, it is. It's very hard being in ministry and trying to do ministry with no money. Ask me how I know. Ask the endless number of other ministries in existence how they know. People today think it's glamorous to be an apostle, but you know what – it is probably one of the most difficult offices to serve in from a financial perspective. When you exclusively cover other leaders, you face the reality that they too are operating in similar if not the same type of work and are also encountering the financial blows that you are experiencing. Simply put...there is often just not enough money to go around. For this reason, every minister needs to know there are people they can count on financially. Whether it takes the form of business owners or professional people, other ministers or ministries, family members, corporate sponsorship, regular grant organizations, a congregation or group of people who are regularly tithing and offering, or somewhere else, ministers need to know they will be able to cover the financial needs of the ministry, their own lives, and the varied expenses that often come out-of-pocket for ministers in the process of doing ministry work. It's also important to recognize creative ways to receive giving, if people do not want to just outright send a check: have them take care of your mortgage payment or a bill you have, your car note or various expenses or purchasing needed for the ministry, gift cards for places of your choosing, or other ways that people can see to it to tend to ministry needs beyond the typical concept of "offering."

Chapter Twenty-Seven

A MILLION REASONS

Therefore seeing we have this ministry, as we have received mercy, we faint not.
– 2 Corinthians 4:1

Many ministers refuse to acknowledge the difficulties present in ministry. There's a reason for this: It doesn't look good. We are supposed to be all perky and in love with everything about ministry, ready to enthusiastically draw everyone to us as if by magnet-force. A bad day? Nah. Personal problems? Forget about it. Questions about the faith? There's definitely no room for those. Most of the ministers I've known over the years are a grand social media display of selfies, family shots, videos, and pulpit poses, all grandly posted in the hopes people will think and believe it's real. Some of the time, it is real. There are many times we are excited, prepared, and ready to take on the world, just as we appear. Then there are other times when we wish someone else would be called and we can go sit down somewhere. Then when we go sit down, we aren't happy with that, either. When we are busy, we're too busy, and when things are slow, they are too slow. Finding a happy medium is hard in ministry, which is why many ministers spend a great deal of their time malcontented. It gives the Apostle Paul's words, **"Not that I speak in respect of want: for I have learned, in whatsoever** *state I am, therewith to be content. I know both how to be abased, and I know how to abound: every where and in all things I am instructed both to be full and to be hungry, both to abound and to suffer need."* (Philippians 4:11-12) a whole new meaning. It's easy to be dissatisfied with ministry, and most ministers wouldn't admit it on their Facebook or Instagram accounts, but many are dissatisfied with the general flow and movement of their ministries.

I confess to the general ministry struggle between contentment and discontentment. One of us has to tell the truth about this thing, so I guess It'll be me. Maybe, if I am to be honest, it wasn't always a struggle: it was a spiral. I'd start out in one place, and any series of negative and discouraging events would wind me back up at the bottom. It seems like if I look back over the years, much of my time has been spent trying to encourage myself into thinking things would be better or get better if I tried hard enough. While I wish I could say this is a rare story, the majority of ministers I know spiral themselves, albeit, in private. They start out in one place, working hard to encourage themselves or receive the encouragement others have to give them, only to find themselves back in the same place they've found themselves before.

We wind up back in bad places, time and time again, because the little bit of encouragement doesn't seem to hold weight against the realities we deal with on a regular basis. It doesn't help that we don't really know how to encourage people, and most of the form so-called "encouragement" takes today is in the form of verbal words that we've already heard a thousand times before. Being told things like:

- "Won't God do it?" (Won't God do what?)
- "Your breakthrough is coming!" (But when is it getting here?)
- "It's your season!" (If it's not mine now, whose is it then?)
- "Turnaround is on it's way!" (Did it get lost?)
- "Don't despise small beginnings!" (What beginning?)
- "Your gifts will make room for you!" (Only if you get out of the way and let them in)
- "God's got great things in store for you!" (Are they hiding?)
- "You're so anointed!" (As opposed to…?)

...Doesn't particularly help a minister who has already heard them a bunch of times. There are a lot of ways we can encourage ministers that don't fall into the scripted version of "encouragement," but when we don't see them...we often feel...restless and discouraged.

As of the writing of this, it has been almost a year since I preached in a church. Sure, I've done plenty of other things, including seminary classes, book writing and publishing, counseling, couples' counseling, and some general visits to people, but not preaching in church has been an adjustment, to say the least. There was a time a few years ago when I was preaching as a visiting speaker almost every month, and that was in addition to all the other regular work I was doing in ministry. Over the past few years, especially since the recession hit, the number of invites I received to speak steadily declined. There are other reasons why speaking engagements have declined: not as many events and too many speakers to select from, not being in any one specific circle, my stance on some current events, and other social changes have all impacted the general circumstances that have led to a definite number of ministry engagements the past few years. Since around 2014, the number I've gotten has steadily declined.

This culminated when we were evicted from our building in 2016 due to a mold infestation. A year-long trial run for a project that didn't quite turn out the way I'd hoped. We went in with a bang and out with one, the difference being the final bang was enough for awhile. I'd gotten word from God about a possible move out of the area, so that meant staying still until that move took place. And stand still, in some ways, I have.

What I've done in many ways is think a lot about ministry, especially if I desired to continue in it, or not. That's a musing I know I'm technically not supposed to admit to, especially in light of the words of other ministers who would say such a musing is wrong. I don't think it's wrong; I think it's honest, and that's probably what's wrong with it. Many of us are at crossroads in our lives where we simply cannot go on any longer like we are and it's at those crossroads that change comes. The problem is that the change that comes is often not like we've envisioned it, and it's frequently far more uncomfortable and disquieting than we might like to admit. Yet in ministry, the pros and cons list we often seek out to assist us in making our decisions don't always add up like they might at other changeable spots in our lives. That's what makes ministry and being in ministry so difficult: we struggle to discern if it's for us, then we struggle to discern how to do it, then we struggle to discern what to do, and then we struggle to do what we are supposed to do. Everything about ministry displays that eternal struggle between God and humanity, finding our place and our purpose in this world, and even though we know the final and ultimate battle has been won by Christ…we assume our position as soldiers in this world.

Lady Gaga is a favorite of mine. I've blogged on one of her songs before, and I knew when I first heard *Million Reasons*, I'd have to do it again; I just didn't know the context. As I drove between Shelby, North Carolina and my apartment in Cary, North Carolina, last weekend, I heard the song on the radio, and it finally clicked. I was stuck in horrific traffic, cars all around me: to the left, the right, the front, the back, for miles. It came on the radio, and I turned it up and sang it too, as loud as I could, not this time for relationship purpose or advice, but for the realities of the answers I'd been seeking in my own ministry experience.

I could easily list you a million reasons why ministry hasn't always worked for me, and why, honestly, I spent a lot of years tired and frustrated with it. People have been difficult, I haven't always found the majority of people I've worked with to be honest and ready to do what ministry requires, and I've watched as most of the people I've known have either walked away from it or landed themselves in a position to stop growing and progressing in it. Ministry's not for wimpy people. It might seem like a quiet profession, but we battle things and deal with things that nobody could ever imagine much of the time. But the answer lies in Lady Gaga's words: no matter how many reasons I might have not to do it, there's really only one question as to whether or not to continue – only one answer – Is this what I have been called to do, or not?

In ministry, there will always be a hundred million reasons why we shouldn't do it: We don't have enough money, we aren't "important" enough, nobody seems to like us, we're too "different," we don't get invited enough, we aren't a part of the popular club or clique, we don't minister like others do, we don't look like everyone else, we aren't called to deal with the same things as everyone else, we don't do things the same, we don't have the same interests or calling, and so on and so forth, down the list of the other 99,999,990 reasons

not to do this. Every day of a minister's life, they wake up with the same reasons, and maybe even some new ones, not to do this. But the song says it best – we only need one good reason to stay.
If we are called, and this is what we are to do, the other reasons do not matter.

So, despite the reasons to stop, to leave, to end it all, we stay. For that reason, encourage a minister you know on today and make those hundred million reasons to walk away seem like a few less.

Section 6 study, discussion, and review questions

- What are essential things coverings need to know about covering other people?

- How do we, as Christian ministers, become "all things to all people" and what does that mean to the Christian minister?

- What things need to be kept in mind when we are leading people overseas? What guidelines should we set up?

- What are some types of leaders to avoid, and why?

- What kinds of people do leaders need in their lives, and why are these people important?

- What kind of resolve to we need to adapt as ministers to survive ministry?

Section 7

APOSTLE MARINO'S APOSTOLIC TESTIMONY

Chapter Twenty-Eight

CROSSING THE JORDAN: MY TESTIMONY AS AN APOSTLE

And when they found them not, they dragged Jason and certain brethren before the rulers of the city, crying, These that have turned the world upside down are come hither also.
— Acts 17:6 (ASV)

Upon my ordination to the office of apostle in 2010, my former apostle randomly opened up the Bible to a verse by which to commemorate the event. She opened the Bible to 2 Kings 2:13-15: *"He took up also the mantle of Elijah that fell from him, and went back, and stood by the bank of the Jordan. And he took the mantle of Elijah that fell from him, and smote the waters, and said, Where is Jehovah, the God of Elijah? and when he also had smitten the waters, they were divided hither and thither; and Elisha went over. And when the sons of the prophets that were at Jericho over against him saw him, they said, The spirit of Elijah doth rest on Elisha. And they came to meet him, and bowed themselves to the ground before him."* (ASV) This verse had a significance that truly came from God – none of us could have ever planned or fabricated its relevance. The years of the calling have brought with it a true transition – a crossing from one side to the other. The resulting anointing has been truly a double anointing. It has brought with it an intense challenge, many difficulties, and many pursuits. It is a walk that has been many years in process, yet is just beginning.

I always remember being interested in God, spiritual things, and religion, even from a very young age. Despite an abusive childhood and many early difficulties, I was intrigued with spirituality. I didn't always understand everything about it, but I knew there was something greater than the things we could see with our natural eyes. By the time I was a teenager, I was strongly interested in religion as a pursuit for life and teaching. I wanted to know God and know about God.

I was the youngest of five children, all girls, born to my parents in upstate, New York in December, 1981. My childhood was, in some ways, very classic of its age. Things were rapidly changing. Technology was expanding, the way we were taught was constantly changing, music was changing, clothing was changing, things were speeding up, and family dynamics were changing. Even the way people worshipped God was changing, as the segue began into what is now classified as the "mega-church" and "televangelist" style of faith and belief. Phil Donahue's popularity began to be replaced by Oprah Winfrey. Nobody had ever heard of reality TV, and movies still had professional actors. The internet was unheard of, something we couldn't fathom, even if we wanted to. Rap, hip hop, and heavy metal began to replace the scene of easy listening music. MTV was not only still cool, it was also innovative, new, and different. The arcade was the place to hang out. Everywhere you looked, change was there: in the streets, on the television, in the schools, in the workplace, in faith and religion, and in the family. There was a sense and spirit of change unleashed on the world.

My family was caught up in this spirit of change like everyone else, and it manifested as it did everywhere else. One of the biggest changes that was notable in the 1980s was a marked change in the way people interacted with one another. Where things used to be about relationship, things were now very much about the individual. Therapy was "in," as was a big emphasis on "not repeating the mistakes of the past." New Agey events and conferences touted the "power within" and the "creative power of visualization." My sisters displayed disrespect with our parents, and their children disrespect with them. There were rumors of eating disorders, drug and alcohol use, and the like that was common of the 1980s.

In other ways, my childhood was very different from the others that I knew. At least, at the time, I thought it was different from the cozy, two-parent households I saw. As the youngest, there is a twenty-two year age difference between my oldest sister and me. My father was a venomous, abusive alcoholic. In hindsight, he was probably a narcissist. He was totally dedicated to his career, his life, and his own impending retirement. He wasn't around a whole lot by the time I was born, but when he was there, he definitely made his presence known. He was no deeper than he seemed on the surface, and had little interaction with us except when it came to extreme and abusive disciplinary measures. My mother, on the other hand, was going through her own metamorphosis, very reflective of the times. She'd learned she was a battered woman watching *The Phil Donahue Show* and came to a point where she knew change had to happen through her. After a few years of attending Al-Anon meetings, my mom decided it was time to move us to a better life. Three days before Halloween in October, 1989, we became something out of a Lifetime movie: my father went away on a business trip and we, left, literally in the night, to the nearest town, about ten miles away. It wasn't long before my father, who was also the town justice, was able to locate us. Even though my mom faced many trials and issues, she never returned to him.

The next several years were a long, grueling battleground complete with family strife, rifts, and issue after issue. Between being bullied at school, visits that seemed to drag on forever, divisions in the family that were never resolved, and many court battles, all of which made my young head spin, I understood things as best I could for my age and comprehension at the time. Maybe one of the best ways I was able to understand – and deal with things – came through my interest in the spiritual realm. I remember having various visions starting around age eight; some were demonic, and some were divine, but I wasn't sure what any of it meant. I also loved to dress my dolls up in their Sunday best and "play church" every Sunday afternoon after mass. I was an altar server, one of only a handful of girls, who first served on the altar in our parish when it was first opened up to girls in 1992. I also wanted to be a priest, even though it was not (and is still not) an option for Roman Catholic women.

I'm not sure what kept my interest in God over the years, which continued to be tumultuous, to say the least, save the intervention of the Holy Spirit. More familial ups and downs, divisions, poverty and consequences for other people's choices made life incessantly chaotic. From the time I was a teenager, I was noted for a bit of a rebellious streak, one that transcended every aspect of my life, including a deliberate desire to be everything opposite of authority's desires for me. I saw many different trends come and go, including my mother's own endeavors into the New Age movement when I was a pre-teen and teenager. If we use the justifications of the world, I had plenty of reasons to desire avoiding a belief in God: separated and alienated family, not really fitting in, especially when the teen years fit; and not feeling particularly accepted anywhere I went. Despite this, I believed. I might not have always believed everything according to doctrine, but I did believe – even if I didn't always understand.

My initial contact with my calling to the apostolic came in January 2003, when I was one month past twenty-one years old. I'd known I was called to ministry since I was sixteen, although I didn't understand what ministry was or how that would relate to my own apostolic call. I had been working as an apostle since I was about seventeen years old, coinciding with around the time I was saved, even though I did not recognize it. Having come out of the Roman Catholic Church officially at age seventeen, I had no concept of being an apostle or of the five-fold ministry. I had heard shades of the term "apostle" used to refer to Paul or Peter on occasion, but that was about it. For the most part, Biblical apostles were referred to as "saints" rather than "apostles." I was thoroughly confused as to who was who in the Bible, believing the Apostle John was John the Baptist. I never gave much thought as to whether or not the apostolic ministry had ceased because it was never discussed. Apostles, prophets, and evangelists remain notably absent from Catholic structure, and teachers are delegated to instruction with children in schools or converts in religious education classes. Pastors were a reference to parish priests, men who were ordained according to Catholic rite and maintained a local parish or a group of smaller parish congregations. They were never called "pastor," but always called "father," in accord with Catholic terminology of the priestly title.

In Catholicism, children are taught minimally about the church's structure. The major emphasis is on priests, bishops, and the pope, with a great deal of time spent on the importance of both the pope and bishops. Cardinals, monsignors, archbishops, the Holy See and the Magisterium were seldom, if ever, mentioned. The office of deacon was mentioned on occasion, and within my own mind, I had delegated them to be big altar boys. Even though we covered the sacrament of Holy Orders in fifth grade religion class, the rite and being called to the rite were not discussed in detail. I remember walking away from the teaching on holy orders wanting to know more about it, especially how someone knew they were called to receive the rite. While the church made "calling" (called "vocation") out to be some great mystical thing, it seemed like something was left out of the process.

To make matters more confusing, we never read the Bible in our religion classes. This is not surprising to those who know anything about the Catholic Church. Because the Bible is not a part of Catholic structure or study, reading and studying the Bible is not part of Catholic indoctrination. When we did hear of the Bible, it was divided into small parts of only a few verses. Other times we learned of "Bible stories" retold in religious education texts. Never was the actual Bible text read or referenced as part of the story. I had never heard of Ephesians 4:11 and did not even know there was such a thing as a "five-fold ministry." While I had severe doubts about Catholic Church structure and their authenticity to the purpose and teachings of Jesus, I had absolutely no clue that God had put authority and structure in place for the purpose of church leadership in the New Testament.

What I learned about Roman Catholicism and its structure, I learned in college. Around the time I was leaving the church, I was taking a college Bible study through Apostolic Preachers College. Even though it was a general Bible study (historical in nature versus doctrinal), I came face-to-face with many verses and passages contradictory to Catholic teaching. While I did not receive great revelation in interpreting the passages, what I saw in the Word made me very uncomfortable with Catholic ritual, structure, and teaching. The more I studied, the more I questioned, which brought me head-to-head with church authorities in my diocese. Studying the history of Catholicism (particularly the Early Church Fathers, who were supposed to confirm Catholicism but instead make the whole foundation look morally wrong and mentally ill) caused me great discomfort with calling myself a part of such a denomination and led me to further question of participation with such a church. Even though the ultimate blow-up between my diocese and myself came over diocesan non-adherence to church canon law, by the time of my voluntary excommunication at seventeen, I knew there had to be more to life and church than Roman Catholicism.

Within one week of my voluntary excommunication, I met a woman through a college religion project who brought me to church with her. It was here that I first accepted Jesus as Savior and was filled with the Holy Spirit back in February, 1999. The church was what we would call "Charismatic," with primitive shades of what we would now call Word Faith teaching. The church was deeply rooted in the "Shepherding Movement," a 1970s doctrinal movement out of Fort Lauderdale, Florida. The Shepherding Movement taught every person within Christianity needed to have a pastor ("shepherd") in order to receive revelation, guidance, and approval from God. The pastor of this small church in upstate New York was seriously immersed in shepherding mentality and truly believed himself to be an essential part to every church attendee's relationship with God. He was cocky, arrogant, and conceited. A former Hollywood screen writer with a resume including a very popular science fiction movie, it was obvious he believed the congregation was blessed that he'd graced us with his presence. He frequently invoked the necessity of obeying him, staying connected with him, and bringing any issues we may have to him for correction. He told people the ministries they were anointed to walk in, what gifts they were to operate in the Spirit, and made it clear that no matter what doubts or issues we may have, we were to never, ever leave his control under the threat of being cut off from God. The church was still informal enough to hold belief in the importance of all believers walking in the Gifts of the Spirit. However, the dictates of who was to do what and receive what rested in the hands of this singular man who was off track of God's purpose for the pastoral role. Even though he himself was subject to a "pastor," his pastor reflected the same concepts and values that he himself espoused. To question or report any wrongdoing within this setup was just like doing so in the Catholic Church: despite any evidence to the contrary, the iron-clad hold of control was not going to dissolve within the structure so set. While the different pastors I heard complained of being overworked and people not desiring to participate in church ministries, there was clearly a part of them that enjoyed the control they exercised. They were unwilling to surrender that control, even if it meant they would spend their ministries burnt out and neglecting their families.

One continuing church theme remained that I did not learn of the apostolic in this congregation. We never discussed the five-fold ministry. In all my time in that church, I never heard the word "apostle" used once. Because the focus was on things being accessible to all, the Biblical apostles were referred to by their first names, and nothing else. Instead of focusing on popes and bishops, we now focused on pastors who seemed larger than life and just as controlling. I tried hard to reconcile the various roles in my mind and believe this to be different from the control I'd seen in Catholicism, but somewhere I knew something was very, very wrong. I just didn't know what was wrong.

In the midst of all this, I started my apostolic work. I had no idea what I was doing or that it was a part of a higher calling. I had no idea what an apostle was or that apostles were still called today. All I did was begin to study the Word intensively and praying for revelation from God about the Word and its meaning. I focused more intensely on my theological studies. In response to my prayers, God gave me the revelation I sought. God started to give me a format and plan, and clear sight of both the positives and negatives of where I was. The church I was attending definitely had its strong points. The people seemed to love God and were sincere in their faith. Several congregation members had been welcoming to me and seemed supportive of my research and the work I wanted to do for God. At the same time, there were very glaring negatives that could not be negotiated when examined as a leader. The congregation was not growing spiritually. There were overtones of racism and bigotry among many members. While the church prayed for revival, it was both stated and unstated through their behavior that the introduction of "different" people into the congregation was unacceptable. There were many doctrinal inconsistencies and obvious confusion in the church, including the pastor, about essential matters of faith and facts. On one occasion, the pastor stated the Twelve Days of

Christmas began on December 12 and ended on December 25. In actuality, they begin on December 25 and run until January 6 (the traditional date for the Epiphany). Then there were the vast doctrinal inconsistencies, from baptism to communion, to matters of salvation and twisting of Bible passages to suit convenience. All I knew were my deep concerns in what I saw and heard. I wanted to give the pastor of the church the opportunity to explain his perspectives and where they could be concretely proven in the Bible. The result was a typed letter, nearly twenty pages in length, in which I thoroughly examined what he said, the passages he used, and showed where, according to the studies I had done, he was in error. I closed by giving him the opportunity to respond and clearly stated I had no bad intention, purpose, or motive. All I wanted to do was receive clarity for both my own search and to make the church better.

The pastor's response was less than receptive. He accused me of having a bad spirit and of doing this prior at another church, with the intent to conform the church to "my viewpoints." His answer to me I should go to another church that was "more suited" to my concepts and he flatly denied any wrongdoing. He gave no credibility to the exhaustive Bible search I'd done, or to the references I provided. What he did instead was accuse me of twisting Scripture around and maligning it to fit with my own viewpoints.

I was infuriated. According to his own words, he was supposed to be the one I brought my issues before, and he in turn, was to bring clarity. More than once, he claimed to be humble enough to accept correction, from wherever it came. While correction was not the primary purpose in my letter, I sought answers. I wanted to understand where he was coming from, because that point was not clear. Likewise, I felt the need to defend myself against his accusations, which were unkind and far from the truth. I did not understand his purpose was to make my letter a personal battle. His goal was to reduce matters to the immature level of personal debate and argument, because he really didn't have a response for the issues I'd raised. In my response to him, I too made it a personal battle. He did not respond, and I did not ever hear from him again. His departure from the church came around the time I sent my second letter to him, in January 2000. Even though I did attempt to report his conduct to his pastor (he had stated he would return to his pastor's church), I never received a response.

Right before this first pastor left, the Lord spoke to me, telling me he would return to our community in New York and would cause division, destroying the existing congregation. The Lord assured me this would be proof that even though I did not understand everything I addressed, I was indeed correct about the character and motive of this individual and the error he taught. As this did not come to play immediately, I pushed the experience aside.

The pastor who replaced the first man was a solid, kind, and sincere man of God. He was eventually rejected by the community. Despite wavering on some issues in the beginning, his sincerity, faith, and love for God drove him on a serious pursuit to better and grow the congregants. He was a true pastor, one who made it known he wanted you to be there and be a part of whatever it was God was doing there. As much as I desired to remain in the congregation, I started to know God was prompting me to move elsewhere. I went, begrudgingly, because I felt like things were just starting to reach a point where I might find something more that I needed...but as hard as it was, I was obedient. I was led to another local church, this time identified as "Full Gospel," also seeking revival, complete with another abusive, controlling pastor and thorough doctrinal error. This pastor was notorious among the region for beating his wife and children; in fact, his first wife had left him years prior due to abuse. He turned around and married a much younger woman, a college student he'd met through a youth outreach he'd done several years earlier. He was an unlearned and uninspired man. I would dare say he was not anointed to pastor; he was not a good speaker, had trouble formulating thoughts, and was not knowledgeable of the Word. His teachings were rambling concoctions of disoriented thoughts. Whereas the other church I'd attended had more freedom in spiritual expression, this particular church was far more observant of rules, regulations, and rigid codes of submission to their leaders. The church members were not as interested in worship or participation, but were fixated on attending church and the need to go to church, no matter what the experience might be. Their place was to go and receive from their leader, and while they were not a "shepherding" church, they had a worship of their leader that I have not even seen anywhere else to this very day. Women had no place or purpose, and were not allowed to minister, preach, or pastor. Nobody could ever explain why they held this position; they just stated it was the way they believed it should be. The pastor was dominating and controlling, believing he was the center of the church and the ultimate authority. On one occasion, he described himself as the "pope" of the congregation.

My presence in this church was not quite as welcomed as it had been in my former church. Being female and expressing an interest in preaching landed me with the label of having a "demon," because they believed no woman could desire to preach and that desire originate with God. The day I was told this by one of the elders in the church left me running to the bathroom to bawl my eyes out at the mean-spirited connotation and accusation in those words. The congregants were very complacent with their pastor and level of understanding, which defined "praise" as running around the room in a manic conga line during worship. Not big on the gifts of the Spirit, this church fell somewhere between evangelical and Charismatic (without Word Faith teaching). They were strong in Messianic overtones, with a lot of focus on the Old Testament and Hebraic understanding. I still never learned about the five-fold ministry. Based on things said to me, I do believe the pastor of this congregation would have rejected apostolic authority as a contradiction of his ultimate authority within the church. Ironically enough, Ephesians 4:11 graced all their documents and official stationery – yet there was no role accepted in the church but that of the pastor!

The Lord had me start apostolic work in this church immediately. I had no interest in doing anything; mind you, I didn't even want to be there. I missed my former pastor and the people at the church I used to attend. Although I was not as welcome or received well in this church, it was obvious the people in the congregation (including the pastor) recognized some sort of authority on me that I did not recognize, nor understand. Looking back, there had to be something to it because they were acknowledging something on me that, according to their own doctrine, wasn't supposed to exist. I was female, young, and clearly not interested in membership with them. They pursued me anyway, seeking my approval and wanting me to endorse their congregation. I was repeatedly asked, by both the pastor and members, "What do you think of our church?" I was unsure of what to answer much of the time and thus my response was, "I haven't been here long enough to answer that question." Throughout my duration, I took notes – lots of notes. I made note of what was said to be Biblical or out of line with claims that had been made about church beliefs. I made myself aware of everything that was both good and questionable. Right before departing, a letter was sent to the church pastor about issues – both pros and cons – raised in visiting that church. It was done in a parallel-style and once again, I was open to dialogue and reply. I never received reply and never attended service at this church again, although many years later the pastor of this church appeared to me in a dream. In this dream, he was apologetic, stating things had just gone to go too far within the congregation to correct them. Even though I never spoke to this pastor again after leaving the church, I do believe this dream, all those years later, was a message about the congregational situation.

After that work was done, God had me move on, yet again. The next church was by far the most uncomfortable experience I'd ever had in a church setting. This particular group was a second-generation family run institution with an extremely high turnover rate. It was notorious for being the area's "last-stop" church, the one people attended when they'd exhausted all other resources. Not much on experience, this could be classified as the most spiritually dead church I attended. Not only was nobody interested in spiritual growth, nobody was interested in reaching out to anyone else, either. It was very obvious outsiders and outside opinions were unwelcome, and that they didn't want to grow the church or change it at all. While revival was yet again the claim of the day, this church probably had about as much chance of having revival as the Yankees would at winning the Super Bowl. It should be no surprise the five-fold ministry was never mentioned. This church, in fact, talked nothing of the pastoral role or any ministerial roles. The experience here was short-lived and very fast-paced: I was in and out within a matter of two months. I continued in taking notes and answering questions and did present the case of severe error and misguided teaching to the leaders who I am sure promptly rejected it.

Right after this experience ended, I preached my first message to a small group in an upstate New York community, about forty minutes from where I lived. About ten minutes into the message, I was promptly interrupted by an older, heavy, rude woman who disliked what I said and felt the right to interject her own opinions and perspectives. Others followed suit and the meeting turned into a berating forum, contradicting what I said. I was asked to leave midway through the event, and I accepted out of concern for what would happen if I stayed.

These four early experiences stand out, as I was doing the work of an apostle incognito. I had no idea I was doing apostolic work. To many, it seemed as if I was trying to usurp authority, but that was not the case. I did what I did with the invitation to discuss and dialogue with those who were there. It was not my intention to take authority that was not mine. I had no interest in taking over or changing the churches present. I just wanted to understand why things were the way they were, and that was misunderstood. In hindsight, I might have interacted differently, but I did the best I knew how to do at the time. The pastors and church leaders I encountered were exercising a misguided authority. They didn't want to be accountable and have to explain themselves, not to anyone. No matter what the reception might have been, there is no question in my mind that those early years were a preparation for the apostolic work which is now and yet to come.

After these initial experiences I spent a number of years running a religious circuit, seeing and experiencing the beliefs and teachings of a number of different religions. My early church experiences caused me to question many core tenets of Christianity, especially the pastor's role and the church's role in the world. I wandered mentally from theory to theory for about three years, including heavy emphasis on New Age ideals. I couldn't fathom a spiritual system that seemed so exclusive, blocking people from hearing what was true because the goal was to make them a carbon-copy of everyone present. In those early years, I met no Christians whole or healed; in fact, all I could see were people who, for the most part, brought all their problems, baggage, and situations along with them. All they appeared to do was change the focal point of their ideology. Such examples caused confusion in my own logical and philosophical mind, not so much about Who Christ was, but who the Christian is called to be in the church and the world.

This search was not in and of itself a negative. While I fully admit some of the concepts I delved into were not true or godly, I also see that through the process I went through, I came to discover what was true. I came to discover truth and Christ on a deeply personal level: recognizing Who He was and that He is the way to God alone. It was a truth that became real to me, which is in essence, what a personal relationship with God through Christ is. It is not becoming our own "pope" or abandoning leadership; it is knowing the essence of Christ and His message for ourselves, which no one can take away! As a result of my awareness of a personal relationship with God through Christ, I desired to pursue my ministry further.

What I did find through my attempts to network as far as church went was a small Apostolic Pentecostal church. For the first time in my life, I was introduced to something that appeared to be genuinely "apostolic," at least that was how it was identified. It was led by a minister who had also experienced the ostracizing of the closed area community. Even though he did not educate me in the five-fold ministry, he did help me begin to see plain and simple truths from the Scriptures, he introduced me to the world of "if you can find anyone in the Bible who was baptized according to Matthew 28:19, we will give you $5,000." I'm always open to a great challenge, but this wasn't one that I won. I learned about the power of the Name of Jesus, about baptism in Jesus' Name, and was baptized in water in 2005. It might not have always been ideal, but this pastor set a powerful foundation within me to *rightly divide the Word of truth*" (2 Timothy 2:15). It was there, at this church, that I learned how to "rightly divide."

Beyond the basics, the belief system, which was an offshoot of the United Pentecostal Church International, was a maze of rules and regulations coded as "holiness": No make-up, no pants for women, no short hair for women, no long hair for men, long skirts for women, and what seemed to be an endless parade of rules and regulations. I'd never encountered "holiness" codes before and I loved the idea that these things they believed and taught had a connection with Biblical times.

It was a blessed place to be until you challenged or broke one of the rules. It also wasn't easy to be a woman in this church, any more so than it had been in some of the other churches I'd attended. If anything, it was worse. The never-ending regulations made it feel as if everything you did was considered a "slip" and you would never be good enough or able enough to go to heaven – forget about being in ministry. I tried to pursue ministry despite the feeling of never being "good enough." This continued until I reached a point where I was so depressed by the oppression I experienced that I sat down and took a good look at myself – and asked if this is truly the kind of lifestyle God would ask of me. One by one, the various codes, legalisms and rules were before my eyes thanks to the different people I met in my life and I was able to see in the Word where the rules just didn't measure up to the "apostolic standards" we were told they did. I was nice and uncomfortable, but not quite there to change all the ways I held dear.

Perhaps the most ironic way that God dealt with me about the legalism of Oneness Pentecostalism was through a testimonial clip I passed on a Catholic program that shared how formerly Protestant ministers had become Catholic. In my minds' eye view, particularly at this place in my walk, I couldn't fathom how such a thing could be possible. I used to watch the show to figure out why someone would ever even be tempted to the Catholic Church, and then one day, a minister on there shot at me, right in the heart. In talking about the Catholic position on tradition, the former Protestant made the statement, "Now let's not pretend Protestants don't have traditions. There are traditions that say women can't wear make-up or jewelry." So then, I was livid. I threw my book across the room at the television set. Maybe the UPCI was right, maybe we shouldn't have been watching television, with the mess like that. Maybe he was right.

He was right, but I wasn't ready to call it quits with the Apostolics, just yet. I was going to circumvent the rules and do something else. My answer? To start a church.

Because the theory of the day was ministry meant being a pastor, I thought the answer to finding my place in the religious spectrum was to become a part of it. I was ordained a pastor in 2002, in between crawling between my quasi-not-so-much membership with the Apostolic church (which I would continue to hold to anywhere I could find one until around 2009) and my own ministry work, which was now attempting to pastor. The endeavor didn't go over real well. My attempt to pastor was a disaster of every sort. Even though the small number of people who attended lauded the preaching and vision, nobody stuck with it. What made matters worse was that no one could tell me why they did not desire to come back. The vast number of people I'd known who expressed interest in ministry participation never even came, and responded badly to the entire effort. I knew trying to start the church was a mistake about seven weeks in, when a chronic complainer voiced yet another complaint about the service that day. He harbored racist thoughts, and complained about using Ron Kenoly's *Ancient of Days* in the service. I turned around to him and point blank said, "Well, we're not singing to you, are we?" He never returned after that day and within a few weeks, everyone stopped coming. I was both discouraged and confused because I thought starting a church was the way to do ministry. Nobody ever visited or returned to service again, and even though the experience was a flop, I continued to keep things going for two more years.

Between running my circuit of visiting churches, trying to maintain my identity as a Oneness Pentecostal identity despite abandoning more and more of their rules, learning about others, and trying to maintain my own church ministry, I was uncertain about what was next for me. I had spent several months contemplating the idea of leaving ministry for awhile and trying to pursue other avenues. By the time 2002 was out, I'd already had many different religious experiences and a number of questions. Even though I had settled a number of my questions over the past few months, I still had more, wanted more, and was curious about more. I was especially curious about my purpose in life.

Being young and immersed in various traditions that criticized and damaged female identity, being good looking, of substantial age, and single led to a ridiculous amount of vanity. My rebellious streak led me to an amazing penchant for older, dangerous men who were everything the Apostolics told me they shouldn't be. At the time, I was involved with a man thirteen years my senior who not only had a wild history of drug use, he also was running from parole and ran the risk of being incarcerated at any time. We'd met in that he was pursuant to me when I had no interest in him and his continual pursuits made me think that maybe I was missing or overlooking something, so I should give him a chance. He had a wild way of manipulating me into feeling guilty for standing up for myself and his questionable spiritual history – part Oneness Pentecostal, part fatalist, part New Ager, part jerk – made him a combination too irresistible for me to resist. Our tumultuous seven-month long relationship was a veritable roller coaster of intensity: fighting, control, opposition, and the infamous making up, all jumbled into what seemed like an exciting, unmistakable, wild ride. With him in tow (or perhaps we should say with me in his tow) I continued working in ministry much in the same way I had prior for a little over a year, with the same lack of results.

Then, it happened.

In January of 2003, one month past my twenty-first birthday, I had a very significant dream in which I saw published books that I'd written where in the byline, I was called "apostle." I then saw a vision of Jesus and after heard a voice calling, saying, *"Come, blessed apostle of God, for all things are now ready."* When I woke up, I was both excited and surprised. I still didn't know what an apostle was and I still didn't know what all this meant. I decided to try and find out. My joy and excitement lasted just until I told the man I was involved with (we were engaged at the time) whose response was less than enthusiastic. He told me, "You can't call yourself that. People will think you're full of yourself. Pick another title." He espoused the theory that it was fine if other people regarded me as an apostle, but because the churches he'd attended debated as to whether or not Paul was an apostle, I could never call myself one. I was a woman, and to call myself apostle would be perceived as conceit. He caused me deep fear for my ministry's successes, especially given the failures I'd already experienced. I decided to call myself "evangelist" instead and move forward with the ministry work. I stopped having church services and let the church go by early 2004, and began pursuing ministry work full-time. I vascillated back and forth between various churches I had gone to in the past, hoping to find something new, somewhere, but without luck. A few months later, I broke off my engagement. It was hard and I did it thinking that I may never well meet someone else. That sounds absurd all these years later, but it was how I felt at the time, and the fear of being alone with an undetermined calling and confusion in my own ranks was more than I wanted to handle.

My ministry attempts post-apostle discovery were no more successful than they'd been prior. I had trouble maintaining a free mailing list for our newsletter. People were irate and angry upon receipt of it, and would call, screaming and yelling about how they did not want to receive it anymore. With no church, I began to see the importance of ministerial networking. My attempts to network with other ministers in my small community quickly became a failure. Area ministers were unwelcoming and not open to seeing me as a minister in the community. They enjoyed their tight-fisted community control and did not want new ideas, younger people, or change in the situation. I was denied ministerial networking repeatedly by men who did not believe women should preach or teach. The female ministers I met were also unwelcoming and competitive, backbiting, and unsupportive. When I wasn't studying, I spent most of my time alone.

In this interim, I met a young man about four years older than me who seriously pursued me, even if it was only for a short period of time. He was my "rebound" guy, the one who I met not long after breaking off my former engagement. I couldn't have told you what it was about him. We had some things in common, but the most glaring thing we did not have in common was our faith. I was a staunch Apostolic Pentecostal in this time, even if I didn't really believe all the things I said I did. My faith in the system was wavering and I had given up many of the exteriors, but at the core of my spiritual understanding, I remained Apostolic. According to the doctrine, he was going to hell because he had not been baptized properly and was not living a "holy" lifestyle. Despite all the warnings and evidence to the contrary, we hit it off, and hit it off, hard. I was ready to take off and see the world with him, until it all came crashing down in a few singular set-up moments that led to our break-up.

I know now it wasn't all my fault, but part of why I believed we broke up was because I drove home his need to become a Christian in the exact same way I was so hard and so furiously. I would spend hours trying to figure out how to get him to see my perspective. I'd been trained to argue my faith. People would hear our incredible-sounding arguments and then want to fall at our feet in puddles of repentance and conversion. I never found that method to be effective, at all. After a particularly difficult experience as a result of this relationship, I went to God and asked why people were not converting. He spoke to me, clear as day, and told me, "Lee Ann, people aren't saved because they agree with you. They are saved because of their relationship with me." I was initially angry. If people would just have done what I told them to do, God and I wouldn't be having this conversation. Then I was angry with God, because He shouldn't have ever had that right to talk to me like that. Here I was, making all these sacrifices, trying to adapt and understand what were really His rules from what were not, and He was speaking to me like that!

I cried for three days. My anger quickly turned inward, leaving me feeling lost and inadequate. I hadn't had good examples for ministry, and even though I had a great educational background, I didn't have the best ministry training, either. When I was ordained to the pastorate, I received no training whatsoever. I never understood about being chosen for a work of God like many of us do today. I knew from this experience I needed to change how I talked to people, how I reached out, how I ministered. My belligerent, angry way was not going to help people find what they needed to in God; it was going to be more of a deterrent. It had to change if I wanted ministry to continue.

It was also hurting my relationships, as I searched for someone who would not only be willing to take me on, but take on a complicated situation that was not resolving itself any time soon. My rebellious streak wasn't always clearly defined, and while I might have been mouthy and difficult as a general rule, I was steeped in traditions that channeled that rebellion into downright difficult much of the time. The traditions caused me to be mean and sour, and I channeled that into a series of bad relationships that were not only detrimental for me, they were killing my ministry. I knew I needed a change, and it was time to get a new focus. I continued to identify as Apostolic, but dropped out of affiliation with any Oneness Pentecostal church, and tried hard to start again, in some semblance of identity.

Cleaning myself up doctrinally gave me strength and purpose in my life and ministry. Even though I was running fast and furious from my apostolic calling out of fear and discouragement, I was finally starting to figure out my ministry was not going to fit in with conventional church concepts. I received great revelation as a result from my encounter with the Lord a few years earlier. I had a revelation that seemed obvious to me, but not obvious to others. I did not understand back then it was my purpose to bring forth this revelation, and tried to fit in with conventional concepts instead. I continued to fight my apostolic realization and revelation, but it gave me the grace to begin working ministry in unconventional ways. It was clear I was not going to be accepted where I was, and needed to start to reach out anyway I could beyond my location. I started working online in ministry later that year, in 2003.

I'd been working in online research since 1998, and I'd started doing online counseling work in 2003, spending hours with people one-on-one. I wrote many writings and devoted time to people claiming to be interested in the ministry work or needing help. I did not find many serious in their pursuits, but was able to work intensely with a few who greatly benefited from the studies and counseling. Things continued on like this, with few preaching dates and speaking engagements (most of which were cancelled beforehand due to disagreements on matters) over a period of a few years. I was still calling myself "evangelist," and attempting to avoid my call to be an apostle at any and all costs. The Apostolics weren't thrilled with such a label for a woman, but I had come to find there were female preachers in Oneness Pentecostalism over the years and while they were certainly not a staple of the faith, it was possible to find them in different places without too much of a stir. I wasn't ready to be that "controversial" yet, so I did what I was better at doing, and that was teaching and interacting with others, even if it was through the internet.

One thing that came from online ministry was an increasing number of leaders who desired to "affiliate with me" or have me "cover" them. I wasn't sure how I felt about this, given that I did not understand apostolic ministry in a right context. The only other times I'd heard the term "covering" were in the teachings of my initial pastor, who was out of alignment with true ministry purpose. We didn't talk about "covering" in the Oneness church. Even though I rejected the idea of being an apostle and covering people, those who sought me out as their covering insisted they needed my covering. I reluctantly started covering people as part of my ministry, teaching them and networking as many of them together as I could. Two were in Africa and one was in Pakistan. I also started a correspondence Bible school which had more than thirty-five students within six months. Several of these students kept contact long after they'd completed the course, and some were sent Bibles. One spoke of being in a refugee camp in Uganda, holding on to the Bible our ministry had sent them, reading it nightly. He told of being in a tent with five other people, all of whom had Malaria. He was blessed and said he recognized God and our continual prayer intercession as the reason he never contracted the disease. This story still remains with me years later, even long after contact was lost with this student.

Throughout this time, I continued to call myself "evangelist." Nobody ever called me by that title. I was frequently called pastor, sometimes called prophet, and occasionally called teacher. People also started referring to me as their "apostle." Most called me "mother" in keeping with their cultural customs. I rejected these labels and became very emphatic about doing the work of God without needing a title. Even though I could see my perspective was unbiblical (as Bible ministers used terminology to describe their ministries), I continued to avoid my apostolic call by avoiding all labels.

I continued covering the first churches that came to me until we began to have issues. Everything that arose pertained to money. No matter how hard I would disciple these people at my own cost, they all wanted money or me to visit them at my expense. All but one were overly interested in having a certificate, proving they were part of our ministry. I have always been against the idea that someone covers your ministry and now the right exists to use their ministry name and teaching as your identity or branch. When these ministries were denied money, personal visitations at our expense, and certificates linking our ministries, two of the three quickly faded away, never to be heard from again. One stayed on with us for a while, and several others were added. By January 2007, I was covering seven churches and one ministry.

One day before leaving New York, I received a postcard in the mail advertising a new church soon to start meeting in my local area. I felt led to call and find out more about it. I protested initially, as I had a lot of duties and responsibilities to fill that day. I was uninterested in making a phone call that might engage me in long discussion. Even though I protested with the Spirit a bit, I made the call. Making that call found fulfillment of the words God had spoken to me before my first pastor left our community several years earlier. He had returned, set to bring about "change" and "reform" to the local area. His slogan? "A new thing has come to the hills!" Within a few months, this man successfully divided the church I initially attended and it never recovered. What God revealed to me was true and always would be such as I stayed with Him.

In January 2007, I moved to western Kentucky at what I thought was God's direction. I'd run the gamut with what I could where I was living in New York, and was ready for a change. Given opportunities were becoming fewer and farther between than they had ever been in years prior, when the opportunity to leave came, I believe it was God. There was more possibility as a preacher, especially moving further south, and I was ready to move on in my life and feel more like an "adult." I had received promise of support and interest from a ministry there, a by-product of the Church of God of Prophecy. Even though I was already in an apostolic position, I was not dealing with it. I still thought the best means of advancing ministry was through a local church group, and as I'd stopped attending church where I was living, I figured the only opportunity to branch out was to find a new area. I had come into the church during an era where ministry mentality believed advancing and developing ministry came through doing anything you were asked by local leaders. If they asked you to type, you typed. If they asked you to clean the bathroom, you cleaned the bathroom. If they asked you to clean the church, you cleaned the church. If they asked you to travel with them, you travelled with them. The basic concept: an individual building a ministry must be willing to do anything of service for those perceived to have authority. If you were very obedient and very good, you would be rewarded with a short talk, teaching Sunday school, or other ministry duty on the ladder of ministry success. The theory mused you would eventually be rewarded with ministry status and acknowledgement within the local community. That local community would then serve as your launching pad into ministry in different areas.

    My experience with this ministry seemed to have promise in the beginning. Church was different in Kentucky than it had been in New York. Faith was not as much of a piety, but more of something that was as natural to the landscape as breathing. The people of this group were my only social connection in Kentucky, which was the end of the world as far as I was concerned. Ministry didn't seem as alien to these people as it had in New York. They seemed supportive and interested in what I was doing, helping me to acclimate and make friends. We seemed to have much in common in ministry style and approach. They even gave me a job as promised (after a long pause where it seemed no job would exist), which was much needed at the time due to financial constraints. I continued to cover churches and ministries, and I built up the covering program through the ministry.

    The promise that seemed to exist initially began to change very rapidly in a very short period of time. My ministry work, however, was the very thing this new ministry seemed to ignore. Despite their claims of interest and respect, they did not acknowledge me as a minister among the congregation or community. It did not matter to them that I was covering other churches and ministries. The hours of service I did for this group did not seem to matter, nor did they seem to take any interest in me beyond the superficial. There were signs that things weren't as they seemed, but at the time, I ignored them. I needed the job they offered and desperately needed involvement with something where I was. The longer I stayed in this ministry, the more duties and responsibilities they farmed out to me, causing me to spend longer hours on their matters and fewer hours on my own ministry. They began expecting me to work weekends, take work home with me, and did not increase my pay. How they treated me also began to change. I went from being treated as an adopted member of their family to the wicked stepchild, unworthy of their interest. Something was starting to feel wrong.

The situation at this church proved disastrous, maybe worse than at any other where I was a formal member. Even though they knew I was in ministry and I was faithful in service to the congregation, I was repeatedly passed over for preaching or public events. They had promised to do a conference with me and kept faltering on that promise, keeping me busy with typing and editing work for a low wage instead. In time, it came out they would not allow me to preach without meeting their personal criteria. Such criteria became an invasion of privacy and a total scrutiny of my life. I was told if I wanted to be in ministry, I had to get married. This wasn't the first time I'd heard this, and it certainly wasn't the last, but it was the time that pushed me over the edge into what became some of the most difficult and personally painful years of my adult life. The constant message I received everywhere I looked was, "You're not enough as you are." There was always something outside of my own God-given abilities that was going to "fix" or complete me to make whatever was perceived to be wrong with me better or different. I heard it in these church members and I heard it on an intimate level, from those closest to me, to the point where I thought I would lose my mind on more than one occasion. It was God that brought me through, brought me through to the breakthrough…but there were many times when I was not sure what was going to happen or what would come of things.

Through their judgment, I learned many things about them which caused me to question their position as leaders. One prominent woman in the group, a preacher and eldest daughter of the group's founder, had been married four times. Every one of her four marriages ended in divorce. The founder and his wife had a terrible marriage, displayed as they sniped and criticized one another. n more than one occasion, the wife would call the founder "stupid" and accuse him of not listening. Another prominent member, the youngest daughter of the founder, was a vial gossip. She would speak badly of others in the congregation at every turn, referring to one of the younger men present as a "cock hound" and "sissified." Complete with a fowl mouth, she and her husband were often at odds, including public fights and name-calling. While I am the first to admit we are all human and we all have issues…it seemed to me these people were in no position to measure my personal or ministerial life by their standards!

Despite what I was seeing firsthand, I had no question that I was going to continue attending the services at the church. I was not going to quit my job, nor was I going to walk away from the connection I believed I needed to have there. On one particular Thursday, I met at the church for their Thursday morning prayer session. There were never more than a handful of people present, and on this particular day, after everyone else had left, I sat behind an older woman who started asking me questions about my involvement with the church. I told her I felt like this was where God wanted me to be for right now, and I was just grateful to be here. She looked at me, straight in the eye, and said, "And when it's time for you to move on, you'll know." Her words shook me to the core, as I had no intention of going somewhere else. I wrote it off as something that would happen in the future, and left it at that.

The following Sunday, I arrived for service, ready for the Word. I had on a pretty aqua-colored suit and white heels, and sat myself in the seat, not expecting anything out of the ordinary to happen. This particular week, a visiting "prophet" from Nigeria spoke. He stated God was going to do a great thing in the Kentucky city I was living in. The room cheered and clapped…except for me. I could only remember years earlier the same revival promises, cheerleading, and false prophetic words spoken in upstate New York. They never happened in New York, and I knew they were not going to happen in Kentucky, either. I told God I could not live through this false revival-seeking mentality again and all of its empty promises and false victories. Just as the woman had prophesied, when the time came to move on, I knew. I knew it was over and it was never going to be what it had been ever again. I walked out of the church and called my then fiancé to come and get me when he finished his shift at work. I never returned again. I left with the founder's youngest daughter owing me $150 for work, which I never received, and extreme bad blood. To this day, I am uncertain of why they turned so vehemently. I never voiced my issues with the group until after I left, in the form of letters sent to the youngest daughter of the founder and the founder's wife. I sent letters in response to accusations made against me, all of which were unfounded and untrue. This process caused me further question and personal despair. I felt judged, criticized, and condemned. I allowed myself to be put through unnecessary scrutiny and my ministry never advanced. It seemed I had a calling which would never be accepted by the mainline Christian community.

I visited three other churches in the two and a half years I spent in Kentucky: an Assembly of God, heavy into Promise Keepers (what we'll call a "God and golf church"); a Methodist Church with a contemporary service that was right up the street and around the block from where I lived; and a Southern Baptist Church. Even though I still identified as Oneness, I never felt any draw to join the Apostolics there in Kentucky. Something about that part of my life was over, even though I didn't acknowledge it as such for a few more years. I felt led to attend none of them regularly, and kept covering the churches and ministries under me. Things followed this course consistently until two neighborhood people came to me, seeking a Bible study. They described feeling unwelcome and unwanted in local churches, and wanted somewhere to go to learn more about the Word. I started the Bible study in my home at their prompting. Those who requested the study never showed up. I worked actively on discipling my family, my mother and other immediate relatives, who were interested in study. I was still uncomfortable with titles and calling myself apostle, and it seemed like no matter what I did, my ministry continued to go in a direction opposite of the way I wanted it to go.

In October 2007, I received a bulletin on Myspace from a

woman claiming to be an apostle about an online ministry taking new members. This woman was my first encounter with a female apostle, and I was curious about this online ministry she spoke about. I'd never heard of an online ministry taking or receiving members. As this was a women's ministry, it sounded interesting. I wrestled with joining anything new, as my experiences within church and conventional structured settings always turned negative. My mother (a prophetess in her own right) gave me advice: if I didn't like it, I could always leave. Hesitant and deeply uncertain, I gave the online ministry a try.

At the time I joined the online ministry, it was very small network of women. There were about twenty-five of us in total. It seemed like a great place to share and discuss among women in ministry, for mutual edification and education. I finally found a place where I could discuss the five-fold ministry and the apostolic. The women present were wonderful teachers, sharing in their knowledge of the office and of ministry itself. Many were deep in dialogue about their apostolic calling and what it meant to them. The women shared their experiences, trials, difficulties, joys, and triumphs. This was not an ordinary ministry experience; it was something extraordinary and different from anything I had experienced before in all my years in church.

It was thanks to the support of various women on this network that I was able to confront the reality I had run from for so long. In looking at the years I'd spent in ministry up to this time, I could not ignore a big reason why I denied being an apostle: I wanted my ministry to fit in with conventional concepts. Standing as a woman was challenging enough in ministry, let alone being a woman and an apostle. I had enough trouble getting the right support without having to complicate things. Through this network, I learned many new technical capabilities that helped me to carry His message further. I was able to break through the years of isolation I'd experienced as a female minister with an apostolic calling. Within a few weeks, I was finally comfortable calling myself what God had called me so many years earlier: apostle. It was not until I could call myself apostle, as God already called me, that my ministry began to change.

At the time, I seemed to connect with the founder of this women's network. When she offered me ministry covering, I accepted it. In December of 2007, it was official: I was under her covering. While I had not been formally covered by anyone in awhile, the way in which this apostle covered me seemed helpful. Even though we held to slightly different doctrinal understandings on certain matters, she did not seem pushy about disagreements we might have had. She taught me some things about the apostolic, and expanded my horizon for it. In other ways, she left more questions than answers. What she was emphatic about was women's ministry, just as I was. Despite our differences, our belief in the importance of developing and supporting women in ministry kept us together. It was considered mutual that I was not just a daughter in ministry, but also a friend and sister in the Lord to her as well. In many ways, I served as an assistant to her, helping her administrate her online networks and with letter-writing and editing.

Thanks to the apostolic acceptance I'd finally come to recognize, many opportunities began to open up. I started radio broadcasting online in January 2008. By July, I received promotional offers from traditional radio stations and was on two stations by September. I also received another offer from an online internet station that December. I started travelling and preaching for the ministry. People started reading things I wrote and was able to gather a loyal following of support. I restructured our requirements for apostolic covering, separating those who were serious about apostolic relationship from those who were not. As a result, much in the ministry relationships changed and improved. In the end of 2008, I began the original study which stands as this book's foundation. I'd learned much about the five-fold ministry, especially the apostles and prophets, but truly wanted to see all the offices and how they fit together. There are many who consider themselves the five-fold ministry rolled into one, but God has given gifts and assignments to each office. We must attend to these gifts, encouraging and enhancing them. If we pursue offices God has not called us to pursue, we cannot fulfill the purpose for which He has called us. I know from my own experience that I made a terrible pastor and evangelist. In pursuit of those, I was not fully able to live out my calling as an apostle. The same is true for anyone who avoids their true calling.

Throughout 2009 and the first part of 2010, I continued my ministry work under the same covering I came under in 2007. I remained an active participant, administrator, and assistant in my former covering's online ministries until April, 2010. While the Lord revealed to me in September 2009 this woman would betray me, I noted a change in her as early as February 2010. I spoke with her one day, sharing with her about my vision for a women's conference. She clearly had no interest in what the Lord revealed to me, and wouldn't hear it out. I did not confront her about this, and remained constant in my support of her and of her as my covering despite what happened. I loved my leader, wanted to support my leader, and wanted my leader's approval. I was used to her mood swings and mental shifts, and knew how to wait it out whenever it would arise. I hated what God had revealed would come and wanted nothing more than to pretend it would not. About a month later, I received a phone call from her, introducing me to a new individual under her covering, so I could participate in his radio ministry. Everything was fine in this conversation. She was gracious and caring, referring to me as a daughter, sister, and friend in ministry. She told me she would call back later that night.

My former leader never called me back ever again. I went on to call her several times, with no response. A few days later I received a message from her online saying her computer had been hacked and she would be making many changes. In response to this, I told her that was fine, and to please let me know what she would want me to do further. At this time, I was broadcasting for her radio show and often running several of her networks alone while she pursued other avenues. It was a divine realization how much time assisting her took with no development to the ministry vision God gave to me. The realization would remain my own, as she never replied to the message I sent her.

Over the course of several weeks, I sent her notes through the mail, emails, and attempted to call her. She replied in no way to any of my attempted contacts. One day I went on to schedule broadcasting for her program only to find she erased every single program I'd recorded for her over the past two years. I then went to sign on one of her online networks only to find I'd been banned from participation. Where I'd been confused and confounded for weeks I grew angry at such deplorable treatment. I sent her a message, stating I didn't know what her problem was, but I was assured God would deal with her. About a week later, I received a biting and unprofessional email, filled with false accusations and rants. She declared that due to what she perceived, we were no longer "in covenant" or able to work together. I was flippantly thanked for my service to her women's ministry, ignoring the many other areas of her ministry I served. She went on to accuse me of disrespecting her, not honoring her, and of not realizing she created me and was the reason I had a ministry today. She blatantly told me, "Before you knew me, you were nothing."

My tendency towards defiance rose again, because before I knew her, I certainly was not nothing. I would not apologize to simply appease her notions when she was fabricating lies. I likewise would not tolerate such deception. Before I knew this woman, I'd spent a number of years in ministry, both online and offline. I could clearly see I had hits and misses in ministry, just like everyone does. When we pursue a true calling from God, we always battle established systems and paradigms that dislike the change God seeks to implement through us. If she could not see that, and not recognize nor appreciate the service I had given toward her and her ministry, there was no purpose in continuing with her as a covering anyway.

This woman did not let the matter go, even though she did stop contacting me personally. She made a vial attack online through her ministry, letting others know I had been dismissed by her and I would no longer be participating. She then went on to post writings where she compared me to the Judas in her ministry, believing God would progressively "kill" me from her life by removing me from her presence.

The world would say I should have been hurt. I was, deeply. More than hurt, I was angry. I didn't understood what had happened to cause things to go so awry. Her intention was to disgrace me and punish me, halting my ministry. It was revealed why she did what she did: my ministry outgrew hers, and she was angry as we began to make progress. Her concept of covering was I was to aspire to be like her, rather than who God would have me to be. While I do not, by any stretch of the imagination, condone her behavior, I see God's hand working in the situation for my good and the good of my ministry. The result of my disassociation with her was blessed and powerful because it was time. Great increase came to this ministry. As she sought to do harm, God used everything she did for the good of this ministry. I can see now, in an ironic way, that while she truly believed God was removing me from her life and ministry, it was the other way around. For the direction I was to take from here on out, God needed to remove her from me. I am blessed for His intervention, and for the many great ministers I have had the honor of working with over the years since I stopped allowing myself to be consumed by the ministry of this one woman.

Life went on and I spent the next three years working to fit in, as much as possible, with the concept and vision of general ministry that I saw around me. I was tired of looking so different from others and just wanted to "fit in" for awhile. Our ministry looked like most others that were out there, and in many ways, we were very much the same as everyone else, covering, leading, and holding on to people who were comfortable and complacent, helping them remain connected. Everything was fine, at least for awhile. I was ordained as an apostle in 2010 by the leader I would have for the next three years. We seemed connected and there appeared to be a general love between all of us. I was steadily publishing magazines and had even published a book. Life was what it was, and ministry had that air, as well. The ministry was growing relatively steadily financially, even though we hadn't had a lot of movement in it for awhile in terms of new people and much "new" coming out of it. Let's face it, most ministries are never rejoicing in the flow of money, but the money we had coming in was regular and reliable, even if it wasn't much. The people who were with me had been with me for an extended period of time, save one new person who breezed in about a third of the way through the year and was already itching to get out by the end of it. That is a story for later, however. As far as ministry outlook went, things were relatively good. No questions asked. I anticipated a great year, one without a lot of hassle, and one without a lot of questions. I assumed things would stay the way they were.

Oh, how things change. One day, one season stopped and another began, all together.

This was all in early 2013, right around the time I was invited to travel to Europe (the Netherlands, to be specific), and minister for a women's conference over there. They were going to host me for the thirteen or so days I was going to be over there and all I had to do was pay for my airfare over there. It had long been a dream and a well-purposed vision of mine to minister in Europe. At the time, I had the money (without question) and the ability to go. I didn't think much about the details of the trip: I wasn't real excited about getting to go to Europe, after so many years of feeling called to go over there. I chalked that up to never being real excited (which, as a rule, I'm not), overlooked the fact that nobody who had planned on coming was able to come with me (I figured maybe they weren't supposed to be there), and moved forward. Most people I knew, although maybe a little hesitant, were encouraging about the trip and excited that I was going.

One thing I started noticing was how gravely unhappy many people were with their churches. It seemed like every time I turned around, someone was upset with something going on where they attended. They would go visit somewhere else, but not feel right about the general spirit in the places. It wasn't just "church hopping," as we often call it. These were sincere, dedicated individuals who recognized something was wrong and they didn't have somewhere to go that was right. They were sick of politics infiltrating the church, both church politics and national politics. They complained that their ministries had been hijacked by Republicans (their words, not mine) and that they felt the church had more of an air of causes rather than genuine Gospel truth. They were tired of having to turn their heads the other way and tolerate negative attitudes about women, unwelcoming attitudes toward people who were not members, even a general feeling that they were all just there because of some sort of upholding of tradition. They didn't want to stop attending church, but they didn't see another option because no matter how many places they tried, they just didn't find what they wanted where they were going.

I started thinking about what they were talking about and I remembered all the times I wished I could have gone to a church in the area without having so many questions asked. Every time I went to a church just as a visitor, I was treated as if I was a non-believer or a rebellious heathen who needed to "submit" themselves to that local ministry and attend every week. Forget the fact that I spent several weekends out of the year on the road or in conferences by this time, and that I do know about ministry order and I was not going to sit up under a pastor as an apostle, because that would be out of order for me to do so. Let's also put aside the fact that I visited the church one time because someone invited me and I wasn't the least bit interested in joining based on what I had seen. I knew that going to visit a church, just to visit, just to be with other people in a moment of need, wasn't an option because of how I would be treated in the process. I began to understand what people were talking about (maybe better than I wanted to admit) and I wanted to create a place for them to go, somewhere where the regular members know God is there, want to bring their friends there, and who recognize the responsibility of keeping that place readily available for those who are seeking something just like it.

I left for Europe in March of 2013, making a layover in New York City to visit a friend of mine, the same ex-boyfriend who had challenged me to accept a different perspective than I'd had all those years earlier, for a few days before I flew out of JFK. While on that trip, I talked to my friend about the vision I had and the kind of place I wanted to create. Sitting on a bench somewhere between Harlem and the Bowery, he said to me, "And you know what you are going to call it?"

"Um, no." I had no idea where he was going with that.

"Sanctuary."

I loved it, and I was ready to move full-steam ahead. In fact, it was thoughts of that work that kept me the whole time I was in Europe. The trip was difficult; I had a bad host and nothing went as planned. I dealt with extreme warfare, venomous and controlling spirits, and a feeling of being isolated. I spent nights in the room I stayed in thinking about exactly how I was going to make this vision, this "Sanctuary" come to pass.

After I got home from Europe, it was as if everything changed. Sanctuary was definitely put on hold. I had trouble focusing, I had trouble thinking, and I had chronic migraine headaches (which I'd had all my life, but hadn't had as frequently as I was experiencing them). I was trying to finish a manuscript that was difficult enough to write about, let alone trying to write on it in that state. I found myself sad and displaced many days, unable to adjust to being back and unable to focus enough to make things move forward. I even considered moving, relocating to another area. If this had lasted for a day or a week, I would have said all right, but it went on for months. Because I didn't understand it, I didn't talk to anyone about it.

About three months passed and I got an inbox from my spiritual leader, or spiritual covering, at that time. She never said much to me and was never real involved in anything that was going on, because she never had to be. She knew I could handle matters and, if I needed something, she would advise to the best of her ability. I had been in ministry far longer than her, and my experience in the ministry not only made her look good, it meant I was an easy cover and she didn't have to do much for me. I was very surprised to receive her inbox, because, as I said earlier, she never said much. In fact, I think in the three-and-a-half years she covered me, she might have directly come to me about things on three separate occasions. This time was the second of those three times, and was in regard to a supposed concern she had about a program I was doing via webcam with the woman who hosted me while I was in Europe. Even though the trip was difficult and did not go well, I still tried to be considerate and kind to the woman who hosted me while in Europe, now that I was back home. Despite our differences we had done our best to make amends, at least on the surface, and treat one another as sisters in the ministry. I told only two people how the trip really went (neither of them being my leader, who I was not comfortable sharing with about it because she seemed to be very good friends with the minister overseas), and let everyone else think things went well. I had no desire to disgrace the woman overseas, or her ministry, even though I had severe misgivings about it. When she invited me to do a few long-distance programs for the internet, I saw no harm in it, especially given my own leader seemed very supportive and encouraging about her work and her ministry. The inbox I received spoke of something very different than what she was relaying to everyone on the surface. It sounded like concern, but what it really was, in hindsight, was manipulation. She told me that she had "concerns" about me working with this minister in Europe, and now felt that she was running a cult over there and the reason I had gone over there was to warn everyone over here about her. She started listing a number of things she didn't like about this other woman, and preceded to tell me that if I continued to work with her, that it would cause her to question my own calling and anointing. She also relayed back to an incident she had run into with a former leader of mine from about six years earlier, when I chose to stay with that leader instead of follow her, because they'd had personal issues among themselves.

    I didn't like the position I was put in, not in the least. I was smart enough to know that I was basically being told – stop doing this, or I will look down on you. The truth was that after doing two or three of the programs with the woman in Europe, I didn't feel right about doing them anyway, and had every intention of finding a way out of doing them, all on my own, but now I felt like I had to do it or it was going to cause problems between my leader and me. I respectfully sent an email to the woman overseas, and let things be where they were at. Simple enough, right? Everything was going to be fine...

Yet I still had a very uneasy feeling that things were not over, and something was still not right. I couldn't tell you what it was. I was about to find out, and what I was about to find out, I was not going to like.

I was right in the middle of trying to take some initiative and meet some new people in ministry when it seemed like things began to heat up, suddenly, all around. The woman from Europe started talking about me to other people and also started speaking against the people who were under my ministry. One woman she told, according to the woman's account, that she was "going to hell" for being "fat" and eating pork. Whether or not this accusation was true, I would never know, because I never had a chance to take it to the woman in Europe to investigate it further. That was because within a day later, all of a sudden, I got an inbox from the woman in Europe that seemed strange to me. It was like she was alluding to a problem that I didn't know existed, but sounded vaguely like things my apostle had been speaking to me. I didn't respond much at the time, but it was obvious from posts that people were putting on their pages that there was some sort of undercurrent going on.

About three days later, I got an inbox from the woman in Europe, telling me that she was no longer speaking to me and that I would understand why. I was deleted and blocked by the time I got home, and when someone covered by the ministry found out, she posted a status on her page on my behalf that blew up in our faces, quickly. Her post, which simply tried to address the mess that was going on and clarifying where people should go if they were having a problem with the ministry, became a battleground between my leader and my best friend (who was not a Christian, but a variation on a Hindu cult), who gave me the name and helped with the vision of Sanctuary. Despite requests for the mess to stop, the two of them went at it for well over an hour. The next day, I woke up to find myself deleted and blocked by my friend and more conniving from my leader. She told me that having a friend like that would drag me to hell and that I shouldn't have friends like that in the first place. I knew at that moment that I couldn't have a leader who would do that to anyone, particularly someone who wasn't a Christian. I was hurt and betrayed by my leader, who was supposed to be there for me and to support me in what I was doing. I was also deeply hurt and felt very betrayed by my friend, who I believed was mature enough to handle any disagreements we might have had and was shocked that he would so easily throw me over because he disagreed with someone I knew. Even though we were long past dating, years and years now, later in time, he'd resurfaced as an essential part of my life a few years earlier, and I didn't know how I could function without him. He unblocked me and re-added me, but things were never the same, and somewhere in there, I learned to live with the new "normal," without my friend, whom I no longer considered to be my friend. My leader, however, became another story. I spent long periods of time in deep, introspective prayer, realizing that had anyone I covered acted like that, they would have been sat down. hat meant I could not any longer sit up under someone who behaved in such a manner. When I respectfully requested to be released, she did so, confirming that everything she had issued ordination-wise remained intact, but was very angry with me for the fact that she felt the woman in Europe "went on with her life," but we were all still here, dealing with this mess. She never apologized for her behavior, nor for her negative witness.

Three weeks later, I received an email from the woman in Europe, accusing me of gossiping about her with my now former leader. Even though I tried to defend myself, I gave up by this point in time. She was never going to believe that I was not the instigator of what happened, even in the face of offering to send her the discussions I'd had with my leader. I was not the one who raised concerns and I even defended her when my leaders said things about the woman in Europe that were false. Alas, I knew that she wasn't going to listen. I accepted that my now former leader was running around as some sort of double agent, causing problems that didn't exist between the woman in Europe and me, and who knows who else. I accepted my defeat. I accepted that this was a battle I'd lost, I didn't know what God had ahead at this point, and all I wanted was my life back. I was sick of the chaos that seemed to encircle me and the way that things were constantly out of control. One of the women who also was involved in the mess, accusing the woman in Europe of damning her to hell, also started attacking me and my leadership in the ministry. While she backed off, quickly initially, I didn't have the strength to fight her at the time. I was also concerned about our finances, because so many things started to rapidly change. I didn't know who else was going to leave or what else was going to happen, so I let things lie – and didn't address her blatant disrespect in the way I should have.

By August, my state of chronic depression and confusion still hadn't lifted. If anything, it had intensified. I had started a new book on evangelism that was flowing well, but otherwise, I seemed to be in constant disarray and conflict. I had to move because my rent kept increasing (a move I didn't really want to make at that time) and had recently met a local minister who wanted to partner together with both of our ministries to start a local church work here in Raleigh. I knew I wanted to get better for that, but I didn't know how to get better for it. Casually speaking about it to a minister I had licensed and ordained right before all this came up, he mentioned to me that he thought what might be going on was witchcraft. After praying with him, the problem did seem to lift and get better, although it did not go away completely. It got better enough for me to think clearly and see what I wanted to do, and from there, I started to set my sights on the invitation to join with this other minister and help start this church. I thought that maybe this would be a way to start to introduce the community to Sanctuary and to the greater work that was coming.

The minister who asked me to work with him was very charismatic, albeit very young, even younger than I was, which, by many church standards, was young. I met him two days before I was being deleted and blocked by the minister in Europe and all hell broke loose with my leader. I'd gone to a pre-ordination ceremony that a friend of mine from New Jersey was officiating at, and since I'd never gotten to meet him in person, I thought it was a great time to do so. The first night I met this minister, he was already offering to share a building he was considering up in Durham, and the woman he was with was a pastor's wife for another church, where he would be speaking the next day. Things seemed fine – he was well-liked, people seemed to throw money at him, he was very good at handling people (which I did not feel I was and I attributed to many of the issues I've had over the years) and he seemed to be a decent speaker – so when I was given the invitation to work on this project, I didn't think a lot about it. There was nothing that spoke he was anything other than he said he was…except one day, in July, when I hadn't heard from him for several weeks. It was like he just fell off the planet. There he was, interested in working on stuff…and then there he wasn't. Out of the clear, blue sky, I said to myself, "I wonder if he's in jail!" Then I said, "Where in the world did I get that from?" I didn't think much about it, again, and pushed it aside.

It turns out, that's exactly where he was. I didn't find that out until very far after the fact, but that's exactly where he was. That was God Who put that thought there, I just didn't realize it.

It was decided I would be the apostle over the church, while the other minister (he claimed to be a Bishop, so that is what I will call him, for clarity's sake) was not coming under my ministry, but would retain his own leadership. Somewhere in here, we were supposed to be doing this together, and both groups that we had would be accountable to both of us. It sounded really good in theory, but its reality was quite different. For one, I suspected people were getting the idea that he was my leader, when that was never the case. Also, from the people that I had met through this man, it seemed like information circulated like wildfire, albeit incorrectly. I didn't attribute that to the leader, because I've had people do the same under me, but I just had the feeling that this entire arrangement wasn't going to last long. I resolved to be open-minded, because I was frequently accused of being too "to myself," and gave it a try to see how things went.

By September, things were off and running with plans for the church. He found a church that was renting out their building for twice per week at the rate of $700 per month. This sounded incredibly high to me for a time-share arrangement on a church, especially given that the church was in one of the worst parts of Raleigh and the building wasn't much to speak of. I also didn't trust the woman who was renting out the space. She seemed way too interested in the money and she seemed dishonest to me. I felt like she was always pulling a "con job," even as far as coming to me without the other minister present and telling me the only reason she wanted to let us use the building was because she liked "my vision."

She was always talking to us individually and sidelining each one of us, causing trouble with the other. I didn't trust her. I tried to talk the other minister out of renting from her, but for whatever reason, he wanted to meet there. So meet there, we did, Saturdays at 12 PM and Tuesdays at 7:30, starting October 2013.

One month into the lease, we were already having problems. The landlord refused to provide us with a copy of the lease and refused to provide us keys to the building, even though they were promised at the lease signing. That meant every single time we were to have a service or a class, we had to wait for an elder of the church to let us in. They would show up late, every week, and cause us to wait, sometimes up to forty minutes post-service time. The people of the other minister's church in Durham refused to leave Durham and attend the church in Raleigh. People not attending meant that we didn't have any money, and contriving the rent out of the few people we had turned impossible, quickly. One week the pastor's daughter came in and threw everyone out of the church during service, telling them they had been there too long and were "over time" (even there were no time restraints on our contract). We were also blamed for damaging equipment that nobody damaged when we were in there. While I don't question that the other minister I was working with had issues and was shady, we were being blamed for things that we were not guilty of doing. After one particularly negative run-in with her, I knew that there was no way we were going to be able to stay there through the lease, whether we had the money, or not. In the meantime, our most disastrous women's conference ever took place in Tucson, Arizona. Our host, who volunteered to have us on her own, dropped the ball quite noticeably and that meant we had a huge overhead – between travel, hotel, and venue – that we made nowhere near back. To make matters worse, one of the women who attended the conference attempted to sabotage it and work witchcraft on attendees who were present. If it wasn't one thing, it was another.

I went home from Arizona both disgusted and disgruntled, because I was always there for this particular leader, even though I had misgivings about her when we met. I figured that, misgivings or not, I had an opportunity to train and make a difference in her life. She wanted me for her leader, she felt God was in it, and I was willing to see how things went. It didn't help that the very next week, it was decided that back home, we would not continue to meet at the church where we had been meeting. Not only did he not make good on his promise to supply a full church and tithes, we had another leader fail to follow through on commitment, and we were out of money and patience. The landlord was going to continue to treat us as she had been, admit no wrongdoing, and we both agreed to take our chances and stop using the building. She threatened to sue, but nothing came of it. According to what I learned, if we vacated the premise, she had the opportunity to re-rent it and she really couldn't do much to us from a legal perspective. I don't even think their "lease" was a legally binding agreement, but I was still very grateful that the matter was not pursued. I knew that if something did come out of it, I would be the one who wound up reaping the harvest, and I was not in a financial position to do so. The ministry and myself were broke at the time, due to all these changes and high expenses. I needed the matter to pass so I could sit back and think about what was next.

I decided that I was not going to move forward with this other minister. I didn't like how he handled his business and I was suspicious by this time that the whole matter of the church was shady, at best. I did some investigation into him and discovered that he had been arrested and charged on larceny three times, and all of those times were within the past two years. I graciously stated that I would not be moving forward with them, but I wished them all the best. I took some time, sat down, and thought.

2014 was rapidly moving in, and I desperately didn't want to have another year like 2013. It's easy to look over all of these happenings and say "Why didn't you" or "Why not," but I know, firsthand, how difficult it is to make decisions when you don't really know what to do. That was how I spent the entirety of 2013 after I got back from Europe. Everyone I was sure was really for me turned out not to be and that left me not sure who to trust…so you start to work with what you have. You take a chance, whether it's against your better judgment, or not, and you see where it takes you. I knew, however, that I didn't want this to continue for another year. This never-ending nonsense was causing me to be not only tired, it was causing me to want to leave ministry. It seemed like everywhere I turned, people were not trustworthy and my attempts at trying to be not so "unto myself," as I was accused, didn't work out. I sat back, did some new writing and published some older manuscripts, and waited.

Around this time, I was being intensely pursued by a local television production company about going on television. Truth be told, I wasn't interested in the least in going on television. Television was expensive and I was going through a long phase of not being sure how I felt about television preachers, period (yes, I am fine with ministers being on television, I wish though that we could have some more moderate viewpoints rather than so many politics and so much extremism). The company, however, wouldn't let up, and no matter how much I expressed that I wasn't sure if I could afford it, they felt that I could sell the show based on how I carried myself alone. The contract wasn't binding; I could leave at any time, so I decided to give television a shot. I thought it might be a sign for a new start, despite my own stubborn concerns about money (that I had whether I did television, or not). I was able to find a sponsor and I took that as a sign.

I hadn't been able to intercept a copy of the program, nor watch it myself because the television station it aired on wasn't played in Cary. Once I was able to see what they were doing, I wasn't pleased with the quality of the program, and I had an assistant who guaranteed we could do the show ourselves and turn out a better product than they were doing. He literally wound up on my doorstep one day in March of 2014, with no place to go, and me being me, I couldn't let him sleep on the sidewalk. He had been ordained by our ministry and seemed eager to be of service and to help, and believed one of the primary reasons he came was to help me launch Sanctuary. He acknowledged I needed help, and was ready, willing, and able to offer it. The truth was, I wasn't crazy about him as a person, and I know that I wasn't his favorite person in the world, either. To him, I was rigid and staunch, and to me, he was flighty and too lenient. Somewhere, in here, however, we seemed to put that aside and make a decent team.

We spent hours – and dollars – on the television ministry as well as hours spent hunting down a building. Even though I had to dismiss someone from the ministry, things seemed to be, for the first time in about a year, looking up. I had a better outlook and was excited about new writing. It appeared that the haunts of the past year, and the problems of before, were gone. I had some local help that, like or not, was willing to work, and I had other people, one woman in particular, pledging to move to North Carolina to also help, which I took as a particularly good sign. This was the same woman I had run into some conflicts with the summer prior and I took her pledge to move as a sign that things were going better between her and me. We had spoken on occasion since our conflict, but things seemed to be peaceable and she seemed to be more respectful. She was getting quite cozy with a mutual acquaintance of ours, which raised my eyebrow, but I didn't worry too much about that. The acquaintance wasn't well-liked by anyone we knew and I knew they had been friends prior to now. Their connection hadn't seemed to threaten her relationship with the ministry, so I just chalked their relationship up to a friendship. I was feeling better, I was doing better, and I was not going to let anyone – or anything – upset that. I had a new covering – in fact, it was the leader from New Jersey that had been a long-time friend of mine – and he was talking about ordaining me as a bishop in addition to my standing ordination as an apostle.

I also was getting a few preaching engagements around the Raleigh area that, while they were not amounting to much financially, were definitely good exposure given I was now on television. One particular church service was extraordinarily sparse, but a woman in attendance at that church seemed to take a liking to me and my ministry. She remained at the ministry she was a part of, following occasional videos and such that I would post online, and buying some things as a very faithful customer through my garment company, Rose of Sharon Creations. We were not friends and were not close, thus I did not think much of her except that perhaps we had a fan, like I've had at many of the churches I've preached at. I moved forward, thinking that maybe things were finally going to improve, not giving much consideration to anyone who was around me or to what spiritually they might be working.

One day in May of 2014, I was on a prayer line when I got word that the woman who had just offered to move to Raleigh to help out with Sanctuary was not, in fact, fine with anything that was going on. She was running around, spreading vicious rumors that were not true, whose root was with the woman she was "friends" with. They were saying that "God" gave some sort of revelation that the man who was assisting me with the television ministry was supposed to be my "spiritual husband" and that I was making plans to move forward with that sort of relationship. Let me say, outright, that if something of this magnitude was true, even sinful, I would admit had I been planning on it…but I wasn't. In fact, it was so far from my mind, it wasn't even funny. It was one of those things that never even was a thought, let alone a revelation. As I stated earlier in this work, I didn't even particularly care for this individual, and he didn't care for me. "Spiritual relationships" were the farthest thing possible from our minds, as much of the time, we had to work to put aside our differences just to do ministry. These two women were off, concocting this mess, and spreading it. Both of them had their papers pulled and I tried to pick up the pieces of the mess they created.

This was easier said than done. The woman who was spreading the rumor was the biggest financial backer of the ministry. Not having her money to rely on every month was going to be a challenge, especially given I didn't know how I was going to replace it. I figured I still had the sponsor and my mom was always regular with her tithes, so we would make do until the finances could be replaced.

A week later, the sponsor I'd had for the television show didn't send his monthly payment. He had been emphatic that God told him to provide sponsorship through September of 2014, and it was now only the end of May. I had to contact him repeatedly, only to get a very annoyed response back that he would put something in the account the following month, but he would no longer be keeping his commitment to the ministry because he was getting married. He never gave his final promised funds, and that was that. To make matters worse, a few days later, my mom also lost her job, and was no longer able to assist the ministry like she had before. I had no idea what was next, I had no idea where I was going, and the leader I now had at the time was of no assistance, whatsoever. His answer to all my problems was to get ordained as a bishop, which never happened because he was both unstable in ministry and personally flighty.

Things continued, although quite unsteadily. I was starting to wonder about my assistant. I had the sinking feeling that he was one way to my face, but another way when I wasn't around. The people who were a part of his vague and leading internet ministry had a tendency to be rather disrespectful toward me. He also seemed to be kicking up. At times prior, he was very respectful, almost to the point of being unbelievably submissive. When he started getting more rude and more vocal, I knew something was up. I now realize that what everyone had been saying about "spiritual husbandry" was equating to a power and control struggle, where he felt he had an authority over me that he did not, in reality, have. Not recognizing that as the root, I did start confronting his behavior, but I didn't confront what was behind it from a spiritual perspective. I didn't say anything directly about what I was sensing from him, but when it was obvious his people weren't lining up properly, I would say something about it. He didn't do anything about what I said, and on more than one occasion, we had an argument. Over all, I watched....and waited...because I knew something was coming.

Over that summer, the woman I had met at the church earlier that April started becoming more interested in me from time to time. She started giving monthly and paying a lot more attention to my postings and event whereabouts in the area, even showing up at a couple of them. A few weeks after, she sent me a copied text message from the pastor's wife at the church she had been attending where the woman had said bad things about her behind her back to the pastor. The pastor didn't defend his church member, who came to me under the guise of being hurt and upset. She didn't make a commitment to my ministry or make it known that she wanted to be covered by me, but was there with some money and as a good customer. We even helped her on one occasion to pay an overdue light bill that was extremely expensive. She was in and out, however, and watched us from a distance as she moved through different phases in her own life, including moving out of her house into an apartment with a friend.

Not much changed in the months that followed. We occasionally went to look at properties, but they never panned out. The finances were not steady, but thanks to several people moved by God, we made ends meet in ministry expenses. Over time, my assistant grew more and more distant and less interested in helping the ministry and keeping his commitments for the television ministry, that was quickly falling apart. My mom finally sold her house. The leader I had at that time was feeling more like someone under my covering than he my leader, and after a particularly negative incident where he tried to usurp my authority with my own people, I also left his ministry. I had long stopped feeling right about the bishopric ordination and was ready to leave him – and all of this mess – in the past.

It was now January 2015, and I resolved the problems of the past years would not, if it killed me, follow me into 2015. Little did I know, there they were, but they weren't panning out like they had before. God had a plan, and I had to trust it...but at the time, I wasn't exactly sure what was going on. I was starting to pick up on the fact, though, that an awful lot of people who were mighty close to me had been "pruned" for the past two years. Most of the people who got axed had been around me for some time, and were supposedly people who would go "all the way" with me and were supposed to be praying. As I went into 2015, I wondered if they were "preying" instead of "praying." It always seemed like there was so much warfare surrounding the ministry and I had a lot of times when I felt like I just couldn't catch a break. I wasn't the type to automatically assume it was as a result of the people who were so close to me, but after the attacks I went through in 2014 and the people they came through, I wasn't so sure.

I had a new group of people who were now coming under the ministry. One was a woman who found a business card of mine in Garner, North Carolina, and felt she had to connect. Even though we never really made much of an official connection, she insisted she was ready to be trained, and I gave her the benefit of the doubt. In the long run, she wouldn't be that relevant to much, except to be dismissed about a year later. Another was the woman I had mentioned earlier, who was following the ministry, albeit from a distance. We could say she was "quasi-covered" for awhile prior to this official decision, which came about because of the woman who found my card and was sure she had to be covered. To be honest, I wasn't sure about either one of them, but I have long been a leader who tries to at least give people a chance. There were four of us in those days who would get together in this area (the two of them plus one other woman and myself) who would get together for spiritual discussions and edification, as I didn't have a church in Raleigh at the time, and I resolved to make sure that we maintained our contact, even without one.

This woman who was now covered by the ministry who had been following me for some time would become most relevant throughout the next year and a half or so. She came to me later that month wanting to start a business, a publishing company, with me. She stated outright that with the vision in ministry I have, I would need more than just the tithes and offerings that were coming into the ministry (which was true) and felt that she could be of help if we worked together toward getting that money. I already had a publishing company, but as I had stated earlier, it wasn't doing poorly, but wasn't setting the world on fire, either. Part of that was due to my hesitancy to take on publishing full-time for fear that it would edge out other things that were just as important in my life, such as my sewing company and, most importantly, ministry. I have always made the commitment to be a full-time minister and part-time everything else, and if there was a cause to question that taking on publishing full-time might impede with that, I wasn't interested in it.

The other realities are that the publishing industry has long changed and people have more options to do things themselves if they are so inclined. This has created a service-based publishing industry that caters more to people who are not willing to take on the technical work of layout and design themselves or who are interested in a distribution platform that they can't do without someone who knows what they are doing. I've been in publishing long enough to know how to do all these different things, but I wasn't sure I knew enough people in order to handle it myself.

This woman echoed the desire to show forth the needed commitment to help bring in clients and to help with the work so that we could turn a profit. What I offered to her was instead of starting an entirely new company to add on the company name she wanted to use as a company imprint. This way, we wouldn't have to file brand-new paperwork and a whole bunch of other messy steps that would complicate things legally. It also meant that I retained legal control over my company in case something came up that merited her dismissal from the work. I wasn't sure how much I trusted her as a person, but I was willing to take a risk on an idea that might help bring in some very much-needed income. I could tell that things were changing around me, again, very fast, and I wanted to be prepared for them. The initial work of the company wasn't much more than setting up logos and business cards, and a little subdomain website to get us up and running. It wasn't overwhelming and wasn't anything I didn't think I couldn't handle. In fact, in the beginning, doing the work was a lot of fun. It was different from what I was used to doing and I had reached a point where I was tired of the unknowns of ministry: you never know if you were going to preach or not, how much you would get as an offering, and waiting forever for people to follow through on their agreements with you as pertain to events and finances. I also was getting tired of feeling like people were always pulling on me for this or for that. I couldn't pray for another person's finances that never seemed to get sorted out. I was tired of feeling like I was wading in a shallow, insignificant pool and was yet drowning in it at the same time. Trying to see where this business went seemed like a good idea, and I was open to it. She was eager as a business partner and ready to get started, and I respected the initiative she took to move things forward in ways she could assist.

My assistant was still sort of around, although rather sketchy in his presence. It had become obvious that he wasn't interested in "assisting" anymore and that he was trying to take authority over me, and, in many ways, subordinate me to himself. I knew by this time these behaviors were a result of the false words spoken in 2014, that even though they did not manifest and were not ever going to manifest as people suggested, they resulted in a spiritual battle for control and headship that was not going to be positively resolved. He had a way of doing what he wanted to do, whether or not I authorized it, and when I started cracking down, he started rebelling. In February 2015, I was invited to attend a church anniversary service held by some dear friends of mine in Burlington, North Carolina. My assistant automatically indicated he wanted to come, of his own free will, recognizing it was a Sunday night and it may very well conflict with his own "online service" (one that was sketchy, at best). When the service and post-fellowship ran over, he became angry and sullen, and refused to speak the entire way back to Durham. He got out of the car, slammed the door, with a sarcastic "See Ya" and did not say another word to me, all week. When I commented on a picture of his, he attempted to start a fight, drag other people into it, and then blocked me when I wouldn't play his nasty game. I revoked his papers due to insubordination and never heard from him again.

And yet...I didn't mind. He didn't do as stellar of a job with the television ministry as he promised he could do, and he kept dropping the ball, time and time again, for months. He needed to go. God just knew that He could do it through his inflated, arrogant ego...because that would be the fastest way to get rid of him.

After he left the ministry, things did immediately change, but it wasn't all for the bad. It felt like a relief. This was the first time someone had left the ministry and it turned out to be a relief, rather than a bad thing. Some of that change I was sensing was starting to come to pass. It wasn't manifesting the way I expected, but change was coming and more was on the way.

The problem with the change that was coming is it was not moving very fast, and it wasn't the change that I was hoping for. Ministry still seemed slow and not moving well, even though the business was a new project. I hadn't spoken much of Sanctuary in almost a year. Save going to look at a few properties here and there, Sanctuary hadn't been much on the table. The focus was always on something else: my assistant getting an apartment, internet services, prayer lines, finding finances, the new business, and the like. Between the warfare and the television ministry (which did not accomplish much), Sanctuary was clearly not a priority, at least not the one it should have been. When my former assistant left the ministry, I declared that I was not going to have another wasted year in this ministry, jumping from one thing to another, looking from one thing to another. It was not going to be another year of the "same." Since I didn't have a lot of help at the time, I didn't know how I was going to make it work. I gave it to God and let it go at that.

In the meantime, things were somewhat quiet on the surface. I came to find out that the woman who was now a business partner of sorts (albeit a subordinate one) who was also covered by the ministry had been doing some work with a local minister I was well-acquainted with from a few years earlier. The bishop I'd worked with in our joint-church disaster was still around, this time maintaining his own congregation that consisted of several men and women from the areas surrounding Raleigh. They were renting an expensive property - $1,200 per month, plus expenses, to be exact – in southeast Raleigh. Somehow she had gotten involved with him and I seriously advised her not to remain connected to him. I told her of my experience and she did not listen. I ended it by saying that I understand that we have different experiences with people and that I was not prohibiting her from helping him out as we did not yet have a church and I understood her interest in gaining experience and being a part of a local congregation, but expected that she would remain aware of who her leader was and she would make sure she maintained her proper balance therein. She stated she understood, and wanted to open up the door for Sanctuary to sublease the property in Southeast Raleigh for half of the rent, half of the time. I decided I wanted to think more about it. Not only was that a lot for a timeshared property, it was a lot of money for us, period, right at that point in time.

It turned out that her involvement with this bishop was far more complicated than I was led to believe. Not only was she not just attending or helping out, I found out later that they had named her the "assistant pastor" and she was involved not just in handling money, but had him living with her. The way I found out was when the bishop got arrested for several counts of larceny, she got arrested, as well. From what I know of the legal process, I think the police were looking for someone to "flip" on the bishop so they could testify and he could get a longer jail sentence. Instead of being cooperative, the woman gave the police a hard time, which equated to the cops hustling her in order to get her to say whatever it was that she knew. Was the evidence circumstantial, certainly, but to me, that wasn't what went through my mind as I got call after call from the county jail about what was going on. Not only did she disobey, she got herself in over her head. As she went through the experience, she assured me that she had learned her lesson. I wasn't so sure. I was very grateful that I learned my lesson with this bishop, and disconnected when I did. Obviously, not everyone was so fortunate.

Around this time, I received a word that it was time to take a project back off the shelf that I'd "shelved." I knew, somewhere inside, that the word was about Sanctuary, but I wanted to make sure. I was planning on axing at least one of the three shelved projects, and I wanted to make sure it wasn't the project I was looking to eliminate. It wasn't, and the word was "take Sanctuary off the shelf." Off the shelf it came, and with it came a flood of ideas and information on how to do the church so it would not become a burden on me and it would not take away from the apostleship. I started putting ideas together and waiting on things. The first thing I tried to do was find a pastor, and a man who came highly recommended became a consideration. He turned out to be connected to the bishop who was now going to jail, and it seemed wise to scrap him as a potential. He had a bad attitude and it was obvious that he wanted to bring his way to the table rather than submitting to the existing vision to get training. We had no potential pastor and I prayed to God that if a pastor was to come to us, to reveal who that would be.

Receiving word that is terribly off has been a long-standing problem in my ministry experience. It seems like with each and every word comes a further question and fewer answers. In looking back, in particular over the original Sanctuary experience here in Raleigh, I can see that I was pushed to do something without full guidance or information, and definitely without the assistance and support to bring it to pass. I had a good vision, but I didn't have enough information to bring it forth. I knew what I wanted to do, and I knew where I wanted to go with things, but the word I was given didn't expound enough to do much successfully.

God was dealing with me, however, and the manifestation of that issue came in the form of opening up our ministry to being inclusive. An inclusive ministry is one that turns no one away, and is welcoming to any and all who do not fit the standard format for traditional church settings: LGBT individuals, women, divorced persons, children of divorce, the elderly, the disabled, and any and all who are ready to hear the message of the Gospel. I knew doing this would be controversial, especially living in the south, but I knew this was an integrated part of Sanctuary, as we offered the place where people could worship God freely, and without question.

In July of 2015, I preached for the last time that year as a guest at someone else's church. It was a great experience, but I knew I wasn't returning there. My message was titled, "Guess Who's Coming To Dinner?!!" and was a foundational establishment for the work of Sanctuary, in inviting people to the table of the Lord without hesitation or discrimination. I had been scheduled to preach in August, but then that got cancelled. There was nothing new on the table and nothing new coming up. I was approaching my eighteenth year in ministry and in addition to being tired, I was finding myself disinterested in the states of the church as they were. I decided that if I was going to do anything, it would be to focus on the business, because I didn't want to live from phone call to phone call and occasional purchase to occasional purchase anymore. If ministry wasn't going to help me to live, I had to take some steps to take care of myself. The new publishing work now on the table was a great way to start. We had our first big client, and I wanted to see where this went.

I didn't connect it at the time, but focusing on the business imprint that we had started together wasn't really what I was supposed to be doing. I had taken Sanctuary off the shelf, but because we didn't have much money at the time and I kept coming up dry when it came to people willing to learn, I didn't know what else to do. Our first big client turned out to be a condescending, controlling, dominating man who I seriously clashed with in personality. The good news is we were able to keep ourselves together enough to produce a great quality of work that he was most pleased with. Despite a rough start, things were moving forward, and seemed to be going in a good direction.

Because I was still open to doing things in ministry (just not as the primary focus), I started looking for a building. It was obvious that I wasn't going to accomplish what I hoped to achieve by preaching hit and miss in other people's churches. The woman who was here, pushing the business and now handling court issues, was also helping out. I was not a leader who abandoned people when they went through, and I felt the best way to handle this was to allow her to go through it while being there to support her through it. We looked for properties, but didn't find much. An opportunity to split the building and work with another minister also came up, but I shut it down before it started. I still didn't have a potential pastor and came to the conclusion that maybe if I built it, the pastor would come.

I do believe this is what God was telling me; there were things about Sanctuary that needed working out and experiences I needed to have to make sure what we offer our leaders-in-training something substantial and purposed. I can't just install people and leave them to their own devices, or consider how to do this work in varied places without some background to consider costs, experience, and needed training. Then the woman I was working with expressed interest in some pastoral training. I was not opposed to that, because I think training can benefit people, no matter what was going on. She was going through an ordeal and I even now believe that ordeal made her genuinely interested in doing something different, even if it was unknown. I left the door open that we would honor her "pastoral" title but she was not going to have automatic access to the pastoral office at Sanctuary and that she still had to go through training. I wanted to see how serious and dedicated she was to the work, and if she was a right fit for actual pastoral requirements. She would be expected to assist in the duties of the church, assist financially, and help promote interest in our church. She was agreeable to this, and I said we can see where things are, later on. I felt this was especially important given she was embroiled in legal issues resulting from her last ministerial connection. Ordination was not discussed, and it was not understood she was not guaranteed an ordination through Sanctuary; it was a wait and see how things went situation.

One day in September, I got a text message about a building on Six Forks Road that was vacant. I'd been through so many other buildings, I didn't think much about it. Talking to the woman who was renting the property, however, was a refreshing change. So many of the people we'd dealt with were nasty and rude, and their buildings were overpriced. When I went to look at the building however, part of me knew this was it. The renters were pleasant and accommodating, and there was something about this building. It was as if it was an upper room experience.

The other part of me was hesitant and unwilling to take this on. I was still in a rather despondent place when it came to ministry, and I didn't want to have a rent bill to take care of every month. I was also handling all of the finances, technical and layout work, ordering, and business aspects of our business. Given this woman's issues with the legal system, I had nothing against working with her as long as she was not going to handle the money or accounts, and she was fine with that. I figured it was better to be safe than sorry later, and I know even to this day that was a good decision.

I left it at that if we were able to raise the money upfront for rent and deposit, I would take a chance on moving forward with Sanctuary. I was so touched that people from all over believed in this work and trusted in what we were doing stepped up and offered whatever they could so we could move forward in this project. And…move forward we did. There was another building I wanted to look into, but could never find anything out about it. The day that I signed the lease papers, I went by and saw it was rented.

I knew God was in this, but I didn't know how, or why. It didn't occur to me that maybe God had something in this situation that He wanted to work out within me.

The building was had, God gave assurance the bills would get paid, and things moved forward. In fact, things seemed good. The bills were paid, the property was being used. We had a Preschool program going one day a week and Sunday worship and Wednesday

Bible study. We had a decent relationship with the landlord. We'd acquired two new clients, both of whom were very promising writers. Overall, it was going in a decent direction.

Fall passed, winter came. With the new year came the same financial responsibilities and a severe lack in clients. The holiday season had put the work in a serious bind. Clients who were scheduled to make payments did not pay and we passed into January with a financial strain. We were experiencing a severe business lull and it was obvious that this other woman who was claiming to be a partner was losing interest in the work. When she ran out of friends to try and persuade to become clients, she stopped attending to business matters. When February came, there was no money to pay for the property.

My mother stepped up and offered to loan us the money. My wanna-be pastor in training and supposed business partner stepped up and offered to pay the rent with money she received from her income taxes, not wanting my mom to pay our bills for us. The day she was to come with the money, she said that her grandchild's father came to town and stole her money, and that she was unable to pay for it. She said instead that she would pay the money back monthly, in installments. She had a book that her son had written and wanted to apply the returned money to the publication of that book. I was willing to do that, and was agreeable. She never paid a dime, and I never published the book.

I was having a hard time feeling right about the story and mentally I looked around at where we were. The church had been paid for monthly due to the extensive amount of work I was doing, and it was being done without the assistance of this woman. She never in the ten months she attended the church ever brought someone to church with her, except grandchildren without their parents who were also disorderly and disruptive. She had stopped bringing the children in her family to our preschool without a word of explanation; one day she just stopped bringing them. I also started noting that she was out of church too often to be considered as pastoral material. She went from being out once every six weeks or so to being out at least once per month. She had money for vacations and things for herself, but she was not interested in business or in the church. I made the definite decision in April that she would not be ordained as pastor. Coincidentally, a month later, she said that she felt God told her it was time to do her ordination. She wanted to have it over the summer, but the date she picked coincided with another project she wanted to do, so she willingly said, "Oh we can postpone it! I'm not going anywhere!" in front of the whole church. Thus, "indefinite postponing" is what was to be done. I did not have the time nor the interest in having a long conversation with her about all the reasons I was not doing the ordination because I knew good and well she was testing the waters. She was a woman very used to having her own way and she knew she wasn't taking an interest in the ministry or in the business. I knew by her spirit that she was trying to be vexing, so I decided to take a different approach: I was going to be kind and nice to her, and the more she rebelled, the more she was going to be treated with love. She was going to be treated as any other church member who was not in leadership and who was attending regularly. If she wanted to leave, then she would leave of her own free will and volition. That also meant she would not be involved in decisions, in who spoke at services, and she would not be working the pulpit.

It took everything I had to take this approach. We had another person leave the ministry in the meantime due to a particularly vicious attack that was wrought on a ministry that I cover a few months earlier. Her departure wasn't a big surprise, but the fact that her money went with her was more of a distress to our financial situation. I was tired of this never-ending attack from within, and being nice to the woman in my own midst was galling to me as a person. I reached a point where I was so angry with her and so infuriated that she had the nerve to show her face like she was doing nothing wrong. It caused me to feel angry and embittered because I couldn't figure out what to do next and was so upset that I had to take time now and deal with this kind of mess, again.

After a particularly disrespectful run-in with her over something I shared from a book I wrote, I decided that I'd had enough and didn't know what to do from this point on. Everything I touched always seemed to turn into a mess and I now had people in my church, my experimental work that was supposed to embody a Sanctuary, that I couldn't stand. I also didn't understand why it seemed to be so hard to find good people to build a ministry work. The past few years, most of the people who had come on board seemed to have so many ulterior and dishonest motives. I didn't see how we were going to get anywhere with such problematic people. Every time we started to grow, we would wind up taking five steps backward.

The monumental, life-changing month that changed everything came in May of 2016. I announced we would be undergoing a reorganization of all things related to the ministry, including the church. The other reorganizations related to business. Even though the woman who was attending my church didn't say much about it, she immediately felt the pinch of the changes. I didn't tell her what the changes were and I also did not reiterate any special privilege to her in regard to any of them. One of the major ones was that I was going to officially be re-advertising my company label, Righteous Pen Publications, instead of promoting the imprint that we were operating under at the time. My reason for this was simple: The majority of our audiences were Christian, looking for Christian books, and were interested in writing devotional or biographical pieces from a Christian perspective. Trying too hard to push a secular imprint wasn't wise and while I reiterated that we would maintain secular imprints, trying to get a Christian audience to take interest in secular materials wasn't helping our advertising rates, and it certainly wasn't going to help us sell books or gain clients. I said it was fine to advertise the secular imprint, but we also needed to embrace the Christian aspects of the company, as well. She didn't protest but I could tell that she was sour about the idea of promoting the company separately because it was an obvious sign that she was going to have less input in the company and in clients than she had before. I also took the initiative to make some changes within the church which edged her out further. These included removal of her name from our websites and any contact information that related to her. I'm not sure if she knew I did this, or not, but if she knew about it, she didn't say anything. I also rearranged the furniture in the church, and made the resolution to plow on, at least to get through where we were.

On May 11, I had a long talk with my mom during a weekly Bible study where our members were no-shows, yet again, about where things were going. The word my mom got about things was that the Lord would show the way and provide answers. I'll admit I rolled my eyes at her that day, because the answer sounded just like a "God thing" to say. I was at a point where I didn't even like what I was doing anymore or who I was dealing with in my immediate circle and that was the answer. I hadn't even preached anywhere in almost a year's time except for my own church, and I had to admit that I wasn't crazy about the material I was using for Sunday service. The Minor Prophets study was interesting as a Bible study, but doing it every Sunday wasn't interesting me much. I kept doing it because I was getting some great insight out of it, but I knew it wasn't doing anything for the church even though the info presented was important, and maybe if they got bored enough, they would stop coming.

Sure enough, May 13 was the day when the answer came. As I sat and entertained the idea of what to preach on that Sunday in the event that our church members did not show up, all of a sudden it dropped in my lap: have we looked for housing in Charlotte? The answer was, of course, no. The revelation that it was time to move to Charlotte – and that the season here was coming to a close – was overwhelming, to say the least. I had no intention of moving and no intention of doing much of anything different, save moving out of the existing property. Leaving the area was never a thought in my mind, so at first, I tried to brush it off.

Brushing it off didn't work. Accepting the realization that moving was coming meant figuring out what was going to happen the next few months. There were four months left in the building lease. I had already decided that we weren't going to renew it when it was up. Where did this move leave this? What was going to happen to everything else? What about the different issues that we had?

I then received word from God that I assumed the old season was over when I went into the property back in October. It's understandable to assume that would be the beginning of a new season because so much seemed new: there were new people involved, new work was coming, and it was a new thing. It was also an underdeveloped vision, one that needed time to work and experience to go with it. I could accept all of that, but it still didn't answer the question as to where I was going to go from here.

The result was a long look at how truly unspiritual my life had become. I was still spiritual, but it had been a long time since I had clearly heard from God about direction. In fact, it had been since the time we first went in the building. I kept hoping someone else would get the word of direction or decision-making to make my life easier, and I was dismayed that it never seemed to come. My life was a maze of trying to raise the rent every month and trying to find new clients so that our funds would be met to keep things going. I was angry at the lack of help I had and I was angry that they didn't seem to care they were not helping like they should. In the reorganization process, I needed to work on reorganizing myself before the distractions came in and took over.

I resolved to let the joint aspect of the business die out on its own while putting effort into my own branding. I also decided that if there was one thing I missed terribly, it was the sewing and crafting work I'd done for years. In years past, it was a main staple of supplemental income. When the recession hit and I stopped travelling as much to preach, the business declined. I knew I could get it back up and while it might not be what it had once been, I knew that internet sales could boost if I would at least work on some sales online.

For the first time in almost two years, I set myself to be busy with productive work instead of focusing on nothing more than trying to raise money and maintain things. I also set myself again to the realization that like it or not, ministry is what I am called to do. Finding some new interest in publishing under my own unique imprints and in sewing gave me some restored interest and hope that maybe somewhere in here, the madness of the season would end. I also started getting preaching invitations again, as soon as I changed my state of mind and realized ministry had to be a priority in my life. They weren't a ton of engagements, but it was more relevant to me that I went from nothing to something all because I had resolved to move in the proper direction.

Things maintained their status quo on the surface. I kept working and reorganizing and we kept moving forward. I had a ton of new ideas and things I wanted to do, but I didn't implement any of them because I knew they were not for this present season. The more this particular woman pushed, the kinder I was, and the harder it got. She gave less and less and spent less and less time at the property, and we saw less and less of her on Sundays. She was missing more church than she attended and her family never came if she didn't attend. Things were tense and awkward and as hard as it was to imagine them getting worse, they did. One day she came and told me she wanted to start attending other services in order to get those people to come to our church. She felt, according to her own words, that going to other places as a fellowship experience would get people interested in the church we had there. I saw through this a mile away, and tried very hard to keep the little composure and tolerance I had for her left in tact. I told her that when the lease was up in two months, she was free to go wherever she wanted and do whatever she wanted, but while this lease was in play, we were going to be at the church. She tried to indicate I wasn't understanding her and the more I shot her down, the more irate the conversation became until I tried very hard to take a gentle tone with my "no." She got the message but when we had a forgiveness service the following Sunday, she apologized for what she did saying that she felt things were said on "both sides" that were wrong, thus implying that she wasn't really sorry. I put on a good front as we had a guest that week and he was a very impressionable young man who needed to see people "practice what they preach." He also loved coming to the church and I didn't want to destroy that for him, so we put on our apologies and moved forward.

About ten days later, a young woman who is a member of our ministry posted on her Facebook page that she was getting ordained. It was a basic ordination that ministers receive after they preach their first sermon entitling them to preach, baptize, and hold communion services. She was a training missionary and in situations that merit being able to perform these things. Instead of being happy for her or coming and asking for clarification, my so-called business partner and pastor-in-training threw an outrageous tantrum. She slugged me online, deleted and blocked me and several other members of the ministry, and removed most of her things from the downstairs office. She never returned to the church and never said a word except to try and get money from the business and to be insulting after she received her official dismissal letter.

But she was gone. I breathed a heavy sigh of relief and wanted nothing more than to move on from things. A part of me knew the season was almost over. Two more months and we would be out of the building, and then the focus would be on relocating, whenever that relocation would come.

For so long, I wasn't pursuing the things I felt I should be doing. In the name of trying to advance things, I had become too open to suggestions and too available to people. I tried to care so much that they took advantage of that. The people who came to "help" weren't there to help, and now all of them were gone: the women spreading rumors in New Jersey and California, the woman in Arizona, my assistant, the bishop I had worked with here, two leaders of mine, the woman in Europe, and now the woman who had come in and wanted to train (but really wanted to be in charge) here in Raleigh. They were all gone; not one was left. Life was to return to normal. Maybe not the same normal as before, but a new one that would usher in the new start and new season.

I spent the next few months trying to sort out the situations I'd been in and learn something from them. The season and all its chaos, however, would rear its ugly head at least once more. I'd been a part of a Christian sorority organization for about three years, and prior to that, I was a part of another one. I was brought into them in a ministerial capacity, one of covering, kind of like a chaplain. At first, I was an honorary member, but when leadership positions changed and scandal hit, I was placed in more permanent positions of authority over the organizations. To be honest, the experience with these groups was never positive. They were different from standard sororities in that they still were under Greek letters and followed a similar structure, but were different in that they espoused Christian foundations, thus avoiding hazing and other matters that would cause a Christian woman to avoid membership with them. I never found these organizations to be very well-run. If anything, they always seemed like a gigantic catfight. I wasn't familiar with Greek culture, as when I was a student at Apostolic Preachers College (later Apostolic University, which I took over in 2004), Greek organizations were strictly forbidden. When the opportunity came up to be a part of them years later, I thought it was a chance to be a part of something bigger, something that would involve networking and meeting others, and to do ministry in a different way. This experience never happened; instead, I found a continuous headache. This culminated when the leader over the organization I was covering at the time (both her and the group, mind you) came and told me that she'd done something very financially irresponsible with the organization's money and our account was now overdrawn. I put my head down, took a deep breath, and said that she needed to make this right. She promised she would, but nearly ninety days later, she still hadn't. I had to intervene and take care of the financial matters, and I made the declaration I was going to disconnect from this organization, as soon as such became feasible.

After the financial situation was resolved, things took a dismal turn in the organization. Nothing was happening for me anywhere else in ministry. If anything, it seemed like the season had lost its steam and was winding itself down. The only thing that was outstanding within my own vision was membership and covering this organization, and I was starting to get antsy as things changed. Multiple people left the organization and I was getting disgusted with the way things were done.

It had always been my job to handle the pledges, or new members, to the organization. I took it over when others expressed disinterest in continuing along with the position, and since they were using materials I specifically wrote for them, it seemed best that I handle these new women. For the most part, we didn't have a bad time. This all changed with a particularly difficult pledge line that was made to wait and grew impatient in the process. One of the women tended to be highly disrespectful, and behind closed doors, in the privacy of the group, everyone was quick to complain about everything and everything. When she came up against me, I sought to establish some order and checked her behavior. The board was divided, with half seeing my point and the other half coming against me. I went to a friend of mine with what was going on and he told me that God would open the door for me to leave, and that when that time came, I would know. It sounded all-too-familiar, like the words that woman had spoken to me at the Church of God of Prophecy ten years earlier. He and I had that conversation on Monday. By Thursday, I had left the organization. It also marked the end of my crazy four-year season that never seemed to end.

Being in a new season, especially given the difficulties of the past several years, has been an adjustment. It doesn't mean that I never have issues or problems like I used to, but that those issues are seen in a different light and handled accordingly, in the light of the experiences I've had and the lessons I've learned. It took me a long time to discover just who I am in this ministry and just who I am as a person. I haven't always made right decisions when it comes to ministry. I have always done the best I could, with what I had, but they haven't always been perfect. I have trusted in the wrong people, I gave my most important intercessory positions to people who should have never had it, and I pursued avenues that did nothing but teach me hard and long-earned lessons. I've let the wrong people get too close to me and allowed them to stick around because I wanted to live my faith, my promise, no matter how difficult it might have been.

Every one of us has gotten sidetracked, misled, betrayed, hurt, or mistreated by someone else. In the church, it has become common enough that we have our own unique brand of hurt, known as "church hurt." There is no such thing as "mosque hurt," or "temple hurt," or "meditation hurt," or even "cult hurt," but there is, very much, "church hurt." When we are people who come to church and seek to be restored or made whole in our lives, many of us, myself included, put the church on par with God instead of realizing it is something to be used by God to promote His Kingdom in this world. If we don't see the difference between the two, it's easy to give up on God and give up on the call He has placed on our lives. It's not error to think we shouldn't have "church hurt," but we do because the church functions via people who are often not as redeemed – or divinely appointed – as they may claim to be. Despite this fact, God is still God and He still works wonders and miracles in our lives. There are good leaders out there today, true leaders who understand what it means to go through, to hurt, and most importantly, to heal. I am so glad that no matter how much I might want to give up on this "ministry thing" and yes, even at times, God, God has never, nor will ever, give up on me.

It is my true desire to understand and present the apostolic office (and Christian ministry at large) to bring forth its truth and veracity in our time. In looking back over so many years of ministry and so many different experiences, I realize how much misunderstanding exists about Christian ministry. Even though people are exploring the five-fold ministry in a way that has never been explored so much before, so much of what I see around me comprises false leadership. People call themselves "apostle" or "prophet" with no true understanding of the offices and what those offices mean. My heart longs to see the five-fold ministry have meaning once again: to see apostle, prophet, evangelist, pastor, and teacher mean something to people beyond being reduced to a title.

Years ago, I started out on one side of the Jordan; now I find myself standing on the other side. It's a different view from over here. My perspective on what it means to be in ministry and to stand as a minister of God is radically different. The ways I handle ministry and Christian leadership are also quite different. God continues to open doors for ministry work, although it's a little different than it used to be. The reality of apostolic ministry is that it isn't fun and frilly. It is a hard job of covering, training, knowing what to embrace and what to let go, what to hold on to, what to correct, and how to handle all situations. It's often an uphill battle as the church continues to spiral more and more out of control in these last days. In a larger sense, I look back and recognize every closed door was closed by God. Every association I was not to further or not have at all dissolved. Every open door does not happen by accident or coincidence, but by His Spirit. Those who I cover in ministry and who I meet are appointed by the Lord for such a time as this. As this is the time, and now is the rising, it becomes more and more essential to trust that, this side of the Jordan, where God desires me to go is indeed where I will go.

I resolve not to abandon anyone, not to disregard anyone, and not to treat anyone in the contemptible way that many treated me. I resolve to walk alongside, rather than stand over and judge. I resolve to be different.

I am still empowered. I am still victorious. I am wiser, I am stronger. I am still here. That's more than I can say for some of them.

And here, good, bad, or indifferent, I shall stand.

References

¹ http://harvestministry.org/100-mission-mottos. Accessed December 19, 2012.

Chapter 1
¹ "Ministry Quotes." http://thinkexist.com/quotes/with/keyword/ministry. Accessed November 30, 2008.
². Strong's Exhaustive Concordance of the Bible, #2427
³ Ibid., #1249
⁴ Ibid., #2537
⁵ Ibid., #1242
⁶ Ibid., #1121
⁷ Ibid., #4151
⁸ Ibid., #615
⁹ Ibid., #2227

Chapter 2
¹ "Inspirational Quotes: Leadership Quotations." http://www.inspirational-quotes.info/leadership.html. Accessed November 30, 1008.
² Strong's Exhaustive Concordance of the Bible, #3381
³ Ibid., #1696
⁴ Ibid., #7307
⁵ Ibid., #7760
⁶ Ibid., #5375
⁷ Ibid., #4853
⁸ Ibid., #5971

Chapter 3
¹"Fuel For Faith: Quotes Collection." http://www.fuelforfaith.com/fuel_for_faith_vault_quotes_category.asp?Category =Influence. Accessed November 30, 1008.

² Strong's Exhaustive Concordance of the Bible, #1320
³ Ibid., #2962
⁴ Ibid., #3538
⁵ Ibid., #3538
⁶ Ibid., #240
⁷ Ibid., #1325
⁸ Ibid., #5262

Chapter 4
¹ "Christian Leadership Quotes."
http://www.poemofquotes.com/religions/christianity/christian-leadership-quotes.php. Accessed December 3, 2008.
² Strong's Exhaustive Concordance of the Bible, #3421
³ Ibid., #2233
⁴ Ibid., #2980
⁵ Ibid., #3056
⁶ Ibid., #2316
⁷ Ibid., #4102
⁸ Ibid., #3401
⁹ Ibid., #391

Chapter 5
¹ "John Newton Quotes."
http://www.famousquotesandauthors.com/authors/john_newton_quotes.html. Accessed December 4, 2008.
² Strong's Exhaustive Concordance of the Bible, #1325
³ Ibid., #652
⁴ Ibid., #4396
⁵ Ibid., #2099
⁶ Ibid., #4166
⁷ Ibid., #1320

Chapter 6
¹ "Elias Hicks Quotes."
http://www.brainyquote.com/quotes/authors/e/elias_hicks.html. Accessed on December 5, 2008.
² Strong's Exhaustive Concordance of the Bible, #5087
³ Ibid., #2783
⁴ Ibid., #652
⁵ Ibid., #1320
⁶ Ibid., #1484
⁷ Ibid, #5807
⁸ Marino, Lee Ann B. "Female Apostles In History."
http://www.slideshare.net/powerfortoday/female-apostles-in-history. Accessed on February 20, 2013.
⁹ ibid.
¹⁰ "Charles Harrison Mason."

http://en.wikipedia.org/wiki/Charles_Harrison_Mason. Accessed on February 20, 2013.
[11] "William J. Seymour." http://en.wikipedia.org/wiki/William_J._Seymour. Accessed on February 20, 2013.
[12] Marino, Lee Ann B. "Female Apostles In History." http://www.slideshare.net/powerfortoday/female-apostles-in-history Accessed on February 20, 2013.
[13] "Charles Fox Parham." http://en.wikipedia.org/wiki/Charles_Fox_Parham. Accessed on February 20, 2013.
[14] Strong's Exhaustive Concordance of the Bible, #782
[15] Ibid., #408
[16] Ibid., #2458
[17] Ibid. #4773
[18] Ibid., #4869
[19] Ibid., 1978
[20] Ibid., 1722
[21] Ibid. 652
[22] Ibid. 1096
[23] Ibid. 1722
[24] Ibid. 5547
[25] Ibid. 4253
[26] Ibid. 1700
[27] McDonnell, Dianne D. "Junia, A Woman Apostle." Fort Worth, TX: Church of God, Dallas-Fort Worth, 1999-2004. Accessed on April 11, 2011.
[28] "Apostle Apphia." http://orthodoxwiki.org/Apostle_Apphia. Accessed on April 11, 2011.

Chapter 7
[1.] "Walter Lippmann Quotes." http://www.brainyquote.com/quotes/quotes/w/walterlipp151321.html. Accessed on December 5, 2008.
[2] Strong's Exhaustive Concordance of the Bible, #4395
[3] Ibid., #3129
[4] Ibid., #3870
[5] Ibid., #4151
[6] Ibid., #4396
[7] Ibid., #5293
[8] Ibid., #4936
[9] "John Climacus." http://en.wikipedia.org/wiki/John_Climacus. Accessed on February 21, 2013.
[10] "Joan of Arc." http://en.wikipedia.org/wiki/Joan_of_Arc. Accessed on February 21, 2013.
[11] "Francis of Paola." http://en.wikipedia.org/wiki/Francis_of_Paola. Accessed on February 21, 2013.
[12] John of the Cross." http://en.wikipedia.org/wiki/John_of_the_Cross.

¹³ Marino, Dr. Lee Ann B. "Female Prophets In History." http://www.slideshare.net/powerfortoday/female-prophets-in-history. Accessed on February 21, 2013.
¹⁴ Marino, Lee Ann B. "Female Prophets In History." http://www.slideshare.net/powerfortoday/female-prophets-in-history. Accessed on February 21, 2013.

Chapter 8
1 "Evangelist Quotes." http://www.yourdictionary.com/quotes/evangelist
² <u>Strong's Exhaustive Concordance of the Bible</u>, #3525
³ Ibid., #2553
⁴ Ibid., #2099
⁵ Ibid., #4135
⁶ Ibid., #1248
⁷ Ibid., #2099
⁸ Ibid.
⁹ Marino, Dr. Lee Ann B. "Female Evangelists In History." http://www.slideshare.net/powerfortoday/female-evangelists-in-history. Accessed on February 21, 2013.
¹⁰ "Anthony of Padua." http://en.wikipedia.org/wiki/Anthony_of_Padua. Accessed on February 21, 2013.
¹¹ Marino, Dr. Lee Ann B. "Female Evangelists In History." http://www.slideshare.net/powerfortoday/female-evangelists-in-history. Accessed on February 21, 2013.
¹² Ibid.
¹³ Ibid.
¹⁴ Billy Sunday." http://en.wikipedia.org/wiki/Billy_Sunday. Accessed on February 21, 2013.

Chapter 9
1 "Randall Terry Quotes." http://www.brainyquote.com/quotes/quotes/r/randallter381770.html. Accessed on December 7, 2008.
² <u>Strong's Exhaustive Concordance of the Bible</u>, #5414
³ Ibid., #7462
⁴ Ibid., #3820
⁵ Ibid., #7462
⁶ Ibid., #1844
⁷ Ibid., #7919
⁸ Marino, Lee Ann B. "Female Pastors In History." http://www.slideshare.net/powerfortoday/female-pastors-in-history. Accessed on February 21, 2013.
⁹"Saint Anthony the Abbot." http://saints.sqpn.com/saint-anthony-the-abbot/. Accessed on February 21, 2013.
¹⁰ "Saint Bernard of Clairvaux." http://saints.sqpn.com/saint-bernard-of-clairvaux/. Accessed on February 21, 2013.
¹¹"Andrew Murray (minister)."

[12] "The Basque Sorera, Sorora or Freila." http://www.womenpriests.org/minwest/freilas_overview.asp. Accessed on September 12, 2014.

Chapter 12
[1] "Leadership Quotes" http://www.christian-history.org/leadership-quotes.html. Accessed on January 3, 2014.
[2] Strong's Exhaustive Concordance of the Bible, #4165
[3] Ibid., #4168
[4] Ibid., #1983
[5] Ibid., #1596
[6] Ibid., #147
[7] Ibid., #4290
[8] Kroeger, Catherine. "The Neglected History Of Women In The Early Church." https://www.christianhistoryinstitute.org/magazine/article/women-in-the-early-church. Accessed on September 12, 2014.
[9] Riss, Kathryn. "Women Pastors In The Early Church." http://www.godswordtowomen.org/pastors.htm. Accessed on September 12, 2014.
[10] "Francis Asbury" http://en.wikipedia.org/wiki/Francis_Asbury. Accessed on September 12, 2014.
[11] "Elder (Christianity." http://en.wikipedia.org/wiki/Elder_%28Christianity%29. Accessed on September 12, 2014.
[12] "Marjorie Matthews." http://en.wikipedia.org/wiki/Marjorie_Matthews. Accessed on September 12, 2014.
[13] "History of Presbyterian Women and Its Publications." http://www.presbyterianmission.org/ministries/pw/about-history/. Accessed on September 12, 2014.

Chapter 15
[1] "Universal." http://www.merriam-webster.com/dictionary/universal. Accessed October 12, 2011.

Chapter 17
[1] African-American Spiritual, Public Domain. Accessed April 5, 2013.

http://en.wikipedia.org/wiki/index.html?curid=1863569. Accessed on February 21, 2013.
[12] Marino, Dr. Lee Ann B. "Female Pastors In History." http://www.slideshare.net/powerfortoday/female-pastors-in-history. Accessed on February 21, 2013.
[13] Ibid.

Chapter 10
[1] "Quotations About Teachers." http://www.quotegarden.com/teachers.html. Accessed on December 7, 2008.
Strong's Exhaustive Concordance of the Bible, #5486
[3] Ibid., #5485
[4] Ibid., #1321
[5] Ibid., #1319
[6] Marino, Dr. Lee Ann B. "Female Evangelists In History." http://www.slideshare.net/powerfortoday/female-evangelists-in-history. Accessed on February 21, 2013.
[7] "Blessed Angelus of Furci." http://saints.sqpn.com/category/saints-who-were-teachers/. Accessed on February 21, 2013.
[8] "Jean-Baptiste de La Salle." http://en.wikipedia.org/wiki/Jean-Baptiste_de_la_Salle. Accessed on February 21, 2013.
[9] Marino, Dr. Lee Ann B. "Female Teachers In History." http://www.slideshare.net/powerfortoday/female-teachers-in-history. Accessed on February 21, 2013.
[10] Ibid.
[11] Ibid.

Chapter 11
[1] "The Biblical Role of Deacons." http://www.baptiststart.com/print/role_of_deacons.html. Accessed on January 3, 2014.
[2] Strong's Exhaustive Concordance of the Bible, #4412
[3] Ibid., #1381
[4] Ibid., #1247
[5] Ibid., #412
[6] Ibid., #1247
[7] "Lawrence of Rome." http://en.wikipedia.org/wiki/Lawrence_of_Rome. Accessed on September 12, 2014.
[8] "Vincent of Saragossa." http://en.wikipedia.org/wiki/Vincent_of_Saragossa. Accessed on September 12, 2014.
[9] "Poplia." http://www.womenpriests.org/deacons/list_arm_syria.asp#poplia. Accessed on September 12, 2014.
[10] "Marthana." http://www.womenpriests.org/deacons/list_pal_egypt.asp#marthana. Accessed on September 12, 2014.
[11] "Saint Sigolena of Arles." http://www.womenpriests.org/minwest/sigolena.asp. Accessed on September 12, 2014.

About The Author

DR. LEE ANN B. MARINO, PH.D., D. MIN., D.D.

Apostle Dr. Lee Ann B. Marino, Ph.D., D.Min., D.D. is an apostle, missionary, apostolic theologian, Bible scholar, women's advocate, feminist, activist, university chancellor, songwriter, worship leader, worship dancer, and Senior Prelate, founder, and visionary for Apostolic Fellowship International Revival Ministries (AFIRM). In acknowledgement of her extensive work in the apostolic, she has been called "the greatest apostle in the modern church." A seminary doctoral graduate of Apostolic Preachers College (now Apostolic University) in Philosophy, Theology, Divinity, and Religion/Comparative Religion, Dr. Marino's approach to preaching, teaching, Spiritual matters, and Scriptural education have touched a generation looking for leadership, connection, and understanding in our modern times.

In nearly two decades of ministry, Dr. Marino has made the joke that she's been "every Pentecostal denomination under the s[un]," college exploration of religion back in 1997 led her to "get save[d] first time," immersing her into a spiritual world of gifts, devoti[on,] spirituality, and an intense call to ministry, sometimes in church[es] that worked – and sometimes in settings that went seriously awry. Through a series of different events, including periods of time in Charismatic, Holiness, Full Gospel, Oneness, Apostolic, and non-denominational, Dr. Marino found her own calling – and her own ministerial identity – in neo-Apostolic, a division of modern Pentecostal understanding that respects and heralds the ancestry of the past, along with vision for the modern-day issues and circumstances the church and the world face today.

Dr. Marino has been in ministry since 1998 and founded Apostolic Fellowship International Ministries (now Apostolic Fellowship International Revival Ministries) in 2004. She was ordained as a pastor in 2002 and as an apostle in 2010. Her experiences have taken her to over five hundred religious services and experiences of all sorts throughout the years, both Christian and non-Christian alike, as she studied and strived to learn what all believe. The work of Apostolic Fellowship International Revival Ministries now extends to all Christian borders, working in different Protestant and non-denominational churches alike. Apostle's vision is about the church now, honoring history while looking forward, and about becoming "all things to all people," that some may be saved. Her fellowship encompasses twenty churches and ministries worldwide, thousands of friends, and includes the work of Sanctuary International Fellowship Tabernacle – SIFT, a church movement dedicated to leading people to God without politics, where she emphasizes relationship, acceptance, experience, and service. In covering, her emphasis is on the unique development of each leader to become all God has for them to be in their specific gifting and ministries. She has preached and taught throughout the United States, Puerto Rico, and in Europe. Affectionately nicknamed "the Spitfire," she is best-known for her work in the apostolic, her instruction for church leaders and ministers, her work in the study of gender, sexual ethics, and human sexuality, and her work in women's ministry through the study of Female Apologetics, established and first taught by Dr. Marino herself. She has spent over twenty years in advocacy, education, and work for and with minority communities, including

, African-Americans, Latinos, and the LGBT community.

...er work is not without acclaim, and she is the recipient of ...ral awards and has been featured in many magazine publications ...d on many radio and television programs over the years, including ...Woman of the Year 2012 and Mother of the Year 2013. As Chancellor of Apostolic University since 2004, her teachings in the apostolic, church history and protocol, Scripture studies, textbooks, and educational materials on many issues of faith, ethics, gender, sociology, church history, theology, and philosophy have reached individuals in over seventy-five countries. Having written over twenty-five books, including her best-sellers, *Ministry School Boot Camp: Training For Helps Ministries, Appointments, And Beyond* (Righteous Pen Publications, 2014), *Awakening Christian Ministry: The Call To Serve Others As We Serve Jesus Christ* (Righteous Pen Publications, 2014), *Stumbling To Nineveh: A Journey Through The Book Of Jonah* (Righteous Pen Publications, 2015); *Discovering Intimacy: A Journey Through The Song Of Solomon* (Righteous Pen Publications, 2015); and *Ministering To LGBTs – And Those Who Love Them* (Apostolic University Press, 2016).

Dr. Marino is editor-in-chief of *Kingdom Now* Magazine and host of the *Kingdom Now* television and radio programs, as well as CEO and designer for Rose of Sharon Creations, CEO of Righteous Pen Media, and Editor-in-Chief for The Righteous Pen Publications Group. She is also a member of the Women's Christian Temperance Union, a historical women's organization with long-held ties to women's rights, ordination, and ministry. Her main website is www.kingdompowernow.org.

www.ingramcontent.com/pod-product-compliance
Lightning Source LLC
Chambersburg PA
CBHW070714160426
43192CB00009B/1185